University and School Connections

Research Studies in Professional Development Schools

A volume in
Research in Professional Development Schools
Irma N. Guadarrama, John M. Ramsey, and Janice L. Nath, *Series Editors*

University and School Connections

Research Studies in Professional Development Schools

Edited by

Irma N. Guadarrama
University of Houston

John M. Ramsey
University of Houston

Janice L. Nath
University of Houston–Downtown

INFORMATION AGE PUBLISHING, INC.
Charlotte, NC • www.infoagepub.com

Library of Congress Cataloging-in-Publication Data

University and school connections : research studies in professional
development schools / edited by Irma N. Guadarrama, John M. Ramsey, Janice
L. Nath.
    p. cm. – (Research in professional development schools)
  Includes bibliographical references.
  ISBN 978-1-59311-700-9 (pbk.) – ISBN 978-1-59311-701-6 (hardcover)
1. Laboratory schools–United States. 2. Teachers–Training of–United
States. I. Guadarrama, Irma N. II. Ramsey, John M. III. Nath, Janice L.
  LB2154.A3U65 2008
  370.71'1–dc22

                               2008013250

Printed in the United States of America

DEDICATION

This book is dedicated to the memory of Claudia A. Balach, for her commitment to the concept and development of PDSs and her leadership in the PDS SIG of the American Educational Research Association.

ACKNOWLEDGMENTS

We are deeply grateful for the hard work and dedication exemplified by the contributing authors. We also extend our sincere gratitude to our colleagues for their support and assistance, and our graduate assistant, Sanghee Choi, who recently graduated with a doctorate degree. We are especially indebted to our publisher, Mr. George Johnson, for his support and patience.

CONTENTS

Part II

PERSPECTIVES ON INQUIRY AND MENTORING

Part III

PERSPECTIVES ON INQUIRY AND MENTORING

Part IV

PROGRAM ASSESSMENT AND EVALUATION

Part V

PAST AND FUTURE CONSIDERATIONS

INTRODUCTION

Irma N. Guadarrama

In the eight years or so that we have served as editors of the Professional Development Schools Research series we have learned a great deal about PDSs from researchers and practitioners from just about every part of the United States. Our current book is the third in the series and one of the most comprehensive volumes in terms of the depth and breadth of themes or topics presented in the 23 chapters. Whereas we can't guarantee it, there is a strong likelihood that upon reading these chapters you will acquire new information and/or fresh perspectives on PDSs, regardless of where you are in the implementation or developmental continuum. Needless to say, we're humbled by the voluminous knowledge represented in this collection, which serves to further underscore or reiterate to our audience that professional development schools continue to be a changing force in the educational landscape, both in teacher education and K–12 schools.

The volume is divided into five parts: (1) program models and issues of implementation that share with the reader how PDSs work within specific content areas or particular program models; (2) research studies on leadership or issues of stability and sustainability; (3) perspectives on inquiry and mentoring; (4) program assessment and evaluation; and (5) past and future considerations—ideas on how we can build upon our experiences and learn from our lessons.

University and School Connections, pages xiii–xiv

The first part, PDS Program Models and Implementation Issues, includes the largest number of chapters. These chapters profile cases of content-area or program-types of implementation. The representation of voices is unique amongst these papers. We contend that these chapters are vital to our understanding of the operational principles of PDSs, even if their research methodology or procedure may or may not withstand vigorous scrutiny. There is no question, however, that the voices emit a passion or excitement from the success of the university and school partnerships that form the basis of each study.

The second set of chapters focus on leadership studies, an important area that demands special attention for the sake of ensuring the long-term success of PDSs. Authors Buchanan, Bleicher, Behshid, Evans, and Ngarupe, elaborate in their chapter on a "culture of respect," which resonates firmly within an environment of a PDS and which is essential for change and/or transformation. The studies in this section offer readers insightful views on the complexity of leadership issues but simultaneously point out how problems can be resolved if and when practitioners meet the new or obstinate challenges.

The third part offers readers four chapters on the role of inquiry in PDSs and/or on successful mentoring practices. Author, Snow-Gerono elaborates on the invaluable function of inquiry in PDSs, a theme that has been re-visited in the previous volumes as well, underscoring the "culture of inquiry" prevalent within this environment.

Part IV chapters on assessment and evaluation contain invaluable information for every PDS. Authors Vare, Small, and Dunlap emphasize the need to develop a "culture of accountability" in PDSs, not unlike what is required of all educational programs if they are to benefit from successful sustainability.

The final two papers focus on (1) the decade-long, evolving journey of a PDS; and (2) an analysis of a selection of research papers from the previous PDS volumes and implications for further inquiry. As our understanding and development in PDSs become more pronounced, it's important to stay on course of a successful, well-planned design, especially when PDSs deal with a multitude of factors and issues. These papers underscore an important lesson: being knowledgeable and proactive in our approach to working within PDSs are essential elements for our success.

PART I

PDS PROGRAM MODELS
AND IMPLEMENTATION ISSUES

CHAPTER 1

LINKING THEORY AND PRACTICE

Teaching Methods Classes in Professional Development Schools

Lourdes Zaragoza Mitchel and Alisa Hindin

ABSTRACT

The purpose of the study was to address the following research questions: Are their differences for pre-service teachers with regards to: (a) planning for instruction, (b) reflections on instruction, (c) perceptions of the ways co-operating teachers supported their lesson development, and (d) their beliefs about teaching literacy. This chapter describes the research and theory that informed this study, the context for the study, and the project design. The authors conclude that there exists substantial differences for pre-service teachers in the PDS setting, as compared to those in the traditional on-campus course, with benefits pointing to a greater transfer of learning and higher levels of reflection on behalf of the PDS participants.

University and School Connections, pages 3–25

INTRODUCTION

Research on teacher preparation programs calls attention to a need for change in the pedagogy of teacher education (Ball, 2000; Korthagen & Kessels, 1999; Wise & Leibbrand, 2001). For example, Feiman-Nemser (2001) suggests that teacher education programs need to link theory and practice and insist that the important question is "how to integrate the two in such a way that it leads to integration within the teacher" (p. 4). Similarly, Ball (2000) argues for intertwining content and pedagogy in teaching and in learning to teach. She maintains that teachers are often left with the challenge of integrating subject matter knowledge and pedagogy in their work.

Although teacher education programs help pre-service teachers to collect ideas, learn theories, and develop strategies, beginning teachers often report that their professional preparation was of little use or practicality (Ball, 2000). McIntyre, Byrd, and Foxx (1996) point out that "the disjointedness of program goals and curriculum may be responsible for the historical ineffectiveness of teacher education because most pre-service teachers are unable to grasp the whole while experiencing the myriad of disconnected parts of the curriculum" (p. 171). Research on pre-service teachers indicates that what pre-service teachers learn in their education course often does not transfer to classroom teaching (Zeichner & Tabachnick, 1985). In a summary of the existing research on teacher preparation, Wilson, Floden, and Ferrini-Mundy (2002) report, "Study after study shows that experienced and newly certified teachers alike see clinical experiences as a powerful—sometimes the single most important—component of teacher preparation" (p. 195). Pre-service teachers are often most influenced by what they see their cooperating teachers do or by their own memories, and often these teacher models are not ideal (Barker & Burnet, 1994; Conner & Killmer, 1995).

One response from policy stakeholders has been to try to draw universities and school districts closer together in true partnerships with professional development schools (PDSs). In these partnerships, pre-service teachers can work in environments dedicated to best practices whereby schools and universities learn from each other. The PDS provides a greater coherence between university course work and field experiences and long-term learning opportunities for teachers. As Pugach and Johnson (1995) explain, "One basic tenet of school-university collaboration is to link the development of prospective and practicing teachers alike. This approach highlights the continuum of development over the course of a career in teaching" (p. 2000).

Although the PDS model is a relatively new concept in teacher preparation, preliminary results show value of this model. For example, Ridley,

Hurwitz, Hackett, and Miller (2005) found that teacher candidates who were placed in PDS sites were more effective first-year teachers than the candidate who did not have this PDS opportunity. In terms of preparation, studies of highly-developed PDS's also suggest that teachers who graduate from such programs feel more knowledgeable and prepared to teach (Sandholtz & Wasserman, 2001). Mantle-Bromley (2002) found that employers also viewed teachers who participated in a PDS as better prepared. Castle, Fox, and Souder (2006) found that PDS student teachers outperformed non-PDS student teachers on a number of areas of their instruction and assessment.

The benefits of the PDS also extend to cooperating teachers who have been found to learn from the pre-service teachers who are placed in their classrooms (Tatel, 1996). As Darling-Hammond et al. (1996) explain, "By creating settings that merge theoretical and practical learning, PDSs may help transmit a common set of expectations that link preparation and practice (p. 460). More recently, PDSs have begun to take a look at student outcomes. Although there is no long-term comparative research on the impact of PDS's on student learning and achievement, Pine (2003) reports findings that PDS students' scores on the Michigan Educational Assessment Program (MEAP) exceeded those achieved by other district schools. Pine (2003) speculates that the focus on student learning at the PDS might explain this difference in student achievement.

Not only is the PDS model supported by research but it has also become a requirement for universities in the United States that seek a national accreditation through the National Council for Accreditation of Teacher Education (NCATE). As described by Darling-Hammond (1995), PDS relationships are "collaborations between school and universities that have been created to support the learning of prospective and experienced teachers while simultaneously restructuring schools and schools of education" (p. 87). Feiman-Nemser (2001) concludes that learning to teach, especially the kind of teaching recommended by reformers, requires coherent and connected learning opportunities that link the university classroom to new teacher induction to continuing professional development.

Although the research on PDSs has begun to show benefits of this model, more research is needed to see how this model can support the learning of pre-service teachers (Lefever-Davis, 2002). The researchers in this current study have been working with PDS sites for the past six years. In order to strengthen partnerships with PDS sites and to better link theory to practice, the methods courses have been taught on-site at the PDSs. The purpose of teaching on-site courses was to work more closely with the teachers and the pre-service teachers in creating a more enriching learning experience for all. This work began in the fall of 2005 by teaching a literacy methods class on-site at a PDS, with pre-service teachers and cooperating teachers learning together. Initial feedback from the pre-service teachers and the co-operating teachers indicated that these courses were more useful because the cooperating teacher modeled many of the practices discussed in the methods class.

The PDS on-site course model seemed to hold promise for the pre-service teachers and their cooperating teachers. A study to compare the experiences of pre-service teachers in an on-site methods course at a PDS and a traditional on-campus course with field experience was designed. The purpose of the study was to address the following research questions: Are their differences for pre-service teachers with regards to: (a) planning for instruction, (b) reflections on instruction, (c) perceptions of the ways cooperating teachers supported their lesson development, and (d) their beliefs about teaching literacy. This chapter describes the research and theory that informed this study, the context for the study, and the project design. This information is followed by a description of the findings and interpretations of how PDSs can support teacher preparation programs. Finally, a reflection follows on what was learned from the study and questions posed for further research.

UNDERSTANDINGS AND PRACTICES: LITERACY METHODS COURSES

Scholars agree that teachers need to have a deep knowledge, or under-standings, of their subject and how to make it accessible to others (Co-chran-Smith & Lytle, 1999; Hammerness & Darling-Hammond, 2002; Shul-man and Shulman, 2004). In this study, literacy is the pedagogical content knowledge of focus. Teaching literacy requires specialized knowledge about language, how children learn and acquire literacy skills, and a variety of in-structional strategies. Yet, the average teacher takes three semester hours or one course in how to teach reading. Although attention has focused on preparation of literacy teachers in documents such as the International Reading Association (IRA) Reading Teacher Preparation Commission Report (Hoffman & Roller, 2001; Hoffman et al., 2005) and National Reading Panel (NRP), few claims about what constitutes effective pre-service literacy education can be concluded (National Institute of Child Health and Human Development, 2000). The IRA completed the only quasi-experimental study of teacher preparation for reading instruction, showing that pre-service teacher preparation does impact beginning teachers. It suggests that effective preparation improves student achievement (Hoffman & Roller, 2001; Hoffman et al., 2005).

The National Reading Panel, commissioned by Congress in the United States to assess the status of research-based knowledge on reading, reported similar findings that certain instructional methods are better than others and that many of the more effective methods are ready for implementation in the classroom (National Institute of Child Health and Human Development, 2000). To become good readers, children must develop phonemic awareness, phonics skills, the ability to read words in text in an accurate and fluent manner, and the ability to apply comprehension strategies consciously and deliberately as they read. With respect to the overall preparation of teachers, the Panel noted that existing studies showed that training both new and established teachers generally produced higher student achievement, but the research in this area is inconclusive about what makes training most effective (National Institute of Child Health and Human Development, 2000). More quality research on teacher training is one of the major research needs identified by the NRP.

Moreover, research on preparing pre-service teachers to teach literacy reflects the same ideas about the mismatch between the university courses and elementary school setting (Wiseman, 1999). For example, teacher candidates report that classroom teachers are using a more "skill-based" approach than is recommended in their university courses (Martin, Martin, & Martin, 1999). Grossman, Valencia, and Hamel's (1997) review on methods courses found that methods courses enhanced teachers understanding of teaching practice but, when in field experiences, teachers often abandoned the focus on subject matter and student learning to concentrate on classroom management.

THE ROLE OF REFLECTION AND CRITICAL INQUIRY

In addition to pedagogical content knowledge, teachers need to develop a set of dispositions (or habits of thinking and action) about teaching, children, and the role of teacher (Hammerness & Darling-Hammond, 2002). Teaching dispositions include the disposition to reflect and to learn from practice. The use of reflection is one means of assisting cooperating and pre-service teachers in giving and receiving feedback, as they question what they are doing and its impact on students. Reflection draws on a constructivist view of knowledge, whereby teachers can thoughtfully review their experiences in order to fully understand and value their professional routine (Collier, 1999; Grossman & Shulman, 1994; Schön, 1996; Shulman & Shulman, 2004; Thomas & Montgomery, 1998). Shulman and Shulman (2004) place reflection at the center of their model of teacher learning, describing reflection as "the key to teacher learning and development" (p. 264).

The role of reflection is also prominent in studies of teacher learning. For example, Freese (1999) found that when teachers are provided opportunities to reflect on their work and to connect their work to research and theory, they are better able to identify areas needing improvement, to consider alternative strategies, and to problem-solve and reason through pedagogical dilemma. Reflecting on their own learning can also help pre-service teachers make their own assumptions about teaching and learning.

The importance of reflection was highlighted by the American Educational Research Association Panel on Research and Teacher Education who recently reviewed more than 500 peer-reviewed studies of pre-service teacher education. Studies, all using case study methodology, documented that methods courses often introduce ideas and concepts that pre-service teachers did not accept (Cochran-Smith & Fries, 2005). The Panel concluded that all these studies provide support for learning and practice that includes theory as well as multiple opportunities to attempt desired practice but suggests that there is a need to go deeper. They concluded that "reflecting on learning by working with individuals or small groups can produce changes in pre-service teachers' ideas about teaching, learning, and the competence of learners, but only if the prospective teachers are engaged with teacher educators who support and practice reflective analysis in relation to what was taught or advocated by the methods course" (p. 316). Reflection has also been identified as a practice used consistently by teachers who were identified as excellent reading teachers (Maloch, Fine, & Flint, 2003).

Taken together, the research and theory on teacher preparation show the complexity of pre-service teacher learning, and this complexity is coupled with discontinuities between what candidates learn in their courses and what they encounter in classrooms. The PDS model helps to address this problem by building connections between universities and schools. Research needs to closely examine the contexts that provide powerful images of good practice while, at the same time, creating positive learning experiences for our pre-service teachers. This means examining learning in particular domains, such as literacy, and focusing on effective learning practices such as deep reflection.

PROJECT DESIGN

Contexts for the Study

In the following section, the three contexts for the study are described: a suburban PDS, an urban PDS, and an on-campus course. A literacy methods course was taught in each of these contexts and the pre-service teachers enrolled in the course completed a 72-hour field placement observing and teaching with guided reflection. Pre-service teachers enrolled in the PDS courses completed their field placements at the PDS, and the on-campus course students completed their field placements at one of a number of local school sites.

Suburban Professional Development School.   The suburban PDS school district, with 10 schools, is located 20 miles from the university. Three of the 10 schools are developing PDS sites (noted as "developing" because they have participated in numerous PDS activities over the last 5 years). The PDS partnership with the university was established in 2001 for the main purpose of renewal and growth for teachers. The leadership believed that changing practices would impact on student learning and provide exemplary opportunities for pre-service teachers. The partnership began with a Goals 2000 grant that provided seed money for initial implementation, and three years later, the PDS leadership continued the relationship with local resources and support. The partnership between the university and the suburban school district was the result of a shared vision based on the assumption that teachers can learn to be more effective about teaching and learning through self-inquiry and critical reflection and that preparing teachers for this lifelong skill begins very early on in the teacher's career.

The school included in this project was an elementary school (K–8) with an enrollment of between 650–700 students with 3 percent of the school population receiving free or reduced lunch. The school was selected to participate in the study because the leadership decided that the project previously held at another of the PDS sites was extremely beneficial and needed to be replicated at the other PDS. Teachers at this school had been involved in PDS activities for four years, and more than half had attended teaching clinics and reflective sessions to discuss lesson implementation and areas for refinement.

Urban Professional Development School.   The urban PDS was organized around the same philosophy as the suburban PDS and provided the partnership with new insights into issues of equity and diversity. This emerging PDS, only into the second year of the partnership, was the only school in the district participating in the PDS. The PDS is an elementary school (K–8) just eight miles from the university and located in this state's largest urban city. This school has an enrollment of approximately 800 students with 60 percent of the school population receiving free or reduced lunch and 95 percent of the student population's first language not being English.

On-Campus Class.   The third context for the study was the on-campus class where students attended class at the college and completed their field placements at a number of schools in close proximity to the university. The university is located in the tri-state region around New York City.

Early Literacy Methods Class

The authors of this study taught the early literacy methods classes. One instructor taught the class at the urban PDS setting and also served as the PDS Coordinator. The other instructor taught at the suburban PDS setting and also taught the on-campus course. The instructors supervised the pre-service teachers at the PDS schools, while other university supervisors were assigned to the other participants. In all three settings, the methods class was held for 14 weeks for two and a half hours per week. The PDS participants spent one day per week from 8:00–3:30 at the PDS completing their methods class and field placement. This schedule allowed pre-service teachers to experience a full school day with instructor and cooperating teachers learning and working together. On-campus participants had varied field-placement schedules, ranging from one day per week to three days per week and were placed at a variety of schools in the local area.

The instructors of the methods courses designed the syllabus together and taught the courses using the same activities, course assignments and texts by Morrow (2005) and Morrow, Gambrell, and Pressley (2003). The instructors met regularly to plan sessions and to reflect on the experience. The course objectives included: (1) addressing the purpose of teaching literacy, (2) best practices that characterize the teaching of literacy, (3) approaches that have shown to be effective in promoting student learning, and (4) practices that address specific groups of learners such as English language learners. Course sessions focused on teaching and applying the key topics recommended by the National Reading Panel as well as topics such as grouping for instruction and instructional strategies for struggling learners (National Institute of Child Health and Human Development, 2000). The course began with a focus on the multiple meanings of the term *balanced literacy instruction,* and this idea was revisited multiple times throughout the course (Mazzoni & Gambrell, 2003). The course was designed to meet NCATE standards and the content and process standards of the state's curriculum.

The concepts and skills were organized around the "big ideas" of the discipline with added attention given to teaching for understanding by developing concepts in depth. For example, instructors introduced the concept of teaching for comprehension, beginning with how the pre-service teachers comprehend text, what the research says, how children learn, how teachers teach (both explicitly and implicitly), how it is assessed, and the impact on learners. The instructors modeled constructivist approaches and strategies, asking participants to build their own knowledge while also considering how their own experiences and beliefs can influence teaching practices.

Participants

Cooperating Teachers.   All K–3 tenured teachers in the two schools were invited to participate in the project. The suburban PDS also included teachers in grades four and five at the request of the school vice-principal. This was the first time that a course had been taught on-site at either one of the two schools. Teachers in both schools had previously attended workshops and/or mentored at least one pre-service teacher. All teachers agreed to participate in the study and to accept a pre-service teacher in their class.

The authors of the study met with the teachers to discuss project goals and expectations and to identify their learning needs (comprehension, fluency, and vocabulary development). This information was used to tailor the three literacy methods class sessions that the teachers attended. Teachers were asked to read selected chapters from the course text that related to the topics of the class sessions. During these sessions, the pre-service teachers had an opportunity to co-plan lessons with the teachers and to hear teachers' perspectives on the literacy topics.

Pre-service Teachers.   All 50 students who were enrolled in the three course sections were invited to participate in the study. Of the 50 possible participants, 43 college sophomores and juniors agreed to participate. Eleven participants were enrolled in the suburban PDS class, thirteen were enrolled in the urban PDS class, and 19 were enrolled in the on-campus class. The PDS courses were opened to all students, as long as they could arrange to have a full day free for the course and field experience. The PDS courses were limited to 13 students (based on availability of classrooms). Pre-service teachers who participated in the study were primarily in their second year at the same university and were completing their first methods course. All the students had completed prerequisite requirements including educational foundations and child development courses. There were no other requirements for enrolling in the PDS classes and grade point averages (GPAs) for the semester prior to enrolling in the class were similar but a little higher for students in the PDS classes. The mean GPA for participants in the suburban PDS was 3.3 (range, 2.8–3.8), for the urban PDS participants was 3.5 (range 3.19–3.94), and for the on-campus participants was 3.25 (range, 2.2–3.93).

All participants completed a 72-hour field placement in grades K–5 or were placed with a special-education teacher who taught multiple grade levels. All participants were required to teach four lessons in their placements. Two of the lessons were taught to small groups or individual students and the other two lessons were taught to the whole class. At the PDS sites, the instructor also supervised the pre-service teachers by formally observing one lesson.

Data Sources

Data for this study consisted of three measures: lesson plans, reflections and surveys. The lesson plans and reflections were selected to see how the pre-service teachers utilized what they were learning in class. The survey was administered at the end of the course to examine perceptions of the experience.

Lesson Plans. Pre-service teachers were provided a standard lesson format used by the college. They taught two whole-class lessons and handed in lesson plans and reflections for analysis. Study participants were asked to voluntarily submit their work for the purposes of the study, and the data analysis includes all work that was submitted. In the suburban PDS, 13 lessons plans from seven participants were analyzed. In the urban PDS, 17 lessons from nine participants were analyzed. In the on-campus class, 20 lesson plans from 14 pre-service teachers were analyzed.

The lesson plan data was coded using the content focus from the literacy course, including the following categories: *instruction embedded in meaningful context, explicit teaching of learning goals, activation of prior knowledge,* and *alignment between the assessment and objective(s).* These areas were selected because they were emphasized in the methods class, reflect current research on best practices in reading instruction (Mazzoni & Gambrell, 2003; Pressely, Rankin, & Yokoi, 1996), and are developmentally appropriate expectations for teacher candidates in their first field placement. Lesson plans were compared for each setting.

Reflections. Pre-service teachers were asked to reflect and respond to the following prompts after they had taught the lesson:

a. Describe how you selected the materials for your lesson.
b. Describe your cooperating teacher's role in your lesson preparation.
c. Provide claims and evidence to support your feelings and impressions.
d. How did the actual lesson compare to the one you planned?
e. How successful was the lesson for the students? What contributed to the success of the episode or what might have interfered with intended outcomes?
f. How would you modify your instruction based on this experience?

For analysis of the reflection data, a rubric developed by Ward and McCotter (2004) for analyzing the reflections of student teachers was modified and used. The expectation was that students completing the first methods class in sophomore year would not have the depth of reflection that would be expected from a student teacher, so we did not include the highest level of the rubric (the critical level). For the purpose of this study, the rubric

TABLE 1.1   Reflection Rubric

	Routine	Technical	Dialogic
	Practice and thought without change	Technical response without changing perspective	Involves questioning and action consideration for others' perspective; new insights
Focus of Reflection	Concern with self rather than students: student control, time, workload	Concern with specific teaching task: planning, management, assessment	Focuses on students not on self. Uses assessment to assess learning
Level of Inquiry	Analysis definitive and generalized	Asked questions of oneself about specific situations but does not probe for further action	Asked questions of oneself and impact on student learning which leads to more questions and action

Source: Adapted from Ward & McCotter (2004).

included assessing responses in the areas of focus and inquiry. A total of 48 reflections were analyzed, with 13 from the suburban PDS, 17 from the urban PDS, and 18 from the on-campus course. Table 1.1, the Reflection Rubric, displays the rubric and definitions for each heading.

Participants also reflected upon the levels of support they received from cooperating teachers during lesson preparation. Data included 40 reflections with 13 from the suburban PDS, 11 from the urban PDS, and 16 from the on-campus course. The data was categorized into four levels of teachers' support. The "No" help category was used for participants who reported that their cooperating teachers did not provide any topic or area for inclusion in the lesson. The "Low" help category was used for teachers who provided a suggestion for a lesson topic or piece of literature. The "Mid-level category" was used when teachers provided the topic and also described how this lesson would fit within the context of the curriculum. The "High" level was used when teachers provided support with a focus on the students' learning needs and curriculum. After coding, the data comparisons were drawn across the three settings.

Surveys.   A Likert-type survey was developed in keeping with Anderson's (1998) suggestions for survey construction to examine pre-service teachers' perceptions of the experience (see Figure 1.1). The survey was administered at the end of the semester using a computer-based program called *Asset*, a Seton Hall University created software program. After finding no significant differences between the urban and suburban participants' responses, the PDS participants were grouped together. Survey data were then

Early Literacy Internship

This survey will be used to assess students' internship experiences.

Figure 1.1 Literacy survey.

analyzed using a one-way ANOVA to see if there were differences between PDS ($n = 25$) and on-campus course ($n = 19$) candidates' responses.

FINDINGS AND INTERPRETATIONS

In the following section, the findings and evidence from the three data sources are described, including: the lesson plans, lesson plan reflections, and the survey.

Lesson Plans

Differences were found between lesson plans in the PDS settings and on-campus course and seen in Table 1.2, Percentage of Lesson Plans Meeting Category Requirements. A greater percentage of PDS participants embedded their lessons in a meaningful context, with more than 94 percent of suburban PDS lessons and 100 percent of the urban lessons meeting this requirement, as compared to 70 percent for the on-campus course. Smaller differences were found in the second category, *explicitly teaching of objectives*, between suburban PDS participants (50 percent) and on-campus participants (45 percent), with the greatest percentage meeting the objective in

TABLE 1.2   Percentage of Lesson Plans Meeting Category Requirements

	N	Embedded in meaningful context	Explicit teaching objective	Activation of prior knowledge	Assessment connects with objective
Suburban PDS	12	100%	50%	92%	83%
Urban PDS	17	94%	82%	76%	88%
On-Campus	20	70%	45%	55%	60%

the urban PDS (82 percent). For the third category, *activating prior knowledge*, the greatest percentages of lessons meeting the criteria were from the suburban PDS (92 percent), followed by the urban PDS (76 percent) and on-campus (55 percent) lessons. In the final category, *assessment aligned to objective*, 83 percent of suburban and 88 percent of urban PDS lessons met the criteria, as compared to 60 percent for the on-campus course. Table 1.3, Evidence for Lesson Planning, provides examples of lessons that did or did not meet the criteria for each of the lesson planning categories.

A closer review of the teaching objectives showed that 55 percent of the on-campus lessons were skills driven (more isolated teaching of phonics and grammar), as compared to 11 percent of the urban and none of the suburban.

Reflections

The reflection data were analyzed, using the rubric, to see if there were differences among the three settings in terms of levels of *focus* and *inquiry*. Teacher support was analyzed using the categories developed to show the continuum from "Low" support to "High" support.

Levels of Focus. PDS candidates' reflections showed a greater *focus* on the dialogic form of reflection, requiring a focus on students as learners rather than a focus on management, self, and the teaching task. Table 1.4, Reflection Data on Focus, shows that none of the PDS reflections were coded as routine (concern with self rather than students) as compared to the on-campus course, where 5 percent were coded as routine. Reflections that were categorized as routine often focused on student control, as in the following excerpt, where one of the participants shared her difficulties with managing her students during her lesson:

My students had just gotten back from physical education and lunch so they were wound up and rowdy. My lesson was a lesson where they had to be quiet and listen to the story. It was hard for them to calm down, and it made me aggravated that they were being so disrespectful during my lesson.

TABLE 1.3 Evidence from Lesson Planning

Context	Embedded in meaningful text	Explicit teaching to the objective	Activation of prior knowledge	Assessments alignment to objectives
Meets criteria	Once I review the components of fluency, I will read story to students, *Mr. Putters and Tubby Fly The Plane*. I will ask students to listen to my reading and let me know whether I am a fluent reader or not. Poem to read later in small groups.	I will call students over to the carpet and ask them if they have ever heard of the word "fluency". I will wait and listen to their responses. Then I will tell them fluency is the way you read. I will give them examples on a chart. Then I will show components and model fluency.	I will have students look at the word fluency and tell me what they know.	I will have students working in small groups. I will give them a poem to read, and then I will ask them to model the reading. The class and the teacher will assess student reading by looking for the components of fluency.
Does not meet criteria	Students will identify clusters with "s" and connect them to letters. Then they will play a game.	I will tell my students that clusters can be found in the beginning of the word as well as the ending. We will then play a game.	First, I will introduce the different types of "s" clusters. I will tell them that the clusters can be found in the beginning of a word.	I will have a worksheet to do "s" clusters.

TABLE 1.4 Focus of Reflections

	N	Routine	Technical	Dialogic
Suburban PDS	13	0	31%	69%
Urban PDS	17	0	35%	65%
On-Campus	18	5%	55%	38%

More than 50 percent of on-campus participants reflected at the technical level, versus suburban PDS participants (at 31 percent) and urban PDS participants (at 31 percent). Reflections at this level show more concern with the teaching task, as in the following excerpt:

> I think this lesson taught me that I need to work on sequencing. It seems like sometimes I'm in front of the class and I have great ideas about how I want the lesson to go, but I end up confusing sequencing. For example, sometimes when I gave them directions or explained a concept, I gave them all the information but did not give it in the most effective order.

This student is thinking critically about his lesson and how he delivered the information to students. He shows reflection on his teaching, but the reflection is not related to his evaluation of the students' understanding of the lesson concepts.

The greatest difference was found in the dialogic reflections, with 69 percent of suburban and 65 percent of urban PDS participants at this level, as compared to 38 percent of on-campus participants. The following is an example of a focus reflection coded at the dialogic level because it moved beyond description and planning to include a focus on student learning.

> The reason the lesson was not very successful for the students was because of the way the lesson was constructed. When we [candidate and cooperating teacher] created the lesson, we tried to include too many parts, which caused us to lose focus on the main objective. When I gave the assessment, I could immediately tell that they [the students] did not get the idea of a summarization that I was trying to teach.

A number of instances were found where students were mentioned in the reflection, but the focus of these comments was on students' level of enjoyment of the lesson. One participant reflected, "I thought my first lesson went marvelous. I felt as though I was very prepared and taught a good and fun lesson. The children seemed to enjoy the lesson very much." Rather than focusing on student learning or the lesson objective, she reports on student enjoyment of the lesson and her own feelings of preparedness.

Similar findings were found in the *inquiry* levels. The inquiry levels examined a pre-service teacher's ability to think and question (beyond describing and generalizing) to allow the reflection to lead them to more questions and ultimately to some action. As Table 1.5, Inquiry on Reflections displays, none of the urban PDS participants and few of the suburban PDS participants (8 percent) showed inquiry at the lower routine level, whereas, 50 percent of the on-campus participants were at this level. The following student's statement exemplifies a reflection that is definitive and does not show any questioning:

> Due to the fact that students' responses were positive and all of my objectives were met, I felt that this lesson was pretty successful. In fact, much of what was planned out on paper actually followed through in the classroom. Thus, I wouldn't modify the lesson because I felt it accomplished exactly what I desired to convey to students in the class.

Smaller differences were found between suburban PDS (38 percent), urban PDS (35 percent), and on-campus participants (28 percent) at the technical level where reflections include questions of oneself but with no thoughts about further action. As the following statement shows, the pre-service teacher questions the success of the lesson but not in a way that leads her to think about possible changes in her instruction:

> One of the things that made me so uncomfortable while teaching my lesson was trying to manage the children's behavior and introduce a new lesson. I tried things like clapping for their attention and one-two-three eyes on me, but they only worked for a couple of minutes then were back to square one.

Substantial differences were found at the highest level of inquiry, the dialogic level, requiring pre-service teachers to question what they were doing and to seek solutions. The majority of suburban PDS (54 percent) and urban PDS (65 percent) participants were at this level, compared to 22 percent of the on-campus participants. The following reflection is an example of an inquiry reflection at the dialogic level:

> If I were to teach this lesson again in the future, I would really try to do this lesson over a period of a few days. When I completed this lesson, although the students were able to produce the end product I was hoping they would, I felt as though there was too much information condensed into a short period of time. Coming back to school the next week, I asked follow-up questions to my students about what a friendly letter was, and many of them weren't able to answer the question for me. I believe that this was because the students were expected to learn and remember too much in a short period of time.

TABLE 1.5   Inquiry of Reflections

	N	Routine	Technical	Dialogic
Suburban PDS	13	8%	38%	54%
Urban PDS	17	0	35%	65%
On Campus	18	50%	28%	22%

This example shows how the pre-service teacher used her understanding of what the students did and did not learn to think about the planning of future instruction.

Teacher Support.   Statements from 16 on-campus, 13 suburban PDS, and 11 urban PDS participants about the ways cooperating teachers supported them during lesson preparation were analyzed and coded according to levels of support. Reflections from some of the participants did not include information about teacher support. As shown in Table 1.6, Teacher Support for Lesson Preparation, differences were found among the three groups. The on-campus course had the only participants who reported no support from teachers (19 percent), as in the statement, "My cooperating teacher told me I could teach the children any lesson that I wanted." In this example, the cooperating teacher is open to the pre-service teacher's ideas but provides no direction for the lesson.

Thirty-one percent of on-campus participants were at the "low-support" level, as compared to 15.4 percent of suburban PDS participants and 18 percent of urban PDS participants. The following is an example of Low Support where the cooperating teacher provides some idea for a topic or material for use in the lesson: "My cooperating teacher let me plan it [the lesson] on my own and merely told me that I should choose a book that went along with the farm theme." The greatest percentage of suburban PDS (69.2 percent) and urban PDS (64 percent) participants were at the "mid-support" level, as compared to the on-campus participants (50 percent). For the Mid-Support category, cooperating teachers provided an idea for a topic and placed the topic within the context of what the class was learning. As the following example shows, the teacher described two possible areas of focus for the lesson, including sequencing and summarizing, and based on what her students would be learning:

> In constructing my lesson plan, I worked with my cooperating teacher on some concepts that would be applicable when addressing the class. At the time I was planning this lesson, Ms. P. informed me that the following week the students would be working on sequencing and summarizing events within a story. Thus, we collaborated on ideas that would be beneficial and relevant to what was going on within the class.

TABLE 1.6 Teacher Support for Lesson Preparation

	N	No Support	Low Support	Mid-Support	High Support
Suburban PDS	13	0	15.4%	69.2%	15.4%
Urban PDS	11	0	18%	64%	18%
On-campus	16	19%	31%	50%	0

Only PDS participants reported "high" level of teacher support, with greater than 15 percent of suburban and 18 percent of urban PDS participants reporting this level of support. The following is one example of a cooperating teacher providing high-level support:

> Mrs. A. made me feel extremely prepared for my lesson. We sat down several times and discussed how I should teach this lesson and the best ways to keep the children engaged. I did feel confident going into the lesson because I felt I put a lot of time and effort into it. We worked over time to put this lesson together and she was very helpful. She modeled ways in which I should do the read aloud the best way possible. She also gave me many suggestions to help me teach the concept of prediction to the students.

In this case, the cooperating teacher worked closely with the candidate on the lesson plan. This comment reflects one of the few that refers to a teacher modeling a practice.

Survey Data

Analysis of the survey data revealed no significant difference between PDS and on-campus course pre-service teachers' perceptions with regards to their interest in pursuing a teaching career, the types of feedback they received from their cooperating teachers, and how well they thought the methods course prepared them to teach literacy. However, the one-way ANOVA of the survey data revealed a significant difference between how well prepared pre-service teachers felt to teach literacy after their field work in the PDS, (mean = 4.28) feeling more prepared, and on-campus students showing (mean = 3.79), $p = .04$.

DISCUSSION

In this study, we found substantial differences for pre-service teachers in the PDS setting, as compared to those in the traditional on-campus course, with greater transfer of learning and higher levels of reflection occurring with PDS participants. Overall, lesson planning by PDS participants showed a higher level of application of concepts taught in the literacy course. Most evident in our findings were lessons with clearly defined objectives, lessons embedded in meaningful contexts that included activation of prior knowledge, and alignment of assessments with the lesson objectives. PDS lessons more explicitly addressed literacy objectives, such as the explicit teaching of a particular comprehension strategy, teaching students how to increase reading fluency, and teaching vocabulary in context.

Moreover, a substantially greater number of on-campus lessons stressed a skills-based approach instead of the balanced literacy approach that was emphasized in the literacy-methods course, and many of the skill-based lessons had no connection to what students were learning and reading. This finding is significant because the most effective literacy teachers embed their instruction in meaningful contexts (Pressley, Rankin, & Yokoi, 1996). Differences in lesson planning could be partially explained by differences in what pre-service teachers observed in their field placement classrooms, although survey data did not reveal any significant difference in pre-service teachers' reports about the practices they observed in the field.

The reflection data also showed differences between the PDS and on-campus participants across levels of reflections. The PDS pre-service teachers' reflections had a greater focus on students as learners and demonstrated higher levels of inquiry as they examined their practice. The participants from the on-campus methods course reflections were more aligned with the research on traditional field experiences.

Consistent with lesson plan and reflection findings, both of which showed a deeper level of development, PDS participants felt more prepared to teach literacy after their field experience. This finding might be connected to our final finding which shows that PDS participants had greater support from their cooperating teachers during their lesson planning. This support might have served to boost participants' feelings of efficacy for teaching literacy. Without this level of support, the on-campus participants might have prepared lessons with an emphasis on how they recall their own literacy experiences as students rather than their new role as teachers. Lortie (1975) called this the problem of "the apprenticeship of observation," referring to the learning that occurs by virtue of being a student for twelve years in traditional classroom settings.

These researchers can only speculate on the reasons for such discrepancies between the two groups of pre-service teachers. One explanation for the differences is the level of connection between the PDS cooperating teachers and the methods course. PDS cooperating teachers not only attended course sessions but also were involved in the planning and decision making for the methods course. PDS cooperating teachers identified their own professional development needs, and these needs were integrated into the course preparation. Including cooperating teachers in the decision-making process and course lessons legitimized their professional role and validated the critical place they hold in teacher preparation. Participating in the course also afforded teachers opportunities to know what pre-service teachers were learning, and pre-service teachers had the benefit of hearing cooperating teachers ideas and questions about teaching literacy. Likely, the most significant factor for explaining differences in lesson plans was the structured opportunities PDS participants had to co-plan lessons with cooperating teachers during the methods class session. Co-planning instruction promoted dialogue, reflection, and alignment of practice.

Another explanation for differences between PDS and on-campus participants could be the role of the instructor in the PDS. PDS participants had the benefit of having the same course instructor and supervisor. This allowed for greater connections between the course material and classroom practice promoting better links between theory and practice. Additionally, the course instructors engaged in ongoing communication with the cooperating teachers that provided the instructors with greater understanding of pre-service teachers' development of practice. PDS participants also benefitted from having a smaller methods class that could have fostered increased communication between the instructors and their students and among the pre-service teachers in the PDS courses.

This research, though limited in scope, does support the conclusion that structurally placing the literacy methods course on-site at a PDS, with cooperating teachers and pre-service teachers learning together and with the instructor serving as supervisor, is a viable alternative for teacher preparation and development. Not only is the pre-service teacher practicing and reflecting in and on action (Schön, 1996) but the cooperating teacher, who contributes to the pedagogical ability of pre-service teachers and who has a significant role in shaping the professional beliefs and practices, is also participating in job-embedded professional development. Our research supports Grossman's (1992) argument that even novice teachers have the potential to make great strides on learning and curriculum—if they have the right context.

Although this study provided evidence that on-site methods courses early in the pre-service teachers' experience might be useful in advancing an agenda for more effective teacher preparation programs, further research is needed. This study took place over a single semester and more attention needs to be paid to transfer of knowledge, reflective practices, and long-term effects. Another variable that needs further investigation is the role that the instructor has on cooperating teachers' levels of support and pre-service teachers' motivation to practice. Although this study did not examine pre-service teachers' prior beliefs, studying prior influences might shed further light into the complexity of identifying best practices. Lastly, since PDS partnerships often include all members of the school community, studying impact of administrator involvement, school culture, and expectations might account for the success or lack of success of an on-site course.

REFERENCES

Anderson, G. (with Arsenault, N.) (1998). *Fundamentals of educational research*. Philadelphia, PA: Falmer Press.

Ball, D. L. (2000). Bridging practice: Intertwining content and pedagogy in teaching and learning to teach. *Journal of Teacher Education, 51*(3), 241–247.

Barker, B., & Burnett, K. (1994). Monetary stipends for cooperating teachers: What do we pay them? *The Teacher Educator, 30*(22), 15–21.

Castle, S., Fox, R. K., & Souder, K. O. (2006). Do professional development schools (PDS) make a difference? A comparative study of PDS and Non-PDS teacher candidates. *Journal of Teacher Education, 57*(1), 65–80.

Cochran-Smith, M., & Fries, K. (2005). The AERA panel on research and teacher education: Context and goals. In L. Darling-Hammond & J. Bransford (Eds.), *Preparing teachers for a changing world* (pp. 358–389). San Francisco: Jossey-Boss.

Cochran-Smith, M., & Lytle, S. (1999). Relationships of knowledge and practice: Teacher learning in communities. In A. Iran-Nejad & C.D. Pearson (Eds.), *Review of research in education* (Vol. 24, pp. 251–307). Washington, DC: American Educational Research Association.

Collier, S.T. (1999). Characteristics of reflective thought during the student teaching experience. *Journal of Teacher Education, 50*(3), 173–181.

Connor, K., & Killmer, N. (1995). *Evaluation of cooperating teacher effectiveness*. Paper presented at the Annual Meeting of the Midwest Educational Research Association, Chicago, IL.

Darling-Hammond, L. (1995). Policy for restructuring. In Ann Lieberman (Ed.), *The work of restructuring schools: Building from the ground up* (pp. 157–176). New York: Teachers College Press.

Darling-Hammond, L., Pacheco, A., Michelli, N., Lepage, P., Hammerness, K., with Young, P. (1996). Implementing curriculum renewal in teacher education: Managing organizational and policy change. In M. W. McLaughlin & I. Oberman (Eds.), *Teacher learning: New policies, new practices* (pp. 442–479). New York: Teachers College Press.

Feinman-Nemser, S. (2001). From preparation to practice: Designing a continuum to strengthen and sustain teaching. *Teachers College Record, 103*(6), 1013–1055.

Freese, A. R. (1999). The role of reflection on pre-service teachers' development in the context of a professional development school. *Teaching and Teacher Education, 15*(8), 895–909.

Grossman, P. L. (1992). Teaching to learn. In A. Lieberman (Ed.), *The changing contexts of teaching: 91st yearbook of the National Society of Education* (pp. 179–196). Chicago: National Society for the Study of Education.

Grossman, P. L. & Shulman, L. S. (1994). Knowing, believing and the teaching of English. In T. Shanahan (Ed.), *Teachers thinking, teachers knowing: Reflections on literacy and language education* (pp. 3–22). Urbana, IL: National Conference on Research in English and National Council of Teachers of English.

Grossman, P. L., Valencia, S. W., & Hamel, F. L. (1997). Preparing language arts teachers in a time of reform. In J. Flood, S. Brice Heath, & D. Lapp (Eds.), *Handbook of research on teaching literacy through the communicative and visual arts* (pp. 407–416). New York: Macmillian Library Reference.

Hammerness, K., & Darling-Hammond, L. (2002). Meeting old challenges and new demands: The redesign of the Stanford Teacher Education Program. *Issues in Teacher Education, 11*(1), 17–30.

Hoffman J. V., & Roller, C. M., & National commission on Excellence in Elementary Teacher Preparation for Reading Instruction. (2001). IRA Excellence in Reading Teacher Preparation Commission report: Current practices in teacher education in the undergraduate level in the United States. In C. M. Roller (Ed.), *Learning to teach reading: Setting the research agenda* (pp. 32–79). Newark, DE: International Reading Association.

Hoffman J. V., Roller, C., Maloch, B., Sailors, M., Duffy, G., & Beretras, S. N. (2005). Teacher's preparation to teach and their experiences and practices in the first three years of teaching. *The Elementary School Journal, 105*(3), 267–288.

Korthagen, F., & Kessels, J. (1999). Linking theory and practice: Changing the pedagogy of teacher education. *Educational Researcher, 28*(4), 4–17.

Lefever-Davis, S. (2002). The preparation of tomorrow's reading teachers. *The Reading Teacher, 56*, 196–197.

Lortie, D. C. (1975). *Schoolteacher: A sociological study*. Chicago: University of Chicago Press.

Mantle-Bromley, C. (2002). The status of early theories of professional development school potential. In I. Guadarrama, J. Ramsey, & J. Nath (Eds.), *Forging alliances in community and thought: Research in professional development schools* (pp. 3–30). Greenwich, CT: Information Age Publishing.

Maloch, B., Fine, J., & Flint, A.S. (2003). "I just feel like I'm ready": Exploring the influence of quality teacher preparation on beginning teachers. *The Reading Teacher, 56*, 348–350.

Martin, M. A., Martin, S. H., & Martin, C. (1999). Pre-service teachers constructing their meanings of literacy in a field-based program. In J. R. Dugan, P. E. Linder, W. M. Linek, & E. G. Sturtevant (Eds.). *Advancing the world of literacy: Moving into the 21st century* (pp. 55–66). Commerce, TX: College Reading Association.

Mazzoni, S. A. & Gambrell, L. B. (2003). Principles of best practice: Finding the common ground. In L. M. Morrow, L. B. Gambrell, & M. Pressley (Eds.), *Best practices in literacy instruction* (2nd ed., pp. 9–22). New York: Guilford Press.

McIntyre, D. J., Byrd, D., & Foxx, S. M. (1996). Field and laboratory experiences. In J. Sikula, T. Buttery, & E. Guyton (Eds.), *Handbook of research on teacher education,* (2nd ed., pp. 171–193). New York: Macmillan.

Morrow, L. M. (2005). *Literacy development in the early years: Helping children read and write*. Boston: Pearson.

Morrow, L. M., Gambrell, L. B., & Pressley, M. (2003). *Best practices in literacy instruction* (2nd ed.). New York: Guilford Press.

National Institute of Child Health and Human Development. (2000). *Report of the National Reading Panel. Teaching children to read: An evidence-based assessment of the scientific research literature on reading and its implications for reading instruction* (NIH Publication No. 00-4769). Washington, DC: U.S. Government Printing Office.

Pine J. (2003). Making a difference: A professional development school's impact on student learning. In D. L. Wiseman & S. L. Knight (Eds.), *Linking school-university collaborations and K–12 student outcomes* (pp. 31–69). Washington, DC: AACTE.

Pugach, M. C., & Johnson L. J. (1995). *Collaborative practitioners, collaborative schools.* Denver, CO: Love Publishing.

Pressley, M., Rankin, J., & Yokoi, L. (1996). A survey of instructional practices of primary teachers nominated as effective in promoting literacy. *Elementary School Journal, 96*(4), 363–384.

Ridley, D. S., Hurwitz, S., Hackett, M. R. D., & Miller, K. K. (2005). Comparing PDS and campus-based pre-service teacher preparation. *Journal of Teacher Education, 56*(1), 46–56.

Sandholtz, J. H., & Wasserman, K. (2001). Student and cooperating teacher: Contrasting experiences in teacher preparation. *Action in Teacher Education, 23*(3), 54–65.

Schön, D. A. (1996). *Educating the reflective practitioner: Toward a new design for teaching and learning in the professions.* San Francisco: Jossey-Bass.

Shulman, L. S., & Shulman, J. H. (2004). How and what teachers learn: A shifting perspective. *Journal of Curriculum Studies, 36*(2), 257–271.

Tatel, E. S. (1996). Improving classroom practice: Ways experienced teachers change after supervising teacher. In M. W. McLaughlin & I. Oberman (Eds.), *Teacher learning: New policies, new practices* (pp. 48–52). New York: Teachers College Press.

Thomas, J. A., & Montgomery, P. (1998). On becoming a good teacher: Reflective practice with regard to children's voices. *Journal of Teacher Education 49*(5), 372–380.

Ward, J. R., & McCotter, S. S. (2004). Reflection as a visible outcome for pre-service teachers. *Teaching and Teacher Education, 20*, 243–257.

Wilson, S., Floden R., & Ferrini-Mundy, J. (2002). Teacher preparation research: An insider's view from the outside. *Journal of Teacher Education, 53*(3), 190–204.

Wise, A. E. & Leibbrand, J. A. (2001). Standards in the new millennium: Where we are, where we're headed. *Journal of Teacher Education, 52*(3), 244–255.

Wiseman, D. L. (1999). The impact of school-university partnerships on reading teacher educators: Important conversations we must have. In J. R. Dugan, P. E. Linder, W. M. Linek, & E. G. Sturtevant (Eds.), *Advancing the world of literacy: Moving into the 21st century* (pp. 81–93). Commerce, TX: College Reading Association.

Zeichner, K. M., & Tabachnick, B. R. (1985). The development of teacher perspectives: Social strategies and institutional control in the socialization of beginning teachers. *Journal of Education for Teaching, 11*(1), 1–25.

CHAPTER 2

BRIDGING THE GAP BETWEEN THEORY AND PRACTICE WITH PROFESSIONAL DEVELOPMENT SCHOOLS

A Department of Special Education's Evolving Journey

Patricia Alvarez McHatton, David Allsopp,
Elizabeth Doone, Darlene DeMarie, Karen Colucci,
and Ann Cranstron-Gingras

ABSTRACT

This chapter is a follow-up to an article published in *Teacher Education Quarterly* (Allsopp, DeMarie, Alvarez-McHatton, & Doone, 2006) in which we examined the impact of a collaborative effort between our university and one of our professional development schools (PDSs) designed to strengthen the linkages pre-service teachers in special education made between their university classes and related field experiences. In this chapter we share subsequent changes and enhancements to our program that have resulted from the data

University and School Connections, pages 27–48
Copyright © 2008 by Information Age Publishing

gathered during the initial study and data we have collected since then. We begin with a brief summary of the history of our Department of Special Education's work with PDSs followed by a summary of the article that provides the foundation for the chapter. Subsequent changes to the model are then described including how the Master of Arts in Teaching (MAT) Program has implemented a unique variation of the model. Finally, we discuss related research we have completed, including implications and our thoughts about future directions.

INTRODUCTION

Research pertaining to professional development schools (PDSs) is situated predominately in the broader general education context (Prater & Sileo, 2002; Rose, 2002; Sapon-Shevin, 1990). The literature that exists on special education and PDSs mainly addresses the integration of general and special education. Additional studies examining the role of special education in reform efforts and special education initiatives within PDSs are needed. This chapter describes such an initiative. It is a follow-up to an article published in Teacher Education Quarterly (Allsopp et al., 2006) in which we examined the impact of a collaborative effort between our university and one of our PDSs designed to strengthen the linkages pre-service teachers in special education made between their university classes and related field experiences.

In this chapter, we share subsequent changes and enhancements to our program that have resulted from the data gathered during the initial study and data we have collected since then. We begin with a brief summary of the history of our Department of Special Education's work with PDSs followed by a summary of the article that provides the foundation for the chapter. Subsequent changes to the model are then described including how the Master of Arts in Teaching (MAT) Program has implemented a unique variation of the model. Finally, we discuss related research we have completed, including implications and our thoughts about future directions.

HISTORICAL CONTEXT

The Department of Special Education at the University of South Florida has a long history of partnerships with local school districts. These partnerships and the lessons we have learned in collaboration with our partners have helped shape and further inform our teacher preparation programs. The foundation for the partnerships began almost 20 years ago with a collaborative research group focused on school reform and comprising department faculty and doctoral students. The group developed linkages to local school districts and collaboratively developed projects with district personnel to address school improvement, K–12 student learning and teacher preparation (Epanchin & Wooley-Brown, 1993, 1995; Evans et al., 1993; Harris & Evans, 1995; Stoddard & Danforth, 1995). Additionally, through relationships built with one local school district and supported by college-wide efforts, our first PDS was established. One of our special education faculty members was the assigned as the PDS liaison with 50 percent of her time spent at the PDS. As the PDS evolved and the partnership strengthened, many lessons were learned that were consistent with the literature on PDSs:

- Not all university personnel find collaborative involvement with schools easy or rewarding—benefits must be clearly perceived and a high priority assigned by both;
- A shared vision and commitment between the partners are extremely important and necessary;
- Honest communication when challenges and ethical dilemmas arise can serve to strengthen the partnership;
- A period of time is critical for university personnel to gain entrée to a school and develop a rapport with school-based personnel (3–5 years);
- Sharing resources can be an effective way to approach school improvement;
- A number of university policies may need to be reexamined when faculty are actively involved in PDSs (e.g., assignments to the partnership);
- The payoffs for partnerships are evident but probably require a longer wait time than universities are used to expecting on traditional cost/benefits models (Evans & Rosselli, 1995; Rosselli et al., 1993).

As we engaged in simultaneous examination and improvement of school-based practices and practices within our teacher education programs, it became evident that developing enough model classroom placements within a PDS to accommodate the size of our teacher preparation program was not feasible. At the time, our special education program was graduating 90 students per year, far too many students for any one school to accommodate in terms of practica and internship placements. Moreover, there were not enough faculty members to both teach core special education courses and supervise students in their practica and final internship placements. Therefore, a different type of PDS was developed, grounded in the lessons we had learned through previous partnerships: A Professional Development School without Walls (Epanchin & Colucci, 2002).

The PDS without Walls was a collaborative effort between our department, the Elementary Education Department at USF, and two local school districts with dual goals of simultaneously improving teacher education and classroom practice with a focus on inclusive practices. The PDS was not bound to one school but stretched across two school districts. It featured school clusters where our special education teacher candidates completed their early fieldwork (practica) and featured a cadre of master teachers (Professional Practice Partners, or PPPs) at these schools who mentored and supervised our teacher candidates in their final internship. School-based site coordinators (teachers or administrators) served as liaisons and supervisors for our students during their three semester-long early field experiences. PPPs completed continual professional development in mentoring to supervise students during their final internships.

Rather than being a PDS bound by the brick and mortar of a school building, this PDS without Walls comprised a learning community composed of university faculty members, school-based cluster site coordinators, PPPs, and teacher candidates. These learning communities met on a regular basis (monthly) to review students' progress, share experiences, and problem-solve. We believed that such a configuration would address issues related to student numbers and that it would establish a viable and sustainable model for special education teacher preparation that would be less vulnerable to personnel and school changes. The PDS without Walls had district commitment and, as teachers/PPPs and site coordinators changed positions and schools within the districts, they still remained in the PDS learning community. As we engaged in our work with the PDS without Walls, we learned several important lessons that continue to inform our current partnerships:

- Nothing happens without commitment of all partners and there must be equitable participation by all;
- Shared objectives are important along with a belief that the shared objectives are more achievable through partnership than through acting separately;
- Self-interest operates in all partnerships; if the partnership is to be effective, the self-interests of all partners and participants must be met;
- Change is complicated and roles and agreements need to be institutionalized;
- Providing opportunities for teacher renewal and respecting the professional knowledge and commitment of teachers is important;
- New individuals brought into the partnership require the partnership to engage in continual reorientation and focus on positive forward movement;
- Dedicated faculty members are integral to the mission of integrating knowledge and practice.

SUMMARY OF COURSE-PRACTICUM DELIVERY MODEL
AND STUDY

After several years, our special education undergraduate program experienced an abrupt and dramatic drop in student numbers. Additionally, while students were consistently experiencing excellent mentorship during their final internships with PPPs, inconsistency among students' early field experiences became noticeable, and a lack of connection between core special education courses and these early field experiences became evident. Altogether, this situation presented the department an opportunity to reflect on our actions and to make adjustments. Due to the lower student numbers, it became feasible for the faculty to be more heavily involved in both course instruction and early field placements. One faculty member expressed an interest in doing this and, after a number of discussions among key undergraduate teaching faculty, a decision was made to pilot a site-based course-practicum delivery model during students' second semester (in which they took their first methods course, Behavior Management). During this second semester, students in the program also completed a practicum in an elementary school setting and were expected to implement an individualized functional assessment and behavioral support plan for one or more students experiencing emotional/behavioral difficulties.

Two additional faculty members, an advanced doctoral student in the Department of Special Education (who taught the characteristics course on *Learning and Behavior Disorders*) and a faculty member in Educational Psychology (who taught the *Learning and Developing Child* course) agreed to collaborate with the other Special Education faculty member to implement the pilot course-practicum delivery model. We partnered with an urban elementary school with which the department had worked previously. Personnel at this school had expressed an interest in collaborating with us on the model and agreed to provide each of the nineteen students a classroom placement with a teacher working in some capacity with students with disabilities—whether it was a special education setting or a mainstream/inclusive classroom setting. We were given a vacant classroom space for our use, and the school's ESE Specialist agreed to serve as the school liaison, with three faculty members to assist in coordinating practicum and course related activities.

The purposes of the model were to: (1) strengthen pre-service teachers' conceptual linkages among the three courses taught during this semester, and (2) to strengthen pre-service teachers' linkages between content in the three courses and their practicum experiences. Courses were taught at the school site on the same days that students participated in their practicum. Through this collaborative on-site PDS course/practicum delivery model, we hoped that special education pre-service teachers would have a more contextualized learning experience where the content they learned was more directly applied to their field experiences. The three instructors met several times to initially plan for the semester. They also met with school staff to get their input and to arrange logistics.

In order to accomplish the goal of strengthening course-to-course and course-to-practicum linkages, instructors reviewed the goals and objectives and assignments that were included in each course. A large overlap of content was noted; therefore, the instructors planned to differentiate how they introduced redundant content. Instead of each person starting with those topics from the beginning each time, a spiraling sequence was established across the courses. Instructors who taught the content later in the semester knew that this particular content was introduced earlier by one of the other two faculty members. This way, they could engage students in building on their prior knowledge and extending this knowledge to deeper levels of understanding/critical thinking. For example, several important behavior management principles were introduced in the educational psychology course, *The Learning and Developing Child*. The instructor of the *Behavior Management* course was then able to build on this foundation by engaging students in applying these principles using particular behavior management practices and helping them to connect the "principles" to the "practice." Students were required to complete a "behavior change project" where pre-service teachers identified a behavioral need of a student in their practicum setting, completed a functional assessment of behavior for the student, developed and implemented a behavioral support plan, and monitored the progress of the student using particular observation methods. Later in the semester, students were provided the opportunity to reflect on their experiences with these practices in their educational psychology course, relating them to the behavior management principles discussed at the beginning of the semester. Furthermore, issues related to dispositions and ways of thinking were exemplified and reinforced throughout all three courses, as each instructor was able to make natural connections across content areas. These linkages across courses and across departments (special education and educational psychology) had not been attempted in such explicit ways before this time.

Data were collected at three points during the semester (beginning, middle, and end) in the form of focus groups and surveys, where pre-service teachers discussed their experiences, observations, and suggestions about participating in this course-practicum delivery model. Results of the data collected supported the success of the model in terms of linkages participants made both among their courses and between their courses and field experiences (Figure 2.1). Allsopp et al. (2006), reported "linkages" as an important theme among participants.

While we believe that we were able to successfully achieve our goal of increasing linkages, the integrated course-practicum delivery model also

Topic	Point in time	Findings
Perspectives of linkages	End	97% reported noticeable to very strong linkages across courses.
		69% reported linkages across courses were greater with new model.
		56% reported behavior management practices observed in their field experience were reflective of what they were learning in their courses.
		44% reported instructional practices observed in their field experience were reflective of what they were learning in their courses.
		70% reported they were able to make more linkages this semester than at their previous practicum experience.
Development of linkage-making across the semester	Beginning	Responses indicated an expectation that the model would provide an avenue for making linkages across field and courses.
		Responses were focused on the role others would play in assisting them in making these linkages. Few if any comments addressed the self as an active learner in this process.
	Middle	Reponses focused on workload and a perceived lack of cohesion across all courses (within and beyond the partnership project).
	End	Responses focused on linkages participants were able to make as a result of the partnership project.
		Responses indicated participants were able to move from "what was wrong" to "what was learned."
Factors impacting ability to make linkages	Middle	Responses focused on perceived lack of empowerment revealing difficulty adjusting to the role of pre-professional and a sense of being micro-managed due to faculty being on-site.
		Responses also focused on logistics (e.g., scheduling, organization, placement, etc...) and how these issues impeded their ability to make linkages.
	End	Responses focused on linkage-making and indicated participants were transitioning from the role of student to novice reflective practitioner.
		Responses also were less personalized as participants were able to provide specific suggestions to improve the model for future cohorts.

Figure 2.1   Findings from the pilot project. *Source:* Allsopp, DeMarie, Alvarez McHatton, and Doone (2006).

had its challenges. At the time of the study, none of the instructors were tenured. Two were members of the Department of Special Education, the department that originally began the partnership with the PDS elementary school and which fully supported the initiative. However, some faculty in the Department of Psychological and Social Foundations questioned the third faculty member with regard to the use of her time related to the need to publish for tenure and promotion. Faculty members were left to wonder whether their willingness to innovate would be embraced (or not) at the point when they went up for tenure and promotion. A second challenge occurred when a small number of students in the cohort reacted negatively to their experience. Their negative responses derived mainly from their displeasure with having to be away from the university during what they deemed as "class time." Additionally, students were not used to having faculty on-site at their practicum. Some students interpreted this as being overly supervised. The negativity from this small group of students was transmitted to the following cohort, which then became a barrier the faculty member had to address in the subsequent semester.

PROGRAMMATIC CHANGES

Undergraduate Program

The collaboration between our Special Education Department and our partner schools continues to evolve as a result of our experiences and new demands from both within the K–20 educational system and beyond. At the undergraduate level, several "logistical" issues were addressed the following year. The *Learning and Developing Child* course was not scheduled during the same semester, so we were not able to continue our course-practicum collaboration with the faculty member from Psychological and Social Foundations. Additionally, one of the other two faculty members in the reported study was not available to teach, due to being assigned a different course load. Therefore, a faculty member from our department, who was not involved with the previous study, agreed to work with the remaining faculty member to build on what was learned from the prior year's work. Two primary changes occurred as a result from feedback received from students. First, students wanted to have their classes held on the university campus instead of at the school site, as was done previously. This response arose from students' expressing that having classes off of the university campus made them feel disconnected from the university and the college student-life experience.

A second change was that the two faculty members agreed to co-teach the two courses linked to the practicum and to co-supervise the practicum.

This change arose from our desire to more explicitly integrate the content and field experience compared to what we were able to accomplish when each faculty member taught the linked courses individually. The two special education courses were taught as a single block and content between the two courses (*Clinical Teaching* and *Behavior Management*) was blended across the semester. Figure 2.2 shows the planning schedule that illustrates how content was blended across the two courses. Each faculty member took ownership for planning and leading class activities for which they had the most expertise. Both faculty members spent one day at the school site where a classroom space was available for their use. They completed observations of students, met with students in the PDS classroom, modeled practices, worked with school faculty, and held a practicum seminar in the PDS classroom once per week. In addition, various school personnel came in during the practicum to discuss school-based practices and procedures (e.g., the school nurse came in to speak about universal precautions and how medicines were dispensed at the school; the assistant principal spoke about emergency situations, what each emergency code meant, and how various emergency situations were handled at the school).

That same semester, the advanced doctoral student who was part of the initial study was assigned to teach the *Teaching Exceptional Adolescents and Adults* course which was linked to the level three practicum. The level three semester focuses on secondary special education settings; therefore, a similar faculty on-site model was developed with a middle school (our first PDS) and a nearby high school. Faculty were at the school during the two days of the practicum, working with our students and fostering existing relationships with the schools' administration and faculty. Based on student feedback, classes were taught at the university rather than on-site, although practicum seminars were held on-site and co-facilitated by teachers from the schools.

The model continued to evolve the following semester. For example, the faculty member who teaches the course on *Mental Retardation and Developmental Disabilities* incorporated a site-based teaching component where approximately eight of fifteen class sessions were taught at a school that serves as an Exceptional Education Center for students with significant support needs. The school's Media Center was made available for use as a college classroom. Students spent the allotted class time at the center where part of the time was devoted to "class" and the remainder was used for students to work with the school's K–12 students in their classrooms. Theory and practice were bridged in various ways but most concretely through a "materials project" that required students to create or adapt materials for a student or students in the K–12 class, taking into account the characteristics of the students in the three adaptive skills areas (conceptual, social and practical), as well as the students' IEP goals. This experience proved to be quite ben-

Week	Date	W & R Practicum Seminar and/or Assignment(s)	Instruction 9:00–11:00 AT	Inquiry 12:00–2:00 PT	Indiv/Assistance 2:00–2:50 PT
1 Class	08/26 T		*Syllabus review and course explanation; Reading tutoring training*		
Practicum	08/27 W (5 hrs)		*Reading tutoring training—EDU 316 8:00 a.m.–2:00 p.m.*		
Practicum	08/28 R (6 hrs)		*Reading tutoring practice—School 8:00 a.m.–3:00 p.m.*		
2 Class	09/02 T		**Beliefs in Discipline (BM)**	Horse Whisperer (BM/CT)	Intro to iBooks (BM/CT)
Practicum	09/03 W (7 hrs 35 min)	*Tour school site; orientation to school policies and procedures*			
Practicum	09/04 R (7 hrs 35 min)	*Begin Informal Assessments instructional module: (1) definitions; (2) overview from big picture; (3) apply to case*			

Note: This figure shows how course content and instructional responsibilities were integrated across the Clinical Teaching (CT) and Behavior Management courses, the Level II Practicum, and related Seminar for the first three weeks. Text in *italics* represents shared responsibility for content, text underlined represents lead responsibility for content by CT instructor, and text in **bold** represents lead responsibility for content by Behavior Management instructor.

Week	Date	W & R Practicum Seminar and/or Assignment(s)	Instruction 9:00–11:00 AT	Inquiry 12:00–2:00 PT	Indiv/Assistance 2:00–2:50 PT
3 Class	09/09 T		• Informal Academic Assessments *(CT)* • Performance Data Collection/Instructional decision-making (BM/CT)	Models/Theories/Research *(BM)*	Functional Behavior Assessment *(BM)*
Practicum	09/10 W (7 hrs 35 min)	*Discuss practicum site's classroom management plans*			
Practicum	09/11 R (7 hrs 35 min)	*Review student IEPs*			
4	09/16 T		• Informal Academic Assessments *(CT)* • Performance Data Collection/Instructional decision-making (BM/CT)	Models/Theories/Research *(BM)*	Functional Behavior Assessment *(BM)*
	09/17 W (7 hrs 35 min)				
	09/18 R (7 hrs 35 min)	*Review student IEPs*			

Figure 2.2 Example of planning schedule showing how content and co-teaching arrangements were integrated across the Clinical Teaching and Behavior Management courses, Level II Practicum, and Seminar.

Week	Date	W & R Practicum Seminar and/or Assignment(s)	Instruction 9:00–11:00 AT	Inquiry 12:00–2:00 PT	Indiv/Assistance 2:00–2:50 PT
5	09/23 T		• Systematic Explicit Instruction *(BM/CT)* • Planning Instruction: *(BM/CT)* 1. Academics (lesson plans, role in planning IEPs) 2. **PBS (PBS Plans, IEPs)**	**Curriculum: *(CT)*** • SSS • GenEd • ESE • **Diploma options** • **State testing** • **District curricula** • **Accommodations and modifications**	
	09/24 W (7 hrs 35 min)				
	09/25 R (7 hrs 35 min)				
6	09/30 T		• Systematic Explicit Instruction *(BM/CT)* • Planning Instruction: *(BM/CT)* 1. Academics (lesson plans, role in planning IEPs) 2. **PBS (PBS Plans, IEPs)**	**Curriculum: *(CT)*** • SSS • GenEd • ESE • **Diploma options** • **State testing** • **District curricula** • **Accommodations and modifications**	
	10/01 W (7 hrs 35 min)	Seminar: Five-skill activity			
	10/02 R (7 hrs 35 min)				

Figure 2.2 Example of planning schedule (continued)

eficial to the students and the Center (such that the same collaboration has continued to the present).

Increasing student enrollment in our department, changes in leadership, and increased teacher turnover at the initial study site required us to rethink the partnership to best meet the needs of our students and our partner schools. We continue to develop relationships with other school sites, thus expanding our placement options while still ensuring a reciprocal relationship among partners in which both benefit.

MASTERS OF ARTS IN TEACHING PROGRAM

A critical teacher shortage led to the development of the Master of Arts (MAT) Program in Exceptional Student Education. Since the MAT program enrolls only currently practicing teachers who are working toward certification in special education, we had to develop both early field experiences and final internships that allowed for this reality, while maintaining a structure that effectively helped our students develop the necessary competencies. It was decided to involve our PPPs (master teachers who take a graduate level course in mentoring) who were already trained to mentor pre-service final intern teachers at the undergraduate level. Our PPPs were willing and eager to expand their roles in the partnership; thus, we were able to extend the PDS model to include the MAT program. We adapted the undergraduate model, such that each MAT student was paired with a PPP who was located at his or her school or a neighboring school. As students complete coursework before embarking on their final internship, they also engage in specific practica where they apply what they learn in their courses and demonstrate their competencies through performance-based products. This is accomplished through the supervision of their PPP, which continues during the final paid internship required of all MAT program students.

Both districts continue to be extremely supportive of the MAT partnership which is evident in the now-shared responsibility of placing final interns for both the undergraduate program and the MAT program. Once a role exclusive to the district, we are now better able to meet the needs of our undergraduate interns in placing them in settings that support their learning needs and work collaboratively with the district in pairing a PPP with a MAT.

SUMMARY OF ADDITIONAL RELATED RESEARCH INITIATIVES

Since the last reported study, several research initiatives have either been completed or are in progress. A faculty member from the Department of

Secondary Education, English Education, teaches her Middle Grades Methods course at one of the sites used for our level three field experience. Over the past several years, we have developed a collaborative venture in which the English Education majors are paired with Special Education majors as co-teaching partners. Both groups participate in an on-site seminar facilitated by both faculty members (Alvarez McHatton & Daniel, in press). At this particular site (USF's first PDS), the relationship has resulted in collaborative ventures beyond placement of interns. For example, both faculty (English Education and Special Education) sponsor a Latina Women's Group which meets once every other week. The purpose of the group is to engage girls in a critical examination of their school-home-community experiences. This project is entering its fourth year. During the 2007–08 school year, a male faculty member will be sponsoring a Latino Men's Group with similar goals. In addition, how middle school students from various service-delivery models perceive their learning environments has been explored and preliminary findings shared with the faculty.

We have implemented a reading initiative in collaboration with our partner elementary schools in which our pre-service teachers work with struggling readers implementing research-based practices and learning about the use of data to inform instruction. Our strong connections with the local districts have led to a para-to-professional program, allowing individuals who currently work in the school system to obtain their undergraduate degree in special education. The paraprofessionals who have graduated from our program have been some of our strongest students, and many of them are continuing for their Masters' degree.

Another project is a one-to-one laptop initiative focused on the integration of instructional technology into teaching and field experiences. The use of instructional technology is implemented into coursework in a developmental model moving from acquisition of technology skills to proficiency using technology for pre-service teachers' own learning as well as their students' learning. Pre-service teachers are required to implement instructional technology during their field experiences and utilize technology to provide access to the general education curriculum by students with disabilities. Their instructional and assistive technology skills are shared with their supervising teachers.

REFLECTION AND INSIGHTS
BASED ON OUR EXPERIENCES

We took an opportunity to reflect on these experiences as teacher educators who have shared common PDS experiences. The discussion was captured by recording what each faculty member said using a laptop computer.

Comments were reviewed and coded, resulting in the emergence of several themes that provide a view of the benefits and challenges of university-school partnerships.

Emotional Impact on Faculty

A theme that emerged quickly in our discussion was the emotional and sometimes physical impact that engaging in PDSs can have on faculty. One faculty member who was part of the initial study recalled being *tired all the time.* Another noted, "*. . . it was draining . . . students were resistant, passive aggressive because of the change*" . . . "*they felt they were guinea pigs. . . .*" Our desire to improve the field experience through the new model was not easily accepted by our students, "*students' expected that their experiences (of support from faculty) were a process that should remain consistent across time*" and across semesters.

Changes in personnel at both the school and the university across time and managing these changes were a major source of stress, "*. . . the second year I was here, I was so burned out from doing this . . .* [there were] *so many variables* [to consider]." Several of us noted that the support received from colleagues who also worked in PDSs was a major source of comfort. When asked why we continue to do it, the response was unanimous, "*. . .* [be] *cause I thought it was the right way to do it.*" The strong conviction that such work was necessary did not diminish concerns about sustainability across the board.

Changes in faculty also increased stress levels as, "*. . . you have to negotiate with each new person who comes along.*" This, along with added responsibilities, made one faculty member note, "*. . . we also have new stuff on our plate, and, when a new person comes along, I am not sure that I have the energy to do it again.*" Changes in the assignment of doctoral students to assist with practicum supervision or TA create the need for additional preparation time, "*. . . like with doctoral students who assist with supervision each semester, there can be a significant change* [from semester to semester]. *It can be like doing a new prep each semester, which can be arduous.*"

Dissonance in Perspective between Faculty and Students

Another theme that emerged was the level of dissonance in perspective between faculty and students about what "practicum" and its related expectations means. For example, when we held classes on the school site, many students did not like this arrangement: "*Students thought they had more work* to do because of the way the classes were scheduled. They wanted to be on campus, be a college student . . . they couldn't separate class from practicum. . . ." The fact that faculty were on-site meant that the students "couldn't sneak out early." Students found it difficult to understand that "class didn't begin and end at a specific time, it extended beyond the class—they want to put things in little boxes."

A common sentiment among students across the last several years has been that they are reticent to see themselves as beginning professionals: "They kept saying I'm not ready to be a professional yet, I am a student. . . ." Some felt that they would become a professional when they "get paid. . . ." noting, "(I'm) free labor (now)."

As we restructured the model over time, students seemed to have a very concrete and simplistic view of what a practicum was supposed to be. Their perception has consistently been that a practicum means "one student placed in one classroom with one teacher." We have tried integrating several clinical experiences as part of the more traditional one-student in one-classroom structure. For example, over the last few years students have engaged in one-to-one reading instruction experiences with struggling readers organized similar to a resource room model. Their students met in a common classroom space for 30-minute instructional sessions, where supervising faculty could observe and provide feedback as students developed knowledge of the reading process and developed beginning reading instruction skills. They came to the "resource room" at different times, based on when the instruction best fits in their student's schedule: "The resource model was not viewed as a field experience [by students] . . . or what students' definition of what 'teaching' is. . . ." For examples, students did not consider the resource room model as ". . . being in the field."

Departmental Differences

Our discussion also revealed differences in how our departments view our investment of time in explicitly linking teaching with practica. One department questioned whether this was a good use of time as it relates to gaining tenure and promotion: "This was new [for one of our departments] . . . [they] questioned me about spending my time wisely before obtaining tenure." A few faculty from the department not involved in this type of teaching have perceived our work as contrary to what they do and how they go about teaching. "A lot of people in the department [said that this person] isn't going to tell me what to teach or how to teach it. . . ." "[they] felt it was an infringement on academic freedom." However, once faculty member saw that what we were doing did not really affect them, this sentiment changed: "Now there are pats on the backs for changes made in how I teach."

Our individual departments have different ways of operating and our teaching and research cultures are somewhat different. In addition to fostering university-school relationships, we also had to foster cross-departmental relationships; we *"didn't know each other, so as much as we were trying to do things* [together] *we had different perspectives . . . different work styles across departments. . . . which may have added to student confusion."*

Team Teaching as a Supportive Structure

The supportive nature of team teaching through our PDS experiences was another theme that emerged from our discussion. An important function of our collaborative teaching structures was that it provided us a process for appropriately addressing student concerns, communicating to them in a unified fashion, and getting feedback regarding questions we might have about our teaching. By:

> . . . hanging out in the portable together, sharing differing perspectives; . . . being able to process together, prevented students from going through the divorced parent syndrome; . . . I remember sitting at the picnic table and processing the experiences we were having with the students; [helping us to] situate the problems [to determine] is it me?

Another important outcome of team teaching was that it provided us a way to plan in a consistent and integrated fashion:

> Together you can talk about what you saw; . . . I feel more confident about what I am doing when I am doing it with someone else, and we have some sort of shared consensus about what you are doing, although you don't always agree; . . . [I was] more aware of program goals and helping students see that my course is a part of their program. . . .

University-Partner School Differences

Yet another emergent theme was the perceived difference between the university perspectives and expectations and those of the PDS. Sometimes school personnel perceived the practicum and what our students were learning in a more positive light than did we: *"While I was seeing all the problems that were resulting, the school's reaction was positive—'they were great,' very pleased by the partnership. The school didn't have the same experience* (as we did)"; *causing one participant to ask: "How does the school's experience mirror our experience with the students? How does that equate with what we see on the other side of the fence?"*

While we, as faculty, saw ourselves as individuals who could collaborate with the school regarding needs they wanted to address, sometimes schools did not react as if they had the same perspective:

> I didn't get the sense that teachers and the school [saw us as a resource], although they liked working with us and getting the students involved. . . . they asked if I was interested here and there but not as if they saw us as a resource for further developing their school. They still saw a dichotomy [between the school and the university]. . . . a few things happened [sought my help] while I was there that was directly related to special education [testing, etc.]. . . . they hired people [to provide assistance] . . . although there were multiple offers [from the university].

This is not surprising as research indicates that schools which function as PDSs often consider the function of PDSs to be related to the preparation of pre-service teachers first and foremost (Voltz, 2001).

The necessity of developing new partnerships in the upcoming semesters due to changing leadership at one of our PDS sites and increasing student enrollment also highlighted the perception of dissonance between the school and university, particularly related to expectations: "*And now* [we are] *trying to develop new relationships with other schools, it is going through that process of what they think practica is,* [viewing it as more than] . . . *that they are getting some students and they have extra hands; . . . getting them to think that we are going beyond that, moving to a reciprocal process.*"

This discussion led one participant to question, "Is it that they view university faculty as part timers unable to understand what it is like to be there every day, day in and day out?"

A discussion ensued that centered on the prospect of linking with schools where previous graduates of our programs served in a leadership capacity and whether such a situation would facilitate the PDS process: ". . . [a previous faculty member] *wrote about that; she was the university liaison for our first PDS. It wasn't until she developed a relationship with the administration at the school that things started to click.*" We pondered, "*What will happen when our students become principals at schools and we move into that school? Would it be different?*" One faculty member noted that he had done ". . . *work at a school where a previous student was now head of the ESE department—she was excited and tried to cultivate interest in her colleagues.*" He noted that "*the entrée was much easier; . . .there were some internal issues that created some difficulties.*" This faculty member also questioned how the fact that our students are special education majors may affect how some teachers at the schools perceive them.

Authenticity

The belief that our teaching and our students' learning was informed within much more authentic contexts was another theme that emerged:

> In a typical model [Psychological and Social Foundations course], even though I try to get the students to go to the schools, usually in my role as higher ed. faculty, I am in the school for one or two hours. In [the PDS model], you were part of the pulse of the school . . . [I] felt I had a better experience . . . I felt like I lived in the school.

Impact on Our Perspectives about Teaching

The impact that participating in a PDS had on our perspectives about teaching and how we generalized these perspectives to other teaching contexts was another theme that emerged. This was particularly true for a faculty member in Psychological and Social Foundations, a department that offers courses to multiple departments but is not traditionally a part of practica experiences offered through initial teacher certification programs:

> A year after [participating in a PDS] I taught the same course in Jamaica and I think the [PDS] experience helped me to incorporate things into my class . . . I would link with places [in Jamaica] . . . people talked and helped me not to make cultural assumptions . . . to allow the context for teaching to enter into my university classroom. . . . I intentionally structured the course so one week we were together then they went out [to area schools]; they brought back [their experiences], and we had two weeks together; my previous PDS experience was a building bridge on changing how I teach; . . . I have not taught the same since having this experience . . . next year I did the same thing with early childhood [program] . . . I had the same type of experience; . . . I think I am a far better teacher when I teach in that context, so now I try to have more experiential experiences, within my courses in which students gather data from their field experiences and they bring them into class where we analyze and discuss them.

Are We Making a Difference?

Finally, comments centered on a final theme. We collectively reflected on whether we were making a difference as faculty. We wondered about the extent to which some of the issues facing schools and universities today were fragmenting the impact of developing and engaging in PDSs (e.g., teacher shortages in particular disciplines; alternative certification routes; high-stakes testing; an emphasis on including students with special needs in general education classrooms without appropriate supports or qualified teachers). Will these issues be short-term in nature or will they continue to affect our recruitment, preparation and retention of special education teachers, and the nature of work with PDSs?

Issues on the university end of the spectrum and the seeming contradictions between those changes and legislative mandates regarding teacher preparation are also a concern:

> Sustainability is a question, changes in the university . . . [the university] is extremely FTE driven, so larger numbers [of students] are required. . . .

> [the] change to a research one university [status] is another question. . . .

These changes also affect the supervision of pre-service teachers, as supervising teachers struggle with the inequity of a professional program versus an alternative certification program:

> Implications for teacher education include supervising teachers conflicted with their role [as supervisors, having to make] decisions of whether a student should repeat a field experience, etc. . . . These decisions severely affect lives, yet others can simply take a test and they are "teachers."

Some discussions we have had with our students and their reflections on their relatively recent experiences in K–12 schools added to our questioning. "More and more of our students say, 'Don't hate me, but I sometimes think about getting a degree in anything, and [then] taking the test to be a teacher.'"

As our time together came to a close, we found ourselves exploring the challenges both entities face as we go about our daily work: "*Thinking about PDSs, it is like we are in a context together but working in separate spheres . . . instead of meshing the worlds together, there is some clashing . . .* [there are] *both similar and different variables affecting what we do.*" Ultimately, working with PDSs is much like working on any relationship. It requires attention, time, and active engagement from all parties: "*It* [the partnership] *is symbiotic in a sense but once we stop working on it, the whole thing falls apart.*"

IMPLICATIONS

We have learned much from our work with PDSs. Successful implementation requires an understanding of the developmental process that our students go through as they progress through their program. The adage of "baby steps" is an important one to remember, as well as the need to structure field experiences so that they have the greatest benefit. Furthermore, as faculty, being aware of the developmental milestones at each level helps us as we attempt to address issues related to the student developmental stage rather than as an indication of personal failure.

The integration of a site-based model, which strengthened our existing partnerships with the districts in our area, has led to stronger internship experiences for our students. The collaboration with schools and each other provides a venue to discuss students' strengths and needs in order to ensure a positive learning experience across all practica and the final internship. Furthermore, this relationship is instrumental when a student experiences difficulties in mastering course and practicum objectives. The fact that faculty are available each week means that issues are addressed in a more timely manner—both supervising teachers and university faculty work in tandem in providing developmental feedback and support to the students.

Finally, the benefit of our collaborative reflection as we embarked on this project was extremely beneficial. Although we strive to maintain open lines of communication, our busy schedules make it difficult to set aside time, as a collective unit, to reflect on our experiences, share our successes and our failures, consider future projects, and learn from each other. Spending time reflecting on our previous experiences and current efforts in some ways re-energized our belief of working with PDSs.

Our discussion reaffirmed the need for flexibility and for looking beyond a traditional model for PDS work. We recognize that sustainability requires sharing information with all partners; this includes university faculty and schools, as well as our students, colleagues within and across departments, and the college. Furthermore, relationships require time—a limited commodity—to maintain. If we believe the reciprocal nature of PDS work is, indeed, necessary for school reform, we need to develop creative opportunities to sustain the partnership.

Because PDS work is multifaceted, there are multiple ways to construct partnerships. Additional research is needed exemplifying these complex and varied relationships so that we can continue to learn from each other.

REFERENCES

Allsopp, D. H., DeMarie, D., Alvarez McHatton, P., & Doone, E. (2006). Partnerships, data collection and teacher preparation: Does an on-site course-practicum delivery model enhance early pre-service teacher preparation? *Teacher Education Quarterly 33*(1), 19–35.

Alvarez McHatton, P., & Daniel, P. (in press). Co-teaching at the pre-service level: Special education majors collaborate with English education majors. *Teacher Education and Special Education.*

Epanchin, B., & Colucci, K. (2002). The professional development school without walls: A partnership between a university and two school districts. *Remedial and Special Education 23(6)*, 349–358.

Epanchin, B., & Wooley-Brown, C. (1995). Sharing the responsibility for educating "homegrown teachers." In J. Paul, H. Rosselli, & D. Evans (Eds.), *Integrating school restructuring and special education reform* (pp. 353–372). Fort Worth, TX: Harcourt Brace.

Epanchin, B., & Wooley-Brown, C. (1993). A university-school district collaborative project for preparing paraprofessionals to be come special educators. *Teacher Education and Special Education, 16,* 110–123.

Evans, D., Harris, D., Adeigbola, M., Houston, D., & Argott, L. (1993). Restructuring the special education services. *Teacher Education and Special Education, 16,* 137–145.

Evans, D. & Rosselli. (1995). Reflections of chapters 14-12. In J. L. Paul, H. Rosselli, & D. Evans (Eds.), *Integrating school restricting and special education reform* (pp. 414–417). Fort Worth, TX: Harcourt Brace.

Harris, D., & Evans, D. (1995). Restructuring for inclusion. In J. Paul, H. Rosselli, & D. Evans (Eds.), *Integrating school restructuring and special education reform* (pp. 322–334). Fort Worth, TX: Harcourt Brace.

Prater, M. A., & Sileo, T. W. (2002). School-university partnerships in special education field experiences: A national descriptive study. *Remedial and Special Education, 23,* 325–335.

Rose, E. (2002). A special issue on school–university partnerships in special education. *Remedial and Special Education, 23,* 322.

Rosselli, H., Perez, S., & Claggett, K. (1995). Becoming a teacher for all children in a professional development school. In J. Paul, H. Rosselli, & D. Evans (Eds.), *Integrating school restructuring and special education reform* (pp. 335–352). Fort Worth, TX: Harcourt Brace.

Rosselli, H., Perez, S., Piersall, K., & Pantridge, O. (1993). Evolution of a professional development school: The story of a partnership. *Teacher Education and Special Education, 16,* 124–136.

Sapon-Shevin, M. (1990). Special education and the Holmes agenda for teacher education reform. *Theory into Practice, 29,* 55–60.

Stoddard, K., & Danforth, S. (1995). Empowering teachers to be responsive to individual differences. In J. Paul, H. Rosselli, & D. Evans (Eds.) *Integrating school restructuring and special education reform* (pp. 322–334). Fort Worth, TX: Harcourt Brace.

Voltz, D. L. (2001). Preparing general education teachers for inclusive settings: The role of special education teachers in the professional development school context. *Learning Disability Quarterly, 24,* 288–296.

CHAPTER 3

TEACHING CONTENT IN PDSs

Investigating Mathematics Preparation

Janice L. Nath and Marion Godine

ABSTRACT

In an attempt to improve the preparation of teachers in mathematics, the authors investigated how teacher candidates best learn to teach the subject within an urban PDS setting. Among the areas studied were teacher beliefs, levels of confidence, amounts of time spent on numerous areas of mathematics and pedagogy, and how PDS settings may be more effective in teaching mathematics methodology.

INTRODUCTION

For the past decade, the issue of mathematics education has attracted as much attention, as it perhaps did during the 1950s following the launch of Sputnik (Associated Press, 2006). After Sputnik, Abbey (2005), first quoting West, writes:

We realized a lead we took for granted was not as much as we thought it was . . . I think that's happening again. We look at our competition and they

University and School Connections, pages 49–64
Copyright © 2008 by Information Age Publishing

are putting a lot of their income into math and science research education. . . . They're recognizing the deficit compared to other countries in the
number of math, science, technology and engineering degrees. They're looking at a number of areas to try to address the shortage because it affects our
whole nation. The federal government is aware of it. The business leaders are
certainly aware of it. (online quote)

A host of calls for better methods and increased time for mathematics for
school children has resulted in special programs, extra stipends for teachers
of mathematics, and state and national initiatives (Chandler, 2007). However, many of these results have been lackluster in increasing knowledge and
scores (Dittman, 2005). One negative issue in teaching new teachers how
to reach students in mathematics may focus on those teacher education
programs that offer few opportunities for mathematics methods to be seen
or used in an actual classroom. Because these methods are taken out of
context in sterile university classrooms, they may seem unrealistic and unus-
able to new teachers. Sutton (2007) believes that teachers have particular
needs and that teacher preparation in the elementary schools is lacking in
mathematics and science. Even though the academic needs may have been
met there still exists a limited application experience. However, using the
professional development school (PDS) model, pre-service teachers can
gain valuable information both from professors of mathematics education
in mathematics methods courses and then move directly into classrooms to
see and try many of these methods with children. Zeichner (2007) noted
that "the focus [of some PDSs] is on improving the pre-service preparation of teachers by closely connecting preparation with real school context
and by attempting to take advantage of the expert knowledge that exists in
schools in addition to that from university" (p. 11).

This study investigated ways by which the PDS model could be superior
to a more traditional model of teacher education within the mathematics
content area. A detailed survey that was administered to teacher candidates in an urban PDS yielded a rich description of the candidates' beliefs,
confidence levels, and amounts of time spent on numerous areas of mathematics and teaching of mathematics. The data were used to determine
ways in which PDS settings may be more effective in teaching mathematics
methodology.

PROCEDURE

Students from a teacher education program located in a large, south/cen-
tral urban area are placed in schools for three "Block" semesters (at least

two of these are in urban PDSs). Student teachers in their third Block can request placements in non-PDS schools, although many teacher candidates opt to stay at their PDS sites and continue there with their student teaching. This study focused upon the first two semesters in which all students are in PDS placements. The mathematics methodology course was taught alongside two other on-site courses (in their school PDS site) during the first of these blocks or semesters. Teacher candidates seeking Pre-K–4 or 4–8 state certification were placed accordingly in a mentor's classroom at either an elementary or a middle school. The semester-long program for the teacher candidates included a three-hour weekly mathematics course and a total of no less than 60 hours in an assigned mentor's classroom. At times during the semester, the instructor "borrowed" classrooms, small groups, and individual children in the school to demonstrate lessons during class time. Course assignments during the semester were tied to activities within the mentor's classroom as much as possible. Pre-service teachers were also asked to teach a minimum of two lessons during the PDS semesters; they were each observed and debriefed by a university supervisor.

A survey was given to all elementary and middle school pre-service teacher candidates who participated in both the PDS and non-PDS components to investigate the amount and quality of mathematics observed, comfort levels in teaching, perceived ability to use mathematical tools such as calculators and manipulatives in the classroom, and other areas. Knowledge of national standards in mathematics was also explored.

Of the 23 surveys returned, one participant was African American, five were White, 12 were Hispanic, one was Asian, and one was Middle Eastern. All responders had completed their course and field experiences at PDS sites.

RESULTS

Because a methods instructor is limited to only his or her classroom hours, it was important to determine how much more knowledge and experience in mathematics the teacher candidates were able to gain by field experience in their PDS placement. In Blocks I and II, where students are definitely placed in a PDS, participants reported more than 300 mathematics lessons observed in mentors' classrooms. Of those, 22 participants reported that the lessons that they observed were focused more upon problem-solving than upon practicing algorithms or drill. Respondents reported teaching a total of 37 lessons in mathematics during Blocks I and II (although teacher candidates also taught lessons in other content areas).

Designing a Mathematics Lesson

The comfort level in designing an effective mathematics lesson had 14 responses as "very" comfortable and nine responses as "moderately." Only one responded as "slightly" comfortable, and no students responded as "not (comfortable) at all." The survey also sought to determine the reason why students felt comfortable designing a mathematics lesson. Students who answered positively to being comfortable with planning mathematics instruction, were asked to discern the percentages of what they believed contributed to their learning (the methods course at the PDS, the PDS field placement, or past experiences). Their responses are summarized in the Table 3.1.

TABLE 3.1   Student Responses to Questions on Sources of Their Comfort Levels on Designing a Mathematics Lesson

	PDS Methods Course	PDS Field Placement	Past Experiences
1–10%	5	6	13
11–25%	4	2	4
26–50%	7	8	3
51–74%	5	4	9
75%+	7	7	2

The kinds of past experiences that they listed were reportedly teaching in a day care and tutoring. In some cases, the respondents indicated that they had maintained strong mathematics abilities throughout their K–12 schooling.

Use of Manipulatives

Part of the mathematics instruction that helps children learn best is instruction with manipulatives. Cathcart et al. (2000) note that:

> Children seem to learn best when learning begins with concrete representation of a mathematical concept. In fact, it is best to provide children with multiple embodiments of the concept. To provide multiple embodiments, the use of manipulative materials is essential in all mathematics classrooms. (p. 23)

The authors note that it is not simply the use of the manipulatives that guarantee success, but the steps that teachers take in planning and teaching with them that helps children gain success. However, teacher candidates who have not had an opportunity to use manipulatives with children have difficulties with their use in their classrooms. This can result in little or no actual use and/or student understanding. Therefore, the survey sought information on the comfort level of students in using manipulatives in teaching mathematics (manipulatives were also introduced in the mathematics methodology course). Fourteen respondents marked that they were "very" comfortable using math manipulates, six indicated a "moderate" comfort level, one noted a "slight" comfort level, and no one responded negatively. When asked to what they attributed this comfort level, the following percentages (Table 3.2) were reported.

TABLE 3.2   Student Responses to Questions on Sources of Their Comfort Levels on Uses of Manipulatives

	PDS Methods Course	PDS Field Placement	Past Experiences
1–10%	1	—	2
11–25%	4	6	4
26–50%	7	7	1
51–74%	—	1	1
75%+	10	2	2

Even though it is hoped that manipulatives are a part of all mathematics classrooms, the authors wanted to determine if manipulates were indeed part of the PDS field experience. The survey asked if students had access to manipulatives in their assigned rooms. Nine reported that they had observed them in their Block I semester, while 14 candidates reported manipulatives available in their Block II placement. Calculator availability was seen much less, with only seven candidates reporting having them available to children in their Block I semester, and 11 candidates observed these in Block II.

It was also important for students to see various types of manipulatives being used. Of course, candidates were in their placements one or two days a week, so they may have missed the use of various types of manipulatives. However, the researchers wanted to see to what types of manipulatives teacher candidates were exposed in their placements. The kinds of manipulatives that teacher candidates observed being used in their Block I or Block II PDS were (1) pattern blocks, (2) Geo Boards, (3) algebra tiles, (4) tangrams, (5) attribute blocks, (6) number lines, (7) Cuisenaire rods, (8) counters, (9) fraction rods/pieces, (10) two color counters, (11) snap cubes, and (12) base-ten blocks. Miras were not seen, in any classroom, while the manipulatives most seen being used in classrooms were pattern blocks (more than 30 times), base-ten blocks, number lines, Cuisenaire rods, and fraction rods/pieces.

Content Knowledge

Mathematics methodology for teacher education candidates can be stressful due, at times, to lack of mathematics content knowledge. Being familiar with the mathematics included in the content cannot be overemphasized, as noted by Cathcart et al. (2000). Therefore, the survey also sought to discover information on teacher candidate comfort level on content knowledge. Eleven responders noted that they felt "very" comfortable with content knowledge, while 11 stated that they were "moderately" comfortable. No one responded that they were "slightly" comfortable, and one replied "not comfortable at all." Table 3.3 shows the percentage to which teacher candidates attribute their comfort levels to content knowledge.

TABLE 3.3   Student Responses to Questions on Sources of Their Comfort Levels on Content Knowledge

	PDS Methods Course	PDS Field Placement	Past Experiences
1–10%	1	—	5
11–25%	2	7	3
26–50%	8	7	3
51–74%	4	2	—
75%+	5	2	2

The Use of the Calculator

One tool that has made a difference in the learning of mathematics is the calculator, and yet "calculators are not being optimally used in classrooms" (Cathcart et al., 2000, p. 6). Yet many teacher candidates may not have had experiences using the calculator with children. Another question tapped teacher candidates' comfort level in teaching with calculators and to what they attribute any positive comfort level in this area. Nine respondents felt "very" comfortable, while nine felt "moderately" comfortable. Six felt "slightly" comfortable, and one felt "not at all comfortable" (See Table 3.4).

In Texas, the amount of "skill and drill" can be of question in teacher preparation due to high-stakes testing prevalent in the State curriculum. Too often teacher candidates do not see full lessons; instead they often observe activities based upon test preparation such as worksheets and practice tests. However, teacher candidates in elementary school PDSs reported very little drill practice in either Block I or II; slightly more drill exercises were evident in middle school PDSs. In fact, teacher candidates reported that "mathematics related to real life" activities were in 100 percent of the lessons they observed.

TABLE 3.4   Student Responses to Questions on Sources of Their Comfort Levels on Teaching with a Calculator

	PDS Methods Course	PDS Field Placement	Past Experiences
1–10%	1	3	4
11–25%	5	3	4
26–50%	3	3	1
51–74%	2	1	1
75%+	4	2	2

Technology use was available in some of these urban PDS sites, particularly in the middle school PDSs. Seventy-eight percent of the teacher candidates reported integration in their Blocks I and II. The technology observed included PowerPoints, calculators, computer programs, games, and various WebQuests.

Part of being successful in mathematics for all genders is making sure that expectations to do well are set for both boys and girls. When asked if teacher candidates observed strategies that address gender equity in their PDS, 20 teacher candidates noted specific instances of this. They referenced such strategies as "modeling, using pictures (of both genders), calling on all, and grouping in mixed groups." Twenty-three participants noted that they believe *all* students were expected and encouraged to be successful in mathematics. Cruickshank, Jenkins, and Metcalf (2003) believe that "effective teachers have high expectations for success and are encouraging and supportive of students (p. 344).

To address their overall change in growth toward teaching mathematics in each placement, 20 participants reported growth in Block I, and 23 reported growth in Block II, with seven of these reporting more than 75 percent positive growth in Block II. When asked to what they might attribute this to, participants listed, for example, manipulatives, "the kids," watching my mentor, the math methods course, more experience, more practice, time in the classroom, planning lessons, managing a class, and another math class.

Self-Efficacy

Confidence is also an important part of teaching mathematics. Self-efficacy is "an individual's belief about his or her capability to succeed at specific task" (Eggen & Kauchak, 2003, p. 393), so teachers who believe in their own abilities are often more effective. To tap this, authors asked candidates who were going into student teaching if they felt comfortable teaching mathematics. Twenty-one participants stated that they were, while no respondents said that were not. Another question that touched upon this concept, asked if they believed that teaching mathematics would be difficult or easy. One answered "very difficult," one answered "difficult," eleven answered "not so difficult" and ten answered "easy."

Teacher candidates were also asked to explain the "best thing" that they had learned from their mentor about teaching mathematics. The following comments were given:

- To be patient and considerate of children' learning style.
- Classroom management and lesson planning.
- She (the teacher mentor) never rushed the students and would take extra time if needed.
- Allow students to use manipulatives.
- Set a high standard and students will meet them.
- Give the students time to explore with manipulatives.
- Using manipulatives.
- Using manipulatives and asking open-ended questions.
- Manipulatives/real life experiences!
- To not be condescending to kids and encourage everyone to try at least.
- The necessity of teaching a concept in various ways.
- Manipulatives and to provide concrete examples.
- Group work, projects, and manipulatives.
- Using real world experiences/using different approaches to gain students interest.
- Involving students to work in groups for problem-solving processes.
- Applying strategies to solve word problems.
- How to "break down" math.
- To use technology, real-life scenarios, have students practice and areas they need.
- She (the teacher mentor) praised children all the time and took extra time to help mentor the tutor.
- As a teacher, you must be excited about teaching to keep you students excited about learning.
- Connect problems to real life situations.
- Integration of basic math into other content areas.

Benefits of a PDS Over a Traditional Setting

Good teachers also learn from their children. In a traditional teacher education program, this element is not possible because classes meet on a university campus. However, the PDS model provides constant contact with children. Teacher candidates had the following to say about what they learned from children's learning of mathematics in their PDS placement:

- They learn much faster using manipulatives.
- Patience and how important the use of manipulatives are.
- Kids want to use manipulatives.
- They can meet high expectations.
- The depth of knowledge I must have.
- I really must teach step-by-step.
- Kids are very responsive and great!
- They are not always on grade level.
- Students learn differently, so do different examples.
- It's hard for a lot of them, and you HAVE to present the same topic differently.
- Ways so you can help more kids.
- They get excited when they truly understand.
- They can be successful if given the opportunity.
- They have varied learning abilities.
- To make math interesting and fun through activities.
- Explain in different ways.
- Each has a different way of working problems, so I learned how they think.
- Make it easy by going step-by-step.

Twenty responders rated their total Block I and II experience as a "5–3" on a 5-point scale, with nine rating it as a "5". Some ideas for improvement given by the teacher candidates were:

- A math concept review class.
- More lessons to be taught by us.
- Observing other classmates in teaching in their classes (you can see lots of strategies).
- More lesson presentations (practice makes perfect). The more we do it, the better prepared we are for student teaching.
- Make sure mentors don't already have too much on their plates.
- Take your math classes while you are in the Block.
- Have us teach each other more.

Limitations

There are some limitations in this study. The return rate was very low, perhaps, because it was given late in the semester in the hope of obtaining a better picture of the entire year. However, many students did not return their survey, and there were few (if any) class periods left to collect them. Teacher candidates also did not respond to every question. All reported answers were given, however. Results may have also been clearer in a comparison study, but all of the students in this program were placed in PDSs.

DISCUSSION

The survey results point positively to many elements that prepare teacher candidates to step into their own classrooms well prepared to teach mathematics after participating in a PDS experience. These include the extraordinary number of lessons in mathematics taught by expert mentors that teacher candidates were able to observe. Teacher candidates also reported the observed lessons as mostly effective lessons and less of the "skill and drill" type. Teacher candidates also were able to teach a number of lessons in mathematics very early in their professional development. This early experience allowed them time to reflect upon their skills as they continue through their program and into student teaching. When students have confidence and are comfortable teaching a content area, this can translate into a teacher who is able to help students understand more readily. The vast majority of those who responded indicated that they were comfortable in designing lessons in mathematics and will be comfortable in teaching mathematics during student teaching. The data on what teacher candidates believe helped them feel comfortable show that it is the partnership, as almost equal numbers of responders credited their university mathematics methods course and the PDS field placement. In mathematics instruction, the effective use of manipulatives in the classroom is paramount. Interestingly, most teacher candidates felt comfortable using manipulatives. Again, the partnership contributed, with the university mathematics course being slightly higher in attribution. It was expected that the university course would be far greater in mathematics content, but the data also shows that the PDS context also contributed to the level of comfort here as well, giving rise, perhaps, to the adage that "one learns it best when one must teach it." The data for comfort in teaching with calculators was consistent with the previous data, underscoring the importance of the joint experiences. A wide range of manipulatives were observed in classrooms; however, it is obvious that there is unequal use by mentors. Some used them often, and others seldom employed a wide variety. One area to work on with PDS mentors is to help them understand how important it is for teacher candidates to observe the use of manipulatives in a mathematics lesson. Of course, many of these are also grade-level specific, so the teacher candidates who were placed in Pre-K and the early grades may have missed out on an opportunity to see certain manipulatives in use. The data also points to the fact that technology has no widespread use in mathematics. One reason why PDSs work as professional development for mentors is that teacher candidates practice methods they have learned in their university course. Perhaps, integrating technology lessons into the teacher candidates' placements would help mentors to see more readily how technology can better be a part of mathematics. The most telling evidence is the comments that students gave at the end of the semester on what they learned from mentors and by working with the children. It was interesting to observe how the teacher candidates had internalized the knowledge from the mathematics methods course, but they acknowledged the source of this knowledge coming exclusively from their mentor and their field experiences. It was most positive that they had, indeed, internalized the knowledge. From the evidence in this study, it is felt that the PDS model has contributed a large amount of positive influence toward teachers-to-be in teaching mathematics.

Teitel (2001) believed that the benefits of PDSs were not well documented, and, without this documentation, they would run the risk of withering away. Zeichner (2007) states that further research should seek to "illuminate the consequences" (p. 14) for those involved at a PDS. This study illuminates the positive consequences in PDSs for teachers-to-be of mathematics and fulfills the mission of the PDS to intertwine college class work and field learning (Koehnecke, 2001). Although the evidence of good mathematics instruction will eventually be in student scores, the amount of positive feedback from the PDS experience indicates that this model is an effective way to help future elementary and middle school teachers of mathematics.

REFERENCES

Abbey, R. (2005). *U.S. encourages study of math, science.* Retrieved August 9, 2007, at: http://media.www.stateronline.com/media/storage/paper867/news/2005/11/01/News/U.s-Encourages.Increased.Study.Of.Math.Science–1518588.shtml

Associated Press. (2006). *Push for math teachers looks back to Sputnik.* Retrieved August 9, 2007, from: http://www.msnbc.msn.com/id/11103499/

Cathcart, G., Pothier, Y., Vance, J., & Bezuk, N. (2000). *Learning mathematics in elementary and middle schools.* Upper Saddle River, NJ: Merrill.

Chandler, M. (2007). *Higher pay urged to fight dearth of math, science teachers.* Retrieved August 9, 2007, at: http://www.washingtonpost.com/wp-dyn/content/article/2007/06/11/AR2007061102110.html

Cruickshank, Jenkins, D., & Metcalf, K. (2003). *The act of teaching* (3rd ed.). Boston: McGraw-Hill.

Dittman, M. (2005). *U.S. students continue to lag behind their international counterparts in math*. Retrieved August 9, 2007, from: http://www.apa.org/monitor/mar05/math.html

Eggen, P., & Kauchak, D. (2003). *Educational psychology: Windows on classrooms*. Upper Saddle River, NJ: Pearson.

Koehnecke, D. (2001). Professional development schools provide effective theory and practice. *Education, 121*(3), 589–592.

Sutton, B. (2007). *Do we need another Sputnik?* Retrieved August 9, 2007, from: http://www.digitaldivide.net/articles/view.php?ArticleID=825

Teitel, L. (2001). An assessment framework for professional development schools. *Journal of Teacher Education, 52*(1), 57–69.

Zeichner, K. (2007). Professional development schools in a culture of evidence and accountability. *School-University Partnerships: The Journal of the National Association of Professional Development Schools, 1*(1), 9–28.

APPENDIX A

Teacher Candidate Survey
of Mathematics Teaching Experiences
in Professional Development School (PDS) Methodology

I am currently in: ☐ Block I   ☐ Block II   ☐ Block III

(Some of the questions below ask question for all 3 Block. Please answer only for the Block(s) in which you have participated).

Grade level you wish to teach when certified: _____

Grade levels of your PDS placement in each Block:
   Block I: _____   Block II: _____   Block III: _____

If you are currently in Block III, are you placed in a **PDS** school for student teaching? ☐ Yes   ☐ No

My ethnicity is: _____

My age group is about: ☐ early 20s   ☐ 30s   ☐ over 30

Please read the following statements and answer questions *related to your field experiences* in your assigned professional development school (PDS). Enter the appropriate information in each blank space or respond appropriately to each question.

1. I observed *about* the following number of mathematics lessons in my PDS assignments:
   In Block I: _____   In Block II: _____   In Block III: _____

2. Did the mathematics lessons you observed seem to be effective over-all?
   Block I: ☐ Yes ☐ No   Block II: ☐ Yes ☐ No   Block III: ☐ Yes ☐ No
   If so, please explain why or why not:

3. Of the mathematics lessons that I observed, *most* were centered on problem solving rather than practicing algorithms or drill.
   Block I: ☐ Yes ☐ No   Block II: ☐ Yes ☐ No   Block III: ☐ Yes ☐ No

4. I taught the following number of mathematics lessons in my PDS.
   In Block I: _____   In Block II: _____   In Block III: _____

5. I feel comfortable designing an effective lesson plan in teaching mathematics:
   ☐ Very   ☐ Moderately   ☐ Slightly   ☐ Not at all

   If I feel comfortable designing a math lesson, it is due to (please add percentages up to 100%):
   _____% PDS Methodology Class
   _____% PDS Field Placement with mentor
   _____% Past Experiences (please explain)

6. I feel comfortable using *manipulatives* in teaching mathematics:
   ☐ Very   ☐ Moderately   ☐ Slightly   ☐ Not at all

   If I feel comfortable using manipulatives, it is due to (please add percentages up to 100%):
   _____% PDS Methodology Class
   _____% PDS Field Placement with mentor
   _____% Past Experiences (please explain)

7. I feel comfortable with mathematics *content knowledge.*
   ☐ Very   ☐ Moderately   ☐ Slightly   ☐ Not at all

   If I feel comfortable with mathematics content, it is due to (please add percentages up to 100%):
   _____% PDS Methodology Class
   _____% PDS Field Placement with mentor
   _____% Past Experiences (please explain)

8. I feel comfortable teaching with calculators in teaching mathematics:

☐ Very   ☐ Moderately   ☐ Slightly   ☐ Not at all

If I feel comfortable using teaching with calculators, it is due to (please add percentages up to 100%):

_____% PDS Methodology Class
_____% PDS Field Placement with mentor
_____% Past Experiences (please explain)

9. I observed that students had access to *manipulatives* in the PDS classroom (check all that apply):

☐ Block I   ☐ Block II   ☐ Block III

10. I observed that students had access to *calculators* in the PDS classroom (check all that apply):

☐ Block I   ☐ Block II   ☐ Block III

11. I observed the use of the following manipulatives *about how many times* in my PDS assignment:

Block I:

___ Pattern blocks	___ Attribute blocks	___ Number lines
___ Geo Boards	___ Base-ten blocks	___ Cuisenaire rods
___ Algebra tiles	___ Two-color counters	___ Counters
___ Tangrams	___ Miras	___ Fraction rods/pieces
___ Snap Cubes	___ Others	

Block II:

___ Pattern blocks	___ Attribute blocks	___ Number lines
___ Geo Boards	___ Base-ten blocks	___ Cuisenaire rods
___ Algebra tiles	___ Two-color counters	___ Counters
___ Tangrams	___ Miras	___ Fraction rods/pieces
___ Snap Cubes	___ Others	

Block III:

___ Pattern blocks	___ Attribute blocks	___ Number lines
___ Geo Boards	___ Base-ten blocks	___ Cuisenaire rods
___ Algebra tiles	___ Two-color counters	___ Counters
___ Tangrams	___ Miras	___ Fraction rods/pieces
___ Snap Cubes	___ Others	

12. I observed strategies that address *gender equity* in my PDS assignment (check all that apply).
☐ Block I ☐ Block II ☐ Block III

What were some strategies that I remember seeing:

13. I observed the integration of technology (computers, calculators, etc.) in the teaching of mathematics in my PDS assignment (check all that apply).
☐ Block I ☐ Block II ☐ Block III

What types of technology did you see?

About how many times did you see them in all of your experiences?

14. I observed that all students were expected and encouraged to be successful in mathematics (check all that apply).
☐ Block I ☐ Block II ☐ Block III

15. On a scale of 0 to 100, how much improvement do you believe you have obtained through your:
Block I: _____ Block II: _____ Block III: _____

To what would you credit most of the improvement?

16. I feel comfortable in my student teaching placement?
☐ Yes ☐ No ☐ N/A

If not, please tell why:

17. I believe that teaching mathematics for me will be:
☐ Very difficult ☐ Difficult ☐ Not so difficult ☐ Easy

18. The lessons I have observed contained about what percentage of direct, skill/drill test preparation:
In Block I: _____% In Block II: _____% In Block III: _____%

19. The lessons I have observed *related mathematics to real life* about how many times?
In Block I: _____ In Block II: _____ In Block III: _____

20. The best thing I learned about teaching mathematics from my *mentor* in my field placement was:
    Block I:

    Block II:

    Block III:

21. The best thing I learned about teaching mathematics from my *children* in my field placement was:
    Block I:

    Block II:

    Block III:

22. On a scale of "5" (excellent) to "0" (very poor) how would you rate each of your experiences in your teaching assignments in terms of learning about teaching mathematics?

    Block I: 5   4   3   2   1   0
    Please explain why:

    Block II: 5   4   3   2   1   0
    Please explain why:

    Block III: 5   4   3   2   1   0
    Please explain why:

23. Please list any suggestions for changes in the program that you believe might help you in teaching mathematics:

CHAPTER 4

PARTNER SCHOOLS

A University Art Education Program and an Expressive Arts Elementary School

Kathy Unrath and Belinda Smith

ABSTRACT

This chapter discusses how students in a university pre-service art education program benefit from a situated learning experience within a PDS. The collaboration is enhanced through mutual membership in the Missouri Partnership for Educational Renewal. The partnership also expands opportunities that create the kind of "simultaneous renewal" (Goodlad, 1990), that sustains and nourishes all constituents of the educational community.

INTRODUCTION

There is common agreement that teachers are likely the most important resource affecting the education of our youth and their training is worthy of careful development. Educators recognize that knowledge needs to be presented in an authentic context in settings and with applications that would normally involve that knowledge. We also understand that learning

University and School Connections, pages 65–78
Copyright © 2008 by Information Age Publishing
65

requires social interaction and collaboration. Therefore, teacher educators value the situated context that a partnership with a PDS provides for both the pre-service teacher and the community of learners in the school venue.

For those focused on the visual arts, Eisner (2002, 1972) reminds us that the preparation needed by art teachers is (and always has been) influenced by our views on the functions we expect art education to perform. Today, our pre-service art educators are trained to provide rich and deep experiences that enable students to view and respond to their world in a meaningful way. In the course of their educational experiences, emerging art teachers discover that they are also teaching reading and writing, history, and math. Art teachers are in a perfect position to provide the connective bonds within their school community of learners and to help students cross the boundaries of discrete content areas. As art students engage in artistic inquiry and creative production, they are opening the doors to the world and learning to see, to be better observers, and to be more aware of the world around them.

At the University of Missouri-Columbia (MU), a fortunate opportunity to prepare the next generation of art teachers opened because of a partnership with Lee Expressive Arts Elementary School located near the MU campus. Lee Elementary has a special mission within the Columbia Missouri Public School System, as it seeks to prepare students to be successful citizens through an enriched arts-focused curriculum. MU Art Education students move into the school for a semester and, while in residence, provide extraordinary opportunities for young students to view and respond to art and to produce art that is intrinsically connected to the classroom curriculum. This rich partnership benefits both parties, as Lee Expressive Arts Elementary School provides the arts enriched laboratory for emerging art teachers to explore and hone their pedagogical skills. Likewise, the faculty and students of Lee Elementary are the beneficiaries of the expertise of the university researchers and an enthusiastic cadre of emerging art teachers.

ART EDUCATION WITHIN MAINSTREAM EDUCATION

Art's place in schools has evolved over time. As early as Plato and Aristotle, the idea of disciplinary integration was understood to be a necessary and integral part of society (Anderson, 1995). However, at beginning of the 19th century the western conception of education placed the arts in a separate field of discipline. Dewey (1917) condemned the suggestion of an essentialist curriculum for the masses because he believed that it provided a rich full curriculum only for the privileged few. Roots of arts integration were revived during the progressive education movement in the early part of the 20th century when a new revolutionary curriculum replaced the earlier fragmented subject-centered program of study. In many of these new schools, students were engaged in what Dewey called "reflective thinking" through problem-focused core curriculum, based on a belief that aesthetic experiences were not unique to fine art objects but an integral part of life (Galbraith, 1995; Tanner, 1989). During the late 1920s and 30s, the view of art education evolved from the idea that art only provided therapeutic experiences for children, and therefore, "the need for pedagogical skills was minimal; art was not taught—it was expressed" (Eisner, 1972, p. 12). By the 1970's, art educators aimed to also foster critical sensibilities and historical understandings "to help children learn to see" (Eisner, 1972, p. 12).

In the 1980s, research findings from the College Entrance Examination Board (1983), the Holmes Group (1986), the National Art Education Association (1986), and the National Endowments for the Arts (1988) supported a more critical role for arts in the educational arena (Davis, 1998; Sautter, 1994). In 1984, Discipline-based Art Education was embraced as the new paradigm for arts education and was promoted and supported by the Getty Center for Education in the Arts (1985). This new vision for art education focused on disseminating a rigorous content-rich template for art curricula that centered on the fine arts disciplines of creative production, art history, art criticism, and aesthetics (Clark, Day, & Greer, 1987). This new vision endorsed increased literacy in all subject areas as this new conceptualization for teaching art encouraged critical thinking, a focus on multiculturalism, and an integrated approach to interdisciplinary learning.

As visual art education enters the 21st century, educational reform is at the forefront of our national agenda (Goodlad, 2000; NAEA, 1999). Today, art education goals are viewed within a larger social context, requiring a more active and critical teaching role. This is the age of educational accountability—with a great deal of emphasis placed on standards and improved performance on tests. Therefore, it is incumbent upon art education programs to provide extensive practice in building deep knowledge in the art disciplines, including critical understanding of art from both a historical and contemporary perspective. What's more, it is now important for pre-service teachers to have experiences reconceptualizing visual culture within the post-modern world.

It is imperative that art education programs provide their students with the real-world experience of working with children in a school setting in order to foster active and critical citizenship in our profession (Beudert, 2006; Freedman, 1994; Freedman & Stuhr, 2004; Galbraith, 1995; Stuhr, 2003; Zimmerman, 1994). How we prepare, develop, and provide educational programs for our prospective visual art specialists must be as complex and authentic as our profession has become, and its training must be situated in context. The goal of a PDS is to create a community where hands-on experience enhances teacher quality and creates critical growth in *all* participants (Carnegie Forum, 1986; Goodlad, 1990; Holmes Group, 1990; Varvus, 1995) as part of a better understanding of that entire community (Galbraith 1995, 2001; Grisham et al., 1999; Hutchens, 1997) and as documentation and study within the art education field (Beudert, 2006).

THE MISSOURI PARTNERSHIP FOR EDUCATIONAL RENEWAL (MPER)

Understanding that PDSs provide unique opportunities for all constituents, the University of Missouri-Columbia sought a new mission for the educational community in Missouri. The Missouri Partnership for Educational Renewal (MPER) was initiated in 1994 to provide a revitalization of educational resources through a partnership among PDSs across the state. MPER's charge is to forge a mutually beneficial partnership between Missouri partner schools and the university to provide a situated learning environment for students and professional development and inquiry opportunities for both educational communities. In 1994, a group of superintendents from 13 school districts across Missouri met with the deans of the University of Missouri-Columbia's College of Education and College of Arts and Science and faculty members interested in forming a partnership between public education and higher education that would mutually benefit both parties. Inspired by Goodlad's (1990) research on school reform initiatives, the Missouri Partnership for Educational Renewal was formed and included: (1) 13 districts, (2) UM-C's College of Education and College of Arts and Science, (3) The Learning Exchange (a nonprofit professional development organization in Kansas City, MO), and (4) the Missouri Department of Elementary and Secondary Education. These stakeholders formulated its membership charter and governing board. MPER's goals (http://mper. coe.missouri.edu) are listed below:

1. Support inquiry into best practices that lead to student achievement for all P–12 students.
2. Utilize empirical evidence to establish policy and direction of program.
3. Support collaborative efforts among the MPER stakeholder groups that focus on P–12 student achievement and quality teacher preparation, primarily through enhanced external funding and grants.
4. Establish programs that enhance the understanding of key groups (i.e., policymakers, communities, school leaders, and parent groups) regarding the educational renewal programs of MPER.

5. Coordinate study of problems of practice as identified by the Governing Board and the Operations Council.
6. Continue with the development of a comprehensive mental health programming for the pre-service core curriculum, the induction year, and beyond.
7. Increase access and ability for distance communication technology.

Soon thereafter, task forces comprising teachers and administrators from partner schools appointed by MPER's Governing Board, produced recommendations that included action plans to provide professional development for partner schools, improve communication across the statewide education system, and designate PDSs that would explore research-driven initiatives. Their initial work helped to define MPER goals and translate those goals into meaningful interactions between and among members leading to improved educational outcomes for Missouri's children. MPER Partner Schools, in concert with the MU College of Education and College of Arts and Science faculty, share a common purpose. Together they seek to educate children and youth, prepare school professionals, provide ongoing professional development, and conduct inquiry into best practices. Both the MPER Partnership and the Teacher Development Program at MU continue to be a driving force in the educational renewal in the state of Missouri. As a result of the collaboration with MPER schools, the MU College of Education developed a new model for its Teacher Development Program (TDP) that was designed to meet the needs of the 21st century learner. The new undergraduate TDP is competency-based and enriched by an extensive field experience component. Skills and knowledge are integrated and spiraled across the curriculum in a sequenced series of experiences that provide students with ever-increasing responsibilities for classroom management and instruction. The mission of the TDP program is explicitly set forth with the following charge:

> The College of Education has adopted three design principles, which guide all College teacher preparation programs both graduate and undergraduate. All courses are organized around problems of practice and provide opportunities for reflection-in-action and reflection-about-action among novices and experts. The evaluation of students must include assessment of performance in complex situations of practice that is appropriate to the practitioner's level of training.

LEE EXPRESSIVE ARTS ELEMENTARY AS A PARTNER SCHOOL

Art Education pre-service students are fortunate to have the opportunity to work closely with the administration, faculty, and students of Lee Expressive

Arts Elementary School, located near the MU campus. After closure of the University Lab School on campus in 1977, The University of Missouri-Columbia's Art Education Program formed a partnership with Lee Expressive Arts Elementary School to provide an authentic field experience practicum for their pre-service students. Thus, our students have the opportunity, as part of their art education methods coursework, to prepare, plan, and implement art lessons. The pre-service art education students spend a semester working with the art teacher in close collaboration with classroom teachers to develop curriculum that is relevant to the needs of the students.

In 1990, Lee Expressive Arts Elementary School adopted an arts emphasis with a clear declaration that "learning through the arts best prepares children for life" (Corn, 1993). Lee Expressive Arts Elementary School now devotes six-to-seven weeks within each quarter to an intensive arts centered teacher collaboration and integration model that involves instruction in science, social studies, mathematics, literacy, and writing through the arts. The art and music specialists are allotted more instructional time with their students during the course of a week (270 minutes), as compared to most elementary schools in Missouri. One-third of the school population is made up of special permission students whose parents chose to enroll their children in an arts-intensive school. Among the advantages of their program are the additional opportunities for students to develop art in the community and work with local and university artists in Artist-in-Residence initiatives. The arts provide Lee's K–5 students multiple pathways through transmediated symbol systems to learn about their world through creative production and critical analysis of the arts.

The research inquiry of Corn (1993) and Smith (2006) have described the educational groundwork of the partnership between Lee School and the MU Art Education Program. Corn's qualitative study documented the curricular change process during the school's inauguration and illustrated the school's course of action in formulating its arts emphasis. Smith's qualitative study of the perceptions of former students and parents of Lee Elementary School, described through ethnographic interviews, the long-term effects of being a student in a school where the arts were integrated into the entire curricula. Smith found that Lee's former students continue to be active in the arts through music and the visual arts and that their parents held very positive views of their children's educational experience.

Art Education Partnership extends to Art Museum

The children at Lee Elementary School benefit from their close proximity to the University of Missouri Museum of Art and Archaeology and, as such, take frequent walking field trips with art pre-service teachers to view the collection first hand. "The experience of a museum visit, from the aesthetics of the architectural setting to the personal encounter with a great work of art, is one with the potential for wonder and awe, creating memorable images for the child" (Walsh-Piper, 1994, p.1).

A vital part of the future teaching responsibilities for art education students will be to lead discussions about art, so it is optimum to provide them with an opportunity to hone their skills in this area. "A visit to the art museum places students in a new position to contemplate art, to ask questions about art, artists, and to discuss art and art making, and to learn about art history, art criticism, aesthetics, various cultures, the museum and a host of other subjects" (Bolin & Mayer, 1998, p. 2). Integral to the museum partnership is the part that museum curators play in training pre-service art education teachers. During this on-site museum component, the students gain familiarity with research materials and professional museum practices, such as archiving and restoration. These students observe and participate in tours, modeled by experienced docents in order to eventually conduct the tours themselves of the museum collection (Unrath & Luehrman, 2007).

The pre-service teachers have an opportunity to translate their acquired insights from the museum education experience into artful discussion practices and ways to stimulate their young viewers at Lee Elementary School. Strengthened by their museum instruction, pre-service art teachers prepare a field trip to the museum for their young students. To make the experience memorable, the pre-service art educators scour the museum galleries, carefully selecting an artist or art collection to share with their elementary students. Seeing the work in a museum setting brings forth the collective power of the art, the dimensions and surfaces of the pieces, the life and context of the artist, and also energizes the understanding of the work by viewing the primary source. MU pre-service art teachers have remarked that taking students to the museum goes beyond the typical classroom possibilities and permits the young students to stand back *and* get up close to see the works for their whole composition as well as their texture and brushwork.

Having determined the art focus, the pre-service art education teachers complete detailed research leading to the production of a portable, interactive "Children's Museum," as it has come to be called, which they also curate. The Children's Museums bring the art back to the classroom so that students have an opportunity to view and discuss additional pieces of the artist's work and are able to compare the artist's work to that of other artists. The MU Art Education students extend this experience when they convey their portable Children's Museums back to the school so that students may interact with them in the art room and in their own classroom. Taking the portable Children's Museums back into the general classroom adds an innovative and exciting dimension to the art teacher's ability to extend children's interaction with art beyond their traditional art time (Unrath & Luehrman, 2007).

The triangulated partnership between the University of Missouri Art Education program, the University of Missouri Museum of Art and Archaeology, and Lee Expressive Arts Elementary School has a meaningful impact on all participants. This becomes evident, for example when MU Art Education students present their Children's Museums at a district-wide professional development event. Lee's principal noted the value of seeing the MU students' work presented to Lee faculty and the attending school district faculty in a formal forum that was a learning occasion for all. The principal explained:

> Some of the best professional development for our own teachers is seeing the new practices that are being taught at the university level. I would say some of the teachers who came (to museum in-service) are encouraged to do some of the stretching and thinking that they saw students do. The presentation of the Children's Museums is a real opportunity to showcase their work and a real professional development opportunity for all the teachers, the kind of renewal that Goodlad was advocating for professional development schools.

Lee's art teacher sees the professional development forum as a chance to confirm and validate the special arts-focused mission of Lee Expressive Arts Elementary School. She stated:

> The Children's Museums give the pre-service teachers a better opportunity to understand the arts as the vital artery of all learning here. It extends the time and thinking about bigger ideas and the natural transmediation process from planning to implementation. The Children's Museum becomes the centerpiece of the art of teaching. It combines what they've learned in their art studio classes, in their art history classes, and puts it all into a teaching form. What I learn every semester from your MU pre-service art teachers is the conceptualization of artful ideas through the research they have done on their Children's Museum. Just like the kids, I learn content from your students. I learn new processes from your students. They have ideas that I would never think of.

BENEFITS/RESEARCH OF THE PDS

The synergistic relationship between the MU Art Education Program and Lee Expressive Arts Elementary School is refined and articulated through a discussion and reflection session at the close of each school year. The role of situated learning (Cochran, DeRuiter, & King, 1993), or real-life educational situations associated with reflective practice (Susi, 1995), are reviewed and summarized by Lee School's principal, visual arts specialists, and MU professors and clinical associates. Graduating MU Art Education students complete exit interview surveys about their pre-service training and field experiences that provide quantitative and qualitative data used for program enhancement. In addition, a study is currently being conducted to determine how novice teachers reflect upon their own development as an art teacher. Through an analysis of certification portfolio synthesis papers, data is being gathered about the specific actions that most profoundly affected the students' perceptions about becoming an art teacher. Therefore, central to our common mission is sustaining consistent communication, fostering a nurturing environment for learning, and providing real-life field experiences which are the connective tissue that support a vital partnership and sustain stakeholders.

Consistent Communication

Maintaining a viable relationship requires a continuous flow of information and feedback. On communication, a principal noted:

> The strong professional development association with MU is something that has always been supported here at Lee Expressive Arts Elementary School. When the school district went forward with the concept of professional development schools within the now 57 MPER Partner Schools, the initiative expanded wonderfully. The strength (of the partnership) depends upon how well the teacher and the professor communicate, and there has been a strong relationship here for quite some time.

Frequent communications between the elementary school's art teacher, university instructors, and pre-service art education students have enhanced the relationship and are reflected by excerpts of participating members (from a university professor):

> You (the art teacher) send the students emails at the beginning of the week to remind them of what is happening, of activities, such as which group is going on a field trip. It makes them feel like a part of the community. You help with their learning of the small details of teaching and invite them to be a part of the life of a faculty member. They feel like such an important part of your art room and your teaching . . . the little things, and the way you do it makes a big difference to my students.

An art teacher commented the following:

> Even after the MU students leave at the end of the semester, I continue to email them. I say, "Just letting you know: Workday on Sunday for the ceramic mural installation, if you're interested, available, want to learn . . . inviting them to continue to participate in community art projects."

Nurturing Environment

As a PDS, Lee Elementary continues to focus on providing a nurturing environment (physically, emotionally, and philosophically) that promotes museum-based and community art learning in a contextually situated environment (Cochran, DeRuiter, & King, 1993) associated with reflective practice (Susi, 1995). The creative environment, established for the past 17 years, has been fostered by Lee's arts focus and has been universally embraced by the faculty, students, and parents (Smith, 2006). The principal aptly explained it in this statement, "the arts are valued here, and it is very powerful. Those who are here gain knowledge that is often difficult to measure, but it helps the students in the community and in knowing themselves." The emphasis on the arts is welcomed by the entire school community, as one Lee teacher commented, "We have a lot of parents who are artists, who come into our school to teach, understand the needs of the arts, and they value the arts." In addition, the culturally-diverse population of students finds the arts to be a vehicle for connecting to the curriculum and learning through multiple pathways. This focus on individual expression creates opportunities to meet the needs for the whole child (Glaeser et al., 2002; Zadny, 2007).

The school building is filled with art on display on every possible surface. Even the art classroom itself, large and located in the basement of the old school, is unique and visually stimulating. The impression of the art room is long lasting and, as one MU pre-service art student recalled, an ideal. She said: "My idea of an art room is one that is lived in and is comfy . . . like the room at Lee Elementary School."

The art teacher describes the message her art room delivers to all who inhabit the space:

> I think that the Lee art room is very different than many other art rooms, in that the space gives the students a vision that they may not have for what the arts can mean in a school, and be in a school, and can mean in a community. Part of the difference MU students see here is the flexibility of the teachers within the integrated arts program.

A former MU student who is currently teaching art recalls Lee Elementary School as a very special place for learners:

> I enjoyed the environment at Lee—teachers and students valued the arts as it was an integral part to their day. Student artwork was displayed all over the school, inside and out, and students were proud of it. Looking back now, after two years of experience teaching in my own art classroom, I can see what a unique and powerful experience the staff at Lee Elementary is providing for their students. As I learned in my pre-service training and have now seen first

hand in my own teaching, students learn and absorb information in a variety of ways. Some are auditory learners, some oral, and some are visual learners. By integrating the arts into every aspect of a students' learning it gives them a chance to encounter the information in a variety of ways.

Real-Life Field Experiences

The role of situated learning has the potential to positively influence the education of pre-service teachers, if these real-life field experiences are embedded in authentic, relevant situations where learning and growth takes place as a result of the activity, content, and culture in which it is developed (Cochran, DeRuiter, & King, 1993). In the preparation of art teachers, Susi (1995) believes, "The trial and error teaching that occurs during these early experiences forms the foundation upon which pre-service teachers' ideas about teaching are built, tested, and refined" (p. 111). The experiences at Lee Elementary School provided opportunities for pre-service art teachers to work directly with students and faculty. In conjunction with these experiences, the university's art program expectations emphasize reflective practice that enables pre-service teachers to translate educational theory learned in their university classrooms into effective classroom practices. In her reflective teaching journal one MU student wrote:

> I think one of the most valuable things that I gleaned from pre-service training was the fact that I was able to have a great amount of hands-on experience working with students. The field experiences provided a setting in which I could actually practice the things that we were learning in our education classes. I was able to see, in real life, the theories from our textbooks and class discussions. My experience at Lee Elementary especially, allowed me to get my feet wet in actually planning and teaching a series of lessons in the art room and at the museum.

The benefits of the infusion of art education students at Lee Expressive Arts Elementary School are summed up by the art teacher and MU Art Education professor:

> It is especially important that the art education students have prepared the Children's Museums with the classroom teachers in mind. I think the most valuable lessons, are the ones that feed back into the classroom with opportunities for many to learn and relearn through the arts. I want them (art education students) to design the curriculum, have the experience of teaching it, and then analyze how it went. It is important to me that their first teaching experience takes place in such a supportive collaborative rich environment. They remember all the little moments that come from the experience. Deep learning about the art of teaching comes from first hand encounters with

children. Their epiphanies about teaching are born at Lee Expressive Arts Elementary School, and that is something that is really difficult to quantify.

CONCLUSION

As with any partnership, continued and systematic evaluation and assessment are necessary for continued growth and effectiveness in the professional development community. This collaborative university and school partnership has produced a finely tuned sense of "community development" among administrators, university faculty, art teacher education students, art teachers, classroom teachers, staff, parents, children, and the community. This alliance with school personnel in the pursuit of integrative curriculum, pedagogy, and intellectual and creative service through arts education has enhanced the MU Art Education program's ability to prepare art teacher candidates in a rich and authentic way that could not be possible outside of this PDS partnership. The synergistic relationship is one that has evolved through real-life professional experiences, consistent reflection/discussion, and inquiry research and has become an invaluable component of the development of the next generation of art teachers at the University of Missouri-Columbia. The following comment from a university art education professor sums up the essential role of experience in the pre-service training:

> My MU art education students are marked by their experience at Lee Expressive Arts Elementary School in an unbelievably positive way. These emerging art teachers will always remember the nurturing environment in which their professional future was born.

Now, the challenge is to nurture the partnership, conduct practical research that furthers program development within the partner school community in order to provide "a better understanding of what it means to teach and prepare art teachers for the future" (Beudart, 2006, p. xi). As Pink (2006) notes, the future is bright for those prepared to participate in the coming Conceptual Age where creative problem-solving and meaning-making will be valued.

REFERENCES

Anderson, T. (1995). Rediscovering the connection between the arts: Introduction to the Symposium on interdisciplinary arts education. *Arts Education Policy Review, 96*(4), 10–12.

Beudert, L. (2006). *Work, pedagogy and change: Foundations for the art teacher educator.* Reston, VA: National Art Education Association.

Bolin, P.E., & Mayer, M. (1998). *Art museums and schools as partners in learning.* Reston, VA: National Art Education Association.

Carnegie Forum on Education and the Economy. (1986). *A nation prepared: Teachers for the 21st century.* New York: Author.

Clark, G., Day, M., & Greer, W.D. (1987). Discipline-based art education. Becoming students of art education. *Journal of Aesthetic Education, 21*(2), 129–196.

Cochran, K., DeRuiter, J.A., & King, R.A. (1993). Pedagogical content knowing: An integrative model for teacher preparation. *Journal of Teacher Education, 44*(4), 263–272.

College Entrance Exam Board. (1983). *Academic preparation for college: What students need to know and be able to do.* New York: Author.

Corn, A. (1993). *Arts integration and curricular change: A case study of five first and second grades.* Unpublished doctoral dissertation, University of Missouri, Columbia.

Davis, M. (1998). Making a case for design-based learning. *Arts Education Policy Review, 100*(2), 7–14.

Dewey, J. (1917). Learning to earn. *School and Society, March 24,* 332.

Eisner, E. (1972). The promise of teacher education. *Art Education, 25*(3), 10–14.

Eisner, E. (2002). *The arts and the creation of mind.* New Haven, CT & London: Yale University Press.

Freedman, K. (1994). *Teaching visual culture.* New York: Teachers College Press.

Freedman, K., & Stuhr, P. (2004). Curriculum change for the 21st century. In E. Eisner & M. D. Daya (Eds.), *The handbook of research and policy in art education* (pp. 815–828). Mahwah, NJ: Lawrence Erlbaum and Associates.

Galbraith, L. (Ed.). (1995). *Pre-service art education: Issues and practice.* Reston, VA: National Art Education Association.

Galbraith, L. (2001). Teachers of teachers: Faculty working lives and art teacher education in the United States. *Studies in Art Education, 42*(2), 163–181.

Getty Center for Education in the Arts. (1985). *Beyond creating: The place for art in America's schools.* Los Angeles: The Getty Center.

Glaeser, B., Karge, B., Smith J., & Weatherill, C. (2002). Paradigm pioneers: A professional development school collaborative for special education teacher candidates. In I. Guadarrama, J. Ramsey, & J. Nath (Eds.), *Forging alliances in community and thought* (pp. 125–152). Greenwich, CT: Information Age Publishing.

Goodlad, J. (1990). *Teachers for our nation's school.* San Francisco: Jossey-Bass.

Goodlad, J. (2000). Educational renewal and the arts. *Arts Education Policy Review, 101*(4), 11–14.

Grisham, D.L., Bergeron, B., Brink, B., Farnan, N., Lenski, S., & Meyerson, M. (1999). Connecting communities of practice through professional development school activities. *Journal of Teacher Education, 50*(3), 182–191.

Holmes Group. (1986). *Tomorrow's teachers: A report of the Holmes Group.* East Lansing, MI: Author.

Holmes Group. (1990). *Tomorrow's schools.* East Lansing, MH: Author.

Hutchens, J. (1997). Accomplishing change in the university: Strategies for improving art teacher preparation. In M. D. Day (Ed.), *Preparing teachers of art* (pp. 139–154). Reston, VA: National Art Education Association.

Missouri University Partnership for Educational Renewal Goals. Retrieved June 22, 2007, from http://mper.coe.missouri.edu.

National Art Education Association. (1986). *Quality art education, goals for schools: An interpretation.* Reston, VA: Author.

National Art Education Association. (1999). *Standards for art teacher preparation.* Reston, VA: Author.

National Endowments for the Arts. (1988). *Towards civilization: A report on arts education.* Washington, DC: Author.

Pink, D. (2006). *A whole new mind.* New York: Riverhead Books.

Sautter, C. (1994). An arts education school reform strategy. *Phi Delta Kappan, 75*(6), 433–437.

Smith, B. (2006). *A study on the impact of an expressive arts elementary school: Perceptions of former students and their parents.* (Doctoral dissertation, University of Missouri, Columbia, 2006). Ann Arbor, MI: UMI Company, *TX 6-385-257.*

Stuhr, P. (2003). A tale of why social and cultural content is often excluded from art education—And why it should not be. *Studies in Art Education, 44*(4). 301–314.

Susi, F. (1995). Developing reflective teaching techniques with pre-service art teachers. In L. Galbraith (Ed.), *Pre-service art education: Issues and practice* (pp. 107–118). Reston, VA: The National Art Education Association.

Tanner, D. (1989). A brief historical perspective of the struggle for an integrative curriculum. *Educational Horizons, 68*(1), 7–11.

Unrath, K., & Luehrman, M. (2007). *Utilizing art museums in university art teacher preparation programs.* Manuscript submitted for publication.

Varvus, M. (1995, January). *The time for "tomorrow's schools of education" is today.* Paper presented at the national meeting of the Holmes Group, Washington, DC.

Walsh-Piper, K. (1994). *Art museums and children in the United States.* Reston, VA: National Art Education Association.

Zadny, S. (2007). A daily engagement with the arts. Retrieved June 22, 2007, from http://www.ascd.org/portal/site/ascd/index.jsp.

Zimmerman, E. (1994). Current research and practice about pre-service visual art specialist teacher education. *Studies in Art Education, 35*(2), 79–89.

CHAPTER 5

LEARNING ABOUT BEST PRACTICES LITERACY INSTRUCTION IN THE CONTEXT OF PROFESSIONAL DEVELOPMENT SCHOOLS

Julie L. Rosenthal, Marie Donnantuono, Dorothy Feola, Mary A. Lebron, Christina Flynn, and Nina Wasserman

ABSTRACT

Professional development schools (PDSs) are schools that have partnered with a university to reach shared educational goals, including improving preparation of pre-service teachers, providing professional development for in-service teachers, using inquiry as the basis for improving practice, and enhancing learning of P–12 students (National Council for Accreditation of Teacher Education [NCATE], 2001). This chapter describes a joint effort by a university accredited by NCATE and several of its school partners to work toward achieving these goals.

University and School Connections, pages 79–87
Copyright © 2008 by Information Age Publishing

79

INTRODUCTION

Many educators draw a distinction between true professional development schools (PDSs) and other types of school-university partnerships (for example those with schools that do little more than accommodate university students as student teachers) (Zeichner, 2007). Although there is no one definition of what a PDS relationship is, some common characteristics appear to be: (1) increased school-embeddedness of teacher candidate development, (2) more time spent in schools by university faculty, (3) a focus on improving instruction for all learners, and (4) a general school climate that advocates for the university-school partnership. Also inherent in a PDS partnership is the empowerment of teachers to become colleagues of, rather than students of, the university professors; this often results in a school culture of professional inquiry and joint accountability for teacher induction (Carroll, 2006).

University partners frequently face difficult decisions about which schools to engage in PDS partnerships and how to offer other school partners some of the same benefits that full PDS partners enjoy. The model described in this study emerged from the desire to rejuvenate relationships with partner schools to better reflect PDS standards while meeting the needs of the individual schools. The project involved the teaching of all sections of our beginning literacy course on-site in several of our partner schools, with classroom teachers serving alongside university faculty as co-instructors for the course. The first few class sessions met on campus to build background in literacy development and introduce assessment and instructional methods. Teacher candidates were then brought into a primary classroom each week for three hours, where they worked directly with beginning readers on literacy tasks. Course co-instructors modeled instruction and provided feedback to teacher candidates. The session began during the latter part of the school day and continued for one hour after school ends. Each candidate taught a whole-class lesson and then groups of students worked on literacy activities led by individuals or pairs of teacher candidates. After school, teacher candidates worked with individual at-risk readers. Finally, candidates and instructors came together for a reflective conversation about instruction, children's progress, and how their experiences related to theory.

This project embraced the spirit of the PDS as a collaborative learning community. The course, embedded in several classrooms with several school partners, supported the learning of candidates, students, and faculty. University and school faculty collaboratively taught the course, and the course curriculum was clearly driven by the needs of the students in the classrooms in which each section of the course is embedded. This model, though much smaller in scale and less expensive than a full PDS partnership, has allowed us to work toward our shared goals of improving teacher preparation, providing professional development to in-service teachers, positively impacting children, and giving faculty more time in schools.

METHOD

Context and Participants

State University (pseudonym) is a suburban campus of approximately 12,000 undergraduate and graduate students and is surrounded by several urban school districts. The university's College of Education has professional relationships with schools in each of the urban districts; it is in two schools in two of these urban centers where this study took place. (The seven sections of the course are taught in a total of five school partners, but data reported here were drawn from only two sections of the course.) The profiles of participating school partners are not unlike so many inner-city schools across the country: overcrowded, with a high percentage of students eligible for free or reduced lunch (ranging from 90–100 percent) and low levels of education among family members. One of the schools serves a high percentage of language minority students with more than 90 percent of students living in homes where English is not the native language. Teachers participating in the program have been teaching between 3–15 years. Teacher candidates enrolled in this course are predominantly European American (approximately 85 percent) and female (approximately 90 percent). University faculty who teach the course are all former classroom teachers with advanced degrees in the teaching of reading.

Data Sources

Data sources for this study included: (1) teacher candidates' weekly reflective journals and weekly instructional plans, (2) candidates responses to an exit survey in which they describe their perceptions of the course, (3) instructors' written observations of children and teacher candidates as they worked together, (4) samples of children's work products from the tutoring sessions, and (5) informal conversations between instructors of the course as well as between instructors and candidates and instructors and children.

Data Analysis

Journals and instructional plans were perused for evidence of ongoing informal assessment and instructional decisions based on outcomes of assessment. The exit surveys were searched for responses which indicated what teacher candidates felt were the benefits and drawbacks of the course format. Written observations were examined for evidence of growth of teacher candidates' content and procedural knowledge over the semester. Children's work samples, including unsolicited cards and drawings that expressed gratitude toward their tutors and the course co-instructors, were examined. Throughout the course, co-instructors shared what they perceived as the strengths and areas of need of the course as a whole as well as individual candidates' performance and the impact on the children with whom they worked.

RESULTS AND DISCUSSION

The preliminary analysis led us to identify four specific areas that we felt have been positively impacted by the format of this field-based course. These include: (1) improved pre-service teacher preparation through increased classroom-embedded teaching and learning experiences; (2) more time spent in schools by university faculty; (3) enhanced student learning; and (4) empowered teachers, resulting in enhanced professional development and inquiry.

Classroom-Embedded Teaching and Learning Experiences

In contrast to traditional, campus-based literacy methods courses, in this class candidates had the opportunity to actively apply their growing knowledge of theory and research on "best practices" to their work with students. Candidates learned how to assess an array of developing literacy skills, including comprehension, word analysis, writing, and oral reading fluency, using formal assessment tools and ongoing observations of the struggling reader whom they tutor weekly for one semester. Teacher candidates learned how assessment informs instruction by planning lessons to address the needs of their student. Throughout the course, candidates reflected upon their experiences and actively make connections between their growing content and pedagogical knowledge and the application of this knowledge to their work with emerging readers and writers. Teacher candidates engaged in inquiry as they try out different instructional practices and then examined and reflected on the impact of instruction on their student. They developed a sense of what "data-driven instruction" looks like when they planned for tutoring sessions week-by-week based on their ongoing assessment of children's needs. This course also contrasts with most practicum and student teaching experiences, in that teacher candidates worked with the same student over the course of the semester. They, therefore, received ongoing, targeted feedback and modeling from their two instructors and benefited from the combination of researcher and practitioner knowledge. As one candidate wrote in her exit poll, "I felt very supported in this class. I could go to my professor with any questions I had. I also talked to the classroom teacher about (student's) needs and she gave me some ideas and materials to use with him."

In one of the partner schools, teacher candidates were invited to attend grade-level meetings, where weekly literacy instructional plans are devised. They got to see first hand how school faculty work collaboratively to plan curriculum to meet the needs of all learners. Teacher candidates were encouraged to use the school's weekly plans, along with results of their own observations and course readings, to plan for their tutoring sessions. This experience provided the dual benefit of involving candidates in authentic school-based planning, while helping candidates to target their tutoring activities to support classroom instruction.

Candidates engage in inquiry as they reflect on student learning and examine the impact of their instruction. Assessment, planning, instruction, observation, and reflection follow a recursive pattern in which candidates are constantly comparing expected outcomes of research-recommended practices with their individual student's performance. As teacher candidates studied learner processes and developed knowledge of research on literacy acquisition, they grew in their ability to make decisions about which instructional practices might work best for individual students. They tested out their hypotheses and then reflected on why approaches are or are not effective, thereby assuming a problem-solving orientation that allowed them to learn from their own practice across their teaching careers (Darling-Hammond & Cobb, 1996). In one section of the course, for example, students closely followed Morris' (2005) tutoring model, which includes sorting words by vowel patterns as a phonics reinforcement activity. One candidate wrote in his journal:

> I think that the use of index cards has been the most effective way of teaching phonics to D. When he reads the words he has to really say the vowel sound to decide which group it goes in. In fact, I have started to use the index cards for much of the word work with D. The index cards make it quick and easy to review miscues and other word work from the week before and we can find words that rhyme from the story.

This early field experience helps to induct pre-service teachers into school culture prior to more formal internships. This course is taken during the semester immediately preceding a more intensive practicum, and candidates become part of the culture in these schools (where they later may serve as student teachers).

More Time Spent in Schools by University Faculty

In true PDSs, university faculty often serve as "Professors in Residence," or clinical faculty, and spend much of their time in the school. University faculty in this capacity might observe student teachers and provide professional development to in-service teachers based on the jointly determined needs of the teachers and staff in the school. This school/university liaison serves a critical role in keeping the university informed about the needs of schools for which the university's candidates are likely being trained. In a school of education within a university, however, only a very small number of faculty are likely to serve in this role. Most faculty members in teacher education programs are responsible for teaching courses (Zeichner, 2007). The literacy course described in this study got more of our faculty out into the schools (approximately seven per semester). While all of our faculty members teaching this course were classroom teachers at one point, some have not been in a classroom for a number of years. It is critical that university faculty stay informed about current school and student needs. Also, for faculty members who are researchers but not necessarily practitioners, time spent in classrooms provides a rich authentic environment in which they can themselves observe theory in practice.

Enhanced Student Learning

In these times of high-stakes assessment, student achievement, as well as the efficacy of university/school partnerships, is judged by scores on standardized tests and whether scores improve yearly. For a program such as this, where children received one hour of tutoring per week for 14 weeks, standardized tests should not be the sole measure of success. Indeed, teachers, faculty members, teacher candidates, and children all provided data about the program's success. Teachers noted that the tutoring program boosted children's confidence. Having someone interested in their well-being and spending time reading and writing with them makes the children feel special, which positively impacted them academically as well as emotionally (Mary, second grade teacher, personal correspondence, 3/24/07; Juel, 1991). Tutoring motivated children to read and write, and tutored children exhibited increased desire to strive in reading and writing. During one semester, several struggling and, consequently, apathetic readers in the program wrote multi-page stories with their tutors, that they subsequently and eagerly read aloud to their classmates. Teachers reported that tutored children seemed more motivated academically (as demonstrated by their increased participation during language arts and throughout the school day). This may have been due to the one-on-one aspect of the tutoring;

that is, during tutoring sessions, children were able to pursue interests that they did not have time for during the normal course of school day. For example, one candidate wrote in her journal, "We began with reading *Animal Moms and Dads.* J. chose this book last week and was quite excited to read it and immediately grabbed the book and started reading before I could sit down." A second candidate wrote, "E. loves *Mercer Mayer* books so I got a few and she was very excited to read them with me. She asked if she could take one home to read and I gave her it."

Children seemed to have benefitted in terms of gaining proficiency in reading skills such as oral fluency, phonics knowledge, and use of comprehension strategies, although further investigation is required to confirm this. Certainly, children engaged in a wide variety of responses to literature as teacher candidates conducted whole class read-aloud lessons. Work produced by children, following read-aloud lessons, ranged from picture painting using artistic borrowing from a Caldecott award winning book to writing their own versions of twisted fairy tales. In this way, children had the opportunity to engage in aesthetic responses to literature that is not always possible in a school under pressure to raise test scores.

Tutored children proclaimed that the experience was a positive one, and many reported that they felt their reading improved. One child gave a card to her tutor on the last day of the program in which she wrote, "Thank you for reading with me. You showed me how to spell and how to write too. You are the best teacher and I want you to be my third grade teacher." They certainly benefitted emotionally from the attention and time spent one-on-one with a caring adult (Juel, 1991). Previous research (i.e., Fitzgerald, 2001; Juel, 1991) has found that one-on-one tutoring, even by minimally trained tutors, has positive effects on children, including (but not limited to) improving academic skills.

Empowered Teachers, Enhanced Professional Development and Inquiry

Cooperating teachers engage in professional development when they share their expertise with teacher candidates. In many of the schools in which this program is embedded, teachers spend an alarming amount of classroom instructional time preparing students to take standardized tests. By modeling "best practices" instruction for teacher candidates and by assessing future teachers and giving ongoing feedback on candidates' instruction, school faculty had the opportunity to reexamine their own extensive knowledge bases. Furthermore, teachers were empowered and experience increased accountability for teacher preparation. As Carroll (2006) found, when teachers become more accountable for teacher education, they are more likely to scaffold candidates' learning about instructional planning and children's thinking and sense making. Cooperating teachers who feel accountable for interns' learning are more likely to view candidates as learners and to provide appropriate activities to help them develop, rather than to view them as deficient or unable to teach.

This course empowered cooperating teachers by including them as co-instructors of the course and involving them in all aspects of teacher education in this course. Teachers provide: (1) feedback on candidates' lessons, (2) conference with candidates about individual student's needs, and (3) materials for candidates' use during sessions. The benefits of an increased accountability of teachers as teacher educators during the course were clear. An unanticipated outcome of involving teachers as co-instructors in the course was their generalized feeling of responsibility for teacher training. Many teachers serving as co-instructors in the course also hosted student teachers in their classrooms. Several of these teachers, following the course's inception, have voluntarily implemented a program in which they meet with their student teacher several times before the start of the semester in order to involve interns in planning and organization and to better orient their student teacher. In effect, as similarly described by Carroll (2006), involvement in this course helps to transform teachers' identities from passive cooperating teachers, following the university's program guidelines, to active teacher educators who take initiative to make their classrooms a context for learning to teach.

In general, this field-based course, which has been in place as a multi-section project for three semesters, has been extremely positive and beneficial for all stakeholders. Of course, few positive experiences are without some short falls. Initially, several university faculty members were not convinced that teacher candidates could learn requisite content when the bulk of their course time is spent working with children rather than with the university professor. After several semesters of all sections of the course being taught on-site, however, even the most vociferously opposed faculty members recognize the strength of teaching and learning in the context of practice. Professors are able to see first hand how the candidates' content and procedural knowledge develop over a semester of applying their growing knowledge to their work with children.

Classroom teachers who worked as co-instructors in this course serve a pivotal role. They helped candidates identify needs of individual students and helped candidates find ways to address those needs. However, teachers who were not accustomed to working side-by-side with university faculty at first tended to demur to the "expertise" of the university faculty member. By involving classroom teachers in every phase of the course from planning to candidate assessment, this dynamic was changed so that candidates could draw from the strengths of both course instructors.

As the course continued to evolve, candidates reported that they, at times, felt overwhelmed with needing to plan for weekly instruction. They worried that, due to their lack of experience, they might not make appropriate instructional decisions. That issue has been addressed in several ways. Candidates now submit their weekly plans to instructors and are given feedback prior to tutoring sessions. Both instructors provided a good deal of modeling as well as materials for use in tutoring sessions and whole class and group lessons. Also, while it is desirable to allow candidates to take the lead in planning, using a tutoring framework (such as Morris' [2005] *Howard Street Tutoring Manual*) greatly helped candidates plan for the tutoring sessions. Candidates continued to plan based on results of assessment, but the guidelines provided in this and other tutoring manuals helped with this process.

Teaching our pre-service beginning literacy course on-site in our partner schools began as a way by which we could meet the individual needs of more of our partner schools and share some of the benefits enjoyed by our full professional development partners. It has grown into what we perceive as an extremely effective and integral component of our teacher education program. Teacher candidates are experiencing improved preparation, university faculty are spending more time in schools, and children are receiving one-on-one tutoring. Cooperating teachers are developing professionally by sharing responsibility for teacher education. This project allows us to work toward achieving the goals for professional development schools set forth by NCATE (2001) and, at the same time, has improved the quality of our teacher education program.

REFERENCES

Carroll, D. M., (2006). Developing joint accountability in university-school teacher education partnerships. *Action in Teacher Education, 27,* 3–11.

Darling-Hammond, L., & Cobb, V. L. (1996). The changing context of teacher education. In F. B. Murray (Ed.), *The teacher educator's handbook: Building a knowledge base for the preparation of teachers* (pp. 14–62). San Francisco: Jossey-Bass.

Fitzgerald, J. (2001). Can minimally trained college student volunteers help young at-risk children to read better? *Reading Research Quarterly, 36,* 28–46.

Juel, C. (1991). Cross-age tutoring between student athletes and at-risk children. *The Reading Teacher, 91,* 178–187.

Morris, D. (2005). *The Howard Street tutoring manual.* New York: Guilford Press.

National Council for Accreditation of Teacher Education. (2001). *Standards for Professional Development Schools.* Washington, DC: Author.

Zeichner, K. (2007). Professional development schools in a culture of evidence and accountability. *School-University Partnerships, 1,* 9–17.

CHAPTER 6

AN IDEA FOR IMPROVING TEACHER PREPARATION

An Interdisciplinary and Online-Enhanced Field-Based Model

Matt Thomas, Carl Grigsby, and Jerry Akins

ABSTRACT

This chapter addresses the design and initial efficacy of a new model for pre-service teacher preparation developed at a Midwest regional university together with a local school district. Initial efficacy is discussed in terms of logistical improvements and general impact on the pre-service teachers and the local school district. This unique model for teacher preparation is structured as a hybrid course block with four overlapping components: (1) traditional classroom instruction, (2) online asynchronous interactive instruction, (3) classroom field experience, and (4) interdisciplinary blocking of complementary courses. The four components of this program design assist with logistical concerns sometimes encountered in professional development school (PDS) settings while facilitating learning for pre-service teachers, supervising teachers, and students in the classrooms. Although this model program is unique and its efficacy is still being examined, it has potential to be replicated in other PDS programs.

University and School Connections, pages 89–97
Copyright © 2008 by Information Age Publishing
All rights of reproduction in any form reserved.

INTRODUCTION

The approaches used in traditional teacher education programs are being closely scrutinized and, in some cases, are under full-scale attack. "For the first time since 1933, Congress has mandated a wholesale cataloging of the work done by the nation's teacher-preparation programs, to understand better the academic content and field experiences provided to prospective teachers" (Blair, 2004, p. 13). The criticisms of traditional teacher education programs are generally threefold: (1) the pre-service teachers are not learning the depth of content knowledge that they need, (2) the pre-service teachers do not have the practical teaching skills that significantly impact student learning, and (3) it takes too long for pre-service teachers to move through teacher education programs and enter the classrooms where there is often a perceived teacher shortage. Despite the incongruity of the third item with regard to the first two, teacher education programs across the country are working diligently to evaluate how improvements can be made in overall teacher preparation.

As reports are emerging about how we can improve teacher education programs, a theme seems to consistently come forth with regard to the importance of field-based experiences during pre-service teacher training.

> In surveys of teachers and administrators, field experience is the aspect of teacher education rated most highly . . . Wilson, Floden, and Ferrini-Mundy (2002) state that field experiences including student teaching are consistently seen as powerful forces in programs of teacher preparation. In teacher preparation programs that require extensive field experience, the retention rate of graduates in teaching after three years is significantly higher than the average (GC&SU unpublished study, 2002). Darling-Hammond (1992) advises that teacher candidates' skills need to be practiced in the context of actual teaching and to be honed under the guidance of supervisors and mentors. (Georgia Deans, 2003, p. 18)

The concept of authentic teacher training also aligns well with the 2002 Carnegie Challenge Paper (Hinds, 2002) on the topic of teacher preparation. The report begins with the assertion that the quality of teaching is the single most important factor influencing student achievement but also claims that not enough is being done to improve teacher quality and that new models for teacher education programs are needed. The model highlighted in the Carnegie report is a "modern clinical model" for professional preparation.

> One conceptual answer is for society to treat teaching like the modern clinical profession that the nation needs it to be, according to Daniel Fallon, chair of the Carnegie Corporation's Education Division and architect of a major new

initiative called Teachers for a New Era. "Education," he writes in an introduction to the initiative's prospectus, "should be understood as an academically taught clinical practice profession, requiring close cooperation between colleges of education and actual practicing schools." . . . The initiative also seeks to transform schools of education into schools of modern clinical practice . . . with clinical residency programs a bit like the residency programs in medicine . . . [This] will provide each beginning teacher with an array of supports, including college faculty mentors and coaches in both teaching methods and academic content. (Hinds, 2002, pp. 3–4)

PDS PROGRAMS, TECHNOLOGY INTEGRATION, AND INTERDISCIPLINARY BLOCKING

In response to calls such as those made by the Carnegie Challenge Paper (Hinds, 2002), an encouraging trend has been emerging in the form of professional development school (PDS) programs. These programs are partnerships between schools of education and local schools that provide pre-service teachers with an increased level of field experiences in their teacher preparation programs.

Teacher preparation programs have moved to partner schools and professional development schools. These working relationships between school-based practitioners with mentoring skills and university faculty with expertise in pedagogy and subject matter provide high quality internship experiences. This type of intensive monitoring for interns is critically important. Teachers most often describe this intensive student teaching experience as being the most critical in their preparation. (Georgia Deans, 2003, p. 19)

As a result of changes designed to improve teacher preparation, particularly with increased field experiences for pre-service teachers, the PDS movement is expanding as evidenced, for example, by the steady growth of National Association of Professional Development Schools (cf. NAPDS, 2006).

However, as PDS-type programs have been started, new challenges have begun to emerge. One of the main challenges seems to be in the area of logistics. "On paper, these induction programs provide novice teachers with mentors, teaching coaches, and other supports; but in practice, these programs are often unworkable and uncoordinated" (Hinds, 2002, p. 10). Additionally, as we move forward to address one set of concerns or best practices and as the PDS model increases field experiences, we do not want to lose track of additional educational opportunities such as technology integration and interdisciplinary blocking of complementary teacher education courses. For these reasons, as we looked at making improvements in our middle school education program at the University of Central Missouri (UCM, formerly Central Missouri State University), we created and have now implemented a somewhat unique PDS model.

Our PDS Model

In the teacher education programs in the Curriculum & Instruction Department of UCM, we have long valued the PDS concept as an integral part of a long-term and highly successful PDS program. We believe that the PDS model described in this paper aligns fairly well with the Standards for Professional Development Schools (cf. NCATE, 2001) and helps address a number of the Missouri Standards for Teacher Education Programs (cf. MoSTEP, 2005). In our PDS program, we focus on professional preparation of candidates, support continuous faculty development, strive to create opportunities for reflective practice focused on improvement of practice, and hope to ultimately improve student achievement. We know that program assessment needs to be continuous and focused; both the Standards for Professional Development Schools and the Missouri Standards for Teacher Education Programs are basic and integral to the assessment design that is being put in place for assessing our PDS interns.

Several years ago, we began brainstorming ways to improve our middle school teacher preparation by looking at content knowledge, incorporating interdisciplinary learning with a focus on contexts relevant to each student. One outcome of this reflection was the decision to develop a new content area literacy class designed just for our middle school education majors. Previously these students had taken a literacy class that was offered for pre-service teachers in Kindergarten through eighth grade, a span that we felt needed narrowing for this particular literacy topic. We thought that while we were already making changes to the middle school program in this way, it was an opportune time to make additional updates, that would include trying to fuse together four areas in a unique and useful way: (1) traditional face-to-face teaching, (2) online instruction, (3) PDS field experiences, and (4) interdisciplinary course blocking. Just such a model was developed and in four semesters of offering, it has been completed. The following summary explains what we have built.

Those Involved: The students involved are those in courses titled, *The Middle School* and *Content Area Literacy in the Middle School*. These two courses are both three-unit classes, and the six units are blocked together to be taken concurrently. This combination is referred to as the "junior block," as it is usually taken during the pre-service teachers' junior year in this teacher education program. The middle school that we work with is a relatively rural school located about five miles from our UCM campus.

The Course Structure/Delivery: The following section describes the new block components.

- Traditional face-to-face classroom instruction takes place periodically both on the UCM campus and at the field-experience site according to a preestablished schedule contained in the course syllabi. This instruction includes attention to the National PDS Standards (NCATE, 2001) and the Missouri Standards for Teacher Education (MoSTEP, 2005).
- The online portion of the course blocking is delivered in an asynchronous online format. A sizeable percentage of the instructional activities take place online, and the students can log on when it is most convenient for them within a set window of time throughout each week. For this online component, there are weekly readings and tasks to be completed all of which is explained on the course website. More information on these readings and tasks is explained and discussed both in the field and in the designated classroom/on-campus meetings.
- The field experience components of the class take place at the middle school where students and professors meet for a majority of the classes. The class time (in terms of the students' official university class schedules) is blocked from 8:00–11:45 a.m. on Tuesday/Thursday. The operating schedule has usually been the following: on Tuesdays and Thursdays from 8:30–9:15 a.m., the content of EdCI 4130 is taught by the professor in the Library Media Center of the middle school. From 9:20–10:15 a.m. (the middle school's secondhour classes) the EdCI 3230/4130 students (who are called "interns") are in the classrooms with the middle school teachers and students. These interns do a number of things during this time, including observation, working with small groups of students, assisting the classroom teacher with a number of teaching-related projects, and teaching at least one lesson during the semester themselves. This lesson is focused on learners and learning and includes instructional planning, delivery of instruction, and reflection upon student achievement. On Thursdays from 10:15–10:45 a.m., the students of both classes and both professors have a "wrap-up" session where various aspects of both classes are reflected upon. The "unused" time from the 8:00–11:45 block is then reallocated to the students for use in completing the online assignments for one of their courses.
- The interdisciplinary blocking occurs as students concurrently complete their field experience requirements for both of the blocked

courses. In addition, the online Learning Modules direct students to compare between what they learn in one of the courses with what they are observing in the middle school classrooms.

Initial Reflections on Program Efficacy

Logistical Concerns. From the university's perspective, this model has addressed logistically the desire to develop a manageable PDS experience that combines the four elements previously described. In particular, it seems that the unique use of asynchronous online instruction for a significant portion of course content makes regular scheduling of field experiences a more manageable task. Rather than teach university-course content at set times and require the field experience components to be variably and individually scheduled (which is the more traditional model but which can lead to uncoordinated and inconsistent field experiences), the field experiences are more regulated and carefully planned. It is the asynchronous nature of the online course delivery that allows us to make this scheduling upgrade. Rather than take the two university classes at set times and hope for the field experiences when available (the more traditional model, leading often to more haphazard field experiences), in our new model one class and the field experience are held at set and stable times and the online class is what switches into the "flexible" category. This offers improved scheduling efficacy because arranging field experiences is necessarily constrained by the time-limits of the traditional school day, whereas the asynchronous online course work component can be completed at any time during the week that best fits the students' schedules. Students, faculty, and the cooperating PDS school seem to appreciate the more stable/consistent nature of the field experiences that result from this new model. We have concluded that combining these courses in this way has led to more consistent opportunities for the interns to build working relationships with the middle school students, to receive mentoring from the supervising teachers, and to receive feedback from university professors.

Pre-service Teacher Experiences. Anecdotally, students who have completed this PDS arrangement are well prepared for their senior block, which is completed at a different middle school, and for student teaching. Course evaluations and informal communication with our students suggest that they find value in having participated in this PDS experience.

Participating School District. PDS experiences can also provide advantages to participating K–12 schools for both the teachers and the students. From the perspective of participating school district, the PDS partnership with UCM has paid dividends in a variety of ways. Prior to embarking on this program, teacher retention was a concern for the district. Less than 30 percent of the district's teachers reached tenure, since quality young teachers would often be lost to higher-paying districts. In the four years since implementation of the PDS program, the percentage of tenured teachers has doubled. Teachers find that they are no longer working in isolation in their classrooms. Instead, they have, at times, one-to-four other educators in their classroom assisting in delivering the curriculum. This program has fostered an atmosphere of collegiality, which the teachers enjoy.

Likewise, having PDS interns in the classroom has had the effect of "raising the bar" from the perspective of teaching techniques. The presence of other adults in the room naturally causes the classroom teacher to be somewhat more intentional about the teaching process. Each teacher wants to model good teaching for the observer(s). The interns then also tend to want to meet the expectation of the classroom teacher when presenting their own instruction to the class. As a result, the overall quality of instruction has increased.

Another trend that is not uncommon involves teachers who have been out of the collegiate environment for a few years. They often fall into teaching patterns that rarely include searching for new, more effective pedagogical techniques. PDS interns bring fresh ideas into the classroom and practice them. The supervising teacher has the opportunity to witness new techniques at work and, in turn, incorporate some of these practices into his/her own teaching process. This infusion of new techniques thus leads to increased quality of instruction.

The PDS program moreover has helped foster a sense of professional pride in the classroom teachers. Teachers and interns collaborate as partners in the educational process. In doing so, the classroom teacher has a role in helping the intern develop teaching philosophies as well as strategies. By knowing the significant impact that they have on the future of the profession, the teachers become empowered.

The sense of professionalism, acceptance, and excitement that come from the students who participate in the PDS program at the middle school also helps build a reputation within the area that the school district is progressive and is an excellent place in which to work. Teacher recruitment has improved dramatically as the number of applicants for each classroom position has more than doubled compared to prior to the implementation of the PDS program. Putting quality teachers in the classroom is much easier for the district now.

Future Research: Further Scrutiny of the Efficacy of This Model

Looking ahead at our PDS partnerships, we are eager to examine more systematically the efficacy of this model on our pre-service teachers, the in-service teachers, and on the middle school students themselves. Our need for this scrutiny seems in alignment with the Carnegie Challenge Paper that calls for the participating schools of education to conduct clinical research on the student achievement gains that result from their graduates' teaching practices. This critical questioning is too often under-pursued by schools of education today (Hinds, 2002).

In order to add to the initial anecdotal feedback that we have received thus far, as presented in this paper, and to begin more systematic analyses of the efficacy of our PDS model, our plans are to look at the following set of multiple-perspective indicators:

- Assessment feedback from the PDS interns (using a newly developed instrument based on PDS Standards).
- Assessment feedback from the clinical and university faculty at the PDS site (using a newly developed instrument based on PDS Standards).
- Analysis of intern portfolio quality.
- Survey feedback from middle school students and their families.
- Analysis of district test scores.

In addition, we would like to seek external funding support for the research.

CONCLUSION

In this paper, we have attempted a number of things. First, we explained some of the current climate of reform in teacher education, including the calls for increased field experience and clinical model designs and how the emergence of the PDS movement is a way to provide some of these increased field experiences. Second, we shared the unique PDS model that we have designed and implemented that attempts to blend together field experiences, traditional instruction, online instruction, and interdisciplinary course blocking. Finally, we have expressed some of our current indicators from both the higher education and local school district perspectives regarding the efficacy of our new model along with ways we would like to more systematically investigate such efficacy in the future. It is our hope that this model may provide some useful ideas for increasing the quality of teacher education. We invite you to join us in this pursuit and would welcome any feedback.

AUTHOR NOTES

This article represents an updated and revised synthesis of two different recently presented conference papers:

Grigsby, C., & Thomas, M. M. (2004, October). *Teacher preparation for the twenty-first century: An interdisciplinary model for field experience.* Paper presented at the FATE conference, Orlando, FL.

Grigsby, C., Thomas, M. M., & Akins, J. (2005, March). *An interdisciplinary and technology-enhanced PDS model.* Presentation made at the Professional Development Schools National Conference, Orlando, FL.

REFERENCES

Blair, J. (2004). Congress orders thorough study of teacher education programs. *Education Week*, p. 13.

Darling-Hammond, L. (1992). Teaching and knowledge: Policy issues posed by alternative certification for teachers. *Peabody Journal of Education, 67*(3), 123–154.

Georgia College and State University. (2002). Unpublished report on teacher retention. Milledgeville: Author.

Georgia Deans. (2003). *Who will teach Georgia's children? A response to the PSC proposed Georgia certification redesign.* Position paper from the Georgia Deans of Schools and Colleges of Education. Retrieved October 7, 2004, from: http://www.gacte.net/documents/Position_Paper_12-2-03_1.doc

Hinds, M. D. (2002). *Teaching as a clinical profession: A new challenge for education.* 2002 Carnegie Challenge Paper, Carnegie Corporation of New York.

MoSTEP. (2005). *Missouri standards for teacher education programs (MoSTEP).* Retrieved May 10, 2005, from: http://www.dese.state.mo.us/divteachqual/teached/standards.htm

NAPDS. (2006). *A brief history of the national association of professional development schools.* Retrieved December 15, 2006, from: http://napds.missouri.edu/index.php?option=com_content&task=view&id=23&Itemid=53

NCATE. (2001). *Standards for professional development schools.* From the National Council for the Accreditation of Teacher Education (NCATE). Retrieved December 15, 2006, from: http://www.ncate.org/documents/pdsStandards.pdf

Wilson, S. M., Floden, R. F., & Ferrini-Mundy, J. (2002). Teacher preparation research: An insider's view from the outside. *Journal of Teacher Education, 53*(3), 190–204.

CHAPTER 7

PROMOTING PROFESSIONAL DEVELOPMENT SCHOOLS

A Study in the Viability of Future PDS Partnerships, Taking the First Step!

Fern Dallas and Suzanne Horn

ABSTRACT

This investigative study of the viability of professional development school partnerships occurred in two phases. An elementary school faculty and university education professors were surveyed to determine whether the potential partners had common beliefs about teaching and learning. The results were nearly identical. Summer focus groups provided additional data. Themes emerging from these discussions included a desire for change and collaboration, willingness to face and overcome barriers with mutual support, and focus on student achievement. Phase two replicated the study in a different location with a different college and a middle school. The findings indicated a gap in beliefs, although the results were still favorable toward forming the partnership. Themes from the summer focus groups were consistent. Implications, limitations, and future research are discussed.

University and School Connections, pages 99–116
Copyright © 2008 by Information Age Publishing
99

INTRODUCTION

As colleges of education seek to improve their practice and graduate the best teachers for our nation's schools, one thing is certain, the best way to learn how to teach is to practice teaching with highly qualified teachers. Professional development schools (PDSs) enable rich collaboration between the higher education professionals, the practicing professional educator, and the new teacher candidate. As defined by the American Association of Colleges for Teacher Education, (Abdal-Haqq, 1997), a PDS is a P–12 school that supports a multidimensional program collaboratively designed and managed by a school-university partnership.

This study occurred in two phases over a period of two years. During the 2003–2004 school year, professors at a small, private liberal arts college in the Southeastern United States sought a more formal partnership with the teachers at the elementary school located in the same small city. The following school year, the study was duplicated in another state under similar circumstances, except the partnership involved a middle school and a different small, private college. The purpose of this study is to describe the beginning steps taken by all the stakeholders to determine the viability of future PDS partnerships using both empirical and qualitative data.

THEORETICAL FRAMEWORK

The birth of the PDS model of teacher education occurred in the late 1980s as a school reform initiative to help close the "achievement gap" in urban schools and raise student achievement in all schools. The Holmes Group (1986) first used the PDS term in its first report, Tomorrow's Teachers, focusing on preparation and support of teachers as well as school change. Education reformers acknowledged the necessary link between quality education for children and quality preparation of teachers. Effective teacher education programs require "a sound theoretical knowledge base integrated with coherent, systematic, authentic, and comprehensive practicum experiences. These components come together in the concept of professional development schools" (Abdal-Haqq, 1997, p. vii).

Previous models of teacher education have consistently involved placing teacher candidates in model classrooms to observe veteran teachers. The final semester of a teacher candidate's education, known as student teaching, most often served as the time where the supervising classroom teacher was given the job of "finishing" the new teacher preparation. This model differs from the PDS. In the PDS, the focus of teacher education has shifted from that of "finishing" a teacher to raising student achievement. While at the same time the teacher candidate is learning to teach, the collaboration of the new teacher, the classroom teacher, and the college or university professor plays a significant role in student achievement (Murrell, 1998).

Teitel (2003) describes the three ways students' learning is enhanced through PDS partnerships:

1. Through better preparation of interns and their enhanced roles inside and outside the classroom,
2. Through professional development and other experiences that faculty, staff, and administrators at the school, university, and other partners have, engaging and focusing them on student learning.
3. Through the direct engagement of PreK–12 students in an improved learning environment (p. xix).

The PDS movement has four goals: (1) raise student achievement, (2) the thorough preparation of educators, (3) quality professional development of teachers, and (4) research and inquiry into improving professional practice. These goals formed the basis of the newly developed PDS standards. Developed through a national research project and field-tested in sixteen very different sites, the National Council for Accreditation of Teacher Education released *The Standards for Professional Development Schools* in 2001. The PDS standards are titled: (1) learning community; (2) accountability and quality assurance; (3) collaboration; (4) diversity and equity; and (5) structures, resources, and roles (Teitel, 2003). Teitel noted that these standards are developmental, and they acknowledge the different stages that PDS partnerships go through. However, how do colleges and P–12 schools begin this uniting of purpose and philosophies? This chapter describes the grant-funded research on the beginnings of a partnership and how the process was replicated at another site in different state.

The following research questions guided this study:

1. Do the necessary components of the PDS model exist to form a viable partnership between a college and the elementary school?
2. Do the necessary components of the PDS model exist to form a viable partnership between a college and a middle school?

METHODS

Data Sources

The first author conducted phase one of this research, and the study was replicated as phase two in the following year by the second author. Each step was the same—as well as the instruments used. The only difference was that the second author partnered with a middle school rather than an elementary school.

The Settings for the Partnerships

Lenoir-Rhyne College is a comprehensive liberal arts institution affiliated with the Evangelical Lutheran Church in America (ELCA) with more than 60 undergraduate degree programs and master's degree programs. Lenoir-Rhyne enrolls approximately 1,500 students from across the country and around the world. The student/faculty ratio is 13:1. Seventy percent of the approximately 75 faculty members hold doctoral degrees (Lenoir-Rhyne College Website, 2006). The PDS partner school is located in the same small city as Lenoir-Rhyne College. It serves grades PreK–5 and houses approximately 343 students and 30 teachers. The school has been identified as a Title 1 school with more than 70 percent of the students qualifying for free or reduced lunch. Approximately 71 percent of the students are on grade level for reading and mathematics.

Spring Hill College from the replicated study is the first Catholic college in the Southeast, the third oldest Jesuit college in the country, and the fifth oldest Catholic college in America. It is a four-year, coeducational, liberal arts and sciences institution in a residential setting. Approximately 70 percent of the students are from outside of the state, including 26 states and one foreign country. During an academic year, approximately 1,500 students are pursuing a degree. The student-faculty ratio is 14:1, and there are approximately 80 full-time faculty members. Ninety percent of the faculty members hold doctorates or the highest degrees in their fields (Spring Hill College Web Site, 2006). The PDS partner school is a middle school located in the same city as the college and serves grades 6–8. The student body numbers at 637, and there are 38 teachers in the school. Sixty-seven percent of the students participate in the free lunch program and 14 percent participate in the reduced lunch program. The school is currently struggling with test scores with less than 50 percent of the student gaining proficiency in mathematics and reading.

Procedures

The study began with establishing rapport and trust with the teachers and administrators at the sites. College faculty visited the elementary and middle schools during faculty meetings and also met with principals to discuss the concept of the PDS. Ferguson (1999) stresses the importance of developing trust as the first ingredient in partnership formation. Both schools enjoyed the previous presence of teacher interns and student teachers in their classrooms for practicum experiences. The researchers presented an overview of PDS research in after-school faculty meetings and asked for volunteers to participate in the research project. The researchers also presented the same overview to the Teacher Educational Council (TEC) and the Advisory Council (AC) (these groups serve as the governing body for the Schools of Education) of the respective colleges and asked for volunteers to participate in the research project. During the spring of 2004, the first author was awarded a faculty development grant to study the viability of the PDS partnership with their proposed elementary school. The following year, the second author was also awarded a faculty development grant to replicate the study. The original grant money was used to create and pilot a PDS survey and form focus groups for additional inquiry. The Potential Professional Development School Survey consisted of 30 items with a Likert scale choice selection with values ranging from "1" "strongly agree" to "5" "strongly disagree." The items consisted of attitudes, beliefs, and best practices about teaching and learning pulled from the colleges' teacher education competencies, the National Board of Professional Teacher Standards, and National Council for Accreditation of Teacher Education and aligned with the INTASC standards, illustrated in Table 7.1.

After minor revisions following the pilot, the survey was given to the faculty members of the elementary school and members of the TEC and AC near the end of the school year. The desired outcome of the survey would be a consistent score on the beliefs and attitudes about teaching and learning that could indicate matching philosophies and attitudes of the partners.

TABLE 7.1   PDS Viability Survey Aligned with INTASC Standards

INTASC Standard	Public School Question	College Question
1. Knowledge of Subject	23	
2. Learning and Human Development	2, 3	2, 3, 11, 17
3. Adapting Instruction	4, 21, 29	4, 6, 21, 27
4. Strategies	16, 19	12, 15, 19
5. Motivation and Management	30	
6. Communication Skills	3, 24, 27	25
7. Planning		
8. Assessment	5	5
9. Commitment	1, 7, 13, 15, 20, 22, 26, 28	1, 7, 9, 14, 20, 22, 23, 24, 26
10. Partnership	8, 9, 10, 11, 12, 14, 17, 18, 25	8, 10, 13, 16, 18

Consistent scores on INTASC standards for commitment and partnerships would also validate the potential for viable partnerships.

During the summer, a randomly selected focus group of teachers and the principal from the elementary school survey completers met twice with the researcher to form a study group with Teitel's (2003) book, *The Professional Development Schools Handbook*, as the focus of discussion. The same procedure occurred in phase two the following summer with the middle school. Those who were willing from the middle school were asked to volunteer, and the principal selected three teachers and a guidance counselor to participate in the summer program (along with the researcher). The book club discussions were tape recorded and transcribed. They were coded for common themes and used for further description of the viability of the PDS partnership. The results of the survey and summer focus groups were shared with the members of the TEC and the AC and the schools in faculty meetings during the following fall semesters.

RESULTS

In phase one, The Potential Professional Development School Survey results from the elementary teachers nearly mirrored the results from the college professors. The survey was analyzed using SPSS software. The survey data for the elementary faculty resulted in a raw score grand mean of 61 of a possible 150. The survey data for the Lenoir-Rhyne professors resulted in a raw score grand mean of 59 of a possible 135 (the professors' survey had three fewer questions than the teachers' survey; see Appendices A and B). Scores closer to one indicated that more aspects of collaboration were present and a more favorable outlook for a potential PDS. The validity (Cronbach's alpha) score for the internal consistency of the survey was .91.

In phase two, *The Potential Professional Development School Survey* results from the teachers differed from those of the professors. The survey data for the middle school faculty resulted in a raw score grand mean of 60 of a possible 150. The survey data for the Spring Hill College professors resulted in a raw score grand mean of 36 of a possible 135. The validity (alpha) score for the survey was .91. The following tables provide the group statistical results and alignment with the INTASC standards.

Results from Table 7.2 indicate the professors and teachers were in agreement on four of the INTASC standards. Both groups were in agreement on every standard; however, the elementary teachers were significantly more optimistic on Standard 2, "The teacher understands how children learn and develop and can provide learning opportunities that support their intellectual, social, and personal development." The teachers were also sig-

TABLE 7.2 Group Statistics for Viability Survey of Lenoir-Rhyne College and Its Partner Elementary School

Standard	Group	N	Mean	Std. Deviation	t
INTASC2	Professors	14	2.11	.46	3.06**
Learning and Human Development	Teachers	24	1.56	.47	
INTASC3	Professors	14	2.27	.56	.59
Adapting Instruction	Teachers	24	2.17	.61	
INTASC4	Professors	14	2.07	.59	−1.56
Strategies	Teachers	24	2.35	.43	
INTASC6	Professors	14	1.29	.47	−3.19**
Communication	Teachers	24	1.83	.54	
INTASC8	Professors	14	2.07	.99	.40
Assessment	Teachers	24	1.92	.78	
INTASC9	Professors	14	2.40	.61	2.03
Commitment	Teachers	24	1.99	.49	
INTASC10	Professors	14	2.71	.57	2.36*
Partnership	Teachers	24	2.29	.43	

* $p < .05$, ** $p < .01$

nificantly more optimistic on Standard 6, "The teacher uses knowledge of effective verbal, nonverbal, and media communication techniques to foster active inquiry, collaboration, and supportive interaction in the classroom." Because of the favorable responses from the survey, the study continued with the formation of the summer focus groups. The survey results were presented at the first meeting of the focus group.

In Table 7.3, the means show that all members were in agreement with the standards, with the exception of INTASC 4, "The teacher understands and uses a variety of instructional strategies to encourage students' development of critical thinking, problem solving, and performance skills," where the middle school teachers felt neutral about the standard and the college professors were in agreement. In INTASC Standards 6 and 9, the t-test shows significant difference. Both parties were in agreement on these standards, but the college faculty members were far more optimistic than those in the middle school. Because both parties seemed to feel in agreement with almost every standard, in particular INTASC Standards 9 and 10, "commitment" and "partnership" (that were the most valued by the researcher as successful to a relationship), the parties decided to move ahead with the summer focus group sessions.

Data from the summer focus groups were transcribed and coded for common themes according to the goals and standards of the PDS model of teacher education addressed previously in the theoretical framework. The

TABLE 7.3   Group Statistics for Viability Survey of Spring Hill College and Middle School Partner

Standard	Group	N	Mean	Std. Deviation	t
INTASC2 Learning and Human Development	Professors	17	2.16	1.50	1.87
	Teachers	25	1.56	.51	
INTASC3 Adapting Instruction	Professors	17	2.27	.60	−1.47
	Teachers	25	2.17	.71	
INTASC4 Strategies	Professors	17	2.07	.40	−3.72**
	Teachers	25	2.35	.78	
INTASC6 Communication	Professors	17	1.29	.62	−2.87**
	Teachers	25	1.83	.63	
INTASC8 Assessment	Professors	17	2.07	.66	−.55
	Teachers	25	1.92	.67	
INTASC9 Commitment	Professors	17	2.40	.43	−2.63**
	Teachers	25	1.99	.50	
INTASC10 Partnership	Professors	17	2.71	.36	−1.29
	Teachers	25	2.29	.54	

* $p < .05$, ** $p < .01$

qualitative data from the phase one and phase two summer focus group meetings revealed six prominent themes.

A Unanimous Desire for Transformative Change

In both phases of this viability study, the participants expressed a deep desire to change their school "from the inside out." One of the elementary school teachers reiterated this idea in the following comments:

> I think it should be transformative. If you are going to do something, do it to the full extent. From some of what I read, some schools didn't do it to the full extent and it trickled out. It didn't sound as much as PDS. They had interns and student teachers and that was about it. We need to go full force and go for full change and see the benefits of it.

The classroom teachers desired transformative change, as indicated by Teitel (2003), rather than just surface change. The common issues concerning transformative change range from managing classrooms, assisting struggling students, motivating students, providing relevant curriculum, and planning lessons. In both partnerships, the public school faculty members desire to be successful in the classroom was a paramount concern. Teachers wanted to connect with the children and their cultures in order to be more successful academically. Teachers felt that work was needed on understanding the cultural mismatch between them and their poverty-stricken students. "Sometimes you'll read about something and you will assume that they understand words or things they've never seen" (middle school teacher). Teachers found that during reading some of the students had no frame of reference for some images and concepts encountered in the text. By gaining understanding of children's frame of reference or lack there of, they hoped to help students and better manage their classes.

An Existing Atmosphere of Collaboration

Each of these potential PDS partnerships already has an existing atmosphere of collaboration among the faculties within the public schools and with their partnering college. Teachers at these schools appreciate the benefits of collaborating in teams for curriculum development, lesson plans, student assistance, parent conferences, staff development, and a host of other reasons. Collaboration also exists between the colleges and the public schools. The colleges have placed tutors, interns, and student teachers at these sites for their field placements. The teachers and principals also felt that working with pre-service teachers was a collaborative effort to produce individuals who would become quality educators. One teacher stated, "I see our responsibility as being receptive to your [the college's] students. Making sure they are treated as learning colleagues so they will feel comfortable." Another middle school teacher commented, "I look at them as 'What if this was my child?' If my child was coming in [to education] what would I want my child to get out of this?"

The consensus was that training tomorrow's teachers in realistic situations, such as these inner-city schools, was important. This was reflected in a comment made by an elementary school teacher, "I know that a lot of things are going to change and that means a whole lot of collaboration on everything and a lot of integration with the school's leadership committee."

A Willingness to Face and Overcome Barriers

The context of both of these potential PDS relationships provides many barriers to success. Some of the issues on barriers discussed in the focus group meetings included cultural differences, financial problems, and scheduling. The first barrier teachers wanted to overcome was between their "middle-class" values and the struggles that their students faced in their life of poverty. Both schools had students whose family incomes qualified them within the level of poverty; thus, their learning success was at-risk.

One middle school teacher commented on her own teacher preparation program experience and the opportunity she and the other candidates had to tour the neighborhood of the students so that they could get an idea of their students' lifestyles. "We saw where everyone lived, we saw the cars that they drove and understood that these were going to be the kids we got. My whole life was awakened when I took a child [from our school] home who lived on . . . Road, and we went in the house and the floor was dirt and that was like, these are the children you are teaching. . . ." Pre-service teachers in the PDS would have the opportunities for staff development and discussions on teaching children from poverty with in-service teachers.

Another barrier addressed in the focus groups was the cost of forming the PDS, revealed in this comment by an elementary school teacher, "That was one of my major questions, the costs involved? What are they?" Teachers brainstormed ways to fund the PDS, demonstrating their willingness to overcome this barrier. Finally, attempting to fit the PDS into the schools' schedules and the colleges' schedules was seen as a potential barrier. The college would have to rearrange course times to fit with the teaching times of the public school teachers. By the end of the summer, most of these barriers had all been discussed or had been completely overcome. One middle school teacher stated, "Coming together as a community seemed to make the problems that seemed impossible, possibly solvable."

A Desire to Support Each Other as Professionals

Teachers and professors in both groups desired that the PDS enhance the level of professionalism and support of the profession. Teachers in the middle school/college partnership decided to continue their summer book club discussion into the next school year. They formed school-wide book clubs, facilitated by the second author. The book clubs were not only seen as a place of staff development but also a place where teachers could support one another in their attempts at trying things learned during the staff development. This was expressed by a middle school teacher, "I think they need to work with the group first. Then they can go back through the book and pick out other things they want to try in their classroom." The elementary school teachers indicated that participation in the PDS would force them to elevate their own practice by the presence of student interns. One of the teachers made the following comment:

> Here are some of the best practices that we feel are ongoing just part of the routine of the school, which is going to raise the bar for us. We will know what they are looking for and it may encourage us to improve our practice. Cause we are not all at the same practice level.

Another elementary school teacher commented:

> Our practices, I think the bar will be raised for us, what we do. Or at least a
> lot of reflection of what we do. A lot of it will be affirmed, what we are already
> doing, will be affirmed. I just think it will make us reflect more.

The teachers viewed the PDS model as an opportunity for the in-service
teachers to strengthen their practice.

A Notion that Everyone on Campus is a Learner

Teachers indicated that it was important that everyone (the in-service
and pre-service teachers, the professors, and the children) is recognized as
a learner. One elementary school teacher commented,

> I think it will make both places stronger institutions and learning places. I
> think it carries a whole lot of responsibility on both places. It's great that we
> are going to have these extra bodies in here, but I feel an extreme responsibil-
> ity that you are seeing the best very model. I know L-R wants to train teachers
> in the very best practices, and so your expectations is to send them where best
> practices are in place. I feel a huge responsibility that we are being good mod-
> els for these students. Our kids are learning from them, and they are learning
> from us and it is a strong reciprocal relationship.

Another elementary school teacher commented about the sense of community in the PDS, "You feel a part of the community and you are going to
feel comfortable and able to ask questions. I remember being in all those
different schools and that is uncomfortable when you are over here, and
there, and here and you don't see anything for the long term."

It was also important to both summer focus groups that all teachers
participate in the decisions about learning how to implement the PDS. Although the summer groups were charged with planning the beginning activities in the PDS partnership, they were concerned that all teachers have a
voice on future activities. A middle school teacher stated, "I think what we
need to do is select for fall and, as we get into it, I would say put the options
up before the staff. Where do we want to go? What works for you?"

Organization was not the only area of concern for the middle/college
focus group. To build a strong community, it was important to the group
that all members were given the opportunity to figure out what we needed
to focus on with in-service and reading professional development. The pre-
service teachers were viewed as a part of the process. It was the expectation
that they would join the book clubs and their feedback on what was helping
them develop was important as well.

An Extreme Focus on Doing What is Best for Children

One of the main tenets of a PDS as indicated by Teitel (2003) is the focus on student achievement. Both partnership groups established this tenet as their main goal for the PDS. One elementary teacher emphatically stated, "I want something that is meaningful, lasting, significant, and that affects students' achievement. Otherwise it's not worth my time!" The principal added, "I think it makes us more of a community. I think having it will obviously help the students learn." The elementary/college group wrote the PDS partnership into their formal school improvement plan for the following year. As a result of the summer focus group's decision to concentrate on raising student achievement, the middle school group decided to study Ruby Payne's (1996) book about teaching students from poverty for their staff development in the next school year.

DISCUSSION

The empirical and qualitative results in phase one and phase two indicate a strong desire by these two public schools to pursue the creation of a PDS relationship. The results of the surveys from the colleges' School of Education faculty and TEC/AC also mirror this desire. Although there was more variance in the survey results from phase two, both groups agreed on key issues, so the study moved into the qualitative phase with the summer focus groups. The survey was also beneficial in that it provided common language for all the groups during the summer discussion, and it reiterated the common teaching standards on which best practices are based. Additionally, the survey also pointed indirectly to The Standards for Professional Development Schools described by Teitel (2003). The significant agreement on the survey by all parties indicated that a PDS relationship could be viable and beneficial to the partner schools and colleges in both phases of this study.

The summer focus groups navigated and negotiated what a PDS should be. From these results, we concur that because PDS partnerships look different in different locations, the partners really need to negotiate from the beginning what will be best for all parties. It is important that all of the stakeholders feel that they are heard and their most important needs are served (Marlow, Kyed, & Connors, 2005). The qualitative results indicated that both groups seek meaningful change as long as the change benefits the students. Discussions focused on Teitel's (2003) work and what "transformative change" would like within a PDS partnership. One of these changes involved the location of where and how college education courses would be taught.

The PDS model of teacher education, endorsed by NCATE, provides a collaborative framework for pre-service teachers to learn and grow in an elementary school and middle school settings as well as the college classrooms. The in-service teachers benefit from this model by elevating their practice, serving as mentors, and conducting action research in their classrooms with the assistance of college faculty, resulting in professional growth and higher student achievement (Teitel, 2003). Fortunately, in both phases of this study, the partnership schools already enjoyed positive collaborations between the schools and the colleges for the purpose of student teaching placements but not professional development of the faculty or action research.

It is the mission of the PDS to intertwine the college setting learning and field learning. Although these field experiences could present barriers to the partnerships, in these cases the colleges were willing to rearrange student schedules so that pre-service teachers could be on the middle school and elementary campuses longer and participate in teaching the students. The classroom teachers acted as mentors. Both pre-service and in-service teachers were expected to work together to learn about students through the discussion they had in the classroom, the use of book clubs, and by in-service training.

The PDS is viewed as a learning community in which all participants better their knowledge about how education works. This collaborative effort is slow and requires the effort to work together as a team (Snow & Marshall, 2002). The collaborative meetings provided an opportunity for the partnerships to brainstorm and discuss ways to overcome many barriers to the effectiveness of the PDS's. Interestingly, the barriers that were discussed were consistent in both phases of the study. Common to both groups were barriers such as funding, staff turnover, course calendars, space, and timing issues.

In summary, the quantitative and qualitative data of this two-phase study provide insight on how PDS partnerships are formed, how partnerships negotiate the earliest stages, how they navigate around possible barriers, and how they set goals for professional development. Schools interested in this contemporary model of teacher education can understand the intricacies involved in starting a PDS from the qualitative results of this study.

IMPLICATIONS, LIMITATIONS, AND RECOMMENDATIONS

This study implies a strong degree of agreement on philosophies, beliefs and attitudes between the elementary and middle schools and the colleges. Based on these consistencies, the results imply that strong partnerships are possibilities and that the PDS model should be pursued. The use of the survey to help gauge the viability of successful partnerships provides a beginning place for potential partnerships in the development of the PDS model. Often schools just need a tool to help determine the potential of a more formal relationship. The survey served as the starting point for decision-making and a foundation for a formal partnership in this study. The summer focus groups outlined the "next steps" for the formation of the PDSs.

One limitation of the study was that the content-area professors did not take part in the summer focus groups with the teachers. It was only education faculty who participated. Content-area faculty and education faculty discussions about the PDS model were separate from the public school teachers. Only the researchers were involved in all the discussions as participant/observers.

Future recommendations for research include following the progress of implementation of the PDS model of these two partnerships. Small colleges have distinct issues different from larger universities when it comes to partnerships. In depth understanding of the actual formation of the PDS could inform the practice of colleges of education across the country as they implement the standards of the PDS model. It would also be beneficial to study the methods and strategies used by these budding PDS's to overcome their identified barriers. How colleges and P–12 schools overcome these issues is worthy of future research.

REFERENCES

Abdal-Haqq, I. (1997). *Resources on professional development schools.* Washington, DC: AACTE Publications.

Ferguson, R. (1999). Conclusion: Social science research, urban problems and community development alliances. In R. F. Ferguson & W. T. Dickens (Eds.), *Urban problems and community development* (pp. 569–610). New York: Brookings Institute.

Holmes Group. (1986). *Tomorrow's teachers.* East Lansing, MI: Author.

Lenoir-Rhyne College. (2006). *Lenoir-Rhyne College Website.* Retrieved January 2006, from: http://www.lrc.edu/

Marlow, M. P., Kyed, S., & Connors, S. (2005). Collegiality, collaboration and kuleana: Complexity in a professional development school. *Education, 125*(4), 557–568.

Murrell, P.C. (1998). *Like stone soup: The role of the professional development school in the renewal of urban schools.* New York: AACTE Publications.

Payne, R. K. (1996). *A Framework for understanding poverty.* Highlands, TX: aha! Process, Inc.

Snow, J., & Marshall, J. (2002). The more things change....: Re-discovering stubbornness and persistence in school-university collaborations. *Curriculum Studies, 34*(4), 481–494.

Spring Hill College. (2006). *Spring Hill College Website.* Retrieved January 2006, from: http://www.shc.edu/

Teitel, L. (2003). *The professional development schools handbook.* Thousand Oaks, CA: Corwin Press.

APPENDIX A

Potential Professional Development School Survey

The purpose of this survey is to gather information about your impressions of particular aspects of school life. Participation in this survey is voluntary and your identity will remain anonymous. Your candid responses are important and valued. Thank you for your time and for sharing your views.

Directions:

Fill in the blank with the number that best reflects your view about the faculty of this school.

1	2	3	4	5
strongly agree	agree	not sure	disagree	strongly disagree

At this school…

1. ____ Teachers are committed to knowing the content they teach.

2. ____ Teachers understand how learning takes place.

3. ____ Teachers use a variety of methods to facilitate learning.

4. ____ Teachers' instructional lesson plans meet individual student needs.

5. ____ Teachers use a variety of assessments to inform future lessons.

6. ____ Classroom instruction is student-centered.

7. ____ Teachers share the responsibility for their students' academic performance.

8. ____ Outside visitors and volunteers are welcomed into the classrooms.

9. ____ Teachers communicate with parents effectively.

10. ____ Teachers collaborate with each other in lesson planning.

11. ____ Teachers are involved in school-wide decision-making.

12. ____ Teachers model lessons for other teachers.

13. ____ Teachers demonstrate high ethical standards.

14. ____ Teachers work independently.

15. _____ Teachers practice research to solve problems and improve their practice.

16. _____ Teachers employ technology for instructional purposes.

17. _____ Teachers willingly share their expertise with college interns and new teachers.

18. _____ Diversity among staff and students is valued and celebrated.

19. _____ Teachers employ direct-instruction techniques as the main teaching strategy.

20. _____ Teachers are constantly learning new ways to improve their teaching.

21. _____ Teachers provide for students with special needs effectively.

22. _____ Staff development at this school is meaningful and implemented.

23. _____ Teachers read current teaching journals for current ideas and research about teaching.

24. _____ Teachers communicate effectively with administration.

25. _____ Lead teachers serve as mentors successfully.

26. _____ Teachers analyze and evaluate their own practice.

27. _____ Teachers express pride in students' efforts.

28. _____ Teachers are satisfied and want to be here.

29. _____ Teachers are change agents and innovators with instructional design.

30. _____ The teaching profession is celebrated.

APPENDIX B

Potential Professional Development School Survey

The purpose of this survey is to gather information about your impressions of particular aspects of teacher education. Participation in this survey is voluntary and your identity will remain anonymous. Your candid responses are important and valued. Thank you for your time and for sharing your views.

Directions:
Fill in the blank with the number that best reflects your view about the faculty of this school.

1	2	3	4	5
strongly agree	agree	not sure	disagree	strongly disagree

At this college…

1. ____ Professors are committed to knowing the content they teach.
2. ____ Professors understand how learning takes place.
3. ____ Professors use a variety of methods to facilitate learning.
4. ____ Professors' instructional plans meet individual student needs.
5. ____ Professors use a variety of assessment strategies.
6. ____ Classroom instruction is student-centered.
7. ____ Professors share the responsibility for their students' academic performance.
8. ____ Professors visit public school classrooms.
9. ____ Professors encourage future teachers to be reflective practitioners.
10. ____ Professors collaborate with each other.
11. ____ Professors model lessons for future teachers.
12. ____ Professors demonstrate high ethical standards.
13. ____ Professors work independently.
14. ____ Professors practice research to solve problems and improve their practice.
15. ____ Professors employ technology for instructional purposes.
16. ____ Professors willingly share their expertise with future teachers.
17. ____ Professors are innovators with instructional design.
18. ____ Diversity among faculty, staff and students is valued in the classroom.

19. ＿＿＿ Professors employ direct-instruction techniques (lectures) as the main teaching strategy.

20. ＿＿＿ Professors are constantly learning new ways to improve their teaching.

21. ＿＿＿ Professors provide for students with special needs effectively.

22. ＿＿＿ Professors participate in staff development of teachers.

23. ＿＿＿ Professors read journals for current ideas and research about teaching.

24. ＿＿＿ Professors analyze and evaluate their own practice.

25. ＿＿＿ Professors express pride in their profession.

26. ＿＿＿ Professors are satisfied and want to be here.

27. ＿＿＿ Professors are willing to be change agents, putting the latest theories into practice.

CHAPTER 8

PROMOTING LEARNING IN A PROFESSIONAL DEVELOPMENT SCHOOL

Helping Students "Get Over the Mountain"

Tina L. Heafner and Melba Spooner

ABSTRACT

This chapter explores the potential of PDSs to impact student achievement through the analysis of a tutoring program situated within a PDS high school. Lessons learned from this experience indicate that PDS relationships engender unique learning situations which increase collaboration, enable specialized and focused differentiated interventions, and promote reciprocal teaching and learning experiences. Communication, guidance, and support as a result of the PDS environment have facilitated construction of an individualized supportive learning community. Data from this study demonstrate the benefits of this unique learning community as increasing student self-efficacy as well as academic performance.

University and School Connections, pages 117–150
Copyright © 2008 by Information Age Publishing
All rights of reproduction in any form reserved.

INTRODUCTION

Collaboration between schools and institutions of higher education in the preparation of future teachers, school principals, school counselors, and any other professional educator who will work with children is a necessity. This is certainly not a new idea or need; in fact, it is a given, established to provide authentic and real-world experiences to the preparation programs that link theoretical bases to the application of practice in school and classroom settings. Genuine collaboration and partnering sounds simple in concept, but it has been proven to be difficult and challenging in reality.

While PDSs are not a new phenomenon, the examination of their impact on student learning is, to some degree. Since the mid 1980's, the literature has provided documentation of university and school partnerships followed by the transitions into a PDS collaboration. Most of the information found, however, has been descriptive about activities and events occurring within the framework of the partnership.

Many organizations have supported the notion of PDSs and concur that for effective teacher preparation to occur the partnership must be done collaboratively so that pre-service teachers get a real world view of what they can expect to happen when they get their own classroom. More recently, attention is becoming focused on the impact of P–12 student learning as a result of the PDS collaborative. The learning community within the PDS is about the teachers, but it also about the learners, with the ultimate goal being to affect student learning in a positive manner. This occurs through more authentic and thorough preparation of pre-service teachers as well as through the ongoing professional development for in-service teachers.

In order to have a long-term impact, it is necessary to look at ongoing efforts within a school that impact the achievement of students and contribute to their success. When the school and university are dedicated to the priority of establishing a community of learners, the focus becomes the learner through the development and support of teacher learning.

The PDS discussed in this chapter is one of eight PDSs affiliated with the university, but is only one of two high schools. This PDS has undergone a self study and has developed a work plan that has grown out of collaborative work between university faculty, school faculty, and administrators. The NCATE PDS standards were used to guide the process of self study and subsequent work plan development.

One need identified by the faculty at the high school was to work on improving student achievement on statewide standardized tests. This became one of the objectives (goals) of those involved in the PDS. Following three semesters of implementation, the results for students (as learners of the social studies curriculum) have a very positive beginning. This chapter describes the benefits of a PDS for all participants. It begins with a needs assessment for students and contextualizes these as struggles that 9–12 social studies learners face. Next, tutoring interventions are described as well as learning outcomes for students, pre-service teachers, teachers, and university faculty. Specifically, interventions are assessed in terms of their impact on student achievement. Finally, unique opportunities afforded by a PDS are described though the following themes: increased communication, access to learning needs, focused instruction, learning liaisons, methods instructor insights, reciprocal teaching and learning, and mentoring.

PROFESSIONAL DEVELOPMENT SCHOOLS

Professional development schools (PDS) have been in the literature for a number of years and promoted by numerous organizations. Defining PDSs is not an easy task because they often involve different projects and specialized goals. The PDS label does not seem as important as the work that goes on between those who are responsible for carrying out collaborative activities aimed at meeting goals for both academic and professional development (Metcalfe-Turner, 1999). In a comprehensive literature review, Teitel (1998) identified the following organizations that provide differing emphasis and different wording to describe PDSs: the Holmes Group, the Carnegie Forum on Education and the Economy, the National Network for Education Renewal, the American Federation of Teachers, the National Educational Association, and the Ford Foundation. Even though descriptions of PDSs differ, these organizations offer a strong convergence around four PDS goals: the improvement of student learning, the preparation of educators, the professional development of educators, and research and inquiry into improving practice (Teitel, 1998).

According to Levine (1998), to do PDS work participants have to relinquish their traditional roles and take on others. For example, everyone in a PDS partnership is both a teacher and a learner, so the usual hierarchies of "who teaches whom" are broken down. Adults, as well as children, at all levels of experience and in all positions are, at times, teachers and learners. Time is used differently in a PDS partnership to accommodate these new roles and responsibilities. For example, school-based teachers need time in their regular schedule to work with intern teachers. Alternatively, university faculty spend more of their time in P–12 schools. PDS work takes on many forms. It may range from the joint design and implementation of curriculum for intern teachers to the development of block scheduling in the PDS partner school or from an action research project targeted at reducing the dropout rate in a PDS partner high school to having university and school-based faculty co-teaching a seminar for intern teachers.

In the spring of 2001, the National Council for Accreditation of Teacher Education (NCATE) published a *Handbook for the Assessment of Professional Development Schools*. In preparation for that *assessment handbook*, NCATE initiated the PDS Standards Project in 1995. The major goals were to: (1) establish a consensus about quality and good practice in PDSs, (2) design standards that reflect that the PDS as a new institution is still evolving, and (3) use standards as part of the development of an infrastructure to support and sustain PDSs (Levine, 1998). Due to the number of growing collaborative partnerships between schools and universities and the need to determine some correlation of effort and outcome, a standards-based structure has become a way of creating a PDS, utilizing those standards that can ultimately be measured for accountability purposes and not just descriptive activities occurring in the school and classroom settings where student teachers and field experiences are taking place.

Advantages of Professional Development Schools with Regard to Student Achievement

Certainly, educators have always placed a high priority on student achievement and accountability issues but, with the onset of the "No Child Left Behind Act," these priorities have been elevated. Since the late 1990s, studies related to PDS effectiveness have gained in number, but the number of studies examining implications for student achievement pale in comparison to those that describe the collaborative nature of the PDS, implemented activities, and so forth. Valli, Cooper, and Frankes (Pine, 2003) found that the greatest focus of the research was on the development of the partnership (23 studies), followed by 14 studies on professional development, seven studies on teacher education, six on the organization and structure of schools, and four studies on the nature of teaching and learning. The point is that there have been minimal research studies posed and conducted to provide insights into the impact of focused PDS practices on student learning outcomes and achievement.

PDSs can have positive results to all the individuals and groups involved. Most PDSs are student-focused and ideally so. Levine (2002) writes that student learning defines the PDS's curriculum and the direction of research and inquiry for teacher candidates and school and university faculty alike. In other words, it is ultimately all about the students.

One of the main advantages of establishing PDSs is the end effect it has on the students. As their teachers gain (hopefully) from the partnership to become more effective teachers, the students reap the direct benefits. In 1999, Abma, Fischetti, and Larson shared a "rewording and reordering" of the NCATE PDS Standards Project's four functions of a PDS to guide the work of PDS evolution. These functions included:

1. Improving the lives, learning, and opportunities for all students.
2. Enhancing the curriculum, structures, school culture, and community ties for the high school and university-level staff and faculty.
3. Preparing new educators in a professional, collegial environment within the context of experiences that they will likely face in their early years.
4. Researching, assessing, reflecting on, and/or disseminating the results of our work (Abma, Fischetti, & Larson, 1999, p. 255).

PDSs are ultimately about the learning acquisition and outcomes of children in the P–12 schools. The work that university faculty do, the experiences that candidates in professional education programs receive, and the professional development of career teachers is very important and integral to the success of the partnerships, but it is the work that is done to enhance those opportunities that brings about learning opportunities for children.

Clark (1999) also provided some interesting insights into some benefits of PDSs as they relate to the preparation of teachers and, ultimately, the student learning. Some of these benefits include:

1. Students enrolled in PDSs perform better than other students on common measures of student learning in basic subjects such as language arts and mathematics.
2. Teachers perceive that professional development obtained through a PDS is more valuable than that obtained in traditional ways.
3. Teacher associations believe that PDSs contribute to the enhancement of the profession.
4. Universities benefit from teachers who are prepared in PDSs because these teachers help enable students to perform more successfully at the university level.
5. Local school districts benefit from PDSs because they reduce recruiting and retraining costs, legal fees, and professional development needs.
6. PDSs help business secure better workers because the students in the schools are better educated, thanks to teachers who were prepared in PDSs.
7. Better teachers make better schools (pp. 24–26).

UNC Charlotte and Professional Development (PDS) High School

At UNC Charlotte, "maximizing P–12 student performance and achievement" is the first goal listed in the PDS agreement with P–12 public school partners. Further, this work is guided by the NCATE PDS Standards (2001) which include:

- Learning Community: We are a learning-centered community with a common vision that supports the integrated learning and development of P–12 students, candidates, and PDS partners.
- Accountability and Quality Assurance: We encourage accountability, both to ourselves and to the public, and accept responsibility for student learning through continuous examination of best practices that encourage inquiry-based practice and reflection.
- Collaboration: We are committed to designing roles and structures that engage us in interdependent and shared practice and work to improve outcomes for P–12 students, candidates, faculty, and other professionals.
- Equity and Diversity: We are dedicated to upholding policies and practices that result in equitable learning outcomes for all PDS participants.
- Structures, Resources, and Roles: We are committed to ensuring programs, structures, and resources to support the continuous renewal and the improvement of all PDS participants, including P–12 students, candidates, members of the school-based and university-based community, and to support the PDS sites and the university as a whole (pp. 55–69).

The Context

The PDS is a suburban high school situated within fifteen miles of the university. The student population consists of approximate 1,700 9–12 students of which 76 percent are Caucasian, 15 percent are African American, 5 percent are Hispanic, 2 percent are Asian, 2 percent are Multiracial and Other, and 0 percent are Native American. Twenty-two percent of the student population is on free or reduced lunch.

The initial teacher preparation program in which candidates in this course participate is designed for history majors who are seeking licensure in secondary comprehensive social studies education (grades 9–12) and middle grades majors who are seeking licensure in middle grades education (grades 6–9) with a social studies concentration. Most content and pedagogical courses within the program are taught on the university campus. An exception, however, is the social studies methods course taught at a local PDS site. The social studies methods course is a required course for all middle and secondary social studies candidates. Candidates enrolled in this course are typically classified as first-semester seniors. The instructor of this course is a full-time professor who also teaches courses in the program on the university campus.

PDS RESEARCH AT THE PDS HIGH SCHOOL

This PDS relationship began with a request initiated through the PDS Committee work plan. Each department was asked to generate a wish list of areas with which they felt UNC Charlotte faculty could assist. The social studies department approached UNC Charlotte with requests for particular needs, which included a workshop on Socratic seminar, help with End-of-Course-Tests (EOCs) student preparation, and support in implementing technology. This request was passed along to the methods professor mentioned above in a university departmental meeting. Upon receipt of the list, this professor initiated contact with the social studies department and plans were made for a professional development workshop on Socratic seminar. First contact proved to be very successful, and the professor was invited to a social studies department meeting to pursue ways in which she could help with improving student performance on the EOCs. EOCs are state standardized summative achievement tests and are administered in all secondary schools. Student EOC performance is used in the accountability assessment of all schools in North Carolina. After much dialogue, the professor offered the option of developing a tutoring program to help at-risk social studies students. The program would focus on student weaknesses in reading comprehension and study skills and habits. The premise of the intervention program was that, if students developed the skills and strategies for learning and understanding social studies, this would translate into higher student achievement in social studies courses and improved student success on EOCs. This tutoring program is the focal point of this chapter.

In North Carolina, state EOCs in social studies include: Civics and Economics and U.S. History. These are offered in tenth and eleventh grade. However, the tutoring program is not limited to only students taking these high-stakes testing courses. The tutoring program targets students enrolled in social studies courses in grades 9–12. The philosophy of the program is to help build students' skills early in their coursework and provide follow-up support as they progress through their studies. The belief is that, if interventions are offered as soon as struggles are identified, then there is a greater chance for long-term impact on student achievement.

This tutoring program is not a typical program. Many undergraduate candidates and much research often tout the inconsistencies between university methods courses and the real world of public schools. Candidates sometimes do not "buy into" the methods that are presented in their pedagogical coursework and perceive these strategies as utopian. To alter this view, the university professor requested that social studies methods be taught at this PDS site. Capitalizing on the reciprocal nature of the PDS relationship, this tutoring program is embedded in the university social studies methods course for middle and secondary candidates. Her purpose was to develop a learning environment in which candidates would learn strategies in the methods course and then apply these with 9–12 students. Not only would the opportunity to work with students offer a taste of reality, but the structure of this class would enable candidates to discuss, critique, and reflect upon the successes and struggles with implementation.

The social studies method course is taught once a week throughout the academic year at the PDS high school during fourth period from 1:00–2:35 p.m. and then methods candidates conduct an after school tutoring program from 2:45–3:50 p.m. The emphases of this tutoring program are improving students' study habits, test taking and study skills, and strengthening students reading comprehension strategies. The tutoring program targets struggling students enrolled in social studies courses required for graduation.

UNC Charlotte candidates are taught methods for improving students' reading comprehension, the importance of establishing the purpose of instruction, and strategies for helping students understand and remember complex social studies content. Other methods covered in the course emphasize self-regulation strategies which help students make connections between study habits and achievement. Methods course content also challenges candidates to critically analyze student preparation for learning content. Metacogntion is a critical component of teaching, and teacher candidates begin their studies with their own understanding of how they learn and make sense of social studies content. Candidates translate their understanding into methods for teaching students. All pedagogy presented in the course is evaluated through the lens of, "How does this method improve student learning and ultimately student achievement?"

Once foundational knowledge is established, candidates then apply and translate pedagogical understanding into real-world learning experiences. Candidates shift from theoretical analysis to pedagogical applications as they walk down the hall to the after-school tutoring program to test the validity and reliability of these methods. Teacher candidates work with students either individually or in small groups weekly, then return to the methods classroom the following week to collaboratively debrief and analyze the effectiveness of their instruction. The instructor offers suggestions for modifying pedagogy to better support identified student needs, recommendations for further reading and research to improve candidate knowledge, and interventions for how to address personal challenges. These conversations often reveal the need for more information to help candidates understand teacher expectations and emphases. Follow-up dialogue is subsequently initiated with the social studies teachers. The opportunity to work directly with teachers and to understand how teachers define importance of social studies content is a unique opportunity for these teacher candidates. Additionally, candidates write weekly reflections of their tutoring experiences. These reflections include student self-diagnosis of strengths and weaknesses, candidate plans for intervention strategies to address student needs, and analysis of the candidate's impact on student learning as measured through qualitative and quantitative methods. This written record serves as a conversational dialogue between the candidate and the methods instructor.

DATA SOURCES AND METHODS OF EVALUATION

To evaluate the impact of this program, both quantitative and qualitative data was collected. Data sources include: student quiz and test scores, student performance on End-of-Course-Tests, student diagnostic questionnaires, student weekly self-regulation guides, candidate weekly reflections, and candidate summative reflections. Data were collected over three semesters, involving eighty-six PDS students and forty university pre-service teachers.

Qualitative data were analyzed through methods of reading, rereading, identification of data patterns, and analysis of patterns through additional reviews of data to establish existence and significance of patterns. Evaluation of data occurred over two months. After patterns were identified and data sorted into domains (Huberman & Miles, 2002; LeCompte & Schensul, 1999), specific examples from the narratives were identified and cited to support each of the emergent themes. Emergent themes were identified as *Diagnosing Student Struggles, Tutoring Interventions, Impact on Student Learning,* and *Unique Opportunities Afforded by the PDS Environment.* Within each theme, data were analyzed for additional patterns. Sub-themes emerged within each overarching theme. These patterns are defined in subsequent sections.

Quantitative data were evaluated using descriptive statistics. Means and standard deviation were analyzed for student diagnostic questionnaires. Student achievement scores were reported for student quizzes and tests where applicable. Overall school performance was included for social studies End-of-Course-Tests scores in comparison to countrywide achievement for all high schools.

RESULTS AND INTERPRETATIONS

Diagnosing Student Struggles

First, data were evaluated as a diagnostic assessment of student challenges and struggles. Themes emerged that suggest that the majority of all students participating in the tutoring program are *struggling readers who cannot decipher importance or see value in the content, have poor study habits, and low self-efficacy.*

Struggling Readers

Data revealed mixed interpretations of how students perceive their reading abilities. Most students identify themselves as good readers because they "read fast," "read aloud well and can read the words," and "I have to be a good reader. I am an actress, and you have to be a good reader to be an actress." Students also add they are good readers when they "read what I like or what interests me." Those who view themselves as poor readers provide reasons such as: "I forget what I read and can't remember it," "I don't like to read," or ". . . the wording is hard to understand."

Despite perceptions as good or bad readers, most students struggle with making sense of what they are reading, with interpreting and comprehending the text, with establishing patterns and relationships, and with making connections to other social studies content. Struggling readers, thus, are identified by their limited use of a few lower-level reading strategies. When students do not understand what they are reading, they: "read," "read it again," "skip it and move on," "get frustrated and quit," "give up," "wait until tomorrow when the teacher goes over it," or "ask somebody."

These struggling learners employ strategies that require the least amount of reading possible. The preferred method of reading was coined by one of the tutors as "search and destroy." The students will identify key words in the reading guide homework, skim the text for the key words, and then copy the words that follow the key words as the answers to the reading guides. These students search for ways to avoid reading and, in many cases, these students do not read at all. When students are introduced to new reading strategies, they want quick fixes and fast tricks that can help them complete their tasks. The tutors have noted that "the students will not use strategies, even if they work, because it takes too much time" and "I tried to get students to do some strategies, and they wanted nothing to do with them because they took more time."

Deciphering Importance

Probably one of the greatest barriers for these struggling learners is that they have not developed the skills to decipher importance in the content. The significance of this weakness is partly related to the content and content materials. Social studies is, by nature, an overwhelming subject, involving a wealth of information about people, cultures, geography, and events. Social studies content is packed with key people, important events, concepts, vocabulary, dates, facts, and maps. Additionally, social studies texts present this plethora of information in an ominous tone that gives the reader the impression that all of the content described is of equal importance. Social studies teachers, too, have a tendency to give the impression that to know social studies, one must know it all. It is easy to understand how the structure of the content and content resources can overwhelm a struggling learner and cause them to get bogged down in the dates and facts.

The struggling learners are not only handicapped by the content, but they are inhibited by their lack of skills. They are poor note takers and have the tendency to copy everything. Students are often allowed to use their reading notes on the reading quizzes. In reviewing these notes, tutors have noted that students write the entire section almost word for word. Even this strategy does not translate to success on the quiz, as students are unable to sift through the lengthy notes to find the answers to the questions. Students also interpret tests in the same manner. They think that they have to know everything and study by reviewing all of their notes rather than trying to highlight important information. For example, they state, "I can't memorize all the stuff. It's just too much," and "I can't memorize all the bodies of water." Struggling learners approach reading and studying with no direction or purpose and are left feeling overwhelmed and inadequate.

Devalued Content

Struggling learners are disengaged with the content. They don't like the content, are not interested in the content, and find the content to be boring or useless. Over three semesters, student average "like" of social studies content was 3.85 (SD = 2.64) on a scale of 1–10 with "1" indicating 'no like at all' and "10" equating to 'like it very much.' Students expressed their dislike of social studies content as: "I don't feel like learning about things back then," "I don't really like dates and maps," and "I just don't understand." When students do like the content, they explained their like as ". . . because it helps me on my test," ". . . because it reflects my grade," or "I need to know this to pass the class."

Interest in the content is also low with an average interest rating over three semesters of 3.69 (SD = 2.54) on a scale of 1–10 with "1" representing no interest and "10" suggesting extensive interest. Students' overwhelming lack of interest is attributed to the content as "boring." They added that social studies is "so boring" because: "I don't care about the past," "I can't pronounce this stuff," "It's a lot of reading and a bunch of study guides," "It [social studies] is just not very interesting. There's no motivation or any interesting literature." There were a few students who did indicate some interest in the content and credited this to the teacher. Student lack of interest in the content is often attributed to student inability to make personal connections with what they are studying. One student explained, "I'm not really interested in civics because I know that I don't need it like I would something else." They do not see value in the content and view it as "a waste of time."

This lack of interest carries over to assignments as well. Students experience disconnect with tasks because they do not see a purpose in doing the assignments. A student commented in reference to studying for tests that "I just don't see the point. . . . I didn't study because I knew that I was going to fail." One tutor stated in a weekly reflection that "The student still continues to perform average on her quizzes. She is struggling with the connections to her readings at home and her quizzes. She thinks the quizzes come straight from the class notes and not the book work. So she asked, Why should I read?" In a later tutoring session reflection, this tutor noted that her student "had not even realized where her teacher was getting the questions from on the quizzes." This disconnect can be attributed to assessment and limited self-regulation skills of these struggling learners. Students often misinterpret "completion" for "understanding" and cannot understand why, if they did the homework, they did not pass the quiz or test. One student offered the explanation that "I didn't do well, but I don't know why. I did all my homework." A tutor commented in a weekly reflection that, "I think their biggest problem is connecting the book to the class notes, next to the quizzes, and then to the tests. To them it is all disconnect." This later point connects to students' study habits.

Poor Study Habits

Most of these identified students have poor study habits. Study habits are defined as time and time management, the study context and environment, and study strategies. For many of these students there seems to be a 30-minute rule: "If I can't get it done in 30 minutes, then it's not worth doing." Students put unrealistic parameters on their time and expect to be able to accomplish any task despite the difficulty levels. Some students allot more than 30 minutes but still have defined time limits. For example, one student studies from 9:30–11:00 p.m. every night. She will not go beyond 11:00 p.m. because she needs her sleep, and she will not start earlier because she has cheerleading responsibilities. For this student, time parameters become a source of frustration, as she gets angry when she is not able to complete her work within these time limits; yet, she does not adjust her habits.

Another issue is time management. As identified above, many struggling students do not have the skills to be efficient readers and study effectively. Their skill deficiencies exacerbate their frustration and enhance feelings of inadequacy and failure. Inefficient studying is often due to a lack of awareness of the connection between study context and the ability to focus. Struggling learners typically do not study in contexts or environments conducive to learning. They report talking on the phone, watching TV, listening to the radio, working with chatty friends or younger siblings as potential detractors to learning. A final barrier is students' lack of self-regulation skills to make connections between study habits, skills, and academic achievement. They say they study, yet they still make bad grades. This is often a result of the use of limited skills (such as reading over notes and rote memorization) in an environment that is not conducive to learning. In most cases, they are not aware of what to do to improve their grades other than employing current strategies and work in existing contexts.

Self-Efficacy

The second most significant factor attributing to low student performance is self-efficacy. Few, if any, of these students believe that they can be successful. One tutor reflected after meeting his student for the first time that "the biggest obstacle that I am going to have with my student is her confidence level. She is worried that she is going to fail and believes that she cannot pass social studies. I had to constantly remind her during our session today that she wasn't going to fail and that there is plenty of time and grades left to pull up her grades." These struggling learners experience a low self-efficacy and consider their academic failure as personal failure. One student commented that "I don't like social studies and I'm not good at social studies. I just can't remember all that stuff." They cannot see any value in the effort they extend and do not realize the limitation of their strategies. They just feel like, "I not going to pass, so what's the point" or "I'm not a good reader, so I just don't read."

If they do not blame themselves for their failure, they blame the teacher. Feelings such as: "the teacher grades unfairly," "the teacher doesn't like me," or "the teacher tries to trick me on tests" are expressed by the students when asked why they did not make the grade they had expected on the assessment. When asked what they could do to improve their grades, many reported that they would "study more." They believe that effort is the only thing that can help them and, sadly, some are unwilling to exert any more effort than they are currently exerting.

Contextualization of the Struggling Learner

To contextualize these five diagnostic themes of student struggles, individual student cases are presented. These cases describe the difficulties and challenges encountered by struggling learners. Five students' stories provide a broader understanding of the commonalities among the participants of the tutoring program. These descriptions are derived from the student self-diagnosis of strengthens and weakness questionnaire that the tutors administer as an interview with students during the first tutoring session. Student responses to during the interview were transcribed by the tutors. It should be noted that tutors were trained in methods of transcription prior to the interview process.

Student 1
[Student 1] finds homework difficult to complete and states that it is not easy. She comments that she has to really look for the answers, and they are sometimes hard to find. She gives homework a rating of "5", with "10" being "impossible to do." She is not interested in the homework and gives a rating of "3" with the lowest possible rating being "1". She does not like the content and gives a like rating of "3" on a scale of "1–10". She comments that she just does the homework to get it done. [Student 1] rates tests as "5" in difficulty. She gives this rating because she "didn't study to my fullest." She suggests that for improvement she could participate more in class and says that she will definitely do this with a likelihood rating of "7." She is very sure that she will make a good grade on the next test if she does this. [Student 1] does her homework every night, but she does not do it until late. She usually starts on her homework around 9:30 p.m. and quits by 11:00 p.m. so she can go to bed. She often gets so frustrated when she cannot complete her homework in this allotted time. Her main strategy for studying is flash cards. [Student 1] says that she is not a good reader because she does not like to read. She states that she would be a better reader if she was interested in the reading. Her main strategy for not understanding is to "read again."

Student 2

[Student 2] says that homework is not easy and requires time to figure out the answers. She gives a "5" difficulty rating to the homework. She is somewhat interested in the homework's content with an interest rating of "6," but said that her interest depends on what they are studying in class. She does like the content and gives a like rating of "6." [Student 2] does her homework and focuses on completion. She considers the test to be average in difficulty with a rating of "5" but has no idea of what needs to be done to improve her test scores. After thinking for a few minutes she responds, "study more, study more." She is "very likely" ("9" rating) to study more and is very sure that she will make a C on the next test if she studies more. [Student 2] does her homework every day as soon as she gets home from school or right before going to bed. Her main study strategy is to try to think of something that she can relate it to. [Student 2] says that she is "sort of a good reader, but I don't read for pleasure." She states that she could be a better reader if she could "make connections to stuff." If she does not understand when she is reading, she will look over it again and she might ask a question.

Student 3

[Student 3] rates the homework as a "7" and gives this high difficulty rating because she is not interested in it. She gives an interest rating of "3" because "I don't see the point in it" and considers the content "boring," but gives an average like rating of "5." [Student 3] finds the tests to be very difficult and rated the difficulty as an "8." She stated that "it's difficult to remember all those definitions and dates." When asked what she would do to improve her grade, she stated that "I'd study more." She says that she is very likely to do this with a rating of "7," but does not expect to pass the next test and is "very sure" she will fail. [Student 3] does her homework every day right after school and works on it until she completes the task. Her method for studying is highlighting, but she cannot explain what she chooses to highlight or why it is important. When asked, [Student 3] says that she is not a good reader, because "I don't like to read very much." She comments that she could become a better reader if she practiced and states that if she doesn't understand something, she reads it again.

Student 4

[Student 4] finds homework very challenging and gives it a difficulty rating of "9". She says that she can find definitions in the glossary, but the rest is too hard. She has absolutely no interest in the homework's content and has "no like" of the content. She gives both a rating of "1" which is the lowest possible rating. She explains, "I just don't see the point. I want to be a beautician. What's the connection with that?" [Student 4] does not think that the tests are difficult (rating of 2), because she "didn't study and knew I was going to fail, so it didn't matter." However, [Student 4] says that to improve her grade she needs to study and be able to understand the importance of the task. She says that she is "likely" to study more ("7" rating), but believes that she will not pass the next test and is "very sure" of her failure. [Student 4] states that she does her homework, but always at the last minutes right before going to bed or even in class. Her strategies for studying are highlighting and sometimes note cards. She really likes to highlight but cannot decipher importance of what she highlighted. [Student 4] states that she is not a good reader and "I don't like reading. It sucks." She does suggest that to become a better reader she would have to be interested in it and wants to see more pictures. When asked what she does when she does not understand, [Student 4] commented that she will skip it or give up. She did say that she might ask the teacher.

Student 5

[Student 5] finds the homework difficult to complete and says that he "doesn't understand it sometimes." He does not like the content of homework and, in general, does not like homework. He gives a "like" rating of "4" and an interest rating of "5" to the content. He commented that he is interested in the content because "it counts as a grade, but I don't like to do it." [Student 5] thinks that tests are very difficult and indicates a difficulty rating of "8". He added that "reading the questions is confusing, because they don't make sense to me." He believes that if he studies more and takes better notes his grades will improve, although he admits that he is not very likely to do this. [Student 5] confesses that he does not do homework every night, but when he does, he works right after he gets home from school. The strategies that he uses to study are to "take notes on almost everything and try to remember it." He does not consider himself a good reader because "reading quietly is hard. I can't figure it out." He suggests that to become a good reader he should "read more, read aloud, and use the glossary or dictionary to look up unfamiliar words." When asked what he would do if he did not understand something he was reading, he stated that he would "think of something similar and try to make connections, but that usually doesn't work."

Tutoring Interventions

Each of the students involved in the tutoring program was paired with a UNC Charlotte tutor. From student questionnaires, tutors diagnosed student struggles and identified plans for intervention to address individual student needs. Interventions were grounded in pedagogical strategies candidates had learned or were learning in social studies methods. Intervention plans were outlined in candidate weekly reflective logs. Each week candidates evaluated the effectiveness of their interventions through student achievement, observations, and feedback from students. The former included either quiz or test scores and the later two focused on student reaction and success in using the recommended strategies. Candidates then either continued with present intervention plans or modified instructional methods to more effectively address student needs.

Patterns emerged from the data analysis of tutoring reflections of tutor interventions. These include *establishing a learning community* for motivating and engaging students, while supporting improvements in student self-efficacy; *introducing self-regulation strategies* to monitor and improve study habits; and *modeling of reading and study strategies*. For each of the emergent themes, data from tutoring reflections are provided to document these interventions.

Establishing a Learning Community

In social studies methods prior to beginning the tutoring program each semester, the social studies methods professor reads the story of *The Little Engine that Could*. She creates an analogy of the story with the tutoring program. The methods professor points out that if students have never been "over the mountain," they will believe it an impossible task, but if they have the right skills (that would be the Blue Engine), they can get "over the mountain." However, skills alone will not be enough. Students also need constant encouragement (such as "I think you can. I think you can."). Student success necessitates a support system that not only equips students with the skills to do but with the verbal reinforcement to keep trying. It takes time, often weeks, for students to start experiencing improvement in grades as a result of the new strategies they are learning. Consequently, the first goal of all tutors is to establish a supportive learning community.

As indicated in the needs assessment, most students struggled with low self-efficacy, believing that their academic failure was a reflection of personal failure. Building rapport with the students was essential in helping them understand that they were not inadequate or inferior, but rather they had not yet acquired the skills necessary for success. Tutors made a concerted effort to help improve student self-confidence and encourage beliefs that success could be achieved. An example of one such intervention follows:

Student 4

Candidate Weekly Reflective Journal: Week 1

Diagnosed Weaknesses:

[Student 4] does not really want to talk about what she needs. She is resistant to advice and just wants to do her homework independently. She has a very negative view about school and feels that nothing will help her and that she cannot do much of what is required. She does not see the applicability of Civics in her life.

Proposed Interventions:

My first goal will be to help [Student 4] see how Civics can affect her in the real world. Next, I need to work on getting her to feel better about her performance in school. I think this will help improve her interest in her studies. One thing that I will have to do is convince [Student 4] that tutoring can help her.

Candidate Weekly Reflective Journal: Week 2

I don't know how much progress we made this week, expect I was able to get [Student 4] to talk about her life a little. She opened up some and that was a nice start. For her to talk about her family, her feelings about school, and her life made a difference.

The learning community which tutors established evolved into a support system for students. Once students had a personal connection with their tutors, they were more willing to listen and apply the recommended strategies for reading, studying, or test taking. This support system encouraged attendance in the tutoring program (with 84 percent of students consistently attending for the duration of the program) and helped students maximize the benefits of the tutoring program. The support system also provided a nurturing environment which constantly reinforced self-confidence with encouragement. Examples from tutor weekly and summative reflections follow.

Student 1

Weekly Journal Reflection: Week 7

I think that [Student 1] is making progress. This is best seen in how she approaches her school work since tutoring began. At first, she didn't think that she could do it and believed that it didn't matter what she did, she would fail the quiz or test. Now she approaches learning with a more positive attitude. . . . I feel that tutoring positively impacts [Student 1]. She has started to understand how she learns. She knows that she understands the content when she makes connections, like connecting the first two letters in bail to remember the number 8 and the Eighth Amendment. She is also trying new ways to study information, mostly thinking up little ways to remember connections. That is how she learns and sometimes she cannot think of connections on her own. It is very helpful to have someone else to help brainstorm possible connections.

Student 5

Summative Tutoring Reflection

When I first met [student 5], he was very nervous about the tutoring program and leery of how I would be able to help him. He was also lacking in his confidence in his abilities as a student. He was very negative about school and his dislike for social studies. He complained that the work was too hard and he did not enjoy learning about social studies. As our sessions continued, he became more comfortable with the tutoring system and with his skills as a student. [Student 5] has shown great improvement over the course of our tutoring sessions. I knew that the first day jitters and nervousness about me and the program would go away as he continued our sessions. He soon became comfortable around me and began opening up and trusting that my methods of studying would help him.

Student 7

Weekly Journal Reflection: Week 7

My student told me today that she made an 86 on her test, which was what we were hoping for and what we had predicted. . . . We spent about half the time talking about the test. We tried to work on vocabulary, but the time was not very productive. She could not focus on her work because of the good grade that she had received.

Introducing Self-regulation Strategies

The next common intervention was the *introduction of self-regulation strategies*. Each week students were asked to complete a self-assessment of their study habits. Students charted (1) their learning environment [study context]: where they studied, when, and if there were distractions; (2) their modes of learning [study strategies] such as resources, methods, and how they studied; (3) prediction of grades and certainty of this prediction; and (4) the actual grade that was made. As indicated earlier, most students were not aware of how their study habits impacted their achievement on quizzes and tests. They did not recognize a correlation between studying and assessments. This was partly attributed to a misunderstanding that completion equates to learning. Many of these students defined their purpose in doing the homework as "to just get it done." Additionally, they justified their poor grades on quizzes or tests because they could not determine what the teacher would ask, or they believed the teacher graded unfairly. The weekly charting of study habits established for students a pattern in what they were doing and how this impacted their achievement. The weekly self-assessment guides also provided quality feedback to students as they monitored changes in grades due to changes in study habits. The importance of understanding self-regulation strategies is outlined in the following examples from tutoring weekly and summative reflections.

Student 1

Weekly Journal Reflection: Week 4

I think we are making progress with study habits. [Student 1] was so amazed this week that changes in study habits do make a difference. Last week, I had asked her to turn off the TV and put down her phone while she was doing her homework. She said that she finished her test corrections in record time. Go figure!

Student 5

Summative Tutoring Reflection

Many of the students that I worked with do not know what, how, when, where, or with whom to study. They often don't even know why they should study. Students have never been taught how to take notes or how to study. Since they don't know how, they just don't. This becomes a huge motivational problem that causes poor performance in class. This also leads them into believing that they are poor learners or poor readers. This is why the tutoring program is so successful. We help prepare students with study skills, and we help them monitor the use of these skills weekly.

Student 2

Weekly Journal Reflection: Week 5

We looked critically at her self-regulation chart. Her predictions for what she would get on assignments were excellent. Her study habits seem to be improving. I think we are making progress in evaluating study habits this week. By looking at the information that we had gone over when we were studying for her test and then looking at the information that she missed, we concluded that questions missed were those not covered during tutoring. This realization made her consider what she was doing outside of tutoring. We talked about what still needed to be done to improve those study habits. . . . I don't think that my student has fully developed metacognition because she is not fully aware of what she is doing in terms of studying or the impact that her individual study habits have on her scores. She is moving in the right direction, but she is not there yet. For example, she did score well on the questions that we had studied in tutoring.

Modeling of Reading and Study Strategies

The final intervention strategy involved tutors modeling and teaching students how to use various reading and study strategies. Methods were individualized, based upon student needs and learning styles. Most students responded best to the least complicated strategies and those they felt comfortable using. Instruction was not limited to the 'how to' for methods but emphasized when to apply strategies and why strategies should be used. Emphases were given to how students could use strategies to help them stay focused on the content, remember the content, and make sense of content. The purpose for learning shifted from preparation for the quiz or test to reading and studying to understand. Some strategies that were employed are presented in the following examples as described in weekly tutoring reflections.

Student 3

Weekly Journal Reflection: Week 3

Today, I demonstrated how to break down the reading section and question the text. I had the student think about what the teacher might ask. She said that the discussion question at the end of the section sounded liked a question her teacher would ask. We read the question and then read the text. We answered every question we encountered while reading on her notes page. I think this really helped her. She had not even realized where her teacher was getting the questions on the quizzes.

Student 2

Weekly Journal Reflection: Week 3

Today we worked on organizing our notes. My student really seemed to need some help with organizational skills. I think the lack of these skills is hindering her learning. We talked about keeping an organized notebook and how to organize notes while taking them. . . . I showed her how to take notes on reading. I read from the textbook and then wrote the information down that I thought was important and organized it into an outline.

Weekly Journal Reflection: Week 4

Today we worked on organizing and making sense of notes that we had already taken. We took out notes from the previous night and talked about how we might organize these. We decided to highlight dates in one color, people in another color, and important events in the last color. Then we revisited what we had done last week. We read the section and took notes on it then we went back over the notes and highlighted these.

Assessment:

Today, I taught my student a new strategy called Highlight and Revisit. I think this will make the notes a much easier reference during the reading quizzes.

Tutoring Impact on Student Learning

In general terms, the tutoring program had a positive impact on student achievement. For all students who consistently attended the tutoring program, all passed social studies and have passed the state standardized End-of-Course-Tests (EOCs) in the both Civics and Economics and U.S. History. Not only did these students pass, but they averaged B's on the EOC tests. Individual student success is also attributing to overall school success. EOC test scores for this school far surpassed other schools in the county. Although conclusions cannot be drawn that the tutoring program was solely responsible for this success, it can be noted that it is one variable that contributed to improving student achievement (as noted below in the PDS's response). See Table 8.1 for countrywide score distributions by school. Scores on EOC tests were significantly greater and exceeded other schools by as much as thirty percentage points. Interestingly after test scores were compiled, the county office contacted the PDS school's principal to inquire as to what this high school was doing that others were not to help their students reach higher levels of achievement. The school's response was that the social studies department collectively requires test corrections and offers a tutoring program targeting struggling social studies learners.

Once scores were released to the public, the social studies methods professor received an interesting phone call in her university office. A very angry mother called to find out, "Why does my son not have a tutoring program for social studies in his high school?" The methods professor explained that she worked with the current high school because it was a PDS school. She also described the nature of a PDS and clarified the parent's questions about how a PDS works. Once the parent understood the PDS concept, the parent asked, "What can I do to get this PDS and a tutoring program for my son's high school?" This conversation speaks loudly to the potential of PDS relationships to improve the quality of education provided for students and the potential for community outreach.

In more specific terms, the tutoring project has helped increase individual student success. Students have improved their quiz and test scores in

TABLE 8.1   End of Course Test Scores by School for Social Studies

Course	High school					
	PDS	2	3	4	5	6
U.S. History	80.7%	52.1%	66.3%	57.8%	59.5%	66.0%
Civics & Economics	82.8%	54.7%	68.0%	73.7%	80.8%	72.8%

Note: These scores include all schools within the county and school system of the PDS school described in this chapter.

social studies. There have also been positive impacts on student self-regulation and self-efficacy. The impact on student learning does vary, based upon individual student struggles. Not all students reflected extensive academic gains as a result of the tutoring program, but they did experience some benefit from the experience. A review of the first five students will help explain the impacts of the tutoring program. Documentation on achievement is provided from summative tutoring reflections.

Student 1

Summative Tutoring Reflection

Student learning improved. I saw cognitive development in her awareness and self-regulation. She was very aware of where she needed help and where she was good in terms of her skills. She had made changes in her study habits that enabled her to work faster and her work was of better quality. The impact on student learning is reflected in changes in her grades. She was making F's when she came to tutoring and is now getting C's. This might not be as dramatic as other students, but she is making progress.

Student 2

Summative Tutoring Reflection

I think [Student 2] was greatly impacted by the tutoring program. She improved her skills in reasoning, predicting, and awareness. She became very good at reasoning out the correct answer to a test question because she was aware of how the test was set up and could predict which choices were definitely incorrect. . . . I saw huge improvements in self-regulation. [Student 2] became aware of what was working and what was not in her study habits. Her grades improved from getting D's and F's to getting A's and B's. She failed the first progress test. We worked hard in tutoring in helping her understand what she missed and why. When she retook the progress test, she made an A. I think that this is a perfect example of the impact on student learning.

Student 3

Summative Tutoring Reflection

I think the tutoring program made a difference for [Student 3]; although I think more could be done. I tried to get her to open up but didn't make as much progress with this as I would have liked. I kept asking how she was doing in class, but she shared little information. Her teacher, however, each week told me that [Student 3] was improving and that her grades were getting better. She was making F's when she came to tutoring and is now getting C's or D's. As long as her grades improved, she showed signs of being more confident in the information and in her abilities.

Student 4

Summative Tutoring Reflection

[Student 4] is an interesting person indeed. After our first meeting, I was actually dreading the next visit with her. She was unmotivated and just down right negative about C&E [Civics and Economics]. . . . So, as the weeks went on I tried different approaches to get her to focus more. Did it work? I don't believe her teacher will see much of an improvement [in her grades]. However, I did find one area where I was able to connect with the student and that was drawing. We learned about a method called visualizing social studies in our methods class. We read an article on smallpox and had to draw an image representing the important parts of the story. I noticed in week 8 that she liked to draw, so I tried out this strategy and she seemed to like that. For the next two weeks she seemed to like coming to tutoring and enjoyed the reading. Near the end we actually started "bonding" and becoming used to each other. . . . I wish we could have had more days together so I could try a little harder to reach her. Someone just has to get to know her and relate. I believe deep down she is interested in social studies but just doesn't want to admit it.

Student 5

Summative Tutoring Reflection

I think [Student 5] improved his self-motivation because he read at least one more time per week because of our meeting. . . . He was making 20's on his quizzes when he first joined the tutoring program. His quiz grades have improved to 25–45–65–100. He consistently makes in the 70's to 90's on quizzes. On his last test, he made an 85. . . . [Student 5] has really mastered double-entry notes. He liked the strategy and was making A's on his quizzes. We have been working on more advanced reading strategies. I think these will help him improve more.

As a final indicator of the positive influence of this tutoring program, comments from a student were telling. [Student 7] asked the social studies methods professor on the last day of her tutoring program, "Could you fail [my tutor], because I need him to work with me in the fall?" This student had also inquired earlier in the semester if the methods professor could require her tutor to come during spring break because she needed his help. As indicated in earlier comments [Student 7] was elated to the point of distraction with her success of an 86 on her last test. It is evident that this tutor and student built a rapport and supportive community of learning. The tutor commented in his summative reflection that, "the tutoring sessions have really helped [Student 7], and she has made great improvements. Her confidence level in herself and in her skills in social studies has improved and she is performing better because of it."

For [Student 7] and others described above, the tutoring program greatly impacted them, both academically and personally. The interaction has taught students that they can "get over the mountain." It would not be correct to suggest that the success of this program is attributed solely to the individuals involved. The reality is that what makes these tutors so successful is the environment in which this tutoring program is situated. Weekly interaction with students can only have limited impact, but when coupled with lengthy exchanges and constant dialogue teachers, tutors are able to get to know their students well, identify struggles, and provide appropriate interventions to address students' needs. Communication, guidance, and support as a result of the PDS environment have enabled tutors to construct an individualized supportive learning community.

Unique Opportunities Afforded by a PDS

Data analysis revealed the uniqueness of the tutoring program as situated in a PDS school by uncovering the following themes: *increased communication, access to learning needs, focused instruction, learning liaisons, methods instructor insights, reciprocal teaching and learning,* and *mentoring.* For each of these themes, supporting data have been provided from tutoring weekly and summative reflections and observation notes from the methods professor.

Increased Communication

The success of this program can to be attributed to the unique learning experiences and collaborations that a PDS environment creates. The nature of a PDS has provided for greater communication among teachers, tutors, and ultimately students. Many of the social studies teachers at the PDS high school were accessible during the tutoring time to answer questions for tutors, provide resources, and make assessments accessible for review. Tests and quizzes are normally not available to students once the papers have been returned. By working with tutors, students were able to review quizzes and tests to identify patterns for determining importance of content and to better understand why they had missed specific questions. This access to assessment proved to be successful for students as indicated previously in the impact on student learning section and with the following tutor's reflection.

Student 9

Weekly Tutoring Reflection: Week 4

My student told me today that she is still not doing well on her reading quizzes. . . . I do not really understand why she is not doing well because when we talk about the material she really seems to grasp what the text is saying. I think next week I will ask [the teacher] for a copy of the quiz and to talk with the teacher to see if there is a better intervention.

Access to Learning Needs

Since tutors are only in the school once a week, they are not able to experience the daily interactions with students and to completely understand the complexity of student needs. The teachers, however, have these insights, and the PDS environment engendered a collaborative dialogue between teachers and tutors. Weekly, the tutors talked with the teachers to better understand how they could help their students. These conversations included discussions of class interactions, homework, quiz or test performance, identifiable struggles, and possible interventions plans. Tutors relied greatly upon teachers to keep them informed of student needs and academic progress.

Student 3

Weekly Tutoring Reflections: Week 3

I think my student is making fairly good progress. We worked more today on her study and reading skills. This was mostly accomplished through finding the information and evaluating what it was and why she got it wrong. I think that the biggest step towards progress for my student was just approaching her teacher to ask what we can do to make her tutoring sessions more useful for her.

Weekly Tutoring Reflections: Week 9

I think I am positively impacting my student's learning because she is showing signs of improvement. She still has a long way to go, but her grades have gone up and she's using more strategies and exhibiting better study skills. I know this not because she has told me but because I have spoken with her teacher about it over and over. She is a very introverted person and does not want to talk about her grades. She is very resistant to telling me anything. If it was not for my conversations with the teacher, I would have no idea of her needs or any clue of what to do to help her.

Focused Instruction

Tutors took advantage of this increased interaction with teachers to ask for clarification of assignments and direction on how they might more effectively help each student. Tutors are at a disadvantage because they work with their students once a week and with limited knowledge of their needs. In contrast, teachers have a greater understanding of student struggles based upon their daily interaction. As a result, teachers became a resource for tutors. Teachers advised tutors weekly of student needs and suggested possible interactions that would specifically address these weaknesses.

Teachers also provided a focus for each tutoring session. For example, when students are asked what they did in class today, the common response is "nothing." When students are asked what they have to do for homework, they reply "I don't know." These are not uncommon comments from struggling adolescents, but a tutor cannot effectively help a student if they do not have a plan of action for the tutoring session. Relying on students as the only source will not enable a tutor to effectively address student needs. Instead, the PDS relationship allows for much more teacher involvement and direction to guide the work of tutors. The result is quality instruction and interventions for students. For example, one student was struggling with essay writing. The teacher suggested that the tutor help the student rewrite the essay that she had written for the test so that she could see what a good essay would be. The tutor responded in his weekly reflection that, "I'm glad that the teacher suggested that we rewrite her essay because it really seemed to help her out. I would never have thought about rewriting an essay, but it was a great idea and it benefited her."

Learning Liaisons

As indicated, the PDS relationship has greatly increased interaction and communication between teachers and tutors. This has an additional benefit in that it has opened communication to students. The tutors have become voices of the teachers and students, thus creating a conduit for communicating student questions to teachers and teachers' expectations to students. Tutors have become liaisons between the teacher and the student. As liaisons, tutors have been able to clarify, interpret, and explain potential confusion or misunderstandings. For example, assessment tended to be a source of confusion for many students. Struggling learners often attributed their failure to not knowing what the teacher wanted or to the unfair grading of their teacher. Tutor liaisons conversed with teachers to learn more about the teachers' assessment system and requirements and to explain student concerns. This role enabled tutors to clarify expectations of teachers and to help break down personal barriers. These are best explained in the example that follows.

Student 2

Weekly Tutoring Reflection: Week 1

My student has a lot of personality conflicts with the teacher, and she did not mind telling me about it. She started off by telling me that she was going to fail history because her teacher did not like her. I know that was something I would need to stop immediately. . . .

Weekly Tutoring Reflection: Week 2

. . . I tried to help my student see that her grades and learning goes beyond a personality conflict with her teacher. I tried to explain that, although there is a personality conflict, the teacher was not 'out to get her.' I think we made progress in this area. I wanted her to see that her learning was something that she could affect.

Summative Tutoring Reflection

In working with my student, I noticed that she did a lot better on her map quizzes when she colored them. This, however, was not allowed by the teacher, so I offered a suggestion that would allow her to meet teacher requirements and still help her study. I encouraged her because she did have Internet access at home, to go home, print a blank map form the Internet, color it, and keep the teacher's map separate. I did not want to undermine the teacher's authority by telling the student to color the map anyway. I did explain to the student the teacher's reasoning for wanting a map that was clearly labeled and easy to read. I explained that if they colored it, it was hard to read the labels. I told her this, and she understood why the teacher wanted the map different from how the student wanted to do it. I also explained that it would be okay to color her personal map. This really seemed to help her do well on her map quizzes and to get along with her teacher.

Methods Instructor Insights

Not only did tutors have the opportunity to interact on a very personal level with teachers, but the social studies methods professor has also been able to build quality relationships with teachers. Teachers have been very willing to allow this instructor to work more intimately with them and have welcomed her into their class for observations and even provided opportunities to teach. They have had lengthy conversations about the students in the tutoring program which have enable the methods professor to better understand the unique needs of each student. The instructor's consistent work in the school has provided the opportunity to learn methods that teachers use and to design more specific interventions to better address the needs of struggling student learners. This knowledge and understanding shaped the instruction provided to students in the social studies methods class that she teaches weekly at this school. The methods professor has modeled these strategies during class time and assigned tasks utilizing these methods for application with course readings. This experience better equipped tutors with the knowledge and skills that they must understand in order to assist their students. The following student's comment epitomizes the value and uniqueness of this tutoring program.

Student 8

Weekly Tutoring Reflection: Week 6

Today we did our reading, but instead of just taking notes we made a timeline of events and a graphic organizer of people, planes, and ideas . . . She seemed to like the idea of having a visual. . . . Next week we are going to try the drawing strategy. I think this will be another visualizing strategy that will help her learn. Plus it is fun. I know because we did it today in methods. This added bonus of fun will be a great motivator. I am not sure how easy it will be to do this strategy with the textbook, and it all depends on the content covered as well. It is worth a try though. Who knows maybe she will really like it and find the strategy useful.

Weekly Tutoring Reflection: Week 7

Today instead of taking notes, we drew our notes. We used the intervention strategy of drawing that we learned in methods last week. We made drawings of what we read and then reread the text and added more to the drawing. Then I had my student write an explanation of what she drew and why she drew it. I asked her what was so important about what she read that she made a drawing of it. She did an excellent job drawing and explaining why she thought the information was important. I think she really understood the information in this section of the textbook.

Reciprocal Teaching and Learning

Tutoring in a PDS environment has created opportunities for university teacher education candidates that have proven to be extremely beneficial. Learning about methods for teaching social studies in a high school classroom created a sense of reality and credence to ideas presented. The skepticism that often accompanies pre-service teachers' attitudes about education classes does not seem to prevail in this methods course. Candidates do question if these "best practices" are applicable and if they would work in a real classroom, but these questions do not last as students are afforded the opportunities to "try out" new teaching strategies in the real world. Their use of these methods is not limited to their own application in homework assignments, but they apply these interventions with real students. They learn the reality of teaching and the uniqueness of instruction as one strategy does not fit all students. They learn to appreciate the wealth of strategies to which they are exposed in this course and to understand the premise of differentiated instruction. These examples from candidate tutoring reflections capture the essence of reciprocal teaching and learning.

Weekly Tutoring Reflections: Week 10

I have had the opportunity to work with three different students thus far in the tutoring program. What is so interesting about these tutoring experiences so far is how many students have the same problems but different strategies work for them. With my first student, graphic organizers confused him more. With my third student, graphic organizers made sense. It is necessary to understand as a classroom teacher that you must differentiate the ways in which you provide instruction so that all students can get the information from it.

Weekly Tutoring Reflections: Week 7

I learned this week that student motivation plays a huge role in achievement, even more than I ever realized. The biggest problem with middle and high school students is a lack of motivation to learn. We must motivate them to learn the content we teach. We must do this by using alternative assessments and instructional methods. We have to find what methods help each student to learn. This is not an easy thing to do, but we have to.

Summative Tutoring Reflection

Now that I am experienced at tutoring, I would make a better tutor in the future. I am familiar with the strategies more after going over them at least three times each. The repetition of teaching students strategies over and over has helped me learn them well. I am comfortable in using these strategies now. I am also better prepared to teach my content. I have learned a lot of content through reading with the students and taking notes. I think I will be a better teacher because of this experience.

Even beyond the utility and effectiveness of methods, teacher education candidates learned a great deal about themselves. Many were uncertain and lacked confidence in their abilities. This unique tutoring experience provided them with a support system and learning community to scaffold their own understanding of pedagogy and cognitive development. All teacher education candidates touted the importance of this PDS tutoring program as an opportunity for professional growth and a valuable education to all participants.

Summative Tutoring Reflection

Through this tutoring program, I have learned a lot about myself and my skills that I have developed. I was worried that the methods that I used with my students would not help her, but after our sessions, I have come to the conclusion that they worked. I have also become more confident in my skills and knowledge of the material. The tutoring program has helped me in my learning of how to become a good teacher and has benefitted me personally as well.

Overall, the tutoring program was a great success for all who were involved with the program. It has helped both the tutor and the students being tutored. These tutoring reflections capture the self-reflective learning experiences of teacher education candidates.

Weekly Tutoring Reflection: Week 6

My student is teaching me more than I am teaching her. I am learning so much about students. I am also learning about how different each child is. Each day confirms this for me. I am also learning that not every student loves social studies as much as I do (a concept hard for us social studies people to grasp!).

Summative Tutoring Reflection

I really learned a lot about myself through this tutoring program. I was really nervous thinking about the tutoring program. It wasn't because I didn't want to do it, but it was because I was putting a lot of pressure on myself. I did not sleep very well the night before the tutoring program began because I did not know what to expect or if the students would be very receptive to us helping them. I found out very quickly that students want to be there, and they are very glad that we are there to help them. . . . The tutoring program has shown me what kinds of things students have the most trouble with in school. Note taking has to be the most troublesome homework task for students. This is something that I will definitely try and cover with my students when I am in the classroom. I will go over all kinds of techniques they can use to take notes in an effective way where they understand the material they have just taken notes on. . . . Once again, this tutoring program has been great and I really learned a lot about what my strengths are as an educator, along with my weaknesses that I will surely work on before I teach.

Mentoring

An unexpected consequence of the relationships that have evolved through the PDS has been an opportunity to mentor beginning and young teachers. During this study, there were three young social studies teachers who were members of the staff that were University of North Carolina at Charlotte students and who were taught social studies methods by the professor who created this tutoring program. One of these was a student in methods the first semester of the tutoring program. She completed her student teaching in this school the second semester of the tutoring program and was hired midyear, prior to the beginning of the third semester of the tutoring program. Her invested interest in the tutoring program is a product of experiencing the program as a tutor. She has on many occasions mentioned how great this program is and strongly encouraged, if not adamantly required, that all of her struggling students attend. She was very visible each tutoring day and was often involved in the tutoring session. She has had a friendly competition with other social studies teachers that she would have a higher percentage of students attending whom she has encouraged than them. Her first-hand experience is also a voice in support of the program.

In addition, the social studies methods professor has been able to serve as a support system for this beginning teacher. Weekly, the two chat about how things are going in her classes. They often discuss challenging students, and the methods professor has the opportunity to share ideas and possible strategies that novice teacher might implement. This young teacher has asked questions about strategies she experienced in methods and how to apply these in her class. The methods professor has also helped this teacher conceptualize her purpose in her instruction. For example, one of her students was struggling on quizzes and had come to tutoring for help. The professor asked him what types of content his teacher emphasized on quizzes and pointed out that every teacher has some pattern to how he or she determines importance. The student commented that he had no idea what his teacher looked for on quizzes. The methods professor then went to this beginning teacher and asked her, "How do you decide what questions to ask on the quiz?" The novice teacher responded, "I just pick out what is important." "But," the professor asked, "how do you determine what is important?" The young teacher once again commented, "I don't know." The teacher thought for some time and confessed that she really had not even thought about this and could not describe how she picked out questions. The professor explained that all teachers have a way of determining what they define as important. After a series of probing questions, the new teacher identified four common things that she emphasized on quizzes: (1) sequence of events (the timeline in each section), (2) location of events (a map usually), (3) important people, and (4) vocabulary [key terms]. She then giggled and said, "Well, you were right. I do have a pattern after all." The two then discussed the role of purpose and significance of sharing the instructional purpose with students. The young teacher commented that she would try explaining her purpose and her thinking more clearly in class. The methods professor then returned to the tutoring program to share with her student the four points he needed to study, and this student made an 80 on his next quiz. He told the university professor that he would have made a 100 if he had remembered to study the timeline, but he had forgotten about that.

An interesting potential outcome of this mentoring relationship has been the positive impact of this new teacher's success in supporting student learning. As scores for EOCs were reported for the third semester of the tutoring program, students in this teacher's classroom achieved the highest average in Civics and Economics among all regular students.

The learning community in this PDS environment encompasses students, tutors, teachers, and the methods instructor. These relationships go beyond the walls of traditional tutoring programs. This learning community has provided opportunities to support teachers, offer suggestions of possible strategies to help students beyond participating in the tutoring program, observing current teaching practices, and experiencing pressures of high stakes testing and accountability. In addition, teachers have been actively involved in the development and instruction of the social studies methods course. They are speakers, presenters, and instructors. This unique learning community has nurtured an awareness and appreciation for the roles that all participants play in this reciprocal relationship.

IMPLICATIONS AND RECOMMENDATIONS

Lessons learned from this experience indicate that to maximize the potential of tutoring programs, it is best that these programs are situated within PDS schools. Increased communication and improved awareness of student needs allow for more focused differentiated instruction. Data from this study demonstrate the benefits of this unique environment as increasing student self-efficacy as well as academic performance. Communication, guidance, and support as a result of the PDS environment have enabled tutors to construct an individualized supportive learning community. This learning community has educated students in believing that they can "get over the mountain."

In response to limited research of the impact of PDSs on student achievement, this study suggests that PDS schools provide a powerful environment for nurturing student development and promoting student academic success. Through increased communication and collaboration PDS relationships evolve into supportive communities of learners. All participants reap the benefits of this reciprocal learning experience, yet students seem to share an abundance of these successes. While good teachers make good schools, good PDS learning communities make great schools.

It is our recommendation that future research be conducted to explore the unique learning opportunities afforded by professional development schools and the potential impact on student achievement. We intend to continue evaluating the existing PDS relationship between this PDS high school and the University of North Carolina at Charlotte to understand long term impacts that this PDS tutoring program can have on the community of learners and ultimately student academic success.

REFERENCES

Abma, S., Fischetti, J., & Larson, A. (1999). The purpose of a professional development school is to make a difference: 10 years of a high school-university partnership. *Peabody Journal of Education, 74*(3/4), 254–262.

Clark, R. (1999). *Effective professional development schools.* San Francisco: Jossey Bass.

Huberman, A. M., & Miles, M. B. (2002). *The qualitative researcher's companion.* Thousand Oaks, CA: Sage.

LeCompte, M., & Schensul, J. (Eds). (1999). *The ethnographers' toolkit.* Walnut Creek, CA: AltaMira Press.

Levine, M. (1998). *Designing standards that work for professional development schools.* Washington, DC: National Council for Accreditation of Teacher Education.

Levine, M. (2002). Why invest in professional development schools? *Educational Leadership, 59*(6), 65–68.

Metcalfe-Turner, P. (1999). Variable definitions of professional development schools: A desire or a dilemma? *Peabody Journal of Education, 74*(3/4), 33–41.

National Council for Accreditation of Teacher Education. (2001). *Handbook for the assessment of professional development schools.* Washington, DC: National Council for Accreditation of Teacher Education.

Pine, G. J. (2003). Making a difference: A professional development school's impact on student learning. In D. L. Wiseman & S. L. Knight (Eds.), *Linking school-university collaboration and K–12 Student outcomes* (pp. 31–47). Washington, DC: American Association of Colleges for Teacher Education.

Teitel, L. (1998). Professional development schools: A literature review. In M. Levine (Ed.), *Designing standards that work for professional development schools* (pp. 33–80). Washington, DC: National Council for Accreditation of Teacher Education.

CHAPTER 9

PREPARING TEACHERS TO SERVE DIVERSE LEARNERS

A PDS/Full-Service Community School Model

JoAnne Ferrara, Eileen Santiago, and Christina Siry

ABSTRACT

This chapter describes the components of a PDS nested within the context of a full-service community school. This PDS enables pre-service and in-service teachers to realize the value of working with partners, including community-based organizations and college faculty, to support the intellectual, social, emotional, and physical growth of children and their families. Teachers in this setting expand their knowledge base about their students beyond the four walls of the classroom through meaningful collaborations with families and community agencies.

University and School Connections, pages 151–161
Copyright © 2008 by Information Age Publishing
All rights of reproduction in any form reserved.

INTRODUCTION

Over the past decade, professional development schools (PDS) have increased in number across the United States, emerging as models for the preparation of new teachers, serving the ongoing professional development needs of experienced teachers, and becoming centers for conducting educational research focused on problem-solving and student learning (Darling–Hammond et al., 2005; Holmes Group, 1990; Teitel, 2003). PDSs are characterized by school/university partnerships that are mutually beneficial to both institutions. This chapter describes a PDS that is nested within the context of a full-service community school. This partnership extends beyond the school/university relationship to provide broader partnerships with local community agencies. In the following sections, the various components of the partnership are discussed, and perspectives from the program participants are included to provide a profile of a PDS in a community school.

Historically, full-service community schools have primarily been located in urban settings or in areas where there are large concentrations of students with limited resources and high socioeconomic needs (Coalition for Community Schools, 2001). As part of their mission, they attempt to positively influence the social, physical, emotional and intellectual growth of children by delivering site-based services designed to respond to the needs of students and their families (Bingler, Quinn, & Sullivan, 2003; Dryfoos & Maguire, 2002; Harkavy & Blank, 2003; Jehl, Blank, & McCloud, 2001). These services require teaming school personnel with various social, medical, and mental health practitioners co-located in the school. Since full-service community schools are linked to healthier and happier children who are ready to learn and more likely to succeed academically (Blank, 2004), it is particularly beneficial to establish school/university PDS partnerships in such settings. The full-service community school provides an excellent backdrop in which to better prepare future teachers as they face the challenges of life in classrooms and, in addition, enables both university and school practitioners to better understand the dynamic interrelationship between school performance and the quality of their students' lives at home and within the surrounding community. Pre-service teachers and veteran teachers in full-service community schools learn the value of expanding their knowledge base about their students beyond the four walls of the classroom through meaningful collaborations with families and community agencies.

PRE-SERVICE TEACHER EDUCATION

Suburban schools are often considered immune to the problems more typically associated with large cities (poverty, residential mobility, and students with limited English proficiency and interrupted schooling). However, as suburban demographics in many parts of the country are shifting, these schools must overcome some of the same barriers to learning as their urban counterparts. As noted by Scherer (2005) in her analysis of the changing demographics of suburban schools, "Suburban school districts are seeing a steady increase in student diversity, larger enrollments, and greater student mobility rates . . ." (p. 7). Consequently, both experienced and novice teachers must now be prepared to meet the challenges presented by changing demographics in many areas throughout the country. As school districts face the challenges of such shifting demographics in these changing communities, PDSs in both urban and suburban communities must find innovative strategies to prepare teachers to meet these challenges.

In order to adequately prepare pre-service teachers to meet these challenges, it becomes crucial to provide them with valuable clinical experiences. Robinson (2006) notes, "Good clinical settings merge theoretical and practical learning and promote the creation of a perpetual community of learners . . ." (p. 2). Clinical practice is enhanced in a full-service community school which often incorporates extended-day programs, summer enrichment opportunities, parent engagement programs, adult education classes, family health services, and other community outreach activities, in addition to strong academic programs and instruction. In a full-service community school, classroom activities and school life are enhanced by the availability of a variety of community resources that provide much needed support for students and their families. The Coalition for Community Schools (Blank, Melaville, & Shah, 2003), in its report, "Making the Difference: Research and Practice in Community Schools," indicates that research confirms what experience has long suggested—community schools work. Evaluations of this model examined the impact of 20 community school initiatives across America, focusing on outcomes that directly affect student learning. Although not all evaluations looked at every outcome, their collective results clearly show that community schools make the difference for students in four important ways:

- Community schools improve student learning.
- Community schools promote family engagement with students and schools.
- Community schools help schools function more effectively.
- Community schools add vitality to communities. (Blank, Melaville, & Shah, 2003)

When engaged in a PDS relationship, the community school model is able to place pre-service teachers at the forefront of effective educational practices that draw upon theory and research on child development. This model also demonstrates how caring relationships embedded within a network of services that are delivered to students and their families in a comprehensive and integrated manner are vital to the success of all learners.

A PDS/ FULL-SERVICE COMMUNITY SCHOOL MODEL

The relationship between Manhattanville College and the Thomas A. Edison Community School in Port Chester, New York serves as an example of a well-developed college/school partnership that prepares pre-service, novice, and experienced teachers. Through this partnership, teachers develop their abilities to meet the needs of the students, the majority of whom are new arrivals to the country and who meet federal poverty guidelines. This preparation has taken place through a number of innovative venues made possible by the established networks that are the fabric of a full-service community school.

The Thomas A. Edison Community School was an ideal setting for initiating a PDS relationship with Manhattanville College. As a public school, it demonstrates the ability to successfully educate a wide range of children, despite the demands of its high-needs student population. The elementary school, located in a suburban community in Westchester County, faces many of the same challenges confronted by those in urban settings including: (1) having more than 80 percent of its population qualify for free or reduced lunch, (2) having nearly half of its 430 students in grades K–5 considered as English Language Learners, and (3) having an overall minority population of 94 percent with the majority of these students representing a multiethnic Hispanic community. Given the demographic characteristics of the school, a two-tiered level of support was instituted for students and their families as part of its full-service community school model. In this two-tiered approach to education, students are targeted on one level and families on the other. This bilateral approach complements the school's mission to support children's readiness to learn by promoting their social, emotional, ethical, physical, and intellectual growth.

The first level of support targets students by providing various social, mental health, and medical services in shared spaces co-located at the school site. Services offered to students include therapeutic counseling, family outreach, dental care, health and wellness education, and general patient care and treatment. As a result of interactions with these agency providers, both pre-service and experienced teachers regularly dialogue with the school-based health center's nurse practitioner, family outreach worker, and counseling therapist and are informed about the impact of students' health and wellness on classroom learning. Students are thus able to obtain the important prevention and intervention services they need in order to experience success in school, and teachers are better prepared to individualize instruction, modify their classroom teaching, and make appropriate adjustments to the learning environment.

The first tier of the Community School model (aimed at providing direct support to students) is reflected in the following PDS components:

- Student teacher placements: These placements serve to increase teacher to student ratios and provide a forum for the infusion of research-based instructional practices within the classroom setting. Student teachers learn the value of sharing perspectives of their students with a variety of professionals from community-based organizations.
- On-site student teaching seminar: Pre-service teachers participate in the life of the community school. They attend faculty meetings and participate in many of Edison's community school events. Thus, they become thoroughly familiar with the expanded role of the teacher in the setting of a community school.
- On-site graduate level literacy and special education practica: These courses, offered in a clinical setting after school, focus on the individualization of instruction for at-risk learners. Practica activities require collaboration among school personnel, college faculty, and the community agency responsible for after school programming.
- An on-site special education course titled, "Introduction to Diverse Learners": This course provides undergraduate, pre-service teachers with first-hand experience in observing and tutoring special needs and classified students in inclusion classrooms.
- An on-site science methods course: This course enables the classroom teachers, a college professor, and pre-service teachers to deliver inquiry-based science learning activities in a co-teaching model, reinforcing the value of instructional teaming for new and experienced teachers.
- Action research projects: These projects, co-developed by graduate students and classroom teachers, encourage the exploration of issues related to teaching students with different learning styles from diverse cultural and linguistic backgrounds.
- An on-site literacy demonstration classroom: This classroom laboratory, hosted by a classroom teacher with expertise in the area of English Language Arts, serves as a center for pre-service teachers to participate in structured observation and small group teaching.
- A special enrichment program for more able student learners: Thematic modules of instruction, developed by college professors interested in working with potentially gifted students from low

socioeconomic backgrounds, provide enrichment exposure and advanced skills development across the content areas.

- Summer programming held at the school site: The Edison/Manhattanville Home Run Summer Program offers enrichment, remediation, social-skills development, and recreational activities for upper elementary students around the theme of baseball. Under the guidance and coaching of an experienced classroom teacher, a cohort of PDS novice or pre-service teachers receive direct support for their teaching and for the implementation of the summer program's curricular goals.
- The Intensive Teacher Institute (ITI): The ITI, sponsored by Manhattanville College, is a certificate program for practicing teachers to pursue ancillary certification in high-needs specialization areas, such as English as a Second Language. As a result of participation in this PDS initiative, 44 percent of the full-time classroom teachers at the school have received graduate level training in teaching English as a Second Language in order to address the needs of its many limited English proficient students.
- PDS liaison: A PDS liaison is assigned to the school assuming oversight responsibility for all PDS initiatives and serving as a member of the school's leadership team. Participation on the school's leadership team with teachers, parents, and other partner organizations helps to blend resources and the expertise of all involved and ensures the sustainability of the community school model.

There are additional supplemental services provided by community-based organizations on this first tier. Manhattanville College conducts a number of undergraduate and graduate courses held at the Edison School aimed at providing enrichment, remediation, and classroom support as part of its PDS partnership. Traditional student teacher placements and course offerings have thus been expanded within the setting of the full-service community school to include a number of unique experiences in teacher preparation. These venues have taken the form of PDS initiatives held at the school site or at the college before, during, and after the school day as well as during the summers. In addition to helping the elementary students and pre-service teachers, these initiatives also benefit faculty members of the college and the school by providing opportunities for sharing best practices, promoting reflective discourse, conducting action research, ensuring the successful induction of newly appointed teachers, and building the school's capacity for improvement by promoting teacher leadership.

The PDS components, which have evolved within the community school, work in tandem with one another to provide a wide array of support efforts

for student learning and the development of future teachers, exemplify in-
ter-organizational collaboration at its best. This partnership has also served
to raise the level of teacher leadership at the school, involving teachers in
professional conferences, special presentations, and college advisory board
memberships.

Recognizing the importance of children sustaining positive and nurturing relationships with pertinent adults throughout their childhood as a
means of nurturing their overall developmental growth, the second level
of support in the full-service community school model at Edison is specifically aimed at engaging families and community stakeholders in the educational process. These support efforts include various intervention and
prevention services for students and their families. Program services have
been developed with the goal of enabling families to make an adjustment
to the culture in the United States, access resources from within the community, reduce levels of stress within the home, pursue opportunities for
self-advancement, and more effectively support their children's learning.
This tier, as reflected in the following site-based programs, also enables pre-
service, newly minted, and experienced teachers to be better informed in
their decision-making, planning, and classroom practice:

- The Edison CARES Program (Caring and Resources, Education and
  Services): This program, sponsored by a local mental health agency,
  provides outreach and case management for families in need of
  social services through a bilingual case manager and therapeutic social worker. Pre-service and experienced teachers regularly dialogue
  with the Edison CARES personnel to share their concerns, communicate with parents, obtain supplementary support services, receive
  progress updates, and plan for appropriate instruction.
- Topical workshops and seminars: These activities, offered by staff
  and representatives from partner agencies, provide needs and
  interest-based informational forums for families on topics covering
  a broad spectrum, including developmental discipline, effective
  parenting, health, nutrition, literacy development, and citizenship.
  Pre-service and experienced teachers jointly plan and present, in
  some cases with community partners, on several of these topics;
  thereby, they become comfortable with working in collaboration
  with outside agencies for the benefit of their students.
- School-based Health Center: This center, which functions as a satel-
  lite site of a local health center serving the poor and underinsured
  within the community, enables students to receive free medical and
  dental services with a focus on treatment and maintaining wellness.
  As a result of the presence of the nurse practitioner and dentists
  affiliated with the center, pre-service and experienced teachers

have gained a deeper understanding of health issues, including the prevalence of obesity and asthma within poorer immigrant populations and have been able to modify classroom activities to better address these concerns.

- Adult Education Classes: These classes, held in the evenings, are available for families and other neighborhood residents eager to obtain a high school equivalency diploma, learn English, or receive job readiness training. Adult education courses are sponsored through the county's Board of Cooperative Educational Services (BOCES) and are held at the school site throughout the year. The program's director serves on the school's leadership team, along with the PDS liaison.

PERSPECTIVES

"Educational research indicates that a common characteristic among effective teachers of low-income students of color is a respect for, knowledge of, and relationship with the home communities of the students" (Hyland & Meacham, 2004, pp. 115–116). The nature and structure of a PDS in a full-service community school provide opportunities for pre-service and in-service teachers to develop these characteristics as they work in tandem with community organizations to support students and their families. Discussions with pre-service teachers, in-service teachers, and college faculty indicate that the relationships built in a full-service community school partnership broaden understandings of what is needed to effectively educate diverse learners. Statements from participants provide perspectives and illustrate the impact of their experiences.

Pre-Service Teachers

A participant in the literacy demonstration classroom:

My experience this semester was priceless. I really feel I became a part of the school community. . . . I feel this experience was more meaningful because I actually got to take part in the literacy activities and the community programs and really got to know the kids and some of their families.

A student teacher's written reflective journal:

Being in this school has helped me to see how important it is to have services for the kids and families located at the school. Last week J. had a toothache and luckily the dentist was in to see him. . . .

A student teacher facilitating a parent workshop about homework practices:

> Community is the word I think of when I recall my experience hosting the parent workshop. The parents in the school really care about their children and come together at every opportunity they can to learn about more helpful strategies for improvement in their own and their children's education. My topic was homework help and I feel that everyone walked away having learned something new—even me!

In-service Teachers

> Dialoguing with the CARES case manager provides insights about what's going on in my students' lives. I understand why someone is off-focus better when I know more about their home situations.

> Having done my courses and student teaching here, I knew first hand what types of support were available for the kids. Now as a first year teacher in the school, I go immediately to the appropriate community partners for help. Most times, I can solve a problem before going to my mentor so that's really empowering.

> As a fifth grade teacher, I know that if my students have been in the school since kindergarten, they come into my class with all of their needs met and ready to learn. If they are going out for services during the day, I don't mind, I support educating the whole child. I guess I am accustomed to these types of services.

College Faculty

The PDS liaison reflecting upon the model:

> After participating in a variety of PDS initiatives, pre-service teachers are exposed to a variety of instructional practices, child support services, and family outreach programs. By the time they get to student teaching, pre-service teachers understand the mission and the culture of the school and appreciate the dynamics of a full-service school. The interrelatedness of the PDS components provides the context for educating the whole child.

The professor facilitating the science methods course:

> Teaching and learning science in this PDS provides opportunities for the pre-service teachers to develop an understanding of the complexities of working

with students with limited English proficiency. The partnership also develops in-service teachers' capacities for teaching science to their students.

CONCLUSION

An increasingly diverse student population is growing up in poverty in the United States (Berliner, 2006). While presenting a host of challenges to both urban and suburban schools, their presence also provides a unique opportunity to transform schools, to promote collaborative problem solving among community stakeholders, and to change the landscape of teacher education. Therefore, the changing needs of children in schools today requires that institutions learn the value of conducting business in different and extraordinary ways (Berliner, 2006). This new reality of schooling compels teacher education programs to educate their future teachers in more authentic settings where they can acquire the strategies and dispositions for effectively working with all students and learn the value of working with a myriad of professionals whose common mission is to support children and families. When the education of teachers takes place in the setting of a full-service community school, those entering the professional are better able to work with a diverse student population and are exposed to a dynamic and innovative paradigm for addressing the social and educational needs of these students.

The PDS partnership that is nested comfortably within a full-service community school facilitates the transmission of new and different norms for a more reflective practitioner, including effectively planning for instruction with a broader view of the child's individual needs, forming focused professional relationships between colleagues to develop a deeper understanding of teaching and learning, engaging the support of families and outside agencies, and, most important, learning to embrace diversity. Teacher education programs that serve to address the changing demographics of students within this context can potentially advance the profession by developing future teachers who are able to ensure the success of all children in any setting (Bullough et al., 1997; Darling-Hammond, 2006; Teitel, 2003, Whitford & Metcalf-Turner, 1998).

REFERENCES

Berliner, D. (2006). *How poverty affects the changing suburbs in the northeast.* Paper presented at The Changing Suburbs Institute Conference at Manhattanville College, Purchase, New York.

Bingler, S., Quinn, L., & Sullivan, K. (2003). *Schools as centers of community: A citizens guide for planning and design*. Washington, DC: National Clearing House for Educational Facilities.

Blank, M. (2004). How community schools make a difference. *Educational Leadership, 62*(3), 62–65.

Blank, M., Melaville, S., & Shah, P. (2003). Making the difference: Research and practice in community schools. *Coalition for community schools*. Retrieved March 29, 2005, from: www.communityschools.org/CSSFullReport.pdf

Bullough, R. Jr., Hobbs, S., Kauchak, D., Crow, N., & Stokes, D. (1997). Long-term PDS development in research universities and the clinicalization of teacher education. *Journal of Teacher education, 48*(2), 85–95.

Coalition for Community Schools. (2001). *Community schools: Partnership for excellence*. Washington, DC: Author.

Darling-Hammond, L. (2006). *Powerful teacher education*. San Francisco, CA: Jossey-Bass.

Darling-Hammond, L., Hammerness, K., Grossman, P., Rust, F., & Shulman, L. (2005). The design of teacher education programs. In L. Darling-Hammond & J. Bransford (Eds.), *Preparing teachers for a changing world* (pp. 390–441). San Francisco: Jossey-Bass.

Dryfoos, J., & Maguire, S. (2002). *Inside full-service community schools*. Thousand Oaks, CA: Corwin Press.

Harkavay, I., & Blank, M. (2003). A vision of learning that goes beyond testing and choice. *Reclaiming Children and Youth, 11*(4), 211–215.

Holmes Group. (1990). *Tomorrow's schools: Principles for the design of professional development schools*. East Lansing, MI: Author.

Hyland, N. E., & Meacham, S. (2004). Community knowledge-centered teacher education: A paradigm for socially just educational transformation. In J. Kincheloe, A. Bursztyn, & S. Steinberg (Eds.), *Teaching teachers: Building a quality school of urban education* (pp. 113–134). New York: Peter Lang.

Jehl, J., Blank, M., & McCloud, B. (2001). *Education and community building: Connecting two worlds*. Washington, DC: The Institute for Educational Leadership.

Robinson, S. (2006). Getting serious about clinical development. *Briefs, 27*(2), 2.

Scherer, M. (2005). Perspectives: Our cities, ourselves. *Educational Leadership, 62*(6), 7.

Teitel, L. (2003). Using research to connect school-university partnerships to student outcomes. In D. L. Wiseman & S.L. Knight (Eds.), *Linking school-university collaborations and K- 12 student outcomes* (pp. 13–27). Washington, DC: American Association for Teacher Education.

Whitford, B. L., & Metcalf-Turner, P. (1998). Of promises and unresolved puzzles: Reforming teacher education with Professional Development Schools. In *1998 yearbook of the National Society for the Study of Education* (pp. 257–278). Chicago: University of Chicago Press.

PART II

PERSPECTIVES ON INQUIRY AND MENTORING

CHAPTER 10

TEACHERS FOR A NEW ERA

A Collaborative University and School District Teacher Training Program

Robert E. Kladifko

ABSTRACT

Principals in our schools today are inundated with accountability, testing, and increasing demands from state and federal authorities and the community. These necessary responsibilities leave little time for the principal's professional responsibility for nurturing future teachers.

Teachers for a New Era (TNE) is a new teacher-training program of the Carnegie Foundation-funded partnership between the Los Angeles Unified School District and the University of California, Northridge. This program provides much needed assistance for principals in their vital role of preparing future teachers.

The TNE "schools as clinics" objective brings university faculty and school staff together at the school site in a collaborative relationship to better prepare university students to be successful teachers and to curtail the attrition rate of new teachers entering P–12 education.

University and School Connections, pages 165–177
Copyright © 2008 by Information Age Publishing
All rights of reproduction in any form reserved.

The following chapter includes a description of the essential elements of the program and reactions from three clinical site principals.

INTRODUCTION

The Teachers for a New Era (TNE) program is a new and refreshing look at training university students to be better prepared to be successful teachers and to curtail the attrition rate of new teachers entering education. In 2002, the Michael D. Eisner College of Education at the California State University, Northridge (CSUN), in collaboration with the Los Angeles Unified School District (LAUSD), was awarded a Carnegie Corporation Grant and developed the TNE professional teacher education program. Currently, the TNE program is also receiving support from the Ford and the Annenberg Foundations.

> The selection of CSUN and ten other institutions to participate in the TNE Initiative signals an urgent and profound response to what has been depicted as a national failure by American higher education to prepare quality teachers. The lack of confidence in traditional teacher preparation is understandable, albeit painful to those of us involved in teacher education over the last few decades. The numbers of poorly qualified graduates of our public schools are increasing. Overwhelming evidence indicates that the single most crucial factor in the academic success of K–12 students is the presence of a motivated and qualified teacher, regardless of the many other socioeconomic factors that do bear upon student achievement. (TNE @ CSUN Project Overview, 2002)

The mission of the TNE program is aimed at the professional preparation of teacher candidates, the improvement of practices, and the enhancement of student learning.

The goal of this CSUN national initiative is to reinvent teacher education through evidence, the engagement with the arts and sciences, and partnerships with LAUSD. To accomplish this, CSUN has embraced the following design principles:

> Principle A—Assessing the needs of learners and training future teachers in approaches to assessment.
>
> Principle B—Creating strong clinical school practice experiences for teacher candidates.
>
> Principle C—Strengthening the collaboration of the arts and science faculty with the education faculty in the design and oversight of teacher preparation programs.

THE ORGANIZATION OF THE TNE PROGRAM

A five-person Executive Committee and a Steering Committee are responsible for the accomplishment of the goals of the program.

Governance

The Steering Committee is an 18-member group that includes CSUN and school district faculty and administrators. The Committee is subdivided into seven Objective Groups and a variety of Working Groups and Advisory Committees and meets monthly during the academic year to determine the course of the program. The goals of the Objective Group Committees are to define objectives and to perform specific tasks and activities under the Principles. Each Objective Group is chaired by a Steering Committee member.

The TNE program has an Advisory Committee composed of leaders in government, the private sector, education, and the community throughout California. It receives reports on the status of the program and monitors its ongoing progress, facilitates its success, and publicizes any matter pertaining to the project.

SCHOOLS AS CLINICS

In 2002, as an assistant professor in the Department of Educational Leadership and Policy Studies at California State University, Northridge, and a former district and school-site administrator in the Los Angeles Unified School District, the author was invited by the Dean of the Michael D. Eisner College of Education to join the Schools as Clinics Objective Team. This team was an outgrowth of the "teaching as an academically taught clinical school practice principle" of the TNE program.

A developmental approach in the preparation of educational personnel was a key ingredient of the program. Educational leaders and teachers must be strong in their content knowledge and the understanding in which teaching and learning takes place. It was understood that the very basis for our clinical sites program was a nurturing school family that would provide an environment where educational personnel could demonstrate and assess the depth of their content knowledge and set achieving outcomes for every pupil.

If a school were to serve as a clinical site, it must be a dynamic learning community and a setting where all participating faculty are committed to the professional growth and mastery of learning by students, educators in training, educational professionals, parents, and citizens. University student teachers were assigned to a clinical site on a full-day basis, thus becoming regular members of the school staff with experiences as close to a beginning teacher as possible. The clinical school must be an officially designated partnership of all necessary constituents and conducive to a developmental approach to education in a diverse environment where all learning is the outcome of inquiry, reflection, and supervised experience.

Levine (2002) talks about considerations in an effort to create schools that tolerate, educate, and celebrate all kinds of minds. In regards to teacher training, he noted that we must change the way we prepare teachers. In discussing teacher education, Levine feels that a teacher needs to be a "lead observer." He also added that teachers have nearly exclusive access to what he calls the "observable phenomena," an unobstructed view into the world of how children learn. Levine and his colleagues have developed a school/program called *Schools Attuned*, which is a broad training experience for teacher candidates. The TNE program includes the components of *Schools Attuned*, such as ongoing assistance, networking, tools, and consultation.

Also considered in planning for clinical sites were the *Standards for Professional Development Schools* written by the National Council for the Accreditation of Teacher Education (2001). These Standards suggest that school learning environments that provide support for candidates and faculty must operate in the context of: (1) meeting the needs of all children, (2) partners sharing responsibility for educators and students, and (3) partners blending their expertise and resources.

THE ORGANIZATION OF CLINICAL SITES

The clinical site schools are partnerships between CSUN and LAUSD. The primary constituents are administrators and faculty from the schools and CSUN students. Learning communities at each clinical site teach, guide, research, enable, enhance, and mentor CSUN students. The following section describes the guidelines to formulate the governance and attributes of the sites.

Expectations

Policies that are implementable and acceptable to the school site, district, and CSUN include the following:

- Faculty at the clinical school are considered university adjuncts as they work with student teachers.

- Faculty at CSUN are considered adjunct school district faculty.
- Faculty at the clinical site and the university have equal opportunity to participate in partnership work, and all are expected to participate.
- Partnership participants are well prepared to provide leadership in designing and facilitating the professional development of others.
- Mentors and fieldwork supervisors are selected from site personnel. Ongoing training and support are provided for mentors and supervisors (e.g., methods, procedures, stipends/course vouchers) by CSUN and the clinical site school.
- Data gathered from the clinical site provides evidence that students are well served through participation in the partnership.
- Flexibility is provided through student teaching experiences at multiple clinical sites at different levels where appropriate. This gives the student experience with multiple mentors, personnel, and varied types of placements so that students have a broad experience.
- Every effort is made to provide a common attendance calendar matching the university and clinical site.
- Observation of professionals in the work environment and students in the learning environment is key to the experience. Observation of the instruction in the classroom, counseling sessions, and IEP meetings without disrupting the classroom is a priority.
- Physical space for university classes to be held on clinical sites and meetings for student teachers, which include dedicated classrooms for mentors and students (as well as office space for the site director and university liaison), is a goal of the program.

THE SELECTON OF SCHOOLS

It was decided that the first clinical schools should be from the same school district, and LAUSD was a natural because CSUN is located within the boundaries of that district. After consideration of all the characteristics for a clinical site, an in-depth investigation of many suggested schools, and collaboration with the Steering Committee, the school principals, and staff, three schools were selected: Monroe High School, Sepulveda Middle School and Langdon Elementary School.

The following criteria were used in the selection process:

1. An elementary school with grades Pre-K to 5, a middle school with grades 6 to 8, and a high school with grades 9 to 12.
2. All schools should be in the same feeder pattern and geographic location.
3. All schools were in an economically disadvantaged area.

4. The teachers and principal of the school must want to participate in our program.
5. All schools should be within a fairly close proximity to CSUN.

CHARACTERISTICS OF THE CLINICAL SITE

Every effort was made to have the clinical sites recognized by the district and university community as sites with a special mission and with responsibilities shared equally by both. Being a clinical site should bring the necessary personnel, funding, support, and facilities to accomplish the mission.

Schools as Clinics Workgroup

Chaired by a member of the TNE Steering Committee, the Workgroup meets bimonthly at one of the clinical sites. Its main function is as an advisory board. The members of this group are the Site Directors, CSUN Site Liaisons, clinical site principals, CSUN Arts and Science faculty, and College of Education faculty.

Site Director

Each school site principal selects a Site Director. *This person is key to the success of the program.* It is suggested that a member of the school staff be selected carefully, as he or she is the key liaison for the program at each school. The Site Director works very closely with the university-appointed Site Liaison and meets with the Workgroup. The Site Director nurtures and assists student teachers assigned to the site as well as selecting and collaborating with mentoring teachers and relieves the principal of much of the responsibilities for student teachers. His/her time is compensated through the TNE program, and the school site and is part of the normal work load of that individual. Allocating release time for this person is important, as is providing a financial stipend.

School Leadership Team

A site Leadership Team is established by both the Site Director and the principal and they meet regularly to conceptualize, design, initiate, and sustain the partnership. Each team varies in size at each school but should have at least five members who represent all constituent groups, such as administration, master teachers, staff, faculty, students (at the appropriate level), parents and university faculty.

Members of the Leadership Team are carefully selected to include experts in their individual professional fields, and those active in professional organizations and current in research and theory. They must be committed to long-term participation and dedicated to the partnership.

Site Liaison

The liaison, a professor appointed by the university, assists the Site Director and principal in facilitating the daily operation of the TNE program at the clinical site. This liaison works closely with school staff and student teachers assigned to that site and is compensated through a reduced workload or stipend provided by TNE.

TABLE 10.1   The Demographics of the TNE Clinical Site Schools

Langdon Elementary School

Year-round Calendar	4 Track
Enrollment	1,176
Number of Teachers	74
API	630
NCLB	PI 3
Free & reduced lunch	100%
Student ethnicity	97% minority

Sepulveda Middle School

Traditional Calendar	
Enrollment	2,160
Number of Teachers	93
API	653
NCLB	PI 5
Free & reduced lunch	81%
Student ethnicity	80% minority

Monroe High School

Year-round Calendar	3 Track
Enrollment	3,400
Number of teachers	150
API	608
NCLB	PI 5
Free and reduced lunch	77%
Student ethnicity	90% minority

THE PRINCIPALS OF THE CLINICAL SITES

To validate and measure the success of the clinical site component of the TNE program, the author conducted a qualitative study that consisted of the development of an open-ended questionnaire and personal interviews with the principals of the three schools.

Semi-structured audio-taped interviews were conducted at their schools, each lasting between one and two hours. The same protocol questions were used for each principal and, when appropriate, probing questions were included to draw additional depth. The purpose of the study was explained and each principal was given a copy of the questions before being interviewed. (See Appendix for the Interview Questionnaire.)

Shortly after the interviews, the author personally transcribed the content of the interviews. Reliability of the data was strengthened through follow-up telephone interviews. Through this analysis, general themes emerged by frequency of the same responses to the questions.

The following is a summary of the interview responses to the questions by the principals of the three clinical site schools:

What is different about the TNE program?
1. With TNE as the catalyst, there is more communication with CSUN through professors teaching their classes on campus, conducting professional development, and collaboration with school site staff.
2. With enhanced teacher training collaboration between the school and university, there is more confidence in the quality of teacher candidates.
3. As a clinical site, we are partners in producing beginning teachers for our school.
4. In the past student teachers were like 'passing ships in the fog.' We knew they were on campus but had no real contact with them. Now they are known as 'real teachers' and become part of our staff.
5. The Site Director provides coordination and organization. We now know when student teachers are here.
6. As a result of the TNE, student teachers spending more time on campus, many more school site teachers have shown an interest in mentoring student teachers.
7. I feel the TNE program is the ideal way to come into teaching.

Has there been improvement in the way your school works with student teachers?
1. The student teachers know the curriculum better and have a more focused approach to teaching.

2. Student teachers attend staff meetings and participate in school events held after hours and on weekends together with staff members.

3. The university seminars that are taught on campus have brought our staff a mutually beneficial collaboration.

What suggestions do you have to improve the program?

1. Organize the assignment of student teachers so it coincides with our Year-Round Calendar.

2. I would like to see even more reciprocal teaching between professors and my school, such as presentations to my students, working in classrooms and providing professional development for my teachers.

3. I would like to see university supervisors of student teachers more knowledgeable about what our school's curriculum goals are for teachers and collaborate with us in supporting our instructional goals in the classroom (i.e., Open Court Reading and Into English literacy programs).

Were there any opportunities for collaboration?

1. Most collaboration took place between Math and Literacy Coaches and the student teachers. The Coaches gave workshops and conducted classroom observations for student teachers.

2. The student teachers participated in faculty meetings, professional development, and weekly grade level meetings along with clinical site teachers.

Selection of the Site Director

1. My Site Director was not a member of my staff. However, the selection of a professor in that position has worked out well because she is a former principal of my school and knew my staff. This way, I did not have to take away someone from my staff to do the job. However, I would rather have a person from my staff who is full-time out of the classroom. Right now I do not have the money to release someone from my staff. (Elementary School)

2. It was absolutely necessary that we have an out-of-classroom faculty member from my staff to handle the Program. (High School)

3. My Site Director came from my staff and was well known at my school. The TNE program supplemented her salary and now she is retiring but will stay in the program and continue to be partly compensated by TNE. Originally, my school paid for a half-time position and TNE provided the other half. (Middle School)

School Site Steering Committee
1. Finding a mutual time to meet is a challenge.
2. It is important to have the principal, university professors, student teachers, and mentoring teachers present and actively participating.
3. The Steering Committee is meeting on a regular basis facilitated by my Site Director. I try to attend when I can.
4. The Site Director keeps me informed about what is going on. We communicate by e-mail frequently. I want the program here, and I will do what I need to do to make it work.

Joint Events
1. The university has invited the school site teachers to many curricular workshops and conferences held on the university campus. It is important that the clinical site teachers know what the events offer for them.
2. One of the most meaningful workshops that my staff took part in was How to Mentor a Student Teacher. I would like to see more.
3. I would like to see much more joint events. I have a classroom at my school (set aside) that I have designated for use by the TNE program for activities such as seminars, workshops, and collaboration meetings.

Commitment from LAUSD for the program at my school
1. The superintendent has shown support for the program through meeting attendance and positive comments.
2. At this time the district is not contributing any additional financial or personnel resources to the program.
3. I think the superintendent is supportive. The TNE program is very creative and the superintendent likes creative programs at my school. We do not have any additional resources provided by the district, but we would only need financial support for the Site Director to sustain the program if the university dropped that support.

Ongoing funding
1. It would be difficult to continue the Site Director position without TNE funding.
2. Funds from the TNE program provide release time for teachers to collaborate.
3. I am not using any funds from my budget for the program. We are just using teacher and administrator time and effort.
4. I would like to see more lucrative stipends for Mentor Teachers who supervise student teachers.

Collaboration with Arts and Sciences
1. Music and Art professors have conducted professional development for clinical site teachers.
2. Professors have been a resource for classroom teachers and have made presentations to P–12 students.
3. I really liked it when the Art Professor brought his CSUN class to a classroom at my school, and the CSUN students worked with my students.

Other
1. To be successful, this program takes time and dedication on the part of the principal.
2. I want the program to continue. My favorite word is "evolution" and I think the longer we work together the better this collaborative program will become for our school and the TNE student teachers.

SUMMARY REMARKS

As a former principal, I firmly believe that the TNE program is a cutting-edge method of preparing university students to become successful new teachers. With all of the requirements and pressures placed on the principal, such as school safety, standardized testing, the No Child Left Behind Act, the community, and so forth, the TNE program and the Site Director are of great assistance in supporting the principal's professional obligation to nurture student teachers. The key to a successful teacher is the extent to which that teacher is able to have a fulfilling student teaching experience involving the entire school site under the mentoring of a Site Director and a Master Teacher.

REFERENCES

California State University, Northridge, Michael D. Eisner College of Education. (2002), *Project overview*. Retrieved July 29, 2007, from: http.//www.csun.edu/tne/ProjectOverview.htm

Levine, M. (2002). *A mind at a time, the right to differ: Schools for all kinds of minds.* New York: Simon and Schuster.

National Council for Accreditation of Teacher Education (2001). *Standards for professional development schools* [Data file]. Available from National Council for Accreditation of Teacher Education Web site, http://www.ncate.org

APPENDIX

Teachers for a New Era
Schools as Clinics
Principal Interview Questions

TEACHERS FOR NEW ERA (TNE)
SCHOOLS AS CLINICS
Principal Interview Questions

Name	Title	School

1. One of the goals of the TNE program was to create a different and more successful approach to working with student teachers at the school site. In what different ways has your school worked with student teachers? Have these changes improved the way your school works with student teachers? What suggestions do you have to improve the process at your school?

2. To the best of your knowledge, did the TNE students have an opportunity to work collaboratively with professionals at your school other than their assigned mentor teacher? Identify some ways that the TNE students worked collaboratively at your site. Identify other opportunities that could be offered as a collaborative experience.

3. Each school in the TNE project selected a Site Director who was funded by a partnership between the school and the university. Please comment on the success and challenges of this effort.

4. One of the objectives of the TNE program was to establish a local School Site Steering Committee at each school that meets on a regular basis. How successful has this been at your school? What are your suggestions for improvement of this objective?

5. Another objective of the program is to establish a series of joint events to build a dynamic learning community with the capacity to work well with student teachers. How successful has this worked? Can you identify joint events that you or your school have participated in?

6. Please identify the Los Angeles Unified School District commitment to the program that you are aware of? What improvements would you like to suggest?

7. On-going and adequate funding for this program partnership is key to the success of the program. How successful have arrangements been for this effort and the sustainability of the program? Please explain.

8. Faculty development at the local school is a mission of the TNE program. What faculty development opportunities have you taken advantage of? What faculty development would you like to see for your school?

9. CSUN professors have been holding seminar classes on your campus. What is your reaction to this arrangement? Do you have any suggestions to improve this activity?

10. The involvement of the arts and science faculty is important in the content and preparation of student teachers. What activities have taken place at your site to enhance this preparation? What are your suggestions for further improvement in this area?

Is there anything else you would like to add about the TNE program?

Created by: Robert E. Kladifko, Ph.D.
Department of Educational Leadership & Policy Studies
California State University, Northridge

CHAPTER 11

FACILITATING LEADERSHIP ACROSS THE LIFESPAN OF A PDS PARTNERSHIP

Anita Perna Bohn and Thomas P. Crumpler

ABSTRACT

This chapter describes a field-based model for understanding and evaluating the predictable stages of a professional development school partnership over the course of its lifetime and poses a series of questions designed to facilitate leadership and promote growth at key points. The model is informed by the NCATE Standards for PDS partnerships and draws on analyses from three data sources: (1) interviews with six leader participants from both sides of a university-school partnership; (2) a program evaluation of the PDS by a *critical friend;* and, (3) reciprocal interviews of the two researchers who, as course instructors in the PDS site, were participant-observers in the research project. The PDS Lifespan Model offers a way for PDS leadership to evaluate the evolving issues and needs of partners in a professional development school and to help participants to understand those needs within a broader conceptual frame.

University and School Connections, pages 179–192
Copyright © 2008 by Information Age Publishing
All rights of reproduction in any form reserved.

179

INTRODUCTION

The professional development school (PDS) has emerged in the last fifteen years as a crucible for school reform, a place where research and practice can combine to provide for the simultaneous renewal of both schools and universities. The establishment of Standards for Professional Development Schools in 2001 by the National Council for Accreditation of Teacher Education (NCATE) attests to the durability, value, and wide acceptance of professional development schools and has also brought welcome rigor to the conceptualization of PDSs. These PDS standards acknowledge the developmental nature of partnerships and offer specific criteria at each of four different stages of development that provide effective measures of PDS accomplishments from beginning through leading levels. Because the PDS standards are designed as benchmarks, the document understandably offers little guidance to university-school partnerships on how to get from "point A to point B" on the road to efficacy. The standards also lack contextuality, wherein an evolving PDS might be able to recognize and even anticipate some of the complex dynamics and conditions that surround a PDS's team-building efforts at various stages of its development.

In this chapter, we describe a Lifespan Model that examines the predictable stages and personnel concerns of a PDS over the course of its development. We also pose a series of reflective questions for each stage, designed to support leadership in facilitating movement and growth at these key points. This self-evaluation process makes the developmental nature of partnerships explicit to participants and provides a basis for collaborative conversations to encourage continued growth. The model is the result of a field-based study of an elementary school level PDS in its seventh year of operation. The model draws on analyses from three data sources: (1) interviews with six leaders in corresponding positions on both sides of the partnership as well as with two of their subsequent replacements; (2) a program evaluation of the PDS in its third year of operation, conducted by a "critical friend" with an international reputation in the area of leadership in partnership development; and, (3) reciprocal interviews of the two researchers who, as course instructors in the PDS site, were participant-observers in the research project. The model offers a way for leadership to understand and evaluate the shifting needs of a partnership and its participants over time and to appreciate them within a broader conceptual frame.

THEORETICAL PERSPECTIVE

This study draws upon the theoretical framework of the NCATE Standards for PDS partnerships in varying stages of development. It builds upon the descriptive work on PDS development by Abdal-Haqq (1998), Fenstermacher (1994), Wilson and Berne (1999), and on work defining the need for studies that synthesize more detailed understandings of the nature of leadership within partnerships (Byrd & McIntyre, 1999; Campoy, 2000; Teitel, 2004). It acknowledges the work of Winitzky, Stoddart, and O'Keefe (1992), and Christenson et al. (1996) and their examinations of the cultural barriers in PDS partnerships and issues of planning and the dynamics of power that lead to tension between the partners (and, in some cases, failed partnerships.) The development of a conceptual model for understanding the PDS over time extends Handler and Ravid's (2001) work on metaphors that approximate the complex nature of partnerships.

Our work on facilitating leadership in partnerships borrows from the team-building theory of Dyer (1995) and Perkins' (2002) organizational theory. Additionally, the work of Spillane (2005) and Spillane, Reiser, and Reimer (2002) on distributed leadership, which argues that leadership can be "both bottom up and top down" (p. 420), also informed our thinking on how leadership in a PDS can facilitate growth over time. Overall, these theoretical studies suggested a need to investigate the patterns and nature of leadership in a PDS partnership that was continuing to evolve. However, neither the university nor the district had thoroughly considered the ways that leadership might shift and evolve as the partnership matured. As we collected and analyzed data over a two-year period, the significance of those shifts began to emerge. Based upon our examination of the data surrounding the shifts, we argue for a new model to better understand and evaluate the specific challenges of leadership in a PDS setting.

METHODOLOGY

This qualitative study investigated leadership in the PDS and examined how the needs and challenges of leadership shifted as partners collaborated to educate teacher candidates within the context of a school district. The emergent Lifespan Model of a PDS illuminates the predictable stages and issues that challenge partners in a PDS. Our objective in this paper is two-fold: (1) to delineate this model so that it can be used for self-evaluation, and (2) to describe a series of framing questions that leadership can pose to facilitate growth at each of the stages.

Data were collected using semi-structured interviews with six personnel who had administrative responsibilities for the professional development school—three from the university and three from the partner school district. These were conducted by one of the co-researchers. Then, the interviews were transcribed by the researchers. The university leadership team members who were interviewed included the site coordinator, the principal overseeing program implementation throughout the district schools, and the district superintendent. The university team included the faculty coordinator and liaison to the PDS, the chair of the department in which the elementary education program resides, and the college of education dean. Following two changes in leadership personnel, additional interviews were conducted with the new chair of the university department and with the new superintendent of schools. Additionally, the researchers are participant-observers and interviewed each other with the same set of questions. A "critical friend" report, conducted two years after the PDS had begun, was an additional source of data, indicating specific dimensions of the partnership where growth was desirable. Data were analyzed to identify salient issues and themes represented in these texts. Member checking also was conducted as the Lifespan Model began to emerge.

Employing an open-coding procedure, we developed conceptual labels to identify patterns in the interviews and to allow for identification of preliminary categories to begin to answer the research questions (Strauss & Corbin, 1990). These preliminary codes were then used to reexamine the data and compile common themes (Strauss & Corbin, 1990). The refined categories were analyzed and compared to existing PDS theoretical models (Handler & Ravid, 2001) and to expert analysis of the relevant issues as identified in the report written by the "critical friend." Five categories emerged from this analysis and were used to further organize these data. These included: (1) issues of development, (2) practices of decision making, (3) tensions between "operating systems," (4) orientations toward leadership, and (5) practices of accountability. These categories were employed to comb through the interview data for confirmation and to expand our own understanding of the nature of leadership in this PDS. In the following section, we provide examples of data culled from the interviews.

DATA COLLECTION AND ANALYSIS

Sample Interview Data

(1a) *University liaison/coordinator:* "Your assignment [as university faculty] is the same as if you're teaching across the hall from your office; you're getting a 3-credit load for it, but there's no additional pay for it, there's no additional time or load assigned for it. . . . So I think there's a problem with that."

(1b) District *Superintendent I:* "If you do not feel that your responsibility is to help this district perform well according to [state] standards, then there shouldn't be a partnership."

(1c) *Mid-level District Administrator:* "A goal as I saw it was, we are a district that will be losing half of our teaching staff during the next 5 to 10 years, and . . . I want quality people to take the place of those people that are leaving . . . so I saw that as a goal and a way we could get the best possible people to work in an exceptionally fine school district. . . ."

(1d) *University Dept. Chair:* "I was looking at what kind of enhanced and quality-driven experience we can provide for our students."

(1e) *COE Dean:* "The initial goal was to improve teacher education. I think it was initially a one-sided goal."

(1f) *University Faculty Member:* "'We want you to fit in with it' was a real problem and I felt really uncomfortable with that, and it was one of those things that, when I had the opportunity to make a choice between teaching there and doing some other things, I made the choice to leave because I would've felt like it was going in a different direction that I didn't really want to be involved with."

(1g) *District Superintendent I:* "We already have a writing program that works. We don't need them [the teacher candidates] to learn any other methods of teaching writing."

(1h) *District Site Coordinator:* "We want the [university] faculty to be able to spend time in our classrooms seeing what's really going on out there . . . we would love participation in our school improvement issues."

(2a) *COE Dean:* "Getting to scale, getting aligned, getting serious about partnerships and that faculty leadership is critical, because it is the only way we're going to have the respect of the field . . ."

(2b) *COE Dean:* "Folks out there in public schools need to start seeing themselves as being in the teacher education business. And we've got to start seeing ourselves as being somewhat in the student achievement business."

(2c) *COE Dean:* "Transferability and scalability. So how do we go the next step from [study site] to having these experiences for more of our students?"

(2d) *University Faculty I:* "It sounds like we have the same goals, which is to produce teachers that help students learn, but that may be an end goal. Most of our work and our process is an interim goal. The university is here to produce the best possible teacher candidates, and the school is concerned with student test scores."

(2e) *District Superintendent I:* ". . . I believe that those of us who absolutely can see what impact and what difference it's [a PDS partnership] is making owe it to everyone else to help define it [for them]." [statement made over 4 years ago when this PDS was still defining itself.]

(2f) *District Superintendent I:* "I know another district right now who is trying to start up a PDS, and they're going about it all wrong."

(2g) *Mid-level District Administrator:* "We did not always understand [university's] point of view because, naturally, we don't live in that arena that they live and work in, and then, in turn, [the university] didn't understand some of our points of view and issues because they weren't living what we were living."

(2h) *District Superintendent I:* "... we haven't really talked about the research aspect yet, but I see that as a leadership function. And it is, in my opinion, about as loosey-goosey as it could be right now. It's just not, we have not clearly defined how the research should be done, what are the requirements that the university has to have in order. . . . And I believe we need to make our research projects tied to our priorities and tied into our results."

(2i) *District Superintendent II:* "I think it [university-led faculty development for district classroom teachers] happens on a regular basis, but I don't look on this as a function of the PDS at this moment."

(3a) *University Dept. Chair:* "After the actual implementation . . . it seems that the steering committee concept or model just fell apart. And I won't say that's anyone's faulty, I think it just kind of, collectively both sides just dropped the ball on it."

(3b) *University Faculty I:* "I was very surprised, for example, to find that there was initially, in my first two years there, no plan for the professional development of the teachers. It may have been a 'trickle down' theory or something. And so I offered to. And I did follow through [but] it wasn't part of the plan."

(3c) *University Faculty II:* "... it's not that those tests are not important, and it's not that teaching some sort of skills and strategies to make those kids successful in the classroom isn't important, but it seems that the district was overly focused on that. . . ."

(3d) *PDS Site Coordinator:* "If the university is having difficulty finding more faculty to assign to the PDSes, we have a number of very good in-house people who would do an outstanding job teaching those courses and would probably love the opportunity to."

(3e) *District Superintendent II:* "I can think of one [teacher] who was almost ready to retire and decided she would go into the professional development school, and it did change her practices. She became more of a facilitator than a director kind of person. If the professional development school can at least take an individual to the next level on the continuum, it has served its purpose as long as the teachers are continually growing."

(3f) *District Superintendent: I:* "... I would go so far as to say that almost all of our actions seem to be driven by that, unfortunately—improved achievement. And that's very difficult to say to another educator, but that's the reality of it."

A Picture of Complexity

As a result of the coding process, a picture of the complexity of sustaining effective leadership in a PDS partnership began to coalesce. An analysis of the interview data revealed the following five themes:

- There were predictable stages in the development and growth of a PDS that pose different challenges to leadership at different times;
- The original planning of the partnership did not consider the need for distributive leadership and decision-making authority among the various levels of administrative responsibility;
- The school district, in general, operated as more of a "closed system," whereas the university was a more "open system," and this difference had significant impact on communication and decision-making efforts;
- The respective partnerships articulate and practice very different orientations toward leadership; and
- The complexities of leadership in PDS partnership go beyond the different cultural orientations and are anchored in the nature of the accountability demanded at each institution.

Using these themes as starting points, we worked to conceptualize a model capable of schematizing and evaluating the patterns of issues and concerns at various stages within the partnership. This conceptualization is metaphoric in nature. As Lakoff and Johnson (2003) have argued, metaphors are embodied in the structures of communicative practice; deploying metaphors helps reveal larger patterns of meaning and aids in seeing these data in a new way. Morgan (1997) also argues that leadership can broaden and deepen its understanding of its own organization and organizational problems through the use of metaphors which can have the power to shape new ways of working.

The emergent model employs a lifespan metaphor that elaborates and contextualizes the developmental stages identified in the NCATE PDS standards and also makes the developmental nature of partner issues and relations visible at each stage. Table 11.1 illustrates the categories and characteristics of each stage for both partners and includes a superscript notation that shows the connections between them and the sample interview data above.

TABLE 11.1 Life Stages of PDS Leadership

Stage	University	School District
Infancy: high need phase; instant gratification needed; egocentrism; no perspective	• Focus on individual (faculty), departmental, or COE needs rather than on partner's needs (1a, 1d, 1e) • Impatience if needs not met immediately (1f) • Inability to recognize the legitimacy of others views (1e)	• Focus on district's accountability goals (1b, 1g) • Partnership exists to meet district's needs (1c) • Inability to recognize the legitimacy of the other's views (1b) • Lack of awareness of univ. faculty workloads and responsibilities (1h)
Childhood: growing awareness of others, attendant social skills; increasing sense of competence and productivity; desire for praise; limited perspective; tendency to be rule-bound	• Eager to disseminate information on accomplishments (2a) • Starting up new PDSs based on this largely untested model (2c) • Emerging recognition of differences and of areas of mutual interest and benefits (2d) • Recognition of need and potential for compromise (2b)	• Seeks community, district and state recognition for accomplishment (2e) • Emerging recognition of differences, desire to compromise (2g) • Difficulty grasping faculty academic freedom issues (2h) • Very limited view of staff development for district teachers (2i) • Rigidity about what a PDS is based upon current model (2f)
Adolescence: sense of self-actualization; desire for autonomy	• College sees itself in a national leadership role for PDSs • Leadership needs are seen as diminished (3a) • Perfunctory district staff development offered (3b) • Little attention to intern instruction in terms of district goals (3c)	• Belief that district now can run PDS program on own (3d) • Lack of recognition of need for continued professional growth for district staff (3e) • Little attention to effectiveness of intern instruction in terms of univ. program objectives (3f)
Maturity: experienced awareness of stages and roadblocks; realization of potential and need for renewal; inquiry research fully supported; evidence of parity in the partnership	• Melding of goals in joint effort or project that is mutually satisfying • Complex and multilayered renewal efforts • Development of a PDS model that fosters communication and supports change • Conducting and dissemination of inquiry research that is truly collaborative in nature	• Collaborative choices about faculty, students, and mentors • Support for teachers as researchers • Systematic, ongoing, and collaborative staff development • Complex and multilayered renewal efforts

FRAMING QUESTIONS FOR WORKING WITHIN THE LIFESPAN MODEL

In this section, we present a series of questions and prompts that those in leadership positions may pose to evaluate the developmental stage of a PDS and to help participants examine the shifting needs and issues of partners at each stage. These questions also function to make the characteristics and issues of the partnership salient to the stakeholders at each point along the lifespan. Leadership poses these questions to stakeholders in order to shift their perspectives in their current stage and to raise other possibilities for working together. These framing questions and statements are designed to help stakeholders see the partnership in new ways and to evaluate their own roles and responsibilities for growth of the PDS.

Infancy Stage

1. In recognition of the high-need aspect of this phase, the following question is posed:
    - *What do you need from this partnership?*
      This question is asked of each stakeholder and then charted so that participants may compare the partner-to-partner perspectives. These needs form the foundation of the partnership's goals (or "wish list"). The attainability of these goals should continue to be explored as the partnership matures.
2. In recognition of the lack of perspective evident in this stage, each stakeholder is asked to respond in writing to the following:
    - *What you don't understand about my involvement in the PDS is. . . .*
      Individual responses are then pooled and drawn out one at a time, as the group identifies whose perspective that might be. Finally, each perspective is placed on a grid to illustrate how roles and even potential conflicts are being defined with and across the partnership.
3. In recognition of the frustration and helplessness partners may feel in the other institution's setting, stakeholders are asked to finish this statement:
    - *When I come into your institution I expect. . . .*
    The perspective is then shifted with the follow-up response to:
    - *When you come into my institution, I expect. . . .*

Childhood Stage

1. In this stage, initial successes or competencies assume out-of-proportion significance.
   - Ask each participant to list the competencies/successes they have experienced in the current stage of this PDS partnership. These accomplishments are presented and acknowledged. Participants are then asked to project one, two, and three years out in describing how they see these competencies/successes being developed and refined at each point, including research agendas or opportunities.
2. In recognition of the need for praise in this youthful stage, the following exercise is offered:
   - Ask each stakeholder to describe what personal or professional contributions they feel they make to the partnership that may not have been acknowledged.
3. In this youthful stage there is a tendency to be rule-bound. To address that, participants are asked:
   - What current structures support the work you are trying to do?
   - What are some other organizational or governance structures that could be created or negotiated in order to continue to offer you as well as others upport?
4. To foster a growing awareness of the perspective of others, the following suggestion is offered:
   - Ask stakeholders who are in similar leadership positions to "introduce" and explain the contributions of their counterpart in the other organization.

Adolescence Stage

1. In adolescence there is an exaggerated sense of one's own competence, skills, and accomplishment—with little room for further development seen. The following questions attempt to put this in perspective:
   - Review what you and others perceived as the original goals [infancy phase] of this partnership. Are those goals still significant? If so, how are they being addressed? If not, how have these shifted to new goals, and what has led to that shift?
   - What expertise, perspectives, and resources does your partner provide you? What are some ways to extend or maximize those resources and build on that expertise as the partnership continues to develop?

- In what ways can or should this PDS be a model for others to follow? What, if anything, needs to happen for that to occur?
2. There is a tendency toward an untimely presumption of maturity
at this stage. In recognition of that, the following activity is recommended.
- As a partnership, compare your current levels of success with the
NCATE PDS Standards' developmental state, called "at standard." How do the partnership's accomplishments align with
the target performance descriptors? Stakeholders would then be
encouraged to formulate a plan to further align their goals with
the Standards.

Maturity

Maturity in a PDS can be said to be achieved when all aspects of its mission are fully actualized: professional preparation of candidates, faculty development, inquiry directed at the improvement of practice, and enhanced
student learning (NCATE, 2001).

A great impediment to maturity of an otherwise functional PDS seems
to be the oft-sited inclination to plateau after achieving modest levels of
success. A few questions design to further the stakeholders' thinking and
action are:

- What evidence can be marshaled to demonstrate that this partnership has reached maturity?
- As this PDS partnership has matured, how has your role as a stakeholder evolved? What have been the expected and unexpected
features of that evolution?
- What is this PDS capable of that it has not yet achieved? How can
you help facilitate that?
- Why should this partnership continue to exist? How long should it
continue to exist?

COMMENTARY ON FOCUSING QUESTIONS & PROMPTS

These questions and prompts are designed to aid stakeholders' understanding of the patterns of development and of the opportunities to stretch
through and beyond those patterns toward a stronger and more efficacious
PDS partnership. Clearly, additional questions can be articulated within this
Lifespan Model. PDS partnerships committed to continued growth and to

insights into the process and stages of change can use this model heuristically to generate further questions and facilitate that change.

CONCLUSION

Several initial findings of this study were consistent with earlier research on PDS partnerships. For example, as Winitzky, Stoddart, and O'Keefe (1992) and Christenson et al. (1996) have found, our data suggests that universities and schools districts bring different cultural orientations to a partnership. Those orientations can result in barriers that prevent growth toward a mature partnership. Our analysis of these interview data indicates that, like Handler and Ravid's (2001) work on the complexity of partnerships, thinking metaphorically affords opportunities to see the development of partnerships in new ways.

The Lifespan Model builds on this previous scholarship and extends it in several ways. First, the model draws on the generative nature of metaphoric thinking (Lakoff & Johnson, 2003) and provides guidance to direct that thinking through the sequence of reflective questions. These questions prompt the stakeholders in the partnership at each stage to unpack the professional relationships, issues, and goals of the PDS so that all the voices are heard. Second, the model provides tools to delve into the existence of different cultural orientations of districts and universities that has been noted in research on PDS partnerships. By facilitating discussions that encourage partners in a PDS to think collaboratively about their professional roles and agendas as the partnership unfolds, the Lifespan Model has the potential to move partners not only to become more cognizant of each other's views but also to gain deeper understanding of the source of those views. Third, the Lifespan Model supports university and district leadership and the complex and shifting demands placed upon leadership as the partnership proceeds through predictable stages of growth.

Perhaps its most important feature, however, is that the Lifespan Model and the accompanying questioning process reach beyond this critical team-building functions to make each developmental stage of the PDS and its attendant features transparent to participants so that self-awareness of the existing developmental stage can promote growth and suggest appropriate direction. Based on the experiences and reflections of the participants in this study, this metaphoric analysis and use of purposeful conversations can be powerful tools to evaluate and guide the development and efficacy of a PDS partnership. While the NCATE PDS standards have been very helpful in underscoring the developmental nature of the PDS, their lack of contextuality offers little illumination of how partnerships can move along the continuum of growth. The Lifespan Model expands the framework of the

NCATE Standards for PDS partnerships by creating a lens through which PDS partnerships may become aware of the dynamics and issues at each stage of development in the effort to understand the complex dynamics of the PDS over time and to avoid some of the predictable pitfalls that can derail their further development.

REFERENCES

Abdal-Haqq, I. (1998). *Professional development schools: Weighing the evidence.* Thousand Oaks, CA: Sage.

Byrd, D. M., & McIntyre, D. J. (1999). *Research on professional development schools.* Thousand Oaks, CA: Corwin Press.

Campoy, R. (2000). *A professional school partnership: Conflict and collaboration.* London: Bergin & Garvey.

Christenson, F. E., Eldredge, F., Ibom, K., Johnston, M., & Thomas, M. (1996). Collaboration in support of change. *Theory into Practice, 35*(3). 187–195.

Clark, R. W. (1997). *Professional development schools: Policy and financing.* Washington DC: AACTE.

Dyer, W. G. (1995). *Team building: Current issues and new alternatives* (3rd ed.). Upper Saddle River, NJ: Prentice-Hall.

Fenstermacher, G. (1994). The knower and the known; The nature of knowledge in research on teaching. *Review of Research in Education, 20,* 3–56.

Handler, G. H., & Ravid, R. (2001). *The many faces of school-university collaboration: Characteristics of successful partnerships.* Englewood, CO: Teacher Ideas Press.

Lakoff, G., & Johnson, M. (2003). *Metaphors we live by* (2nd ed.). Chicago: University of Chicago Press.

Morgan, G. (1997). *Images of organization.* Thousand Oaks, CA: Sage.

National Council for Accreditation of Teacher Education. (2001). *Standards for Professional Development Schools.* Retrieved December 7, 2006, from: http://www.ncate.org/public/standards.asp.

Perkins, D. (2002). *King Arthur's round table: How collaborative conversations create smart organizations.* Cambridge, MA: Harvard University Press.

Spillane, J. (2005). *Distributive leadership.* San Francisco: Jossey-Bass.

Spillane, J., Reiser, B., & Reimer, T. (2002). Policy implementation and cognition: Reframing and refocusing implementation research. *Review of Educational Research, 72*(3), 387–431.

Strauss, A., & Corbin, J. (1990). *Basics of qualitative research: Grounded theory procedures and techniques.* Thousand Oaks, CA: Sage.

Teitel, L. (2004). *How professional development schools make a difference: A review of research.* Washington, DC: National Council for Accreditation of Teacher Education.

Teitel, L. (1997). Changing teacher education through professional school partnerships: A five-year follow up study. *Teachers College Record, 99*(2), 311–334.

Wilson, S., & Berne, J. (1999). Teacher learning and the acquisition of professional knowledge: An examination of research on contemporary professional development. *Review of Research in Education, 24,* 173–210.

Winitzky, N., Stoddart, T., & O'Keefe, P. (1992). Great expectations: Emergent professional development schools. *Journal of Teacher Education 43*(1) 3–18.

CHAPTER 12

A SCHOOL/UNIVERSITY PARTNERSHIP

Please Don't Stop (PDS)

Fran Greb, Tara Snellings, and Marie Smith

ABSTRACT

This chapter focuses on a school/university partnership where teachers, student teachers, elementary students, and university faculty collaborate to inform practice. These stakeholders are engaged in simultaneous renewal through collaborative endeavors. The focus of this collaboration is on the building of community through implementation of components of the Responsive Classroom approach developed by the Northeast Foundation for Children.

INTRODUCTION

School/university partnerships are the cornerstone of the teacher education program at Montclair State University (MSU). These partnerships are built on the philosophical foundation of the New Jersey Network for

University and School Connections, pages 193–201
193

Educational Renewal (NJNER, 1994), an affiliate of the National Network for Educational Renewal (NNER). In short, "The New Jersey Network for Educational Renewal promotes the simultaneous renewal of schools and the education of educators through a collaboration between and among Montclair State University and member school districts as equal partners" (NJNER, 1994). In this model, classroom teachers and university professors collaborate as teacher educators, researchers, and seekers of best practice to meet the diverse needs of students. This collaborative process examines site-specific issues with the hope of effecting positive change, often through action research.

Approximately five years ago, one of MSU's partner schools, an elementary school joined MSU's College of Educational and Human Services in the development of a formal professional development school (PDS) partnership. The elementary school's student population included children whose first languages at home are Spanish, Mandarin, Gujarati, Farsi, Korean, Russian, Japanese or French. The formal PDS agreement was built on a foundation of previous personal and organizational relationships which, according to Darling-Hammond (2005), often bodes well for future success.

Forming and sustaining partnerships can be challenging because of many factors, including differences in school/university schedules, personnel changes, and demands on teachers' already limited time. The partnership in this study is no exception. The principal who began and supported the partnership was reassigned to another school, grant funding ended, and the elementary school faculty was adjusting to a new principal. However, a cadre of committed teachers, realizing the benefits of collaborative efforts, continued to seek a community for inquiry previously established at the school. The framework for this community of inquiry was enhanced by the presence of an on-site university faculty member as a PDS liaison, an on-site teacher as a PDS coordinator, and an active PDS council of teachers, parents, university faculty, and a union representative. This community of inquiry became a proponent of action-research (Calhoune, 1994) on topics that included character education, cultural understanding, classroom community, and emotional intelligence. This led to the PDS applying for a grant for training in the Responsive Classroom (RC) approach to community building.

"The Responsive Classroom approach is built around five components that integrate teaching, learning, and caring in the daily functioning of the classroom" (Elliot, 1995, p. 1). The components include cooperation, assertion, responsibility, empathy, and self-control. The development of social skills through the RC approach is based on the premise that "how children learn to treat one another is as important as what they learn in reading, writing, and arithmetic" (Charney, 2002, p. 413). Through an Inquiry Project Grant (IPG) from MSU, teachers received both one-day and week-long training in the philosophy and pedagogy for implementation of the Responsive Classroom approach. After the initial training, a year-long teacher study group made up of school faculty, MSU student teachers, and the PDS liaison convened on a monthly basis to share ideas, inform practice, and discuss implementation of the program. An observer could walk into a classroom and see students engaged in components of the Responsive Classroom, including Morning Meetings, greetings, community building activities, and practicing social skills focused on development of cooperation, assertion, responsibility, empathy, and self-control (C.A.R.E.S).

TEACHER-RESEARCHERS

One of the contributing authors of this article is a fourth-grade teacher and recent MSU graduate whose interests were congruent with the RC approach. "Students often carry emotional baggage, and teachers cannot expect them to dump this baggage at the door and come in ready to learn. Students need to know that others care about them and need to learn to respond and care for others" (Snellings, 2004). Another coauthor is both an experienced teacher and a clinical faculty member, the MSU designation for cooperating teachers who complete MSU's formal mentoring program. Both teachers attended the introductory, one-day Responsive Classroom (RC) training session. After the training, they looked to the work of Ruth Sidney Charney, Teaching Children to Care (2002), a text for MSU's pre-service teachers, as a resource for learning more about classroom community building through a Responsive Classroom approach. This approach is distinctive due to its emphasis on community building on a daily basis through those structured activities mentioned earlier. Next, four additional teachers received week-long Responsive Classroom training through an MSU grant and shared this information at monthly faculty meetings.

THE PROCESS/CHRONOLOGY

This PDS collaborative community has been involved in action research for several years. Previous work focused on a state initiative for the understanding of the relationship between emotional intelligence and academic performance. This research was subsidized financially by an action research Dodge Grant from MSU. Action research involves classroom teachers in data collection to inform practice. The study focused on elements of children's emotional intelligence (such as awareness of one's feelings, managing feelings, and problem solving). The school's theme became "Learning to care, caring to learn."

Next, a teacher and the school's guidance counselor at this inquiring, action-minded school community heard about the Responsive Classroom approach. A visit to a site in New Jersey provided an opportunity for several teachers and a student teacher to see this approach in action. Convinced that this approach was applicable to this PDS, the teachers requested RC training. Seven teachers, the MSU Liaison, and the new principal attended a one-day introductory workshop conducted by The Northeast Foundation for Children, founders of the Responsive Classroom approach. Teachers began to implement components of RC and met informally to collaborate and discuss their questions, successes, and ideas. For example, some teachers were conducting Morning Meetings and were acknowledging each child through greetings. The entire class individually greeted each child by name through chants, poems, and/or song. This daily acknowledgment of the individual child is based on the belief that, "The degree to which one's psychological needs are met determines how much of one's energy and attention is available for learning" (Rim-Kaufman, 2004).

Eager to learn yet more, monetary support was requested and granted through an MSU Inquiry Project Grant (IPG) for week-long RC training. The PDS liaison and six teachers, including the coauthors, attended a week-long summer training program. Upon returning to school, a study group was proposed. All faculty members, including student teachers who were interested in learning more about the approach, were invited to attend. A majority of the staff and student teachers participated in the sessions. During this year-long study, the authors designed and implemented a Responsive Classroom research agenda. Although components of the program were implemented in many classrooms, this research focused on two classrooms—a fourth grade and a fifth grade belonging to the coauthors.

METHOD

Social skills data were collected prior to the implementation of the Responsive Classroom approach. The researchers/teachers began collecting data utilizing the Social Skills Rating Scale (SSRS), a nationally normed behavior rating scale by Gresham and Elliot (1990) that assesses the behaviors and frequency of children's social skills. A pre- and post-intervention design with approximately an eight-month implementation period was the primary design for this work. The SSRS-Student form allows students to complete a self-assessment of their social skills. The social skills subscales are Cooperation, Assertion, Responsibility, Empathy, and Self-control (C.A.R.E.S.).

According to Gresham and Elliot (1990), the SSRS assesses the following five behavioral types:

1. Cooperation—helping others, sharing materials, and complying with rules.
2. Assertion—initiating behaviors, asking for information, responding to action of others.
3. Responsibility—regard for property and work; ability to communicate with adults.
4. Empathy—concern and respect for other's viewpoints and feelings.
5. Self-control—behaviors that emerge in conflict situations; also non-conflict situations that require compromise.

The elementary level of SSRS, targeting grades 3–6, was administered, and students were instructed to think about how often they exhibited the target behavior ("never," "sometimes," or "very often"). The data were analyzed using percentile ranks and then compared to a standardized group. The SSRS statistical manual stipulated that performance registering one or more standard deviation below the sample comparison group indicates that the student exhibits fewer social skills than the average for the standardized comparison group. Performance registering within one standard deviation above or below the standardization norm indicates that the student exhibits as many social skills as the average for the standardization sample comparison group. Performance one standard deviation or more above the standardization sample comparison group indicates that the student exhibits more social skills than average for the standardization sample comparison group. Since the students had been working with components of character education in their classrooms, including development of social skills, these researchers did not feel comfortable focusing on performance at the average level; rather the focus was on students reporting that their behavior was at higher levels ("more") for reported social skills as compared to the norm (Gresham & Elliot, 1990). In essence, the teachers were "raising the bar" by concentrating on the existence of "more social skills" for students in this study.

The fifth grade teacher, through the use of a teacher-constructed checklist of observed behaviors, collected additional anecdotal data.

FINDINGS

Examination of the fourth grade data ($n = 14$) indicates improvement in three out of the four indicators with a total of a 14 percent increase in behaviors at a level that is "more than expected" for the age group (Table 12.1).

TABLE 12.1 Percent of Students Performing at Higher than Average Level: Pre and Post (Grade 4; N = 14)

	Pretest	Post Test	% of Increase
Cooperation	14%	29%	15%
Assertion	29%	36%	7%
Empathy	7%	7%	0%
Self-Control	21%	36%	15%
Total:	29%	43%	14%

TABLE 12.2 Percent of Students Performing at Higher than Average Level: Pre and Post (Grade 5; N = 16)

	Pretest	Post Test	% of Increase
Cooperation	25%	44%	19%
Assertion	25%	63%	38%
Empathy	31%	69%	38%
Self-Control	31%	56%	25%
Total:	44%	56%	12%

TABLE 12.3 Percent of Students Performing at Higher than Average Level: Pre and Post (Grade 4 & 5; N = 30)

	Pretest	Post Test	% of Increase
Cooperation	20%	37%	17%
Assertion	27%	43%	16%
Empathy	20%	37%	17%
Self-Control	27%	37%	10%
Total:	37%	50%	13%

The fifth grade ($n = 16$) displayed improvement in four out of four of the indicators (Table 12.2) with a 19 to 38 percent increase in reported social skills. Their greatest growth was in Empathy and Assertion. Improvement is seen in all areas when the fourth and fifth grades are combined, with the greatest growth in Empathy and Cooperation (Table 12.3). Statistics can only tell a part of the story.

The following are examples of student responses regarding implementation of the RC approach:

- I feel safe sharing my feelings.
- The meetings encouraged me to be myself, and this helped me with my problems.
- The class was understanding of how I felt.
- I listened to others and realized that I can talk out problems with the person I am fighting with.

Additional data were collected in the fifth grade class through the use of a checklist for weekly totals of observed social skills. In this classroom, the teacher, student teacher, and students noted an increase in occurrences of greeting of classmates, controlling impulsive behaviors, and complimenting peers. The teachers indicated that these skills were observed during Morning Meeting and throughout the day. Reportedly, students were seen making a concerted effort to use targeted social skills, a positive tone in the classroom was observed, and a feeling of community among the students was apparent. The range of increase of observed social skills was from 14–27 percent. Similar examples of building of classroom relationships were the focus of the September 2003 edition of *Educational Leadership*. In that issue, Kriete (2003), stated, "The sense of belonging, caring, and trust developed during Morning Meetings is a foundation for handling every lesson, every transition time, every lining-up, every upset, all day and all year" (p. 70).

DISCUSSION

Students, teachers, university faculty, and student teachers have benefitted from this collaborative endeavor for building community. Although the numbers of students in this study are small, the implications are far-reaching. These fourth and fifth grade students self-reported a 10 to 17 percent increase in social skills at a level that is more than the average for the standardization sample comparison-group. These elementary education students are benefitting from the collaborative school/university partnership which provided training for their teachers, implementation of the Responsive Classroom approach, opportunities for teacher research, and on-site university presence for teacher support and collaboration. Students can be heard greeting each other, sharing, and displaying examples of C.A.R.E.S (Cooperation, Assertion, Responsibility, Empathy, and Self Control). The teachers are implementing a program and gathering data to examine program effects. The student teachers are observing and assisting with the implementation of the program. Students in university classes are learning about community building from their professor who is on-site at the elementary school. The RC approach is being modeled in MSU's student teacher seminars and curriculum courses, many of which are on site. Additional students are being introduced to community building at MSU's annual Early Childhood and Elementary Education Conference. Graduates of MSU are implementing the program in their classrooms. This PDS has benefitted all stakeholders by the establishment of a collaborative relationship focused on extending educators' knowledge through experimentation, risk-taking, and a commitment to long-term learning.

In fall 2004, *Teaching Tolerance*, a publication of the Southern Poverty Law Center, devoted the entire journal to the topic of building community in our schools. The journal begins with an editorial by Holladay, interim director of the Tolerance Programs of the Southern Poverty Law Center, celebrating the birth of her daughter, Zoe. "We hope that Zoe can join a school community that embraces the wondrous spirit of every child, where she and her peers are lifted up, academically and emotionally, and where the tenets of sharing, caring, fair play are guiding principles" (p. 5). This PDS partnership provided an opportunity for teachers to become researchers by focusing on the tenets of sharing and caring through a responsive classroom approach. Together, the school and the university effectively engaged in professional development and research serving the needs of a diverse student population.

REFERENCES

Calhoune, E. (1994). *How to use action research in the self-renewing school.* Alexandria, VA: Association for Supervision of Curriculum Development.

Charney, R. (2002). *Teaching children to care: Classroom management for ethical and academic growth, K–8.* Greenfield, MA: Foundation for Children.

Darling-Hammond, L. (Ed.). (1994/2005). *Professional development schools: Schools for developing a profession.* New York: Teachers College Press.

Elliott, S. (1995). The responsive classroom approach: Its effectiveness and acceptability. *Responsive classroom evaluation project.* Washington, DC: Center for Systemic Education Change.

Gresham, F. M., & Elliott, S. N. (1990). *SSRS: Social Skills Rating System.* Circle Pines, MN: American Guidance Service.

Holladay, J. (2004). Starting with community. *Teaching Tolerance, 26*(2), 5.

Kriete, R. (2003). Start the day with community. *Educational Leadership, 61*(1), 68–70.

New Jersey Network of Educational Renewal. (1994). *Mission statement.* New Jersey Network of Educational Renewal. Retrieved November 4, 2005, from: http://cehs.montclair.edu/academic/cop/njner.shtml

Rim-Kaufman, S., & Sawyer, B. (2004). Primary-grade teachers' self-efficacy beliefs, attitudes toward teaching, and discipline and teaching practice priorities in relation to the responsive classroom approach. *Elementary School Journal, 104*(4), 321–341.

Snellings, T. (2004). Unpublished paper.

CHAPTER 13

RE-CREATING TEACHER EDUCATION THROUGH LONG-TERM PARTNERSHIPS

Carole Walker, Catherine K. Zeek, Martha M. Foote, and Gilbert Naizer

ABSTRACT

This chapter describes the collaborations between university and public schools within a PDS that have resulted in high quality teacher education. Research results indicate that practices being implemented in public school and university classrooms are effective. Quantitative results documenting the success of the PDS include: (1) high teacher retention rates, (2) teacher appraisal ratings showing that novices meet or exceed professional standards, and (3) class passing rates on student achievement tests that meet or exceed district and state averages. These data support the conclusion that collaborative practices within the partnership have not only allowed our PDS model to remain remarkably stable over time but they have also meant it is neither stale nor stagnant.

University and School Connections, pages 203–220
Copyright © 2008 by Information Age Publishing
All rights of reproduction in any form reserved.

INTRODUCTION

Partnerships define and support our undergraduate teacher education program. Centered within a thriving professional development school, the program operates in urban, suburban, and rural school districts in northeast Texas. The PDS, launched in 1991, maintains its original goals while continuing to evolve to meet the needs of the partners. This article describes the organic partnership (Dixon & Ishler, 1992) that distinguishes the PDS, traces the implementation of structures and programs in response to partners' input, and presents quantitative and qualitative measures of its effectiveness.

THE PARTNERSHIPS

Professional development schools connect universities and public schools as partners in teacher preparation, supporting pre-service and novice teachers as they attempt to integrate practice and theory in their early teaching experiences and also providing research-based professional development for in-service teachers (Boyer, 1986; Carnegie Forum on Education and the Economy, 1986; Goodlad, 1987, 1993; Holmes Group, 1986, 1990; Levine, 1992; National Commission on Excellence in Education, 1983; Wise & Darling-Hammond, 1987; Zeichner, 1992). Our undergraduate teacher education program, one of the largest in the state, began its move to a PDS model in 1991 with support from a Texas Education Agency grant and participation from faculty in the Department of Elementary Education (ELED; now the Department of Curriculum & Instruction), the College of Education, the College of Arts & Sciences, and teachers and administrators in key school districts. From its beginning, the PDS focused on providing more time in "real" classrooms for pre-service teachers, improving professional development opportunities for in-service teachers, and raising the achievement levels of public school students. With these areas of focus in mind, the Advisory Board defined the mission and goals of the PDS (see Table 13.1) and formed a design team to implement them. In this section, we describe layers of partnership that are integral to the PDS design.

PARTNERSHIP BETWEEN UNIVERSITY AND PUBLIC SCHOOLS

A central tenet of the partnership is that university and public school members are full and equal partners in planning and implementation (Linek & Sampson, 1996). The PDS design integrates these voices through the

TABLE 13.1 Mission and Goals of PDS

Mission	Goals
To provide, through a collaborative commitment, relevant field-based teacher education and staff development programs in a way that integrates research-supported, innovative teaching and assessment practices with technology so that educators share a common vision of improving the learning and achievement of all students.	1. redesign pre-service teacher education as a comprehensive field-based program; 2. increase the use of technology for instruction; 3. integrate technology with best teaching practices in a more effective manner; 4. improve the quality and relevance of staff development; 5. align graduate education with teachers' professional growth needs; and 6. maximize K–12 student learning by addressing the needs of a culturally diverse population.

design of the pre-service teachers' field-based year, the PDS governance structure, and the development of a district-based Induction/Mentoring Academy.

The Field-Based Year

From the early stages of designing the PDS, both university and public school partners sought to include extensive classroom experience for pre-service teachers. The public school partners, in particular, suggested that pre-service teachers would become more proficient in planning, classroom management, instruction, and professionalism, thereby increasing their effectiveness during their first years of teaching. The PDS includes two full semesters of intensive field-based experiences for seniors. In the first semester, interns spend two complete days each week in a classroom and one day in a university-based seminar, while the second-semester residents follow a two-week schedule that includes nine classroom-based days and one university-based seminar day. Pre-service teachers receive support and input from both school-based and university-based teacher educators, working at two grade levels with two experienced mentors (public school teachers who include them in planning, teaching, and school activities). University liaisons, who work with interns and residents in only one school, prompt pre-service teachers to connect their practical experience with their campus-based seminars and coursework. Liaisons establish deep relationships with mentor teachers during weekly on-site visits, using both formal team meetings and informal classroom visits to identify concerns and progress. During midterm and final portfolio conferences each semester, liaisons and mentors develop consensus grades for the interns or residents in their college courses as well as identifying the interns' and residents' growth and needs relative to five proficiencies adopted by the state: (1) equity in excellence for all learners and (2) learner-centered knowledge, (3) learner-centered instruction, (4) learner-centered communications, (5) learner-centered professional development. Support for pre-service teachers and their mentors are provided throughout the PDS governance structure.

PDS Governance Structure

The governance structure of the PDS includes five collaborative groups. The foundation of these groups is in the classroom level Instructional Leadership Team (ILT). Each pre-service teacher is part of an ILT, consisting of the pre-service teacher, the mentor teachers, and the university liaison. The ILT reviews the pre-service teacher's classroom performance, monitors progress toward goals, and discusses members' concerns. For example, several years ago input from ILTs and districts resulted in assigning letter grades rather than *Satisfactory/Unsatisfactory* for the courses embedded in the internship and residency semesters. More recently, ILTs began to provide evidence of residents' technology expertise to document equivalence among centers—a requirement for SACS accreditation. While these school-based committees focus primarily on classroom-level issues, they also monitor adherence to PDS operating procedures, suggest changes based on their experience, and provide evidence of meeting program accountability standards.

The Advisory Board meets annually to review PDS structure and organizational issues. A change in the middle school level certification program is an example of an action taken by the Advisory Board. Initially launched in 2003 as a residency-only program, it was modified to add an internship semester. Mentor teachers, familiar with the success of the two-semester elementary program, advocated strongly for that level of preparation, and the Advisory Board adopted the proposed change.

In 1999, the partners formed a Centers Council to consider procedural and programmatic changes suggested by district input, survey and test results, and legislative and other mandates. Members provide broad-based input, and include: (1) center coordinators [university faculty based in each ISD]; (2) the chair of the Curriculum & Instruction department; (3) faculty in psychology, special education, and arts and sciences; (4) representatives from teacher certification; and (5) school district personnel. The council meets several times each semester to adopt center-level changes and recommend program-level changes to the appropriate decision makers.

The multi-level structure of the PDS locates maximum decision making in the ILTs. Each of the other components supports the ILT, recognizing that critical learning happens at the point of impact, namely the classroom. Through these groups based in schools and districts, individual sites retain primary responsibility for developing strategies that best serve their pre-service teachers, mentors, and public school students.

After 15 years of operation, the initial three school district partners have increased to 13, and the university has added three branch campuses, but the structures remain in place. With a focus on building long-term partnerships and monitoring results, key practices were replicated and institutionalized as the PDS expanded. For instance, interns and residents are clustered in a few districts rather than widely dispersed, and they must interview with district personnel for placements rather than being assigned by the university.

As the PDS emerged, traditional lines of responsibility and authority blurred. University partners realized and appreciated that the mentor teachers were teaching pre-service teachers through their daily classroom experiences, while mentors noticed and adopted newer strategies and best practices that the pre-service teachers brought from the university (Foote, Zeek, Walker, & Fleener, 1998; Zeek, Foote, & Walker, 2001; Zeek & Walker, 2006). Teacher education has evolved into a shared process among the partners, and *teacher educator* is a role shared by mentors and university faculty (mentors teach lessons during intern and resident seminars, veteran mentors train rookies at the school level within the districts, and university liaisons use teacher stories of *best practice* to determine *next steps* for professional development during portfolio conferences, seminars, and workshops).

Bright Beginnings: A District-based Induction/ Mentoring Academy

As the partners grew as reflective practitioners, shared insights not only led to changes in pre-service education but also to the migration of proven practices into the in-service program. In 2002 in the second decade of the collaborative, one of the original partner districts piloted an induction program for first-year teachers and their mentors as an adjunct to the existing PDS. A district administrator convened a design team of mentors, principals, a representative of the regional education service center, and university teacher educators and administrators. The Academy, launched in August 2002, had five goals, rooted in district needs and state mandates: (1) provide a quality system of support to new teachers, (2) ensure the application of best teaching practices, (3) establish a plan for continued professional growth, (4) reduce the cost of teacher turnover to the school district, and (5) retain high quality teachers.

Although the leadership in the district has changed, the Academy continues to thrive. Named *Bright Beginnings* in 2006, it aims to scaffold novice teachers during the transition from student to teacher by adapting the original structures for mentoring and public school/university partnership. In the PDS, two mentors at the same school (but at different grade levels) work as a team with the pre-service teacher and university liaison during the internship/residency year. The Academy design team, in accordance with state guidelines (SBEC, 2003), adopted a mentoring team composed of two teachers from the inductee's grade level and school: one veteran mentor and one rookie mentor, a second year teacher who completed the Academy the previous year. This mentoring triad integrates the veterans' years of experience with the more recent experiences of the rookies, providing an environment in which to promote and celebrate the growth of both master teachers and novices.

The Academy provides novices with orientation to the district and the profession using *The First Days of School* (Wong & Wong, 2004), seminar-based professional development, mentoring support under a structured framework (SBEC, 2003), peer support, and observation of master teachers. Another benefit for inductees is a $250 stipend to implement action research projects focused on their students' motivation. Through the Academy they earn six graduate semester credit hours that may be used toward a master's degree, and professional development hours that they can apply when renewing their teaching certificates in five years. The mentors also receive ongoing professional development applicable to their certificate renewal, peer support, and a $500 stipend. A university teacher educator (a liaison for the past eleven years in the pre-service program) is the "teacher-of-record" for the seminars through which the graduate credit courses are delivered (with other members of the design team, particularly mentor teachers participating in the teaching team).

Because of the value perceived by stakeholders, all first-year teachers in the district, whether fully certified or seeking certification through alternative routes, participate in the Academy with both veteran and rookie mentors. Although the number of first-year teachers in the Academy fluctuates based on vacancies, Academy participation has grown steadily since its inception in 2002 (see Table 13.2).

Bright Beginnings provides classroom-based support for novice teachers, as well as encouragement for them to integrate university course content into their teaching. As they support the beginners, the mentors continue their own professional growth. Growing from the success of the PDS and the district's needs, the Academy is an evolving example of the value of this long-term partnership.

TABLE 13.2   Participants in the Bright Beginnings Induction/ Mentoring Academy

School Year	Mentees	Mentors
2002–2003	16 in PK through 9th grades	16 Veterans in PK–9
2003–2004	16 in PK through 8th grades	16 Veterans, 8 Rookies
2004–2005	34 in PK through 12th grades	33 Veterans, 10 Rookies
2005–2006	16 in PK through 12th grades	16 Veterans, 7 Rookies
2006–2007	26 in K through 12th grades	24 Veterans, 9 Rookies

The first level of partnership, then, within the PDS is between the university and public schools. At this critical level, input from all partners guides decision-making. The partners focus on learning: at both classroom and school levels for pre-service teachers; for veteran educators, both mentors and liaisons; and for public school students. The partners share responsibilities for program evaluation, using both quantitative and qualitative measures to document the success of the PDS. Results of these assessments are discussed later in this paper.

Partnerships Between Colleges and Departments

Teacher preparation is a shared responsibility at the university level. Faculty members from both colleges and multiple departments within the colleges have developed a culture of collaboration in program design, course development, and modifications. Examples are found in course and program modifications required by the move to a PDS, joint participation in teacher preparation initiatives at the national level, and, later, state-required changes in certification levels.

When the PDS model was originally formed in the early 1990s, several new and modified courses were developed to build on the field-based format of the new program. Two courses taught by the psychology and special education departments in the field-based seminars provide evidence of initial cross-departmental collaboration. The courses were developed in response to related sets of input. State guidelines called for field-based experiences in cultural diversity and understanding, as well as knowledge of instruction for students with disabling conditions. However, mentors and liaisons noted that, while interns' coursework addressed teaching a diverse population, they were unprepared to use the strategies they knew in the public school classrooms. Interns reported that their knowledge of diversity was theoretical and limited to "definitions" rather than equipping them to "know what to do in the real world" (Sampson & Robertson,

2004, p. 11). The new courses supported pre-service teachers as they connected their theoretical understanding with situations they encountered in their mentors' classrooms.

Courses offered through the College of Arts & Sciences were collaboratively designed by teams of faculty from both colleges, particularly in mathematics and science. Using the State Educator Standards as the starting point, the teams integrated appropriate pedagogical practices with the content-based knowledge and skills that graduates should demonstrate. When state changes in teacher certification levels (adopted in 2000) called for an extensive review of programs and course, the established patterns of collaboration in the university-led faculty from departments in both colleges to develop standards-based courses that were focused on the needs of pre-service teachers in the new programs. For example, the newly authorized programs for certification in middle level (grades 4–8) mathematics and science connect a major in the content area with a strong pedagogical grounding. Faculty members from education, mathematics, and physics attended workshops and sought grants for course development and evaluation. Faculty members from the same areas also developed an innovative course for the Early Childhood–4th grade certification program that highlights hands-on, inquiry teaching and is co-taught by education and science faculty members. Three additional certification programs—in bilingual education, English as a second language, and special education—also crossed lines between departments and/or colleges. Cross-college teams continually monitor the effectiveness of the courses by reviewing passing rates on state certification exams, student comments, and field observations focused on application of learning.

At the national level, this university is a long-term participant with several other universities in a Collaborative for Excellence in Teacher Preparation funded by the National Science Foundation. Through this effort, faculty in elementary education, mathematics, and the sciences have jointly attended professional development related to effective teacher preparation. Outcomes include course development and modification that integrates best practices as well as a vision instrument that science and mathematics faculty used for self-reflection. They later modified the instrument to create a course survey for students (Naizer, Stuessy, & Price-Blount, 2003). Comparing faculty and student perceptions of the courses led to further modifications in content and pedagogy to better prepare these pre-service teachers.

The Colleges of Education and Arts & Sciences are active partners in teacher preparation, striving to make a difference in the state through our efforts. Our graduates' success on their initial certification tests and as novice teachers, which are presented in the next section, demonstrate the positive results of the joint focus on teacher preparation.

EVIDENCE OF PDS SUCCESS

Ongoing program evaluation comes naturally in the PDS, providing evidence of success and suggesting new areas of focus. Whether the goal is analyzing quantitative assessments or probing qualitative input, the partners share responsibility for measuring the performance of pre-service teachers, novice teachers, and public school students. From the program's inception, both quantitative and qualitative evidence have documented the positive impact of the PDS on all three groups. In this section, we present findings from the range of assessments conducted.

Quantitative Evidence

Quantitative measures include pre-service teachers' passing rates on state certification exams, novice teachers' ratings on annual district appraisals, and passing rates of public school students on the state achievement test, all based on the most recent data available. Results have also been collected for novices and their mentors participating in the Bright Beginnings Academy and are presented separately below.

As one of its learner outcomes, the PDS assesses whether pre-service teachers completing the program develop the knowledge and skills in pedagogy measured on the initial certification tests. The most recent results (2004–2005) document high passing rates for first-time test takers: 95 percent of the 352 EC–4 test-takers and 98 percent of the 81 4–8 test-takers passed. Both rates exceeded the 92 percent criterion set by the partners.

For annual teacher appraisals, the partner districts use instruments which rates teachers as *Exceeds Expectations, Proficient (meets professional standards), Below Expectations,* or *Unsatisfactory* in eight domains of classroom interaction and professional development. Table 13.3 summarizes 2005 appraisal results for 107 purposefully selected first-year teachers in PDS partner districts. Sixty-one of the novices completed the PDS program; 46 completed

TABLE 13.3   Teacher Appraisal Results for First-Year Teachers in Partner Districts

Score Categories	PDS Program Completers		Completers from Other Programs	
Exceeds Expectations	17	28%	3	7%
Proficient	44	72%	37	80%
Below Expectations in Some Areas	0	—	6	13%
Unsatisfactory	0	—	0	—

programs at other institutions. All of the PDS program completers received ratings of *proficient* or *exceeds expectations* on all domains appraised, while completers from other institutions received fewer *exceeds expectations* ratings and a few *below expectations* ratings.

The final quantitative measure reports on passing rates on TAKS, the state achievement test, of public school students in classes taught by first-year teachers in the partner districts. In 2004–2005, passing rates for students of PDS program completers consistently met or exceeded district and state averages and were substantially higher than those for students of teachers trained at other institutions (see Table 13.4).

Test results were available in 40 instances for PDS program completers and in 43 instances for those completing programs at other institutions. Student passing rates of PDS teachers met or exceeded district averages in 34 of 40 instances (85 percent) and met or exceeded state average in 35 of 40 instances (87.5 percent). Students of teachers prepared in other programs met or exceeded the district and state averages in fewer instances: 24 of 43 instances (56 percent) at the district level and 21 of 43 instances (49 percent) at the state level.

Contained within the teacher appraisal and student test data reported within this section are results from participants in the Bright Beginnings Academy. The partners have documented new teacher retention rates, annual performance appraisals, and student achievement since the Academy opened in 2002, providing ongoing evidence of its impact on participants and their students. Retention rates for novice teachers who participated in the Academy are impressive. The district reported that after the first year (2002–2003), 87.5 percent of first year teachers remained in the district and 100 percent remained in the profession. After the second year, 75.8 percent remained in the district and 96.6 percent in the profession. State-wide statistics suggest two-year retention rates in the profession of between 75.4 percent and 84.4 percent (Charles A. Dana Center, 2002).

Tables 13.5 and 13.6 present results of Academy participants on annual appraisals and TAKS passing rates. All of the novice teachers met or exceed-

TABLE 13.4 2004–2005 TAKS Passing Rates for School Children Compared with District and State Averages; First-Year Teachers

Certification Program	Teachers	State Tests Given	Class Passing Rate Below Average		Class Passing Rate At/Above Average	
			District	State	District	State
PDS	16	40	6 (15%)	5 (12.5%)	34 (85%)	35 (87.5%)
Other	20	43	19 (44%)	22 (51%)	24 (56%)	21 (49%)

TABLE 13.5   Bright Beginnings Mentor and Inductee Teachers' Summative Appraisal Scores

Groups	Exceeds Professional Standard (score of 90–100)		Proficient (Meets Standard) (score of 75–89)		Needs Improvement (score below 75)
	N	Percent	N	Percent	
2003					
Mentors	16	100.0%	0	0	0
Inductees	7	58.3%	5	41.7%	0
2004					
Mentors	15	87.9%	2	12.1%	0
Inductees	6	50.0%	6	50.0%	0

TABLE 13.6   TAKS Passing Rates for School Children of Inductee and Mentor Teachers in Bright Beginnings

Teacher Groups	Number of Tests Given	Below District Rate	At or Above District Rate	Below State Passing Rate	At or Above State Rate
2002–2003					
Inductees	12	7 (58%)	5 (42%)	7 (58%)	5 (42%)
Mentors	6	4 (67%)	2 (33%)	4 (67%)	2 (33%)
2003–2004					
Inductees	8	4 (50%)	4 (50%)	2 (25%)	6 (75%)
Mentors	10	5 (50%)	5 (50%)	7 (70%)	3 (30%)
2004–2005					
Inductees	10	7 (70%)	3 (30%)	7 (70%)	3 (30%)
Mentors	14	4 (29%)	11 (72%)	7 (50%)	7 (50%)
2005–2006					
Inductees	5	2 (40%)	3 (60%)	4 (80%)	1 (20%)
Mentors	8	4 (50%)	4 (50%)	2 (25%)	6 (75%)

ed professional standards on their appraisals, while their students' performance on state achievement tests was comparable to that of their mentors' students.

For each of these measures, Academy participants meet or exceed district expectations. High new teacher retention rates, annual performance appraisals on which new teachers "meet" or "exceed" professional standards, and passing rates on student achievement test results that often exceed district and state averages, document the program's effectiveness.

Qualitative Results

Ongoing assessment, analysis, and reflection determine the effectiveness of both the pre-service and in-service teacher education programs in our PDS. Our qualitative evaluations go beyond the quantitative data to explore changes in participants' practices and thought processes. This section presents results from two qualitative inquiries: focus groups and teachers' narratives of practice using methodology developed within the PDS.

Focus Group Findings

In 2003, the partners convened focus groups to assess the value of the program and partnership (Walker, Bennett, Cardwell & Pool, 2004). Mentors, district administrators, and principals from partner districts responded to questions including: What elements distinguish our program as a quality program? Across districts, the partners named the importance of: (1) a two-semester field-based program; (2) experiencing the first days of school in the public schools, even though that is before the beginning of the university semester; (3) weekly site visits by university liaisons and decision-making by the ILT; (4) letting the voices of all the participants be heard when solving problems; and (5) classroom experiences in at least two assignments at different grade levels with two different mentors during the two semesters in the field. These elements closely align with the mission and goals initially identified in 1991. The consistency over time and across districts is noteworthy in a climate characterized by frequent change, the tendency to revert to tradition, and the frequency with which state and federal mandates determine practice. As they reported their conclusions, as though speaking in unison, the participants said, "Don't change the program. Field-based is the way for successful teacher education."

Transactional Inquiries

Developed within the PDS, transactional inquiry evolved from initial program evaluations. Early conversations with mentors revealed they saw themselves as supporting and improving the next generation of teachers (Zeek & Meers, 1996). Follow-up conversations confirmed that mentors recognized their critical role as front-line teacher educators and decision-makers (Foote, Walker, Zeek, & Filkins, 1997). Perhaps most striking was their eagerness to tell stories of their experiences and to talk with each other about mentoring. More than one remarked, "We thought you'd never ask" (Fleener, Walker, Foote, & Zeek 1998). Since then, pre-service, novice, and veteran teachers have analyzed their own and others' narratives of practice to explore what one colleague calls the *why behind the what* of their actions and results.

Transactional inquiry allows practitioners at all levels to respond to and reflect on a narrative and on others' responses to the narrative for the purpose of informing and guiding further inquiry (Zeek, Foote, & Walker, 2001). The strategy has theoretical roots in narrative inquiry (Clandinin & Connelly, 2000; Jalongo & Isenberg, 1995; Lyons & LaBoskey, 2002) and transactional theory (Rosenblatt, 1978). Through telling their stories and reflecting with peers on the lessons embedded in them, participants articulate their thought processes and may revise their conceptions of effective teaching and learning (Richert, 2002; Zeek & Walker, 2004, 2006). While supporting novice teachers, university and public school teacher educators have written, read, and responded to teachers' narratives of practice through transactional inquiry. In the process they point out evidence of growth and need for growth for the storyteller and themselves, and identify strategies to support professional development. The stories and themes that continue to emerge highlight valuable lessons: teacher leadership grows out of mentoring (Foote et al., 1997); the PDS structure taps teachers' wisdom and provides more complex measures of success than standardized measures allow (Foote et al., 1998); teachers take responsibility for their own professional growth (Zeek & Walker, 2004); and longtime mentor teachers become teacher educators (Zeek & Walker, 2006).

Over the past decade we have collected and analyzed narratives of practice in the same districts in which we collected and analyzed quantitative results. Their stories and the insights they gained from analyzing others' stories added depth to the quantitative data. In this paper, we share three stories written by teachers trained within the PDS to explore the classroom environment and from which their students' high passing rates state achievement tests developed. All describe student-centered, integrated lessons they intentionally planned and reflectively evaluated during their first year. The effective practices found in the novices' stories suggest that the theory they learned in university-based classes and workshops has become routine practice in their own public school classrooms.

Mrs. Martin's Story. A fourth-grade teacher wrote about *quick quotes* in writing which she used during her first year of teaching in a Title I school in a partner district. Her students' passing rates are among those reported in the previous section and were above the state average in reading, mathematics, and writing.

> Since I teach fourth grade, the main lessons that I know impacted my students throughout the year were writing. Bless their hearts and mine, when they arrive from third grade [where there had been], so much emphasis on

reading and math their writing is less than desirable. They . . . act as if you are pulling their teeth [which might] excite them more because of the Tooth Fairy. . . . That is where my success begins.

My first year of teaching, I went to a conference in Austin. It lasted a couple days, which honestly gave me some great thinking time. Every session I went to basically dealt with writing, since I felt that "I" myself needed help. . . . During one of the sessions they mentioned using quick quotes. They even gave us examples of ones to use. I figured if I could get others that would interest and make sense to 9 or 10-year-olds then maybe they would be more willing to write. With the quick quotes they would be timed and I would only listen to their ideas which made me have to look past conventions, but at least they would feel more comfortable writing freely.

The first few times I did it, my students that were struggling only wrote a few sentences. They weren't willing to share with our class when time was up. I did notice that even though right away they were not writing much, they seemed more excited then they had ever been. I continued to do two quotes a day and sometimes I would have them respond to poems. They began to really think deeply and their writing expanded each time. Eventually, they were the first ones to raise their hands and share. With this lesson it did not happen overnight, but with time there was a significant improvement in their writing. Sometimes persistence and patience pays off in the end.

Mrs. May's Story. A third-grade teacher in another of our partner districts wrote the second story. Her story tells of curriculum integration of literacy, art, and social studies as well as using parents as partners. Her student's TAKS results were also exemplary.

Early in the school year, at the small country school, [my 14 students] were piling into my oversized classroom. . . . I was nervously, preparing the maps lesson. . . . I knew that I wanted to involve their parents in some way because they just don't volunteer for any thing. The children walk in with very eager looks on their faces. They are "country," plain and simple. I love it!!!

When they all got seated, . . . I walked around looking at each of them with a smile on my face and said, "I have something very important to share with you." We began by talking about directions and standing up and pointing north, east, south, and west. As the lesson went on, the kids started talking about where they lived and how far from the school, who they lived by, and whether or not they lived close to the Dollar General.

I was loving it all. Then I stopped them and said, "I want to know where you live. Do you think you can tell me by drawing it? . . . And, of course, there's a catch. You get to do the project with your parents." . . . I handed out the parent pack, which including the requirements, instructions, and rubric. The kids were excited, and some said they would begin immediately: "You know we like to draw, Mrs. May."

As two weeks passed, the kids were talking about it everyday. They would tell their friends about what they did with the parents the night before on the project.

When all were turned in, the greatest part was sitting down [individually with the children] as they explained what they had drawn with their parents. They knew exactly where everything was, including the Dollar General, Post Office, trailer parks, and many others.

I was thrilled to see how much they had actually learned from their parents about maps, directions, and where they live. The parents took part in their learning. Most importantly, my one student who doesn't say anything, was able to use his artistic manner and draw the most detailed picture with every landmark near his home. He even said more than one sentence to explain his drawing. That was more that he had said in six weeks! I also had the parents fill out a form on what they got from the lesson. [They wrote] that they learned a lot from their children [and that they hadn't] worked . . . on homework in a long time. . . .

Mrs. Morrison's Story.   Another third-grade teacher, whose students had excellent TAKS results, wrote the last story. It tells of insights growing out of her tutoring experiences. Her lesson integrates both literacy and social studies linking instruction throughout the school day into a coherent whole.

I was tutoring the third graders after school, when it occurred to me that they did not know how to read a map. . . . So I decided to teach a lesson on maps. We read and discussed *Alexander and the Terrible, Horrible, No Good, Very Bad Day.* Then I [explained] that we could make a Character Map which will help us identify Story Elements and Characters. Once we created the story map, I held up a City of Lenore Map and we talked about what a city map shows us. Towards the end of the lesson we compared and contrasted the City Map and the Character Map.

My students learned a lot from this lesson. In the end they were able to describe a map and its purposes, distinguish between a city map and character map, and relate the character map to the city map. Later on, we broke into small groups and did a few more activities relating to the two maps. I had about ten Bloom's questions on index cards that the groups had to answer and share with the class. I felt very happy with this lesson when I assessed it. I actually got observed on this lesson and received a great overall rating.

The stories three novice teachers told about their students' learning are stories of reflection about their instructional design and how it worked or could have been improved. They provide examples of research-based practices being implemented and describe how these practices resulted in student engagement and learning or in the teacher recognizing needed revision of a lesson's design. Veteran teacher educators' transactional inquiries using these stories resulted in "next step" recommendations. As inquiries continue, we plan to implement increasingly sophisticated designs to explore how teachers' practices are shaped by the collaborative support systems in place and how these systems, with their embedded protocols for interactions, can lead to an even higher quality teacher education and public school student engagement.

CONCLUSION

The evidence presented in this paper comes from multidimensional research and yields an initial understanding of the layers of the organic collaboration in this PDS. The robust partnership engages university and public school partners in developing and monitoring courses and programs, mentoring pre-service and novice teachers, and provoking reflection and professional development for mentors. Quantitative and qualitative results indicate that the practices being implemented in university and public school classrooms are effective.

Perhaps the most exciting conclusion is that, while our PDS model has remained relatively stable over the past 15 years, it has not become stagnant or stale. Built into the model are structures for collaboration that encourage ongoing program evaluation and refinement that are based on issues and needs identified by any of the collaborative groups: ILTs, campus groups, center council, advisory board, and university faculty teams. This systemic process provides for discourse and reflection within the PDS and has led the partners to listen at a deeper level to both public school students and pre-service teachers, a practice called the *pedagogy of listening* (Rinaldi, 2001).

Our research suggests that ongoing conversations and a deep level of listening form a critical venue for ongoing advancement of teaching. As our nation embraces the need for P–16 initiatives and continuity in educating our students (Haycock & Huang, 2001), the institutionalized professional development school model we describe here is ahead of the curve. The model supports the reflection, collaboration, and evidence-based decision-making needed to support all learners. Years of collaboration have resulted in the integration of theory and practice and the development of a pedagogy of listening throughout the PDS. Further, our persistence in collecting, analyzing, and reflecting upon both quantitative and qualitative research findings has kept our PDS on track, dynamic, and moving forward in response to the needs of all the partners.

REFERENCES

Boyer, E. L. (1986). *High school: A report on secondary education in America.* New York: Harper & Row.

Carnegie Forum on Education and the Economy, Task Force on Teaching as a Profession. (1986). *A nation prepared: Teachers for the 21st century.* New York: Author.

Charles A. Dana Center. (2002). *Texas Beginning Teacher Support System evaluation report for year three, 2001–02.* Austin, TX: Author.

Clandinin, D. J., & Connelly, F. M. (2000). *Narrative inquiry: Experience and story in qualitative research.* San Francisco: Josey Bass Publishers.

Dixon, P. N., & Ishler, R. E. (1992). Professional development schools: Stages in collaboration. *Journal of Teacher Education, 43,* 28–34.

Fleener, C., Walker, C., Foote, M., & Zeek, C. (1998, February). *We thought you'd never ask: Mentor teachers tell their stories.* Paper presented at the meeting of the American Association of Colleges for Teacher Education, New Orleans, LA.

Foote, M., Walker, C., Zeek, C., & Filkins, K. (1997, February). *Leadership development through mentoring: Professional development with—not for—mentor teachers.* Paper presented at the meeting of the American Association of Colleges for Teacher Education, Phoenix, AZ.

Foote, M., Zeek, C., Walker, C., & Fleener, C. (1998, December). *Using stories and "transactional inquiry" to tap the wisdom of teachers: Nonlinear assessment in a standardized world.* Paper presented at the annual meeting of the National Reading Conference, Austin, TX.

Goodlad, J. I. (1987). *A place called school: Prospects for the future.* New York: McGraw-Hill.

Goodlad, J. I. (1993). School-university partnership and partner schools. In P. G. Altback, H. G. Petrie, M. J. Shujaa, & L. Weis (Eds.), *Educational policy. Vol. 7, No. 1: Professional development schools* (pp. 24–39). Newbury Park, CA: Corwin Press.

Haycock, K., & Huang, S. (2001). Are today's high school graduates ready? *Thinking K–16, 5*(1) 3–17.

Holmes Group. (1986). *Tomorrow's teachers.* East Lansing, MI: Author.

Holmes Group. (1990). *Tomorrow's schools: Principles for the design of professional development schools.* East Lansing, MI: Author.

Jalongo, M. R., & Isenberg, J. P. (1995). *Teachers' stories: From personal narrative to professional insight.* San Francisco: Jossey-Bass.

Levine, M. (1992). A conceptual framework for professional schools. In M. Levine (Ed.), *Professional practice schools: Linking teacher education and school reform* (pp. 8–24). New York: Teachers College Press.

Linek, W. M., & Sampson, M. B. (1996). Collaboration between public schools and universities: Success through voice and choice. *Illinois Reading Journal, 24*(1), 7–17.

Lyons, N., & LaBoskey, V. K. (Eds.). (2002). *Narrative inquiry in practice: Advancing the knowledge of teaching.* New York: Teachers College Press.

Naizer, G., Stuessy, C., & Price-Blount, K. (2003). *Using the TxCETP vision for effective teaching and learning.* Paper presented at the annual meeting of the School Science and Mathematics Association. Columbus, OH.

National Commission on Excellence in Education. (1983). *A nation at risk: The imperative for education reform*. Washington, DC: U.S. Department of Education.

Richert, A. E. (2002). Narratives that teach: Learning about teaching from the stories teachers tell. In N. Lyons & V. K. LaBoskey (Eds.), *Narrative inquiry in practice: Advancing the knowledge of teaching* (pp. 48–62). New York: Teachers College Press.

Rinaldi, C. (2001). The pedagogy of listening: The listening perspective from Reggio Emilia. *Innovations in Early Education: The International Reggio Exchange, 8*(4),1–4.

Rosenblatt, L. M. (1978). *The reader, the text, the poem: The transactional theory of the literary work*. Carbondale: Southern Illinois University Press.

Sampson, M. B., & Robertson, H. (2004, October). *A reflective discussion of the evolution of a professional development center: Preparing literacy teachers for a diverse society*. Paper presented at the 47th Annual Meeting of the College Reading Association in Del Ray Beach, FL.

State Board for Educator Certification. (2003). *TxBESS framework: Beginning teacher performance standards: A developmental continuum*. Austin, TX: Author.

Walker, C., Bennett, T., Cardwell, M., & Pool, A. (2004, September). *Teacher mentoring/coaching: Value-added research in a school-university collaborative teacher induction program*. Paper presented at the eighth annual Conference on School-University Partnerships, San Antonio, TX.

Wise, A. E., & Darling-Hammond, L. (1987). *Licensing teachers: Design for a teaching profession*. Santa Monica, CA: RAND Corporation.

Wong, H. K., & Wong, R. T. (2004). *The first days of school: How to be an effective teacher* (3rd ed.). Mountain View, CA: Harry K. Wong Publications, Inc.

Zeek, C. K., & Meers, P. J. (1996). Teachers' reasons for becoming and continuing as mentors in a field-based teacher education program. In S. L. Knight, N. J. DeLeon, & C. S. Reese (Eds.), *The Texas School University Research Collaborative: Proceedings of the 1995 Forum* (pp. 11.24). College Station: Texas A&M University.

Zeek, C. K., Foote, M., & Walker C. (2001). Teacher stories and transactional inquiry: Hearing the voices of mentor teachers. *Journal of Teacher Education, 52,* 373–381.

Zeek, C. K., & Walker, C. (2004). Teaching fluently: Exploring teaching practices in divergent certification programs. In J. R. Dugan, P. E. Linder, M. B. Sampson, B. Brancato, & L. Elish-Piper (Eds.) *Celebrating the power of literacy: Yearbook of the College Reading Association* (pp. 94–110). Commerce, TX: College Reading Association.

Zeek, C. K., & Walker, C. (2006). There's nothing easy about mentoring: Mentors as teacher educators in an established professional development school. In J. R. Dangel (Ed.), *Research on teacher induction: Teacher education yearbook XIV* (pp. 279–293). Lanham, MD: Rowman & Littlefield Education.

Zeichner, K. (1992). Rethinking the practicum in the professional development school partnership. *Journal of Teacher Education, 43,* 296–307.

CHAPTER 14

PROFESSIONAL DEVELOPMENT IN ACTION

Getting People to Get Along

Merilyn Buchanan, Robert E. Bleicher, Sima Behshid, Charmon Evans, and Linda Ngarupe

ABSTRACT

This study took place at a professional development school (PDS) that opened in 2002 as a K–5 public charter school in collaboration with a local public university in Southern California. The exploratory interpretive study examined how teachers defined professional development and collaboration from their own perspectives. Group interview data and direct field observations were conducted and analyzed employing grounded analytic techniques. Teachers expressed that they were meeting their expectations for personal professional development and felt empowered and renewed to teach in accordance with both research findings on best practices and their own craft knowledge based on years of teaching experience.

University and School Connections, pages 221–248

INTRODUCTION

> It just takes one question and then there are ten people working on it as soon
> as you walk out the door. You know it's kind of contagious. (Elaine, a teacher
> at the professional development school in this study)

Professional development schools, by definition, provide for the professional development of their faculty, in addition to the preparation of student teachers. It is therefore important to understand how professional development is conceptualized by teachers who commit their expertise to creating a successful and effective professional development school (PDS) setting. This study examined teachers' voices as they express their professional development needs and expectations and how their multiple needs are met and supported within the PDS setting.

We view professional development from a socio-communicative perspective (Bleicher, 1998). This perspective is founded on the tenet that it is the people (not the place or structure) that make it work. Yet, the place and structure must allow and support professional development in multiple manifestations. This presupposes collaborative environments. However, collaboration does not occur by simply putting people together in a room to accomplish common tasks. It calls for the initiation of supporting organizational structures along with a personal willingness to understand, or make sense of, what needs to get done in a workplace setting. Research suggests that sense-making is created by individuals, framed by who they are, what they value, and their identities—as well as by their prior experiences and the cultural, organizational, and structural contexts in which they are situated (Yanow, 1996). This implies that the individual histories of the participants give rise to unlimited interpretations of professional development. Weick (1995) explains that sense-making is creating a "good story" as a person integrates multiple sources of information in a way that is personally meaningful and rational. As such, sense-making stories have the power to change lives (Noddings, 1996). Because teachers have shared elements in their personal histories and school contexts, there will be similarities in the sense-making stories they tell. Accordingly, several themes are embedded in how teachers in this study make sense or tell the story of their professional development school experiences. Our research is informed by the research literature on professional development schools, teacher professional development, professional learning communities, and collaboration.

THEORETICAL FRAMEWORK

Professional Development Schools

The National Council for Accreditation of Teacher Education (NCATE, 2001) outlines five characteristics that distinguish and define a professional development school (PDS). One characteristic is the unique environment that a PDS creates to support a professional learning community. This includes fostering collaborative relationships that allow individuals to share responsibility for good school practices. The PDS infrastructure should be crafted so that it utilizes supporting structures, resources, and roles to achieve the collaborative goals of a professional learning community. Furthermore, a PDS should forge innovative partnerships between K–12 schools and higher education, engage in inquiry about teaching and learning, and promote the professional development of educators (Holmes Group, 1995). A PDS serves the same function for teacher candidates as in-service faculty and, by doing so, creates opportunity to reform education. Inquiry into effective teacher professional development models can help frame such reform.

Teacher Professional Development

Most educators report participating in some form of professional development (PD), spending an average of 8 hours or less annually in PD activities (Lewis et al., 1999). The traditional approaches to professional development, such as workshops and one or two day conferences, are increasingly regarded as relatively ineffective (Corcoran, 1995; Darling-Hammond & Baratz-Snowden, 2007; Fetter, 2003; Guskey & Huberman, 1995). Despite this, the same narrow view of PD has persisted (Monahan, 1996). Lewis et al. (1999) found that teachers who were involved in frequent cooperative planning and collaboration with their peers more often reported feelings of confidence and being well prepared to work in a modern classroom. Good and Brophy (2008) endorse such collaborative activities. "Through working with peers, teachers can exchange ideas and improve instruction throughout the school. . . . Teachers must be cognizant about how other teachers in the same school teach" (p. 443).

Before collaborative activities can be considered in a school, we must recognize that teachers in any school are at different stages of their development due to both years of practice and personal growth, resulting in differing needs and concerns. These stages are typified by teachers' years of experience and distinguished by qualitatively different sets of attitudes, beliefs, and behaviors (Huberman, 1993) and concerns (Fuller & Brown, 1975).

Stages of Teacher Development

Fuller and Brown's (1975) seminal account of teacher development identified dominant concerns of individuals at each of four stages of becoming a teacher: *pre-teaching concerns, early survival concerns, teaching situation concerns*, and *pupil concerns*. We focus here on the third and fourth stages of development. In the third (*teaching situation concern stage*), the concerns are on personal limitations in subject matter content knowledge and what kind of examples teachers give or what materials they provide to help students' learning. The fourth and final developmental stage is characterized as *student concerns*. In this stage, the teachers turn away from their own teaching performances and focus almost entirely on student learning with attention centered on developmentally-appropriate instruction and the social and emotional needs of students.

In another professional model, Perry (1970) names the final stage of teacher development as the *committed stage*. Teachers in this stage begin to accept uncertainty and alternative viewpoints. The *committed stage* can be characterized by teachers working in professional teams where they can learn from their peers without feeling challenged and defensive when opinions, preferences, and practices differ. The key for successfully working together in professional teams is effective communication (Bleicher, 1998).

Professional Dialogue and Teacher Empowerment

Good and Brophy (2008) point out that communication is broader than teachers simply sharing information. They refer to a "sense of community amongst teachers . . . based on information obtained in carefully planned and coordinated discussion with other teachers" (p. 444). While dialogue by itself may be insufficient, it is nevertheless a central component of professional support. Glatthorn (1987) defined "professional dialogue," as follows:

> Professional dialogue occurs when small groups of teachers meet regularly for the guided discussion of their own teaching as it relates to current developments in education. The objective is to facilitate reflection about practice, helping teachers become more thoughtful decision makers. (p. 143)

Creating a strong professional dialogue is central to building a foundation for teacher empowerment; a direct vehicle to achieving empowerment is engagement in collaborative professional development within schools (Good & Brophy, 2008). Glatthorn (1987) used the term "cooperative professional development" to describe "a process by which small teams of teachers work together using a variety of methods and structure for their own professional growth" (p. 143). Cooperative professional development is more powerful when it includes "colleague consultation" (Goldsberry, 1986) and "peer coaching" (Brandt, 1987). These different peer-centered techniques describe ways that teachers can work together to achieve professional development goals. Engaging in professional dialogue implies a common school-wide community language that accurately reflects group-held experiences, beliefs, and attitudes. Professional dialogue, teacher empowerment, common experiences, and group-held beliefs begin to define the professional learning community.

Professional Learning Community

A professional learning community (PLC) is characterized by Eaker and DuFour (2002) as an "environment fostering mutual cooperation, emotional support, personal growth, and a synergy of efforts" as a way to transform a school. A learning community is the core of a PDS. A PDS is "a learning-centered community that supports the integrated learning and development of P–12 students, candidates, and PDS partners through inquiry-based practice . . . (which) results in improvements in the practice of individuals and of the partnering institutions" (NCATE, 2001, p. 9).

While the beneficial aspects of learning communities are well documented, there is little information to provide guidance in creating and developing professional learning communities (Hord, 2004). However, there are an abundance of suggestions for approaches based on the documented experiences of other institutions which may help in forming such communities (Boyd & Hord, 1994; Floden, Goertz, & O'Day, 1995; Kruse & Louis, 1995). What emerges from these examples is that creating a learning community environment requires hard work. It demands intense commitment and persistence.

Establishing a PLC is a cultural shift for a school. It is a new way for teachers to work in order to refocus attention on learning rather than teaching for both teachers and students. It requires a form of collaboration that enables PLC members to attain and sustain focus and self-accountability. The key is how to establish effective collaboration.

Collaboration

Long (2004) reports that the structures supporting long-term professional partnerships are not commonly evident in K–12 settings. We contend that, because of the multiple responsibilities faced by teachers, collaboration can be burdensome unless participants' values, common objectives, and shared work are considered in addition to engaging in dialogue. Research has found that one of the key elements that must be included in K–12 settings is scheduled time during the day for teams of teachers to engage in collegial meetings (Roberts & Pruitt, 2003).

Educational growth for teachers is likely to be optimized when there is support from other professionals (Darling-Hammond & Baratz-Snowden, 2007; Richardson, 1998; Sarason, 2002; Sarason & Lorenz, 1998). Building a learning community calls for teachers to collaborate as active participants who exercise professional influence in the decision-making process. John-Steiner, Weber, and Minnis (1998) offered a definition of collaboration in a PDS setting:

> ...a true collaboration represent(s) complementary domains of expertise.... There is a commitment to shared resources, power, and talent: no individual's point of view dominates, authority for decisions and actions resides in the group, and work products reflect a blending of all participant contributions. (p. 776)

PURPOSE

The purpose of the study was to examine how teachers defined professional development and collaboration from their own perspectives as integral members of a PDS that has already established a degree of success among stakeholders (such as teachers, students, parents, and local community partners). The study picks up the theme of nurturing collaboration as a foundation to establishing a healthy professional learning community.

CONTEXT OF THE STUDY

In 2002, the University Preparation School at CSU Channel Islands (UPS), then a K–5 public charter school, and its partner California State University Channel Islands (CSUCI) both opened their doors to students. Bringing a new public university campus to the region and proposing a charter school PDS was strongly supported by the County Superintendent of Schools and the county's 23 school district superintendents. In the fall of 2006, UPS began to expand to include a preschool and a middle school. The school offers a dual language/language enrichment program to 650 students. In its charter, University Preparation School at CSU Channel Islands described its mission in terms of a professional development school.

UPS hosts an exemplary continued professional development and research environment in which teachers, student teachers, and University faculty collaborate to develop learning experiences, strategies, and activities to benefit all children. Opportunity to participate in professional development and research opportunities is very attractive, causing a competitive application process. Faculty comes from several of the County's school districts with three or more years' leave of absence, allowing them to maintain their seniority, salary, and benefits. Teachers who stay for their entire tenure return to their districts with a greatly enhanced repertoire of skills, experiences, and knowledge.

Students are taught in multi-age clusters that loop in a two-year cycle which supports a developmentally appropriate environment where students can move freely as their program and skill needs change. The children participate in a variety of fine arts programs, including music, art, drama, and band, as well as enrichment classes in literature, culture, agriculture, and sculpture. Multilingualism is a key component in the educational philosophy. Some students are in dual language classes, a 50/50 model focusing on bi-literacy, while others are in a language enrichment strand receiving approximately 1½ hours of Spanish per week, focusing on conversational skills. The 2007 student demographics reflect the local county region. There are 55 percent Hispanic, 22 percent English learners, 38 percent socioeconomically disadvantaged (with an excess of 40 percent of students receiving free or reduced lunches), a 5 percent migrant population, and 10 percent special education students at UPS.

While opportunity to work at the school remains appealing and competitive, a new institution with rotating staffing brings challenges, especially if the professional development mission of the school is to be effectively enacted in a way described by Darling-Hammond (1994):

> . . . creating settings in which novices enter professional practice by working with expert practitioners, enabling veteran teachers to renew their own professional development and assume new roles as mentors, university adjuncts, and teacher leaders . . . to engage jointly in research and rethinking of practice, thus creating an opportunity for the profession to expand its knowledge base by putting research into practice and practice into research. (p. 128)

The multiple roles available for teachers within a PDS have been shown to result in feelings of enhanced professional fulfillment (Johnston, Brosnan, & Cramer, 2000).

Alongside providing an exemplary innovative curriculum in a dual language setting, the teachers have had to create culture, build collaborative teams, craft professional development, and meet the myriad demands of a PDS—all in an environment of frequent teacher turnover. Some faculty members are stimulated by the complexity and seek solutions to the constant challenges. Others find the setting too complex and the challenges a constant strain and leave during their period of tenure, compounding the dilemma of scheduled teacher turnover (Behshid, 2007; Evans, 2007).

METHOD

Design

In line with the theory-building orientation of this research, an interpretive design (Erickson, 1998, 1986) was implemented. Interpretive research analyzes actions from the participant's (emic) point of view. This approach was chosen since only the participants themselves could communicate their perceptions of what professional development was from their unique perspectives and how it was working for them at UPS. One author, in the role of a participant observer, could then triangulate her direct observations and interpretations of participants in various professional development contexts at UPS, both formal and informal.

Participants

The 25 participants in this study were teachers at UPS, a professional development school in Southern California with a total faculty of 30. The data were collected over a two-semester period during the normal academic school year. Two of the authors were among the participants. One of the authors was able to draw upon her five-year formal position as the University Liaison to UPS since its founding. As such she was able to assume a participant observer role in this study.

Data Collection

Initially, teachers were interviewed in four groups. These occasions were videotaped. The groups normally met during ACTT (Active Collaborative Team Time). Other data sources were the fieldnotes of the participant observer (author 1) and discussions among the researchers that triangulated with the teacher interview data.

Analysis

Grounded theory (Strauss & Corbin, 1997) techniques were used to negotiate meaning and develop explanatory models. Interview data were analyzed for emergent themes about what participants were defining as professional development and what aspects had been successful for them personally. Several methods were employed to insure quality and trustworthiness in data collection, analysis, and reporting. A researcher in the role of participant observer allowed for continuous data collection and prolonged engagement in the field (LeCompte, Preissle, & Tesch, 1993). Member checks (Guba & Lincoln, 1989), asking participants to agree or disagree with various interpretations arising from the study, strengthened the validity of capturing the emic point of view.

FINDINGS AND DISCUSSION

We asked teachers, "What has been working for you? Tell us some of your success stories." Analysis of responses led to a categorization of elements of PD that seemed to be embedded within their normal teaching day. Teachers expressed this as professional development-in-action, and we will discuss the power of this concept in this findings section.

Reality (Induction)

I was very scared at first. I'm feeling better now (Rosa).

Lack of confidence, being out of their comfort zone, and other emotive expressions characterized teacher reflections about being new at the school. These were framed as challenges and were followed by realizations of what they felt helped them to overcome the challenges.

I was way out of my comfort level. (Rosario)

. . . it was a huge learning curve for me. (Jane)

I have never worked so hard in my life. Working here is tough. (Robin)

Numerous expressions like these indicated an emotive response to a new teaching situation. The construct of self-efficacy, expressed as a feeling of confidence, was the essence of these statements and led to the framing of new experiences at UPS as challenges.

> There's the challenge of specific curricula areas and/or grade level assignment. (Raul)

> It's a challenge, we are all learners, we learn every day and every single minute—along with the kids. (Sally)

> It's hard when you are having . . . the challenge of a rotating staff. (Elaine)

After framing their new experiences in terms of challenges, teachers often mentioned general personal attributes that they felt were required to overcome them.

> You have to have lots of patience and time. (Mary)

However, teachers were quick to go beyond these general personal attributes that helped overcome challenges. There was a general consensus that it was not just about what you have to do, but it's also about what other people could do for you that was important to overcoming challenges.

> Luckily, I had a great team that really took me under their wings, they had a lot of experience, great team work and a lot of collaboration and (they) really help me survive that first year. (Jacki)

There was acknowledgment that success in overcoming challenges involved a process of induction. Further, this induction was a two-way responsibility of the new teacher and established team members at the school.

> . . . when new teachers come they have to have their breathing time to adjust to the school, so when those (new) teachers are ready to move forward there has to be a sense that the other teachers need a break. So that's still a huge struggle. (Maria)

Established teachers recognized that the new teachers needed to have an adjustment period. Newcomers and veterans were often referred to as operating "on different body clocks" in terms of teaching in the PDS school environment. Very quickly, discussion about induction into the unique challenges of teaching in a PDS led to defining just what professional development was for each individual and collectively how it was embodied within the school community. At UPS, beginning a dialogue about what defines professional development and how to help newcomers settle in constitutes the beginning of creating a professional dialogue (Glatthorn, 1987).

Professional Development-in-Action

One expression used to describe this notion that everything felt like professional development at UPS was "Professional Development-in-Action" (PD-in-Action). There was a strong sentiment that, when one came to work each day, there was a sense that every part of the day was in some way related to professional development. This ranged from informal hallway discussions to more formalized activities both in and outside of classroom teaching.

Two formal events that took place on a regular basis during the school year were grade-level Active Collaborative Teams and school-wide Councils, which will be discussed in this section. In addition, there was a third area that is traditionally a strong focus of the PDS—interactions with student teachers.

The three elements—teaming, sense of community, and making public for peers and student teachers reflections on one's own practice—were considered the "glue" that binds PD-in-Action together. Organizational structures were put in place that supported each of these three elements. Teaming was particularly well supported by Active Collaborative Team Time (ACTT). Sense of community was centrally supported by school-wide Councils. Working with a student teacher each semester provided teachers the opportunity for self-reflection on their own practice for the express purpose of teaching how to teach. Teachers talked about teaming, sense of community and working with students teachers not as three separate entities but as a seamless source for professional development which they coined PD-in-Action.

In Figure 14.1, at the intersection between ACTT and Council, teachers who go to ACTT take information to Councils. Teachers bring local team concerns to a Council setting and take school-wide policies back to ACTT.

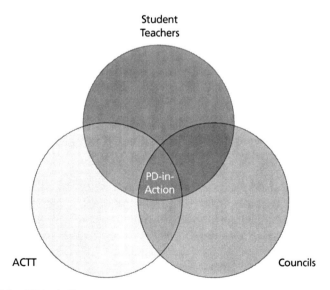

Figure 14.1   PD-in-Action.

The overlap areas between working with student teachers and ACTT and working with student teachers and Councils is where student teachers learn how schools work and how grade-level teams create curriculum and plan for instruction at the local level. In the classroom, student teachers work in a dyadic team relationship to gain training and the wisdom and art of teaching from veteran master teachers. In return, they often share the latest pedagogy and content knowledge from the university with their master teachers. An equally important element of team building is the growth of camaraderie. This is nourished in all three of the overlapping regions in Figure 14.1.

ACTT: Teaming

ACTT, an acronym for Active Collaborative Team Time, occurred three times a week for an hour. It was set aside for teachers to meet in grade level teams. This was a key event for building a team in the smaller grade level groups. In order to allow for this time, the principal had organized for content area specialists to take classes so that the teachers could meet during the regular school day hours on these three days. Sitting in on an ACTT meeting, it becomes obvious to an observer if the group coalesces. Elements such as respect for expertise as well as personal communication skills are keys in the ability to work together in ACTT. Teachers expressed the following outcomes achieved through their participation in ACTT: focused on student needs; achieved induction at team level; enriched knowledge and skills; enhanced collaboration; and valued expertise and resources.

Sally and Joan's summary of the benefits of participating in ACTT is representative of their colleagues.

> We have one of the finest working teams of six. We have total utter respect for each other; we value each other's expertise. As teachers, as colleagues we can give and take and have really interesting dialogues. (Sally)

> We trust . . . are open . . . comfortable giving ideas. . . . If there was no ACTT, I think I would be in my room all the time and be struggling to keep going. (Joan)

Teachers expressed a feeling or attitude of respect that bridges between trust and valuing expertise. Maria expresses this idea below. She is referring to her close working relationship with her dual-language partner and an acknowledgment of content area strengths in each other.

> We have this relationship that works really well and have our own weaknesses and strengths and even with the two languages of instruction. We both know that I am better with the math instruction and she is better at the concept

building and we can rely on one other to help, we complement each other. . . . We can talk to each other without hurting one another. (Maria)

These ideas about respecting expertise and trusting one another are not givens in a workplace. Particularly the idea of not hurting one another (an attitude of caring) was a strong sentiment that was frequently expressed. We contend that a culture of respect is a foundation that must be nurtured in any workplace before one can expect trust and/or valuing expertise to be a possibility. Based upon the teachers' responses, we see several characteristics that a person should exhibit to be a member of a culture of respect:

1. Display interest in others (helpful workplace buddy—does things with others even if it does not benefit personally—support the team).
2. Be dependable (somebody you can depend on to do their part of the job).
3. Value workplace colleagues for more than knowledge and work.
4. Be willing to try things out and critique each other.

We agree with Clarke and Hollingsworth (1994) that not all teachers are at the same stage of readiness to participate in certain professional development activities. We recognize that not everyone feels inclined to participate in the development of a culture of respect. On the other hand, we presuppose that the existence of a strong culture of respect can be a powerful influence, affecting where a person may be on the respect continuum. We are certain that such an environment leads to positive PD and therefore, positive student outcomes are a win for all.

> If you want to come here, it assumes that you are a certain kind of teacher and maybe that's why we all get along so well. (Raul)

Despite our PDS attracting "certain kinds of teachers," it is also acknowledged, as evidenced in the Reality section, that newcomers needed time to adjust and acquire the culture of respect prevalent in the school. This is provided for through the opportunity to interact with other teachers on a daily basis. Social interactions build everyday ways of working together that begin to define a culture of respect and mutual trust among members. Time is required for newcomers to develop trust in their new colleagues as well as to learn the ways they work together in all aspects of the school. This is an important prerequisite for implementing any of the effective professional development strategies specified by McLaughlin (1990), Clandenin and Connelly (1991), Diamond (1991), and Fraser (1990).

I think being safe and being able to fail is what makes us able to be successful. If the lesson didn't work, it doesn't mean you failed, it means you need to tweak a little and go to people and ask what worked for (them) in this area and not say, "This didn't work the first time so we have to move on." . . . if it didn't work the first time for another person, you know what did and didn't work for you, so you can help. And I think with having the freedom here how to work within the standards . . . the freedom that we can be creative in the classroom, allows us to take risks which benefit our children. Maybe we wouldn't have tried certain things at another school, but here we can (Ana).

Learning comes from permission to experiment, fail and try again. (Elaine)

When something goes wrong, there is no blaming. Its more, "What can we do to help?" (Rosario)

Teachers felt that they could try things out and fail, but this is taken to the next stage in Rosario's idea of "no blaming" when something goes wrong. This is another aspect of working in a culture of respect that allows positive PD to happen.

The notion of experimentation in a blame free environment ties in with risk taking discussed in the Expectations section. It is also supported by research such as DeLange (1992), which concludes that time to experiment and take risks is fundamental to effective professional development. This is the trust issue that we contend is one of the positive outcomes of creating the culture or respect that underpins teaming.

. . . you have to have people with open minds, who are willing to listen, who are willing to accept other people's ideas and give value to them (Sally).

This is another critical component in the development of a culture of respect.

With everything, you have more than one brain working on an idea and figuring things out. That is the number one thing. (Ellen)

Each teacher recognized different critical elements that made the ACTT work for him/her. Ellen expressed the idea that many hands make light work. Teachers talk about being open-minded and good listeners, which is certainly a key piece to establishing a culture of respect within a team setting such as ACTT. Ideas cannot simply be brainstormed and left on the table at meeting's end. They need validation in an ongoing discursive manner. Eventually, a summing up of possibilities and pitfalls needs a group-decided direction to act on one or more of the ideas. These are steps to developing Glatthorn's (1987) concept of professional dialogue.

I saw the opportunity to learn from a lot of people, and after a while I realized I was one of the people that would be contributing to the conversations and those learning opportunities. (Raul)

Many comments were made about the need to recognize people's strengths and how expertise was shared in many situations.

We pool our resources or knowledge and skills to help students. (Ellen)

... we have our own weaknesses and strengths. You see that played out when you see us teach. (Maria)

Maria expressed the idea that was not enough to stay in one's own classroom and teach well but that there was a need to take the opportunity to go see how somebody else engaged students in the learning process.

Being able to walk into someone else's room and see what works, or even to think 'I didn't think it would have worked that way', is very powerful learning. (Rosa)

The idea was emphasized that sharing, showing, and not just telling is a powerful, classroom-based professional development activity that is the heart and soul of PD-in-Action. Ashley provides a definition of PD-in-Action:

... we have experts on campus and see what they are doing in their classrooms. ... Here is our professional development—here is what we are doing. (Ashley)

Once expertise resources are established and recognized, how are they shared around the school? In our PDS, there are different avenues to access each others' expertise. Access can be accomplished through conversation in ACTT or by walking into other classrooms and being able to see expertise-in action, or both. This was another key element of PD-in-Action.

In ACTT, we were talking about teaching writing . . . Joan went to the Writer's Workshop Institute. I was trying to visualize the classroom set-up. Penny said she'd cover my class while I visited Joan's when they were doing Writer's Workshop. I tell you, she was wonderful, it was better than a hundred explanations. (Robin)

Although building community is all premised on a culture of respect and the access to the resource of group expertise, it is more than just pooling resources. Putting people in a room does not mean that effective teaming occurs. In a PDS, we do not see the shared labor that accomplishes the ongoing maintenance of school (life getting done through deciding whose turn it is for yard duty, the library schedule, etc.) as enough. The ongoing development of a culture of teaming is the foundational work that must be consciously and publicly supported for an institution to deserve the label of professional development school. Just as it takes time to work through challenges, time is needed for the PDS culture to develop and PD dialogue to happen. As one teacher put it, "Sorry, there is no shortcut, it just takes time."

> After about a month and a half, things started to gel and change . . . we meet every ACT time of course, and Gwen and I meet maybe on a Thursday or a Tuesday to see how our week is going because we're kind of partners, and they (other two team members) meet quite a bit on their own. (Rosario)

You need time to focus on developing a public professional dialogue, the substance of which is shaped by the group's specific local needs.

> Our communication and collaboration time has to be focused on students to make it work. (Sally)

Teachers acknowledged that cooperation (sharing resources) and collaboration are different. In many schools one can be found at the exclusion of the other. But we contend that both must be present to achieve a culture of respect.

> Sharing and collaboration are two different things and we do both. (Jill)

It is not enough for one person to want the idea of collaboration; just as getting people in a room together is not enough to get the process going. A critical mass of people is needed behind the idea of cooperation and collaboration to get the job done in a way that is not only founded on respect but sustains and strengthens that respect as well. People need a motive or clear goal in mind in order to want to engage in collaboration. People contribute in different ways but equitably.

> . . . we're not all the same in what we do, but we complement each other. (Raul)

This maintains a sense of fairness that is required—one has to play his/her part in maintaining an equitable workplace—everybody pulls their weight.

> We all are working hard and love it, and we are there to support each other. The whole sense that we are all on the same team and have a positive attitude and are giving the very best for the kids, and for ourselves, is wonderful. (Lillian)

Building community involves an element of not taking one another for granted in the daily hustle and bustle of running a school. Our roles and responsibilities are supported both by organizational structures and a personal component of respect established considerately and carefully over time with intention (Bleicher, 1998). A culture of respect supports trust and the valuing of expertise (the freedom to experiment without fear of failure or blame for failure) allows for the opportunity to create an equitable workplace. If people work hard and know that they will experience a personal benefit in the long run, there is a happy, productive workplace.

Councils: Sense of Community

Councils are once a week events that allowed teachers to meet in larger across-grade level groups. The purpose of Councils is to work on school wide areas of concern as well as provide for small group professional development. Councils allow cross-phase, multi-grade interactions and input from individuals. The time required for Council meetings was gained from banked time derived from shortened break times and other time saving devices that allowed students to be dismissed earlier each Thursday of the week. Teachers expressed the following as attributes and benefits of Councils: encourages cross-phase collaboration; facilitates shared decision-making; creates a common vision; builds school community; ensures authentic professional development experiences (PD would emerge from local as well as personal needs rather than from an outside mandate); and develops a common history and culture.

> We . . . I . . . love the community approach here, the whole collaborative feel is just a part of what UPS was built on. I think that has been one of the strongest pieces of our groupings here at UPS. (Rosa)

Teachers described a sense of community at the whole school level that seems to be primarily derived from participation in Councils. This gives each grade level team member a sense of place in the whole world of the school. Participation in a Council allows teachers to go beyond the narrow view of their own grade level to the broader whole school picture.

> So everyone here seems to know so much about the school and the way it is organized and the way that it is run . . . It is not just a community setting at your team level (ACTT), it is a community all the way throughout the whole school. (Raul)

Teachers expressed some aspects of what a school community might be. This involved shared knowledge among school members as to how the school is organized, who does what and for what purpose. It is well known that teachers often are isolated in their own classroom activities and life-world (Cochran-Smith & Lytle, 1992). Participation in Councils gets them out of their local setting (e.g., their own classrooms and ACTT) and involved as a member of the total school community.

> At the community level teachers get together in Councils and come up with big ideas but in a way that allows for individual expression. (Diane)

Much of how teachers function in ACTT gets carried over to Council. As in ACTT, decisions are shared, but how they get actuated is different. From ACTT, they are implemented more or less directly into teaching practice or curricular planning. From Councils, decisions and big ideas are brought back to the ACTT team for ratification or enactment. Participation in Councils facilitates making changes to school wide practice and making changes to one's own practice. As such, Councils are a bridge between school reform and classroom practice.

> . . . not everyone is doing the same thing and it might not fit my students, but we have the experts on campus and ask them questions about what they are doing in their classroom. We get a hands-on status rather than just looking at the book and saying, "OK this is how you are supposed to do it." Well if "this" didn't work, we can actually see it—see why. Here is our professional development. Here is how we are doing it. (Jacki)

The expert knowledge to which teachers have readily accessible is expanded through Councils. Individuals can utilize expert knowledge but still have the freedom to enact big ideas in ways that are meaningful to their teaching context. This is a significant step in their individual PD because it builds on their personal PD goals.

Councils are larger groups than ACTT. Initially, Councils were more difficult than ACTT to keep on track to produce constructive results. They need more facilitation to ensure equitable participation and input of ideas from each member of the group.

> We needed more focus and clear goals for our Council to make it more effective. (Penny)

> It would have been more productive if we had clearly established goals and objectives in our Council ahead of time. (Gwen)

Teachers' proposals support Good and Brophy's (2008) advice, suggesting that the foundation for building a "sense of community amongst teachers" . . . rests on "carefully planned and coordinated discussion with other teachers" (p. 444). Guided discussion reduces the possibility that dialogue degenerates into unproductive verbal posturing (Clark & Peterson, 1986).

> There were certain individuals who dominated. They had to be the centre of attention and nobody knew how to manage their behavior, which caused people to regard Council meetings as a waste of valuable time. (Ana)

In response to such concerns, UPS administration selected a cohort of teachers who were involved in a Masters program in leadership and administration. They attended a professional learning community summer institute that facilitated leadership training (DuFour, Eaker, & DuFour, 2005). The participants returned with an understanding of the importance of establishing group norms (Bleicher, 1998) and with a set of techniques to ensure more equitable involvement. Council members reported immediate benefits.

> Each member of the Council was valued and discussions were of quality. (Mary)

> Each person enjoyed the camaraderie of the group. (Ellen)

> Overall, there was a stronger understanding of topics after a Council meeting. (Joan)

Reported changes in the evaluation of the Councils' effectiveness may have resulted from the increased in length of time teachers had been participants. What is evident is that getting Councils to work effectively requires hard work and personal effort on the part of each member.

> I have never worked so hard in my life and working here is tough. (Larry)

> We are all working hard—and love it and we are there to support each other. (Phyllis)

> Everyone is working together. We're all pulling in the same direction. (Irene)

Working with Student Teachers

Student teachers and other pre-service university students enter UPS classrooms to learn to teach. This area of PD-in-Action gives meaning to the notion that teaching at the PDS was like having professional development experiences all day long. This corresponds to Darling-Hammond and McLaughlin's (1995) proposition that a characteristic of effective professional development is that teachers are involved "both as learners and as teachers," and one way this occurs is to "engage teachers in concrete tasks of teaching, assessment, observation, and reflection that illuminate the processes of learning and development" (p. 592). The findings in this section are presented in three parts: *reflection on practice*—Me teaching them; *gaining knowledge*—Me learning from them; *teaming with student teachers*—Us learning together.

On reflection on practice: Me teaching them

> When you are working with student teachers it really forces you to think of what you are doing and why you are doing it and what research is behind it. (Rosario)

There is an expectation that in working with student teachers, teachers are going to debrief their actions and, to some degree, make public their reflections to the student teacher.

> I really try to think about what I'm doing and reflect. I've become a more reflective teacher. (Sally)

> The role is expanded, you are not just a teacher. Personally, I have become a much more reflective teacher. (Raul)

What UPS teachers were doing with their student teachers was debriefing the common experience they had just had with them and sharing knowledge. "I ask, 'Did you notice what I did, and do you know why I did it?'" (Penny). Teachers' questioning of student teachers about their own practice gives rise to self-reflection upon what they are doing and why.

The teachers in this study were not novices. The majority came to the PDS setting as experienced master teachers with long histories and have engaged in multiple in-service activities. On the Fuller and Brown (1975) continuum, it can be expected that some faculty might be in the *teaching situation concern stage* of development. At this third stage, focus is largely on one's own teaching performance but with a concern for providing the best materials and examples to enhance. Alternatively, teachers in our PDS setting might be expected to be at the fourth and final developmental stage, characterized by *student concerns* whereby focus shifts almost entirely to student learning with attention centered on developmentally appropriate instruction and the social and emotional needs of students. This final stage is in accord with constructivist and problem-driven beliefs about effective teaching.

From Perry's (1970) perspective, the work with student teachers highlights that teachers are beginning to accept uncertainty and alternative viewpoints and this is illustrative of the *committed stage* of teacher development. The uncertainty comes when a "model" lesson does not come off perfectly and there is a need to explain to the student teacher what went wrong and how it was fixed it or will fixed in the future. The source of alternative viewpoints could be student teachers asking questions or from peers suggesting other ideas during ACTT or in Council meetings or as a result of classroom observations.

Reflective practice allows for continual development in all areas, including growth in content knowledge and pedagogical habits of mind. As these areas mature, teaching confidence strengthens (Bleicher, in press). It is recognized that student teachers are not given enough specific instruction in or practice with reflection (Bleicher, Correia, & Buchanan, 2007). In the UPS setting, this is, in part, being counteracted when a teacher consciously models reflection for the student teacher.

On gaining knowledge: Me learning from them

> So, we have a student teacher in each of our classrooms—which is a big help. We learn so much, I wish they could be here for the whole semester rather than eight weeks! (Jane)

> When I was a student teacher, I might have been the new kid on the block, but I will never be more current than I was back then. (Elaine)

> I'm able to converse with and get information from the student teachers as well as teaching them. I think that gives you a real professional teaching experience. (Raul)

Student teachers do more than provide additional assistance for teacher and students. Interacting with student teachers provides opportunities for the mentor teacher to learn and reflect (Sundli, 2007). This creates favorable conditions for the renewal of UPS teachers' own professional development as they assume the role of mentor (Darling-Hammond & McLaughlin, 1995). Often student teachers are viewed as a professional responsibility that can be burdensome on time (John-Steiner, Weber, & Minnis (1998) and, in results-driven settings, on student learning outcomes. This is not the case at UPS. Most UPS teachers mentor and supervise a student teacher each semester. They are disappointed if they do not have a student teacher assigned to them.

Having student teachers in the classroom challenges the teachers to articulate not only how to teach but "why" they teach things the way they do. This naturally leads to teachers being more reflective and purposeful about their decisions in the classroom. A residual outcome of being under the continuous scrutiny of student teachers is more conscientious instructional decision making. As student teachers complete their coursework assignments within the UPS classroom, the mentor or master teacher has the opportunity to revisit theory, pedagogy, and methodology. As theories evolve and change, the master teacher is kept abreast through student teacher interactions. Student teachers view the young students with a fresh perspective which helps the master teachers see children through different eyes.

> Watching student teachers implement knowledge gained in their coursework offers us a chance to analyze and evaluate the implementation of strategies from an objective perspective that can later be applied to our own teaching. (Diane)

Through the student teacher, UPS teachers gain currency in pedagogical ideas, contemporary research, and intellectual renewal. Thus, learning from student teachers counters the criticism of teachers' failure to remain current with theories on research and teaching, which Cochran-Smith and Lytle (1992) see as an obstacle to teacher research being "a legitimate and unique form of knowledge generation and a profound means of professional growth" (p. 299).

On teaming with student teachers: Us learning together

> The nice thing about having a student teacher is you can work with each other and share things. (Rosario)

The language Rosario uses, "work with each other," indicates a collegial rather than a supervisory relationship. While the degree of collegiality between the mentors and their student teachers is not on par with the critical friend relationships formed through ACTT, the teaming process and benefits are similar. Working with a student teacher allows a version of peer-coaching or colleague consultation (Goldsberry, 1986) similar to that experienced from ACTT in which peers might visit one another's classrooms to conduct PD-in-Action. It is also provides a context for the type of professional dialogue described by Glatthorn (1987) which facilitates reflection about practice in a way that helps teachers become more thoughtful decision makers. By including student teachers in planning and reflection, both before and after instruction, the student teacher is able to participate in an authentic professional dialogue with the teacher. For the teachers, they become better decision makers through the effort of making their usually private reflections public through professional dialogue with their student teacher.

CONCLUSIONS AND IMPLICATIONS

Based on what we learned from this study, we draw at least six conclusions with direct implications for other professional development schools.

1. Achieving some degree of PD-in-Action elevates a school's PD awareness level. This leads to unexpected results and benefits. Teachers themselves express that everything they do at the school is PD, including their everyday work as a classroom teacher.
2. Establishing a professional learning community is key to developing PD-in-Action. Collaboration is the essence of a professional learning community. A level of caring for one another and valuing expertise within a community are central tenets for collaboration.
3. Creating a culture of respect is pivotal to achieving collaboration. This means developing respect for each other on a personal level and trusting that there are others one can turn to and who will come to you for your expertise and to help get the job done. Effective teaming hinges on respect.
4. Developing and maintaining a culture of respect requires professional dialogue. Communication is hard work. Not only does time need to be set aside to develop professional dialogue, but one has to establish and continually revisit community rules for discourse to ensure that everyone's voice is heard and has equal time on the conversation floor.
5. Supporting a culture of respect, requires mechanisms that allow for frequent, formalized, and systemic meeting time to occur during regular school day hours. The principal is indispensable for creating the time and funding for such an organizational structure.
6. Distinguishing between the benefits and purposes of internal and external PD is an important step in the process of establishing PD-in-Action. By and large, external PD provides technical training that may or may not be incorporated into teaching practice. Professional explanations and information are delivered to teachers, but they do not have the opportunity to engage in professional dialogue. Internal PD involves the exchange of ideas through professional dialogue, thereby affording more teacher ownership and decision making. It empowers teachers to implement their own professional development which they plan to utilize in their own classroom teaching practice.

To take any definition of professional development (PD) that tries to describe what effective PD should be in a PDS has questionable validity. In concert with Hord's (2004) conclusions about professional learning communities, we contend that PD must be defined by the PDS community of practitioners. That is not to say that teachers should ignore theory and research findings. Teachers interested in creating PD-in-Action should select the pieces they want, make them their own, and meld them together with their own experienced-based knowledge.

One indicator of PD-in-Action is how teachers redefine the typical school work day. When describing their work in a PDS that has achieved PD-in-Action, such as UPS, teachers tend to use professional dialogue that blurs the boundaries between classroom teaching and professional development activities. Being successful means communicating and acting in new ways that match your goals. It means taking risks with the support of critical friends in safe environments. These are aspects of an effective professional learning community which must, first and foremost, develop a deep culture of respect for all its members. It then follows naturally that the unique mission of the school will engage all teachers to work collaboratively toward shared goals to achieve community-valued student learning outcomes and move teachers to Fuller and Brown's (1975) fourth stage of *student concerns* or Perry's (1970) *committed stage* of development. Focusing on the PD in a PDS, members of a professional learning community will constantly strive to improve their professional dialogue to support these professional development goals that lead to valued student learning outcomes.

Being successful is marked by teaching to high standards not standardized teaching. It is all about being open-minded, taking charge of shared decision-making, and trusting one's own expertise as much as others'. For a school of dedicated teachers, all actions and all discussions finish with student learning outcomes firmly in the center of focus (Rutledge, Smith, & Watson, 2003).

> It is really the students that drive the curriculum rather than the text book. (Phyllis)

> We share what work best for kids . . . our conversations revolve around what is best for kids and how to best fit the learning environment to each student. (Sally)

As the teachers so enthusiastically put it, "professional development, its all about helping students not yourself." The conversation always seemed to come back to concerns for student learning, which is a good thing (Fuller & Brown, 1975). As Ashley so aptly claims, "Everything that I do here is PD." All the teachers we interviewed at UPS support her sentiments unanimously.

> I think the most valuable thing in coming from a more structured to an open environment was that it has stretched me to do things I have never done before. (Raul)

Once an atmosphere of respect and trust is established, it enables participants to focus on one another's areas of expertise and allows professional dialogues to take place often with good effect. We see culture-building in a school as the horse. We see the cart as great curriculum and teaching that goes on in the school. We see the payload being carried in the cart as student learning. We believe the adage that it is critical to keep the horse before the cart. In a school that keeps the cart where it belongs, we see a happy, productive school where teachers eagerly come to work, not only motivated by the love of teaching children but by the joy of learning together as a professional learning community.

REFERENCES

Behshid, S. (2007). Master's Thesis in progress.

Bleicher, R. E. (in press). Nurturing confidence in preservice elementary science teachers. *Journal of Science Teacher Education.*

Bleicher, R. E. (1998). Classroom interactions: Using interactional sociolinguistics to make sense of recorded classroom talk. In J. Malone & B. Atweh (Eds.), *Aspects of postgraduate supervision and research in mathematics and science* education (pp. 85–104). Mahwah, NJ: Erlbaum.

Bleicher, R. E., Correia, M. G., & Buchanan, M. (2007). *Service learning: Building commitment to becoming teachers.* ERIC Document Reproduction Service No. ED (494 939).

Boyd, V., & Hord, S. M. (1994). *Principals and the new paradigm: Schools as learning communities.* ERIC Document Reproduction Service No. ED (373428).

Brandt, R. (1987). On cooperation in schools: A conversation with David and Roger Johnson. *Educational Leadership, 45,* 14–19.

Clandinin, D. J., & Connelly, F. M. (1991). Teacher as curriculum maker. In P. Jackson (Ed.), *Handbook of research on curriculum.* New York: American Educational Research Association.

Clark, C. M. (1988). Asking the right questions about teacher preparation: Contributions of research on teacher thinking. *Educational Researcher, 17,* 5–12.

Clark, C., & Peterson, P. (1986). Teachers' thought processes. In M. Wittrock (Ed.), *Handbook of research on teaching* (3rd ed., pp. 255–296). New York: Macmillan.

Clarke, D., & Hollingsworth, H. (1994). Reconceptualising teacher change. In G. Bell, B. Wright, N. Leeson, & J. Geeke (Eds.), *Challenges in mathematics education: Constraints on construction. Proceedings of the seventeenth Annual Conference of the Mathematics Education Research Group in Australasia (MERGA)* (pp. 153–163). Lismore, New South Wales: MERGA.

Cochran-Smith, M., & Lytle, S. (1992). Communities for teacher research: Fringe or Forefront? *American Journal of Education, 100,* 298–324.

Connelly, F. M., & Clandinin, D. J. (1990). Stories of experience and narrative enquiry. *Educational Researcher, 19,* 2–14.

Corcoran, T. C. (1995). *Transforming professional development for teachers: A guide for state policymakers.* ERIC Document Reproduction Service No. ED (384600).

Darling-Hammond L. (1994). *Professional development schools: Schools for developing a profession.* ERIC Document Reproduction Service No. ED (364996).

Darling-Hammond, L., & Mclaughlin, M. W. (1995). Policies that support professional development in an era of reform. *Phi Delta Kappan, 76,* 591–96.

Darling-Hammond, L., & Baratz-Snowden, J. (2007). A good teacher in every classroom: Preparing the highly qualified teachers our children deserve. *Educational Horizons, 85,* 111–132.

Day, C. (1999). *Developing teachers: The challenges of lifelong learning.* Philadelphia, PA: Falmer Press.

De Lange, J. (1992). Critical factors for real changes in mathematics learning. In G. Leder (Ed.), *Assessment and learning of mathematics* (pp. 305–329). Hawthorn, Victoria: Australian Council for Educational Research.

Devany, K., & Sykes, G. (1988). In A. Lieberman (Ed.), *Building a professional culture in schools.* New York: Teachers College Press.

Diamond, C. T. P. (1991). *Teacher education as transformation.* Philadelphia: Open University Press, Milton Keynes.

DuFour, R., Eaker, R., & DuFour, R. (Eds.). (2005). *The power of professional learning communities.* Bloomington, IN: National Education.

Eaker, R., & DuFour, R.(2002). *Getting started: Reculturing schools to become professional learning communities.* Bloomington, IN: National Educational Service.

Erickson, F. (1986). Qualitative research on teaching. In M. C. Wittrock (Ed.), *Handbook of research on teaching* (3rd ed., pp. 119–161). New York: Macmillan.

Erickson, F. (1998). Qualitative research methods for science education. In B. J. Fraser & K. G. Tobin (Eds.), *International handbook of science education* (pp. 1155–1173). Dordrecht, The Netherlands: Kluwer.

Evans, C. (2007). Master's Thesis in progress.

Feiman-Nemster, S., & Floden, R.E. (1984). *The cultures of teaching. Occasional paper no. 74.* ERIC Document Reproduction Service No. ED (251423).

Fenstermacher, G. D. (1994). The place of practical arguments in the education of teachers. In V. Richardson (Ed.), *Teacher change and the staff development process: A case in reading instruction* (pp. 23–42). New York: Teachers College Press.

Fessler, R., & Christensen, J. (Lead Authors and Eds.). (1992). *Teacher career cycle: Understanding and guiding the professional development of teachers.* Needham Heights, MA: Allyn & Bacon.

Fetter, W. R. (2003). *A conceptual model for integrating field experiences, professional development schools, and performance assessment in a world of NCATE 2000.* ERIC Document Reproduction Service No. ED (472396).

Floden, R. E., Goertz, M. E., & O'Day, J. (1995). Capacity building in systemic reform. *Phi Delta Kappan, 77,* 19–21.

Fraser, B. J. (1990). Factors affecting school change: Lessons from the transition program. *Curriculum and Teaching, 5,* 55–61.

Fuller, F., & Brown, O. (1975). Becoming a teacher. In K. Ryan (Ed.), *Teacher education* (74th yearbook of the National Society for the Study of Education) (pp. 25–52). Chicago: University of Chicago Press.

Glatthorn, A. (1987). Cooperative professional development: Peer-centered options for teacher growth. *Educational Leadership, 45,* 31–35.

Goldsberry, L. (1986). *Colleague consultation: Another case of fools rush in.* Paper presented at the annual meeting of the American Educational Research Association, San Francisco.

Good, T., & Brophy, J. (2008). *Looking in classrooms* (10th ed.). Boston: Allyn and Bacon.

Guba, E. G., & Lincoln, Y. S. (1989). *Fourth generation evaluation.* London: Sage.

Guskey, T. (1985). Staff development and teacher change. *Educational Leadership, 42,* 57–60.

Guskey, T. R., & Huberman, M. (1995). *Professional development in education: New paradigms and practices.* ERIC Document Reproduction Service No. ED (394215).

Henninger, M. L. (2007). Lifers and troupers: Urban physical education teachers who stay. *Journal of Teaching in Physical Education, 26,* 125–144.

Holmes Group. (1995). *Tomorrow's schools of education: A report of the Holmes group.* ERIC Document Reproduction Service No. ED (399220).

Hord, S. (2004). *Learning together, leading together: Changing schools through professional learning communities.* New York: Teachers College Press.

Huberman, M. (1993). Linking the practitioner and researcher communities for school improvement. *School Effectiveness and School Improvement, 4,*1–16.

Inman, D., & Marlow, L. (2004). Teacher retention: Why do beginning teachers remain in the profession? *Education, 124,* 605.

Johnston, M., Brosnan, P., & Cramer, D. (2000). *Collaborative reform and other improbable dreams: The challenges of professional development schools. SUNY series, teacher preparation and development.* ERIC Document Reproduction Service No. ED (481274).

John-Steiner, V., Weber, R. J., & Minnis, M. (1998). The challenge of studying collaboration. *American Educational Research Journal, 35,* 773–783.

Kruse, S., & Louis, K. (1995). *Teacher teaming—opportunities and dilemmas.* ERIC Document Reproduction Service No. ED (383082)

LeCompte, M. D., & Preissle, J., with Tesch, R. (1993). *Ethnography and qualitative design in educational research* (2nd ed.). Orlando, FL: Academic Press.

Lewis, L., Parsad, B., Carey, N., Bartfai, N., Farris, E., Smerdon, B., & Greene, B. (1999). *Teacher quality: A report on the preparation and qualifications of public school teachers.* NCES Report 1999080.

Long, S. (2004), Separating rhetoric from reality: Supporting teachers in negotiating beyond the status quo. *Journal of Teacher Education, 55,* 141–153.

McLaughlin, M. (1990). The Rand change agent study revisited: Macro perspectives and micro realities. *Educational Researcher, 19,* 11–16.

Monahan, T. C. (1996). Do contemporary incentives and rewards perpetuate outdated forms of professional development? *Journal of Staff Development, 17,* 44–47.

Morimoto, K. (1973). Notes on the context for learning. *Harvard Educational Review, 10,* 245–257.

NCATE. (2001). *Standards for Professional Development Schools.* Washington DC: National Council for Accreditation of Teacher Education.

Noddings, N. (1996). Stories and affect in teacher education. *Cambridge Journal of Education, 26,* 435–47.

Perry, W. G. (1970). *Forms of intellectual and ethical development in the college years.* New York: Holt, Rinehard & Winston. Teachers Change

Richardson, V. (1998). How teachers change. In *Focus on basics* (pp. 1–10). Boston: Focus on Basics.

Roberts, S., & Pruitt, E. (2003). *Schools as professional learning communities: Collaborative activities and strategies for professional development.* Thousand Oaks, CA: Corwin Press Inc.

Rutledge, V. C., Smith, L. B., & Watson, S. W. (2003). *NCATE, NCLB, and PDS: A formula for measuring success.* ERIC Document Reproduction Service No. ED (474946).

Sarason, S. B. (2002). *Educational reform: A self-scrutinizing memoir.* ERIC Document Reproduction Service No. ED (472632).

Sarason, S. B., & Lorentz, E. M. (1998). *Crossing boundaries: collaboration, coordination, and the redefinition of resources.* ERIC Document Reproduction Service No. ED (412660).

Scherer, M. (2001). Improving the quality of the teaching force: A conversation with David C. Berliner. *Educational Leadership, 58,* 6–10.

Strauss, A., & Corbin, J. (1997). *Grounded theory in practice.* Thousand Oaks, CA: Sage.

Sundli, L. (2007). Mentoring—A new mantra for education?. *Teaching & Teacher Education: An International Journal of Research and Studies, 23,* 201–214.

Townsend, J. S., & Pace, B. G. (2005). The many faces of Gertrude: Opening and closing possibilities in classroom talk. *Journal of Adolescent and Adult Literacy, 48,* 594–605.

Weick, K. E. (1995). *Sensemaking in organizations.* Thousand Oaks, CA: Sage.

Yanow, D. (1996). *How does a policy mean? Interpreting policy and organizational actions.* Washington, DC: Georgetown University Press.

PART III

PERSPECTIVES ON INQUIRY AND MENTORING

CHAPTER 15

INQUIRY-ORIENTED MENTORING IN AN ELEMENTARY PROFESSIONAL DEVELOPMENT SCHOOL

The Case of Claudia

Diane Yendol-Hoppey and Nancy Fichtman Dana

ABSTRACT

While a great deal of attention has been given to the adaptation and development of an inquiry stance toward teaching and learning in the PDS, less attention has been focused on applying the tenants of an inquiry stance to the process of mentoring. This chapter reports on a year-long case study of one mentor teacher in a PDS whose approach to mentoring was consonant with the underpinnings of the teacher inquiry movement. Four components of an inquiry-oriented approach to mentoring are described and analyzed: (1) Co-planning; (2) Co-teaching; (3) Co-reflecting, and (4) Co-problem posing. Implications for supervision and mentoring in the professional development school are discussed.

University and School Connections, pages 251–273
Copyright © 2008 by Information Age Publishing

251

INTRODUCTION

Professional Development Schools (PDSs) are innovative school-university partnerships designed around the notion of simultaneous renewal for prospective and practicing teachers as well as teacher educators (Darling-Hammond, 1994). Two decades ago, in the political environment of *A Nation at Risk* (National Commission on Teaching and America's Future, 1983), and *A Nation Prepared* (Carnegie Forum on Education and Economy, 1986), the Holmes Group (1990) began advocating for the PDS concept as a movement to professionalize teaching and teacher education. Since that time, the PDS movement has gained momentum and spread as a powerful means for preparing teachers and creating a nexus for theoretical and practical work in schools (Darling-Hammond, 1994; Hoffman, Reed, & Rosenbluth, 1997; Levine & Trachtman, 1997).

The Holmes Partnership (1990) states that general guiding principles for creating PDS sites must include a commitment to making reflection and inquiry a central part of the school (Holmes Group, 1990). Hence, one critical component for all members of a PDS is engagement in teacher inquiry (Dana & Silva, 2002; Dana, Silva, & Snow-Gerono, 2002). In addition and developing alongside the PDS movement, the teacher inquiry (or, more formally, teacher research) movement, has been touted as a critical tool for generating knowledge about teaching and learning and furthering educational reform efforts (Carr & Kemmis, 1986; Cochran-Smith & Lytle, 1993, 1999; Kincheloe, 1991; Lieberman & Miller, 1990; Miller, 1990). Two of these researchers, Cochran-Smith and Lytle (1993), define teacher research as "systematic, intentional inquiry by teachers" (p. 5), while McKernan (1988) suggests that teacher research is the "rigorous examination of one's own practice as a basis for professional development" (p. 154). Teacher researchers gain a better understanding of why they behave as they do and, consequently, make better choices in their classroom practice (Oberg, 1990). Inquiring professionals seek out change and reflect on their practice by posing questions or "wonderings," collecting data for insights, analyzing the data along with reading relevant literature, instituting changes based on new understandings developed during inquiry, and sharing findings with others (Dana & Yendol-Silva, 2003).

The ultimate goal of engagement in teacher research is to create an inquiry stance toward teaching. To achieve this stance, teachers must first understand the inherent complexity of teaching. Given this complexity, it is natural and normal for teachers to face many problems, issues, tensions, and dilemmas as they practice. Rather than "sweeping the problems under the carpet" and pretending they do not exist, reflective teachers embrace problems by deliberately naming them, making them public, studying them, and making a commitment to do something about them.

An inquiry stance actually becomes a "professional positioning" that is owned by the teacher, where, because of the inherent complexity of teaching, questioning one's own practice becomes part of the teacher's work and, eventually, a part of the teaching culture. By cultivating this inquiry stance toward teaching, teachers can play a critical role in enhancing their own professional growth and ultimately the experience of schooling for children. According to Cochran-Smith and Lytle (2001):

> A legitimate and essential purpose of professional development is the development of an inquiry stance on teaching that is critical and transformative, a stance linked not only to high standards for the learning of all students but also to social change and social justice and to the individual and collective professional growth of teachers. (p. 46)

While a great deal of attention has been given to the adaptation and development of an inquiry stance toward teaching and learning in the PDS, less attention has been focused on applying the tenants of an inquiry stance to the process of mentoring, which, according to Wang (2001) is "one of the most important strategies to support novices' learning to teach and, thus, to improve the quality of teaching" (p. 52). What does *an inquiry-oriented approach to mentoring* look like? To address this question, we embarked on a year-long case study of one mentor teacher in a PDS whose approach to mentoring was consonant with the underpinnings of the teacher inquiry movement.

METHODOLOGY

Procedures and Data Collection

This study is interpretive in nature (Erickson, 1986) and draws on case study methodology (Stake, 1995) informed by both ethnographic (Wolcott, 1994) and phenomenological (Denzin & Lincoln, 1994) lenses. This methodology focuses the spotlight on the ways one mentor teacher came to know and carry out her work with a prospective teacher over a ten-month period in a PDS.

Using a unique case selection procedure (Goetz & LeCompte, 1984), the case mentor teacher was selected from a pool of six veteran teachers serving as mentors in a PDS partnership with our university. In this case, the unique attributes included: (1) the intern/mentor dyad's negotiation of a successful and exemplary learning context as perceived by intern, mentor, and university faculty; and (2) the mentor's approach to inducting a new teacher into the profession, emerging as consonant with the underpinnings of the teacher inquiry movement early in the PDS year. Through this process, one teacher (Claudia) and her intern (Julia) were selected for participation in this study. It is also important to note that this case study of Claudia was a part of a larger study exploring the work lives of mentor teachers in a PDS. This larger study yielded data and interpretation of other exemplary forms of mentoring (Yendol-Hoppey, in press; Yendol-Hoppey & Dana, 2006) as well as issues veteran teachers face as they assume the role of teacher educator in PDS work (Silva & Dana, 2004).

The data sources used to understand Claudia's work as a mentor teacher included: (1) journal entries written by Claudia and her intern Julia, (2) weekly fieldnotes, (3) interviews, (4) e-mail, (5) meeting minutes, and (6) observation sheets. In addition, Claudia participated in three semi-structured interviews focused on her experiences working as a mentor. Julia, Claudia's intern, participated in ongoing informal weekly discussions with one of the researchers and engaged in a single semi- structured interview near the end of the school year. The tape recordings of each interview were transcribed, allowing for accurate reporting of the participants' responses and enabling the researchers to interpret specific responses in the context of the entire transcript.

This paper presents a description, analysis, and interpretation of Claudia's work with her intern, Julia, as it unfolded throughout one entire school year in a first-grade PDS classroom. This accounting of Claudia's mentoring was member-checked to ensure trustworthiness (Patton, 1990).

Setting: The PDS Context

The PDS in this study is located in the Northeastern United States and is the result of a Holmes Partnership commitment between a Research One University and a local school district. Pre-service teachers complete an undergraduate internship where learning to teach is accomplished through teaming with a mentor teacher for an entire school year (Silva & Dana, 2001). In addition to teaching alongside their mentors, interns engage in seminars and coursework conducted in school sites to earn 30 credits. During the fall semester, interns take twelve credits of methods instruction: three credits each of math, science, social studies, and classroom learning environments. The fall and spring field seminars, including a focus on teacher inquiry and practicum experiences, comprise the additional 18 credits. This PDS program departs from the traditional initial teacher preparation program in three important ways: (1) the mentor and the intern team to teach children throughout an *entire* school year, (2) mentors work closely with teacher educators to plan the intern teacher education curriculum on an individual basis, and (3) mentor and intern engage in teacher inquiry (Dana & Yendol-Silva, 2003).

The Participants

Claudia is in her fourteenth year of teaching first-grade children in two different schools within the same district. Claudia received her own pre-service teacher training in a setting similar to today's PDSs. After getting her undergraduate degree in psychology and philosophy, she went back to the university for a one-year intensive Master of Arts in Teaching Program, coupled with a full-year of teaching in the university lab school. Claudia believes her own mentor teacher was excellent because she provided a supportive and caring context for teaching. Claudia's own positive pre-service teaching experience contributed to her interest in working with prospective teachers, and she draws upon memories of her own mentor teacher and learning to teach experiences as she now mentors new teachers in the PDS (Koerner, 1992).

Claudia is highly motivated when it comes to her own learning and enjoys taking course work when there is a topic that she is interested in exploring. As a classroom teacher, she is committed to providing a context and stimulus for children to actively construct knowledge. She uses child-centered pedagogy such as cooperative learning, conflict resolution, peer tutoring, and student problem solving as daily instructional techniques. According to Claudia, building a relationship with her intern is a necessary component of mentoring in the PDS:

> I really feel like Julia and I are moving through the year together. In the old experience there was still a separate feeling because they were in and out, and we didn't have as much involvement in the university work. This is a much closer relationship personally and professionally because you really spend a lot of time with this person. It is more intimate, so to speak, because you are together so much. . . . It is not disconnected and disjointed. (Claudia, interview B, 416–424)

Julia, Claudia's intern, is a capable, bright, reflective, and energetic young woman. As with many prospective teachers, she has struggled a bit with classroom management, but overall she is strong and plans well in her work with children. Claudia describes what she sees as Julia's beliefs, philosophy, and approach to teaching:

> She has really refined observational skills, and she is very reflective. She does a lot of question asking, and she has got a real curiosity about her teaching. She wants to know why. I think she holds certain beliefs philosophically that she really sticks to and doesn't succumb to going back into the traditional mode when things get tough. (Claudia, interview B, 113–121)

Claudia shares Julia's philosophical beliefs and level of commitment to these beliefs:

> There is a certain "telepathy" because we think a lot alike. I think we are very similar in philosophy, and we value the same things. We are both focused on intrinsic motivation. We try to make our relationships with the kids the focus in our room, and we both feel that way. I think we just have similar values about learning and how it looks and feels in the classroom. (Claudia, interview B, 651–656)

Julia is always well prepared and actively identifies ways she can contribute to the classroom activities by asking for specific roles and enthusiastically accepting new responsibilities. In combination, these intern characteristics have allowed Claudia to develop a strong sense of confidence in Julia's work and to forge a professional relationship with Julia that has allowed an inquiry-oriented approach in mentoring to emerge in this context. This inquiry-oriented approach to mentoring, as it emerged in this case study, is defined by a four-component cycle that Claudia and Julia spiral through together throughout the PDS year: (1) co-Planning, (2) co-Teaching, (3) co-Reflecting, and (4) co-Problem Posing. This four-component cycle is presented in Figure 15.1.

Undergirding this cycle are three fundamental elements that parallel fundamental elements of the teacher inquiry movement—(1) embracing teaching as inherently complex, (2) risk-taking, and (3) constructing new knowledge about teaching and learning. These elements, as well as the four-component cycle, are described in detail utilizing salient quotes and excerpts from field notes in the next section of this paper.

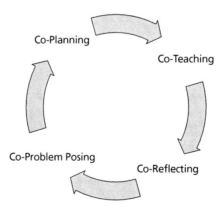

Figure 15.1   Claudia's Cycle of Inquiry-Oriented Mentoring.

FINDINGS

The Look and Feel of an Inquiry-Oriented Approach to Mentoring

As discussed in the introduction to this paper, the ultimate goal of the teacher inquiry movement is to create an inquiry stance toward teaching characterized by recognizing teaching as an inherently complex activity. Similarly, one key premise to Claudia's inquiry-oriented approach to mentoring is sharing a recognition of teaching as inherently complex with her intern from the very start of their work together. To create a context where Julia and Claudia can spiral through the four components of an inquiry-oriented approach to mentoring (co-planning, co-teaching, co-reflecting, co-problem posing) in concert with one another, Claudia feels Julia must feel comfort with exploration and experimentation as well as realize that dichotomous concepts like "right" and "wrong" are rarely useful in learning to teach. Julia shares her impressions of Claudia's take on "right" and "wrong":

> I think that Claudia doesn't think there is a right or wrong way to teach but one that fits her beliefs and personality. That is what she wants me to find. There might be a right way for her, but I think she is open to other ways to teach. If it works for the kids and the teacher, that is how she would define right or wrong. (Julia, interview, 233–236)

Because teaching is so complex, devoid of the existence of a definitive "right" and "wrong" in the teacher inquiry movement, teachers position themselves professionally as questioners and risk takers, naming problems and dilemmas and studying them in a systematic, intentional way. Similarly, risk-taking is key to whom Claudia is as an inquiry-oriented mentor teacher. Encouraging risk-taking in Julia is another critical component to creating a context where Julia and Claudia can continue through the four components of an inquiry-oriented approach to mentoring together. Julia further describes Claudia as:

> . . . someone who is open to new ideas and willing to take risks. She is always encouraging me to take more risks. I think she takes risks in her own teaching. She will say, we will try it, but I don't know if it is going to work. (Julia, interview, 92–95)

Finally, in the teacher inquiry movement, teachers construct valuable knowledge about teaching and learning through raising and studying questions. This construction of knowledge becomes a natural process. Similarly, as they spiral through the four components of inquiry-oriented mentoring, Claudia wants Julia to understand the process as natural:

> I think one thing I want Julia to know is how easy it is to teach. In a sense it is a natural process. . . . This is all about natural dialogue and conversation. . . . It is truly a joint experience and it really isn't technical. . . . You need to come back to learning as a natural process, you know, discussion, dialogue, process-oriented activities, thinking, and thinking about your thinking. (Claudia, interview B, 82–90)

Claudia actualizes "discussion, dialogue, process-oriented activities, thinking, and thinking about your thinking" as she and Julia plan, teach, reflect, and pose problems with one another throughout the school year.

Co-Planning

From the very start of the internship, Claudia engages Julia as a partner in co-planning, the first of four components in the Cycle of Inquiry posed by this paper. Claudia and Julia regularly met for an extended period of time on Sunday afternoons to plan for the following week. This extended Sunday planning session was followed up during the week with frequent dialogues to refine and adapt instruction.

At the start of the internship, Claudia gives Julia insight into how she thinks about her own planning or teaching during these planning meetings. This takes the form of talking out loud in front of Julia so that Julia can gain insight into the teaching process and ultimately draw on that knowledge in her own teaching. For example, as part of the planning process Claudia said, "Julia, you have to realize that I am thinking out loud, and I am really just refining my ideas as I speak" (field notes). Julia recognizes the importance of Claudia talking or thinking out loud as they plan:

> I think she talks a lot out loud to me so that I understand her thinking, and I am the one who listens. (Julia, interview, 264–265)

As Julia moves from *listening* to Claudia's thinking to *engaging as a partner* in brainstorming the possibilities for lesson development, Claudia assists Julia in planning ways she might individualize instruction for different levels of learners as illustrated in this field note excerpt:

> Claudia and Julia talked about the organizational set up of the writing station and brainstormed the type of writing activities that Julia might use. Some of these connected to the current social studies unit. I asked Claudia about

how she prepared Julia for the different types of writers who would arrive at the center since the four groups she would work with were ability grouped. Claudia shared that she reviewed the types of things that she expects from each group and, then, in some specific cases for each child. She did this to highlight the differences in writers as well as how Julia could approach them as writers. At this point, she sent Julia to the writing table to gain some experience working with the children and construct an understanding of who each child is as a writer. Claudia and Julia would then discuss issues as they came up. (field notes)

As a part of the planning process, Claudia acknowledges moments in her work with Julia when she needs to be directive and provide specific feedback or instruction. Typically, Claudia provides this type of direction when she thinks Julia needs information or understandings that are beyond her current developmental perspective. In order to continually ascertain Julia's developmental perspective, Claudia believes communication during planning is critical. For example, early in the year Julia may not have been able to notice particular children's inappropriate behaviors as she taught because she was so consumed with the act of "doing" the teaching. However, through thoughtful communication during planning, Claudia is able to direct Julia in particular ways:

> If something is not working I am going to hear about it from Julia. So when I keep hearing about it, I am thinking I can then help her with what I hear her saying. For example, I hear management repeatedly so I say, this is what we are going to do. . . . Two-way communication is real important because I get to know some things that maybe she doesn't even realize she is saying but she says them several times. (Claudia, interview B, 522–526)

Claudia believes that direct feedback during planning is also influential as a way of enriching an already strong lesson:

> Even when she is doing a good job with her teaching, there are some times that I want to guide her along. Like if I notice that she might want to take this thinking a little further. This is a good opportunity to ask another question, "How can we get a little more mileage out of the lesson?" (Claudia, interview B, 163–167)

By stretching and challenging Julia during the planning, Claudia moves Julia beyond the minimum level of competence typically sought by cooperating teachers (Lemma, 1989).

During the planning process, Claudia also deliberately decides when to share materials and resources with Julia and when to encourage Julia to identify and explore other materials for instruction:

> Teacher resource books should be shared with the interns so they have some-
> thing to spin off of. That is our job as a mentor. It will give them some back-
> ground knowledge and conceptual understanding as well. That should be a
> major role of the mentor because you do have experience and familiarity with
> materials. (Claudia, interview B, 573–576)

Although Claudia recognizes the role she plays in sharing resources, she
also realizes there may be times to withhold resources so that Julia has the
space to independently identify and develop useful resources on her own.
Therefore, Claudia purposefully builds into co-planning a space for Julia to
develop independence as a planner, necessary for the day that her mentee
will have her own classroom.

In summary, co-planning, the first component in the Cycle of Inquiry,
is characterized by the following actions taken by the mentor teacher: (1)
setting aside a particular time to meet with the intern for the purpose of
planning; (2) "talking out loud" during planning so the intern can gain
insight into veteran teacher thinking; (3) helping to develop lessons collaboratively with the intern; (4) providing direct feedback to address problem
areas as well as to enhance teaching skills that are strong; and (5) sharing
resources that are pertinent to the planning at hand.

Co-Teaching

From the outset of the internship, Claudia engaged Julia as a partner
in teaching. In order to engage Julia as a partner, Claudia reflected on her
own teaching process and the ways she hoped this process would translate
to Julia:

> When I teach something for the first time . . . first, I become familiar with the
> new material myself. Then, after going through it, I compile the material in
> my head. The same things that stick out in my thinking are the things that
> other people highlight, but I don't know that until after I go through it on my
> own. I try the activities and then I refine them. With my experience this year,
> I will refine them some more . . . trying the refinements and then reworking
> and rethinking. That is the same thing I want Julia to do. I want her to have
> some information and then jump in at some point and try. Then go back and
> forth trying and rethinking. You know it is kind of like whole language. Whole
> language is about giving a context and exposing kids to reading and litera-
> ture. But then, you need to bring the children to the text and zero in on the
> skills. And then go back and forth between the whole and the part. (Claudia,
> interview B, 401–417)

Claudia creates a space where both she and Julia "jump in and try" the
act of teaching together very early in the internship year. She starts Julia out

in small group instruction. The students in the classroom are divided into four groups and rotate through four language arts stations each morning. At two of the four stations, the learners work independently. Claudia teaches at the reading station and asks Julia to teach writing at one station at the same time Claudia teaches reading. In this sense, co-teaching involves capitalizing on two adults in the classroom to provide small group instruction to different groups simultaneously. Instruction by mentor and mentee can be tailored to the unique attributes of each different group of learners. This arrangement also creates the context for Julia to "jump in and try" teaching in developmentally-appropriate ways for a novice teacher and, subsequently, to "go back and forth trying and rethinking" as she teaches adaptations of the same writing lessons to four separate groups of learners.

Claudia has a sense of Julia's teaching, even when she is teaching at the same time. This concept of "indirect observation" is similar to the notion of a teacher having "eyes in the back of her head":

> Even though she is usually teaching at the same time, she has an idea of what is going on all around the room. She may not know the details but she has a general idea. Julia shares that after her lessons they talk, and Claudia asks questions and she asks Claudia questions. (field notes)

Since they plan together, Claudia knows what Julia's teaching objectives and activities will be even before the lesson begins. This understanding of the lesson, paired with their collaborative teaching style, creates an approach to supervision that is somewhat unique to inquiry-oriented mentoring. Understanding this intuitive approach to mentoring provides insight into why written observation sheets are not as highly valued and often rarely completed by mentor teachers. The power of Claudia's "eyes in the back of her head" approach to supervision comes from her intimate understanding of her intern's abilities, their collaborative planning, a collegial relationship, and the intuitive nature of their work over an extended period of time. Claudia begins her mentoring using this intuitive sense of whom Julia is as a teacher as a starting point for observing, and then Claudia follows up these "observations from afar" by engaging Julia in conversation. By acknowledging and recognizing Claudia's ability to "know" at some level about Julia's work without direct observation, mentoring as a form of supervision can take less structured paths.

Claudia also acknowledges the importance of Julia taking on a multitude of teaching roles:

> I think that the interns need to get a feel for the many roles a teacher has and what it takes to get each of the roles done. I think the mentor needs to make sure that they have many experiences, not always teaching small groups, or working at the writing stations, or on recess duty. The roles need to rotate.

> That is real important that the roles change and that takes a lot of organiza-
> tion. (Claudia, interview B, 627–631)

One role Claudia engages Julia in throughout the internship is whole
group instruction. However, rather than one teacher delivering the whole
group instruction, both mentor and mentee teach as a "tag-team":

> We really have a community in our classroom, not just with the kids, but with
> us too. That allows us to play off of each other and jump in and support and
> add to each other's teaching. There are many times when I need Julia to help
> me do something. We talk to each other as we teach, "Now Miss T is going to
> come around and hand out the papers." It doesn't have to interrupt instruc-
> tion. . . . It is working off each other. I try to include Julia a lot—"I don't know
> Miss T, it is awful noisy in here today. What's going on?" The students just
> play right into that. It also keeps them on their toes. (Claudia, Interview B,
> 169–176)

At the start of the internship, it was more typical for Julia to take a supportive role and Claudia to lead during their tag-team whole group instruction. However, as the PDS year progressed, both Claudia and Julia would
move in and out of supporting and leading roles as they collaborated to
deliver whole group instruction:

> Julia and Claudia stood near the center of the room as the children busied
> themselves at their seats. They talked quietly to each other posing alternatives
> to how to organize the activity and what kind of feedback to give the children.
> Julia and Claudia collaborated to give directions to the children. They seemed
> comfortable in "feeding off" of each other. The interaction is supportive and
> appears to be reciprocal in nature. While the children work, they share ideas
> about how to help the children with creating the Paddington Bear and then
> they cooperatively offer advice to the children. (field notes)

In summary, co-teaching, the second component in the Cycle of Inquiry,
is characterized by mentor and mentee teaching different small groups of
students simultaneously as well as mentor and mentee "tag teaming" during
whole group instruction. Claudia appreciates Julia's willingness to play the
role of collaborator in the act of teaching. A natural outgrowth of collaborating on the act of teaching is debriefing the teaching experience after
delivery of a lesson. Claudia and Julia co-reflect.

Co-Reflecting

From the outset of the internship, Claudia engaged Julia in reflecting
on practice. Schon (1989) describes reflection as largely a solitary action

occurring in two time frames. "Reflection on action" occurs after an action as a way of thinking about a completed lesson. "Reflection in action" occurs during a lesson. Zeichner and Liston (1996) and Day (1993) suggest that the solitary nature of the reflection process described by Schon is limiting and acknowledge the dialogic nature of reflection. The dialogic and collaborative nature of much of Claudia and Julia's reflective conversation indicate the social dynamic of reflection and suggests a movement from Schon's concepts of "reflection in action" and "reflection on action" to a socially constructed "co-reflection in action" and "co-reflection on action." However, for Claudia and Julia, engagement in dialogic co-reflection on action depended upon the space for solitary reflection to occur first.

For example, Julia comes to understand early in the internship year that as much as reflection on action with Claudia is critical and important to learning to teach, she must be patient and honor Claudia's time to regroup and think for herself during the school day before they co-reflect on a lesson.

> I learned not to talk to Claudia during snack time very early in the internship year. That was hard because sometimes I would see something during stations and want to ask her about that. But it was too hard to talk then, and I know Claudia valued that time for talking to the children and regrouping. (Julia, interview, 312–315)

Although lunch time might be a logical time to engage in reflective dialogue on action, Claudia spent much of her lunch period in the classroom alone gathering her thoughts:

> Claudia mentioned how she really needed time to regroup after spending a very intense morning organizing and interacting with everyone. She also mentioned that she is a person who likes to have quiet time to think and to gather her thoughts. (field notes)

After the children leave for the day, Claudia and Julia return to the room and work independently trying to clean up and gather their materials for the next day. This is a valued component of the day:

> We don't talk that much right after school. In fact, sometimes long stretches of time will go by where we are independently working and thinking. But we are both just doing our stuff. I know Claudia needs time to herself to think and plan, and she is talking to the children and me all day long. She needs some time to regroup and do her own thing. (Julia, interview, 338–343)

Similar to co-teaching, one way that co-reflecting on action plays out for Claudia and Julia is that each honors the others' time and space to think about particular lessons that occurred during the day. In essence, they each have times (during snack, during lunch, and immediately following dismissal) when they are reflecting on the day simultaneously, but silently and independently. It is after this independent simultaneous reflection that they engage in dialogue and discuss their thinking with each other.

Interesting, as the internship year progressing, Claudia intentionally and purposefully pulls Julia back from teaching responsibilities and places her in the role of observer. This action is antithetical to many student teaching programs where student teachers begin as observers and then slowly take on teaching responsibilities until they successfully "solo" for the final weeks of the semester. Claudia's thoughtful repositioning of Julia from teacher to observer later in the internship year is a tactic Claudia enlists as an inquiry-oriented mentor to stimulate deeper and further co-reflection on action with Julia.

During the year, Claudia realized that, although Julia had made tremendous progress in her teaching and was actually quite competent, she felt responsible for moving Julia beyond the level of competence. She believed that moving Julia beyond competence could be facilitated by returning Julia to an observational role in areas where she was excelling. As a result, Claudia shifted Julia's role in various activities away from the "doing" of teaching back to the "observing" of teaching. This shift offered Julia the opportunity to observe from a new developmental position that resulted in her noticing new aspects of the teaching/learning context. For example, since Julia now had experience teaching, the observations provided the opportunity for Julia to make connections by juxtaposing her own teaching with Claudia's teaching. This allowed Julia to compare and contrast their approaches and raise questions about her own teaching. This technique facilitates Julia's continued learning about teaching beyond the level of competence and brought the reflective dialogue Claudia and Julia engaged in after school to a new level.

In addition to facilitating reflection *on* action, to facilitate co-reflection *in* action, throughout the internship year, Julia and Claudia would dialogue with one another during the teaching act. At times, however, Claudia also intentionally and purposefully refuses to answer some of the questions Julia poses as they reflect in action:

> To some extent, I know Julia looks at me traditionally, like I have the answers and she looks to me to tell them to her. Whereas I feel, she really has a lot of answers, and some of it she needs to get by doing. She has the major things thought out but now she needs to work on the details . . . Sometimes she will ask me a question as she is teaching and I will just put my head down so that she has to decide. (Claudia, interview B, 128–135)

Claudia deliberately disengages in co-reflection in action because she wants Julia to learn to problem solve as she teaches.

As Claudia mentors, she experiences a tension between when to give Julia specific feedback and when to let her independently problem solve. Her decision regarding when to use each is connected to her beliefs about knowledge construction being a critical component of intern growth. To these ends, Claudia encourages Julia to consider possibilities thoughtfully, take thoughtful risks, carry out the lesson, and then revise as evidenced in the following:

> The intern needs to put some thought into what they are doing, so it isn't solely trial and error. However, I do believe in trial and error and risk-taking, but there is thought going on before each trial. Someone that is thinking rather than just trying. . . . That is the pattern. (Claudia, interview B, 103–108, interview)

Julia seems to understand the responsibility of coupling trial and error with thoughtful reflection as she is mentored by Claudia:

> I know I have to do it wrong to find out it is wrong. I think Claudia believes this too. A lot of times she just lets me think about my choice because she knows that I am figuring out what works myself as I experiment. She thinks that I learned from my mistakes. (Julia, interview, 230–233)

While Claudia makes deliberate choices during co-reflective dialogue to not answer Julia's questions and let Julia make mistakes, Claudia discusses the important role Julia's voice plays in Claudia's own reflection as she poses questions about teaching. For example, Claudia shares that Julia will ask questions about past, current, or future lessons. In response, Claudia often asks Julia for her thinking, and then together they brainstorm specific solutions or ideas. Claudia believes that Julia's questions raise her own thinking on that topic to a more conscious level because the questions require her to make her own thinking explicit for Julia. Claudia's own thinking about teaching often evolves through this process. Hence, just as Claudia serves to take Julia's level of self reflection to deeper levels as the internship year unfolds, Julia takes Claudia's self reflection to deeper levels as well. This reciprocal reflective relationship leads to greater learning, and shares similarities with the literature of critical friends. Sagor (1993) defines critical friends as:

> A person who has your interests at heart when she gives you constructive criticism. This person's outside vantage point allows her to see your weaknesses better than you can, but because this person is a friend, she's likely to be critical of your weaknesses in a positive way. She is critiquing you because she cares about you. (p. 46)

Through co-reflection, Claudia and Julia form a caring relationship that enables them to embrace the complexity of teaching and learning to teach and problem solve together throughout the PDS year. To the inquiry-oriented mentor, however, the process of problem solving with a mentee must not overshadow another critical attribute of inquiry oriented mentoring—problem posing. Schon (1989) highlights the difference between problem solving and problem posing:

> In the process of problem solving . . . problems of choice or decision are solved through the selection, from available means, of the one best suited to the established ends. Here we ignore problem setting, the process by which we define the decision to be made, the ends to be achieved, the means which may be chosen. (p. 10)

In summary, co-reflecting, the third component in the Cycle of Inquiry, is characterized by the following actions taken by the mentor teacher: (1) safeguarding time such as snack, lunch, and after-school for intern and mentor to reflect silently and independently; (2) repositioning the intern from the teacher to an observer role late in the internship year to stimulate deeper reflection; and (3) deliberately not answering interns' questions so the intern learns to problem solve on her own. The process by which a teacher identifies, defines, and frames a problem is of central importance to learning. Claudia brings to her mentoring the keen ability to pose problems or issues in her work.

Co-Problem Posing

From the start of the internship, Julia noticed that problem posing was a critical component of teaching through her observation of Claudia in the process. According to Julia,

> . . . posing problems is a part of what Claudia does everyday . . . One example she tells me about is how she wonders about something, and then she goes home and really thinks about it, and then she tries something. There is action with the thinking. Doing something new and trying new ways. (Julia, interview, 415–419)

Claudia shares the following comments about making her work problematic:

> I understand making my work problematic is looking at things that don't run smoothly and looking at things year after year. Teaching is not static. We are dealing with human beings, and those interactions are not static. So you

constantly have to be looking at the uniqueness of your classroom community and adjust accordingly. I think making your work problematic feels interesting to me. (Claudia, interview B, 427–433)

Throughout the school year, Claudia constantly investigates her own development as a teacher by making her work with specific children problematic, by posing questions to herself, observing carefully, thinking, and making changes. She invites Julia to be a part of this process by sharing her wonderings out loud with Julia, and asking Julia to articulate wonderings of her own.

Perhaps the most visible way Claudia and Julia problem pose together was during the second half of the internship year when Julia was required to conduct teacher research as a part of the PDS responsibilities. As discussed earlier, teacher research is a vehicle for developing a problem-posing stance to teaching and has been defined as "systematic and intentional inquiry by teachers" (Cochran-Smith & Lytle, 1993). In this case, Julia took the lead and shouldered the responsibility for monitoring and completing the research. However, Claudia co-participated in the inquiry as they selected a wondering, attended a conference together that supported their inquiry question, and engaged in dialogue, planning, and interpretation of the data as it was collected.

Julia and Claudia's research question focused on a particular child who had poor auditory processing skills and auditory memory but excellent visual processing skills. This child was struggling with all subjects, but was especially discouraged and falling behind in reading. In contrast to most of her peers, she did not know many sounds and confused many letters of the alphabet. Claudia and Julia also noted that this struggling child loved to sing and was extremely musical.

Although the official focus on teacher research during the PDS year did not begin until January, Claudia began the problem-posing process of crafting a teacher research question with Julia in October:

Julia and I discussed our inquiry project back in October, so she really had time to think about it. I think if everyone was thinking about that from the beginning it would help. (Claudia, interview B, 7–12)

From October through January, Claudia and Julia observed this child and engaged in an ongoing dialogue to contemplate how they might problematize the struggles she was experiencing as a learner in their classroom. This illustrates the careful deliberation necessary to frame a good problem. As a result of engagement in this careful deliberation with Claudia over many months, Julia framed her teacher research in the following way:

> After witnessing the Instructional Support Process and observing Meg strug-
> gle throughout the year with reading, I wanted to find a way to help her. The
> first thing that came to my mind was music. I not only noticed that Meg was a
> wonderful singer but that she remembered songs very easily, so I hoped that
> music might work well with her auditory memory and processing difficulties.
> I hoped there was some way I could connect music to reading. I wondered,
> "In what ways could I utilize music to help Meg become a better reader?"
> and "How might music help her combat some frustrations when reading and
> boost her self esteem?" (Julia, Teacher Research Report, p. 2)

Claudia was clearly supportive of this classroom-based research and emphasized the value of collaborating in inquiry:

> I think the beauty of the whole inquiry is the fact that we collaborated on the
> work together. Julia and I did a lot of talking about the student through the
> inquiry project, although she had more of the formal responsibility. But I
> think that the collaboration is more productive than both of us doing teacher
> research alone, in isolation. (field notes)

Julia also values their collaboration on teacher research. She believes
that the research might have been less meaningful if she had worked alone
because she didn't have the same experience base from which to draw as
she observed and made sense of the observations. When Julia collaborates
with Claudia in thinking about this child, Claudia provides alternative insights and often deeper meanings behind some of Julia's sense making of
the observations.

In turn, Julia's presence in Claudia's classroom spawns a different teacher
research project for Claudia. An area of problem posing to which Claudia
devoted prominent attention throughout the school year was "How can I be
an effective teacher educator?" Claudia demonstrates a passion for inquiring into her role as a teacher educator:

> This is really exciting. I am trying to see if I can teach someone else to teach.
> This allows me to broaden my teaching and brings me out of isolation. (field
> notes)

Claudia's commitment to Julia's growth makes inquiry into her work as
a teacher educator important. Throughout the year, as Julia collects and
analyzes data on the struggling learner in their class, Claudia informally
collects and analyzes data related to her question—"How could I become
a better teacher educator for Julia?" Through this process, Claudia partici-
pates in an ongoing form of informal inquiry, a type of problem posing into
her own work as a teacher educator, that introduces a new level of reflection
into Claudia's work life as a mentor teacher in the PDS. Stanulis (1995) discusses a similar situation in a Michigan State PDS where reflection reached

a new level when teachers examined their own roles as teacher educators. To these ends, Claudia's problem-posing stance facilitates growth for both her and Julia as they collaboratively frame questions, explore alternatives, collect relevant data, and cycle in and out of the problem posing, reflecting, planning, and teaching components of an inquiry-oriented approach to mentoring together.

CONCLUSIONS

Working side-by-side with her intern Julia, Claudia crafts a form of mentoring that merges her roles of inquirer and teacher educator, allowing both Julia and Claudia to adopt an inquiry stance to their collaborative work. Underpinning this stance is a recognition of the complexity of teaching, a context that supports risk-taking and experimentation, and a focus on construction of new knowledge. These underpinnings provide the prerequisites for Claudia's cycle of inquiry-oriented mentoring.

Based on this foundation for inquiry-oriented mentoring, Claudia and Julia offer insights into the process of spiraling through the four component cycles that include co-planning, co-teaching, co-reflection, and co-problem, posing with new knowledge construction occurring upon each rotation. Claudia and Julia's experience provides a description of each of these components as well as introduces some salient elements that emerge within each phase of the cycle. For example, within the co-planning phase, Claudia provides both *directive* and *stretching* feedback depending on Julia's developmental needs at that specific moment. During the co-teaching phase, Claudia uses a variety of strategies including station teaching, team teaching, and one teach-one observe and introduces the concepts of *indirect observation* and *observation from afar*, providing insight into the type of observation typically valued by mentor teachers. In moving to the co-reflection phase, Claudia's work introduces the importance of beginning with *solitary reflection* before moving to *collaborative reflection* focused on the social construction of knowledge. An additional feature of this mentoring component is Claudia's *intentional repositioning* as a tool for providing an experiential text for deepening Julia's reflection on teaching. Finally, collaborative problem-posing existed as a daily, natural outgrowth of their co-reflection. However, Claudia and Julia's work provides an example of how the problem-posing dialogue that existed within their shared work space can serve as a *springboard for practitioner inquiry*.

Although inquiry-oriented mentoring shows promise as a tool for novice and practicing teacher knowledge construction, we are left with a few significant questions. For example, are all mentors and interns capable of engaging in this style of mentoring? What are the strengths and weaknesses of this approach? What are the barriers and facilitators to using this approach to mentoring? What are the prerequisite knowledge, skills, abilities, and dispositions necessary for mentors and interns to possess in order to engage in this approach? What do novice teachers learn as a result of receiving this type of mentoring at various stages in their development? Are there particular points in one's career when this approach is most viable? These and other related questions need further exploration.

Claudia's inquiry-oriented approach to mentoring is consistent with the work of Garmston, Lipton, and Kaiser (1998) who suggest that one of the functions of supervision is to develop an individual educator's potential for learning. They suggest that an inquiry-oriented supervisory process, similar to Claudia's approach to mentoring, will result in "self-directed practitioners who engage in a problem-posing, problem-solving stance toward their practices" (p. 245). They add:

> Supervision of this type requires an understanding and application of psychological dynamics that is developmentally appropriate and challenges individuals toward a greater ability to think abstractly, work strategically, and operate with a clear, conscious intention. It will require supervisors to become continually more conscious regarding their own thinking and meaning making, to engage in reflection regarding their own practice, and to model self-directed, problem-solving behaviors. (p. 245)

Sharing many of the same qualities of inquiry-oriented supervision, this study serves to explicate what inquiry-oriented mentoring looks like and the ways this approach to mentoring supports novice teacher development. Garmston, Lipton, and Kaiser (1998) suggest that this is the type of supervision that will result in Sergiovanni's (1992) vision of a "day when supervision will no longer be needed" (p. 203). The case of Claudia and Julia bring mentors, interns, university researchers, and teacher educators one step closer to that day. Yet, a great deal of additional research is needed to understand the complexities of co-planning, co-teaching, co-reflecting, and co-problem posing. With each research study that is conducted on inquiry-oriented mentoring, we gain insights not only into the process of mentoring but the implications powerful mentoring has to make traditional forms of supervision obsolete. Inquiry-oriented mentoring holds a great deal of promise to improve and transform initial teacher preparation and practice. Because of the explicit focus on teacher education and inquiry as well as the intensity of field experiences in professional development schools, PDSs provide a unique context to learn more about mentoring and new forms of supervision. The PDS context holds tremendous potential for learning not only for novice and veteran teachers but for researchers interested in transforming supervision and mentoring for new teachers (Yendol-Hoppey & Dana, 2007). The transformation of supervision and mentoring within the PDS context will create much more powerful experiences for novices that serve to accelerate their growth and development, ultimately leading to stronger teaching in all of our schools.

REFERENCES

Carnegie Forum on Education and the Economy. (1986). *A nation prepared: Teachers for the 21st century: The report of the Task Force on Teaching as a Profession.* Washington, DC: The Forum.

Carr, W., & Kemmis, S. (1986). *Becoming critical: Knowing through action research.* Geelong, Victoria: Deakin University Press.

Cochran-Smith, M., & Lytle, S. L. (1993). *Inside/outside: Teacher research and knowledge.* New York: Teachers College Press.

Cochran-Smith, M., & Lytle, S. L. (1999). The teacher research movement: A decade later. *Educational Researcher, 28*(7), 15–25.

Cochran-Smith, M., & Lytle, S. L. (2001). Beyond certainty: Taking an inquiry stance on practice. In A. Lieberman & L. Miller (Eds.), *Teachers caught in the action: Professional development that matters* (pp. 45–58). New York: Teachers College Press.

Dana, N. F., Silva, D. Y., & Snow-Gerono, J. S. (2002). Building a culture of inquiry in professional development schools. *Teacher Education and Practice, 15*(4), 71–89.

Dana, N. F., & Silva, D. Y. (2002). Building an inquiry oriented PDS: Inquiry as a part of mentor teacher work. In I. N. Guadarrama, J. Nath, & J. Ramsey (Eds.), *Forging alliances in community and thought: Research in professional development schools* (pp. 87–104), Greenwich, CT: Information Age Publishing.

Dana, N. F., & Yendol-Silva. (2003). *The reflective educator's guide to classroom research: Learning to teach and teaching to learn through practitioner inquiry.* Thousand Oaks, CA: Corwin Press.

Darling-Hammond, L. (Ed.). (1994). *Professional development schools: Schools for developing a profession.* New York: Teachers College Press.

Day, C. (1993). Reflection: A necessary but not sufficient condition of professional development. *British Educational Research Journal, 19*(1), 83–93.

Denzin, N. K., & Lincoln, Y. S. (1994). *Handbook of qualitative research.* Thousand Oaks, CA: Sage.

Erickson, F. (1986). Qualitative methods in research on teaching. In. M.C. Wittrock (Ed.), *Handbook on research of teaching* (3rd ed., pp.119–161). New York: Macmillan.

Garmston, R. J., Lipton, L. E., & Kaiser, K. (1998). In G. R. Firth & E. F. Pajak (Eds.), *Handbook of research on school supervision* (pp. 242–286). New York: Simon & Schuster Macmillan.

Goetz, J., & LeCompte, M. (1984). *Ethnography and qualitative design in educational research.* San Diego: Academic Press.

Hoffman, N. E., Reed, W. M., & Rosenbluth, G. S. (1997). *Lessons from restructuring experiences: Stories of change in professional development schools.* Albany: State University of New York Press.

Holmes Group. (1990). *Tomorrow's schools: Principles for the design of professional development schools.* East Lansing, MI: Author.

Holmes Group. (1986). *Tomorrow's teachers.* East Lansing, MI: Author.

Kincheloe, J. L. (1993). *Teachers as researchers: Qualitative inquiry as a path to empowerment.* New York: Falmer Press.

Koerner, M. (1992). The cooperating teacher: An ambivalent partner in student teaching. *Journal of Teacher Education, 43*(1), 46–56.

Lemma, P. (1993). The cooperating teacher as supervisor: A case study. *Journal of Curriculum and Supervision, 8*(4) 329–342.

Lieberman, A., & Miller, L. (1990). Teacher development in professional practice schools. *Teachers College Record, 92*(1), 105–122.

Levine, M., & Trachtman, R. (Eds.). (1997). *Making professional development schools work: Politics, practice and policy.* New York: Teachers College Press.

McKernan, J. (1988). Teacher as researcher: Paradigm and praxis. *Contemporary Education, 59*(3), 154–158.

Miller, J. L. (1990). *Creating spaces and finding voices: Teachers collaborating for empowerment.* Albany: State University of New York Press.

National Commission on Teaching and America's Future. (1983). *A nation at risk.* Washington, DC.

Oberg, A. (1990). Methods and meanings in action research: The action research journal. *Theory into Practice, 29*(3), 214–221.

Patton, M. Q. (1990). *Qualitative evaluation and research methods.* Newbury Park, CA: Sage.

Sagor, R. (1993). *How to conduct collaborative action research.* Association for supervision and curriculum development, Alexandria, VA: Author.

Schon, D. A. (1989). A symposium on Schon's concept of reflective practice: Critiques, commentaries, illustrations, quotations. *Journal of Curriculum and Supervision, 5*(1), 6–9.

Sergiovanni, T. J. (1992). *The moral dimensions of leadership.* San Francisco: Jossey-Bass.

Silva, D. Y., & Dana, N. F. (2001). Collaborative supervision in the professional development school. *Journal of Curriculum and Supervision, 16*(4), 305–321.

Silva, D. Y., & Dana, N. F. (2004). Encountering new spaces: Teachers developing voice within a professional development school. *Journal of Teacher Education, 55*(2), 128–140.

Stake, R. (1995). *The art of case study research.* Thousand Oaks, CA: Sage.

Stanulis, R. N. (1995). Classroom teachers as mentors: Possibilities for participation in a professional development school. *Teaching and Teacher Education, 11*(4), 331–344.

Wang, J. (2001). Contexts of mentoring and opportunities for learning to teach: A comparative study of mentoring practice. *Teaching and Teacher Education, 17*(51–73).

Wolcott, H. (1994). *Transforming qualitative data: Description, analysis, and interpretation.* Thousand Oaks, CA: Sage.

Yendol-Hoppey, D. (in press). Mentor teachers work with prospective teachers in a newly formed professional development school: Two conceptual illustrations. *Teachers College Record.*

Yendol-Hoppey, D., & Dana, N. F. (2006). Understanding and theorizing exemplary mentoring through the use of metaphor: The case study of Bridgett, a gardener. In J. R. Dangel (Ed.), *Induction and mentoring in teacher education: Teacher education yearbook XIV* (pp. 111–123), Lanham, MD: Scarecrow Press.

Yendol-Hoppey, D., & Dana, N. F. (2007). *The reflective educator's guide to mentoring: Stengthening practice through knowledge, story and metaphor.* Thousand Oaks, CA: Corwin Press.

Zeichner, K. M., & Liston, D. P. (1996). *Reflective teaching: An introduction.* Mahwah, NJ: Lawrence Erlbaum Associates.

CHAPTER 16

PROFESSIONAL DEVELOPMENT SCHOOLS

Mentoring Checklist to Enhance Effective Practices

Jennifer E. Aldrich, Sharon L. Lamson, Beverly Wallace, and Sherrie Carter

ABSTRACT

Faculty at our institution and our public school partners actively collaborate to improve the learning experience for the interns in our profession development school (PDS) sites. A Pre-Service Teacher Observation Log Guide (Checklist) for mentoring interns was developed and piloted. This chapter presents the expectations and concerns of the clinical faculty that mentor interns, the development and use of the checklist, and the results obtained from it. Qualitative data from the mentor teachers at four levels and quantitative data from student completed Checklists are included. The purpose of the collaboration, the Checklist, and the study was to promote effective practices in the professional development of pre-service teachers.

University and School Connections, pages 275–293
Copyright © 2008 by Information Age Publishing
All rights of reproduction in any form reserved.

275

INTRODUCTION

People believe that well prepared teachers are the best hope for school reform. Teacher education is an important component of education reform since effective teachers produce higher student learning. Therefore, calls for reform in education have exerted pressure to change the system of education of teachers (Association of Teacher Educators, 1986; Cobb, 2001; Goodlad, 1990; Ishler, 1995). School reform efforts have proposed that future teachers attain knowledge and experience from practicing teachers in collaboration with university teacher educators. The professional development school (PDS) program at one regional Midwest University is a field-based approach in which education majors spend several hours a week the semester before student teaching working in public school classrooms.

PDSs not only prepare future teachers and students but also support clinical faculty's (practicing teachers) and university faculty's learning. Linda Darling-Hammond (1998) wrote, "Teachers learn best by studying, doing, and reflecting; by collaborating with other teachers; by looking closely at their students and their work; and by sharing what they see" (p. 8). Professional development school collaborative partnerships take time to develop but can make a difference in continued professional growth of teachers and pre-service teachers. The collaborative efforts between our university faculty members and clinical faculty at several professional development schools support the National Council for Accreditation of Teacher Education (NCATE, 2001) standards.

NCATE developed standards that address the desired characteristics of professional development schools. One of the five standards used to describe the purposes and principles of the PDS centers around collaboration (NCATE, 2001). The elements of collaboration include an ability to synthesize ideas, practices, and emotional investment of a diverse group with diverse goals and often become key to the success of many PDS programs. Thus, we used the NCATE definition of collaboration to guide our PDS partnership work. NCATE (2001) defines collaboration thus:

> PDS partners and partner institutions systematically move from independent to interdependent practice by committing themselves and committing to each other to engage in joint work focused on implementing the PDS mission. They collaboratively design roles and structures to support the PDS work and individual and institutional parity. PDS partners use their shared work to improve outcomes for P–12 students, candidates, faculty, and other professionals. The PDS partnership systematically recognizes and celebrates their joint work and the contributions of each partner. (p. 23)

The specific collaborative activities of the partnership of clinical faculty, university faculty, and pre-service teachers described in this chapter support the ideas of the NCATE standards and strive to improve learning outcomes for P–12 students by preparing effective future teachers.

The purpose of this chapter is to share the way that faculty at our institution, along with our public school partners, maintained an active network that fostered collaboration, resulting in the development of the Pre-service Teacher Observation Log Guide (called "Checklist"), used for mentoring interns in Professional Development School sites. In this chapter, we present the expectations and concerns of the mentor teachers who worked with interns in their classrooms, and we focus on how a newly developed mentoring Checklist was employed and evaluated during the 2004–2005 school year. The overall purpose of the collaboration and the Checklist was to promote effective practices in the professional preparation of pre-service teachers.

BACKGROUND

Over many years at this institution, university and clinical faculty (mentor teachers) have worked together with student teachers. This usually entailed moving university students from undergraduate coursework into the schools for a traditional student teaching semester under the supervision of clinical faculty and a university supervisor. Frequently, the university supervisor was an adjunct faculty member whose only responsibility to the university and teacher education was the supervision of student teachers and a lunch during the middle of the semester. University supervisors and clinical faculty were rarely trained in any depth on the state standards used for evaluation, the objectives and goals for the various programs within the university, or the specific needs of individual classes. In addition, the hosting districts, with more thought to district needs than to university or student teacher needs, selected clinical faculty members. Thus, university supervisors and clinical faculty often supervised from a generic set of guidelines, usually based on their own experiences in the classroom.

Changes to the status quo are evident. The early childhood, elementary, and middle school majors in the Department of Curriculum and Instruction experience a semester-long professional development school (PDS) experience before they have their the traditional semester-long student teaching experience. The PDS interns (pre-service teachers) spend approximately 4–6 hours per week in public school classrooms with mentor teachers where they apply the information learned in their PDS senior block classes.

Because of long-term and complex collaborations within and between PDS sites, we engage in sharing and matching expectations. These include the standards and goals, expectations of the classroom, and the ways to share the information with interns that is organized and useful. Thus, university faculty and mentor teachers collaboratively envisioned, developed, reviewed, and implemented the Pre-service Teacher Observation Log Guide (Checklist) to guide university faculty, mentor teachers, and interns during the PDS semester.

TRAINING

Training I

During the 2004 PDS Annual Summer Institute for Professional Development School sites, the new Pre-Service Teacher Observation Log Guide (Checklist) was presented to the entire mentoring faculty as a way to work with both PDS interns and student teachers. The training session lasted one hour at the beginning of the Summer Institute. The primary author of the Checklist, a third grade teacher and PDS site coordinator, introduced the Checklist and explained why it had been developed. She told the 110 participants that the impetus for the checklist had been her experience with a student teacher who did not make satisfactory progress in the classroom. The student teacher kept saying to her mentor, "But you never told me." The classroom teacher thought she had, but she had no record of the conversations and no evidence to support her memory. Thus, the teacher began a list of items she discussed with her PDS interns and student teachers, which then morphed into the checklist.

Another reason for developing the Checklist was the fact that most student teachers and PDS interns and their mentor teachers started out talking about the student teaching process and progress, but invariably the conversation moved to the children in the classroom. This natural inclination reduced the amount of time devoted to discussion of other professional responsibilities; thus, the Checklist would anchor discussions about professional growth.

As presented to the PDS Summer Institute participants, the Checklist was offered as a tool to focus discussions with mentees and to provide opportunities for the mentees to ask specific questions and to observe specific behaviors from the perspective of a well-rounded educational professional, not just the person who is transmitting discrete pieces of information to children. While the original impetus for the Checklist targeted student teachers and PDS interns, the use and research of the Checklist focused on PDS interns.

Training II

The second part of the training at the 2004 Summer Institute consisted of the participants taking time to read the Checklist and to discuss it with each other. This discussion enabled the teachers and administrators to operationalize their understanding of the items and to think about how the process could be implemented in their own classrooms. After about twenty minutes of discussion, the participants asked a few clarifying questions and brought forth four points the development team had not considered. The first point was, "Who would handle the paper trail?" Some felt that the classroom teacher should initiate all discussions and keep track of the Checklist; others felt the pre-service teachers should demonstrate their burgeoning professionalism and initiate the conversations and manage the Checklist. Yet another group felt that it should be a shared relationship. At the end of the discussion, it became apparent that the person who initiates the specific conversations and handled the paper should be an individual mentor's decision, based on the mentoring style of the teacher and the preparation level of the pre-service teacher being mentored.

A second point was that, even though the Checklist had been designed in a way that it could be used at any level of teaching (from early childhood through high school) there may be more variation in those levels than first thought. The Checklist might need to be modified, based on the data collected at the end of the school year to see if, in fact, grade level made a significant difference in the topics for mentoring pre-service teachers.

A third point centered around the discussion at the middle school level, that the university faculty and mentor teachers already had many of the items of the Checklist already included in their forms and procedures. As a result of this discussion, the middle school university faculty members modified their previous forms to be subsumed by the Checklist or used the Checklist as a central record keeping document.

A fourth point was brought forward by the secondary educators, when they stated that using the Checklist presented unique challenges for the secondary PDS. The secondary educators immediately saw items, particularly those relating to section E (*Special needs and services*) as problematic. Due to the way that issues pertaining to students with special needs are handled at these educational levels, the mentor teachers and administrators felt that allowing pre-service students access to documentation needed for discussion would violate students' rights to confidentiality.

Alternately, university faculty brought up a positive point about the checklist. They pointed out that some of the topics on the Checklist were discussed during the building tour given by the principal; by the teachers who come to the class to speak on various topics such as assessment, discipline, professional development, and special needs; and during class by the university faculty. Thus, the PDS interns could receive the information from the Checklist from multiple sources that would reduce the burden on individual mentor teachers.

After the discussion phase of the training, two of the university developers talked about the procedural aspects of the process and the data collection process at the end of each semester. The human subjects review approval process was shared, and the dissemination of the needed forms, color-coded for grade level, was explained.

Post-Training Conversations

The training ended at that point, and the rest of the evening's program continued. It was interesting, however, that the conversations continued about the Checklist, and many participants sought out the developers and thanked them for the effort. The overall feeling was positive. Several PDS sites chose to incorporate additional study of these items as part of their commitment to the PDS study groups. Several principals stated that they intended to use the Checklist with their new teachers. The district superintendents in attendance encouraged their administrators to use the Checklist. All in all, the initial response to the Checklist was positive.

PILOT STUDY

Method

A pilot program to evaluate the value of the "Pre-service Observation Log Guide" (Checklist) was initiated in the fall of 2004 at ten PDS sites. The instrument used was a 41-item Likert scale checklist (see appendix for the checklist). Within the categories of routines, curriculum, discipline, instruction, special needs and services, professional development and potential opportunities, this Checklist addressed the concepts of respect, organization, duties, responsibilities and intern initiative during the spring 2004 semester in eight PDS sites.

University faculty supplied and explained the Checklist to the interns at their individual PDS sites. The interns (n = 192) were asked to check off each item that was addressed during their semester in the PDS placement. The mentor teachers, university faculty, or guest speakers (i.e., principal or guidance counselor) addressed the items, and interns recorded their in-depth involvement in various items. University faculty collected the Checklists from PDS interns at the end of the fall 2004 and spring 2005 semesters. A research assistant tabulated the data. In addition, the qualitative feedback and comments from the mentor teachers were collected at the 2005 PDS Annual Summer Institute. The results of the pilot study are reported in three categories: mentor teacher qualitative feedback, analysis of the Checklist, and descriptive statistics (Gall, Borg, & Gall, 1996).

At the end of the first year, the mentor teachers at our professional development school (PDS) sites met for the 2005 PDS Summer Institute. The Checklist was introduced at the 2004 Summer Institute and presented as a way to work with both PDS interns and student teachers. It was discussed and evaluated by the mentor teachers. However, the focus of implementation and discussion about the Checklist centered on PDS intern experiences. The following are salient comments from each group of mentor teachers.

PDS Sites

Early Childhood.   The early childhood PDS grew into two sites. The first site was one building with all kindergarten classrooms. There were eight (of ten) mentor teachers at the 2004 PDS Annual Summer Institute. The second early childhood PDS was established in the spring of 2005 with classrooms from preschool through second grade. The mentor teachers did not attend the 2004 PDS Summer Institute but received training by the university faculty member and participated in the Checklist.

Elementary.   There were five elementary PDS sites in four different school districts. Each PDS site was unique with preschool through fifth grade, first through third grade, or fourth and fifth grade classrooms.

Middle School.   The middle school PDS sites were in two different school districts. Because of the small number of interns at the middle school level, both sites only had students in the fall semester.

Secondary.   The PDS model was used at one rural location at a small high school. This site provided valuable service to the university and PDS collaboration, in that new procedures were often tried there first and then moved to other secondary locations after refinements were in place. The Checklist provided an opportunity for secondary educators to discuss, perhaps for the first time, what a list of items to begin conversations with PDS students might look like. The consistency that such a guide offers was, in itself, something new for many secondary educators, who tended to be so focused on their specific content that they forgot that some discussion points are relevant, regardless of that content. The Checklist provided a wonderful opportunity for these educators to begin thinking about what is important to talk about with PDS students.

RESULTS

Qualitative Feedback

Early Childhood Mentor Teachers.   At the 2005 PDS Annual Summer Institute, the early childhood mentor teachers reiterated that the Checklist was a good tool to guide PDS interns and mentor teachers in their conversations. The mentor teachers reemphasized that the Checklist would be useful to track important topics they have discussed with their interns and so the interns would know what questions they might need to ask. However, they still believed that the PDS intern should have the responsibility of maintaining the Checklist and initiating dialogue in regard to the items on the Checklist. Another reason the mentor teachers felt the PDS interns should take responsibility was that the Checklist was designed as a learning tool for the interns. The mentor teachers restated that they were very willing to talk with the PDS interns regarding the information on the Checklist but felt the interns should guide the conversation based on their specific needs. Consequently, the early childhood mentor teachers agreed to support the PDS interns as they completed the Checklist, but the initiation of dialogue and physical placement of the Checklist would be the individual responsibility of the PDS intern.

Elementary Mentor Teachers.   At the 2005 PDS Annual Summer Institute the mentor teachers reported that the Checklist worked very well for establishing baseline questions for the interns to initiate collaborative conversations with the mentor teachers. During the semester, the mentor teachers took turns giving a 30–40 minute presentation to the interns once a week. The mentor teachers were encouraged to use the Checklist to help determine topics for the presentations. The elementary interns and their mentors kept track of what topics were covered; both the intern and the mentor teachers were encouraged to make time for collaboration around the topic.

In addition, the elementary mentor teachers reported that some of the Checklist topics were geared more for student teachers rather than interns. The mentor teachers decided that they would continue to use the Checklist with some revisions to help facilitate PDS interns' growth.

Middle School Mentor Teachers.   The mentor teachers felt that the Checklist provided a focus for the important performance behaviors for each intern. The Checklist, they believed, addressed the important classroom activities and the required performances of each intern. Further, they felt that the Checklist, introduced at the outset of the semester, laid out for the interns a thorough set of expectations of performance and overview of the complexity of teaching. The mentor teachers had, for the most part, used the Checklist to plan their feedback for the interns assigned to their classroom and to frame the conversation during instructional planning time. However, some of the mentor teachers discussed quality indicators used in the Checklist to address more of a summative assessment for the interns. They saved their evaluative responses until the end of the semester. This helped them to clearly articulate to the interns their strengths and areas for growth.

Mentor teachers at both middle school PDS sites indicated that the Checklist encouraged continued conversations with the PDS university faculty, themselves, and the interns. However, both sites indicated that they only used selected indicators because several did not seem appropriate to the middle school level. They supported the change of the heading from "teacher initiated" to "conversation initiated." All of the participants looked forward to continuing the use of the Checklist but in site-specific modified ways. The mentor teachers became familiar with the Checklist and comfortable enough with its use to integrate it into the regular rhythm of the PDS experience.

Secondary Mentor Teachers. Ownership of the Checklist continued to be a point of concern. The secondary PDS mentor teachers discussed the Checklist, and the group began to modify the Checklist to meet the specific needs of secondary interns and their mentor teachers. This discussion continued through the fall semester. At that time, the group decided that the list should be reintroduced during the fall 2005 semester. Items that were eliminated included much of the IEP information as well as grade book information, since the group could not come to consensus on a consistent way that these could be handled across disciplines and in the various grade level classrooms.

Also, the secondary mentor teachers decided that each mentor teacher would use the modified list as a private checklist for PDS intern-initiated discussion points. These lists would be compared among the mentor teachers at the end of the fall 2005 semester and to determine which Checklist items were discussed and which were not. Then, specific items would be modified or eliminated. Second, the pre-service teachers would be responsible for formally completing the Checklist with an additional column for identifying which elements they saw as important to them and which items they thought would be better discussed during the student teaching semester. During the spring 2006 semester, the PDS mentors would study the pre-service teacher data. Comparisons made between what pre-service teachers thought were important and what their mentor teachers believe were important to professional development revealed interesting findings.

YEAR ONE CHECKLIST STATUS AND MODIFICATION

Even though the PDS mentor teachers were fairly adamant that they did not want to be responsible for keeping the Checklist, they did think that the

Checklist was a valuable tool for initiating conversations with their mentees. As the Checklist continued to be revised, it became easier to use for both the mentor teachers and the PDS interns.

The Checklist developed a different look at each educational level. While many items continued to be similar, some were modified in significantly different ways. For the Checklist to serve its purpose, it needed to reflect the context of the educational level, as well as the local school context. One suggestion was to make it into a checklist without the developmental scale.

University professors must also be consistent in the use of the Checklist, making it a part of their instruction and record-keeping to enable their pre-service teachers to use it effectively. As new professors and adjuncts assumed responsibility for PDS sites, training would have to occur for the sake of consistency of instruction. With the above realizations, the university faculty and their mentor teacher partners continued to work together to facilitate the effective professional development of pre-service teachers.

Year One Student Quantitative Responses

During the fall of 2004 and the spring of 2005, Checklists were completed by PDS early childhood, elementary, and middle school pre-service teachers. In general, the results were not surprising. Consequently the researchers concentrated on a few salient items to discuss in this paper but included the graph representations for all 41 items on the Checklist (see Figures 16,1, 16.2, and 16.3). [Note: The graphs represent the number of responses (left column of numbers), mean of scores (right column of numbers, and each of the 41 Checklist items (along the bottom). The round shaped points represent the mean for each of the Checklist items, and the square points represent the number of responses.]

Because the PDS experience occurs the semester before student teaching, the researchers predicted that students would assign a value of "1" ("mentor teacher initiates discussion with pre-service teacher") on a few items, and a "2" ("mentor teacher models the skills for pre-service teacher"), and "3" ("mentor teacher guides practice for pre-service teacher") on most items. In contrast to these options, "4" ("pre-service teacher independently demonstrates the skills") would require the students to engage in activities usually reserved for the student teaching semester. There were some surprises, however. For example, there were very few items that received a value of "3," indicating that the mentor teachers were not guiding students enough to practice skills. Instead, PDS interns reported gaining knowledge and seeing the skills modeled. This was of concern because in some skill areas the learning curve is steep, and if students were not given opportunities

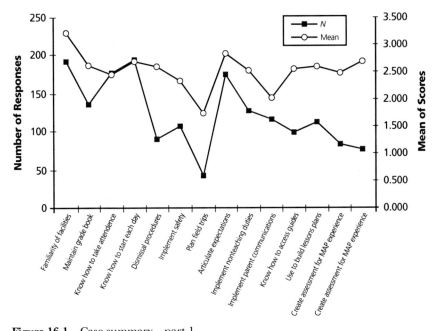

Figure 16.1 Case summary—part 1.

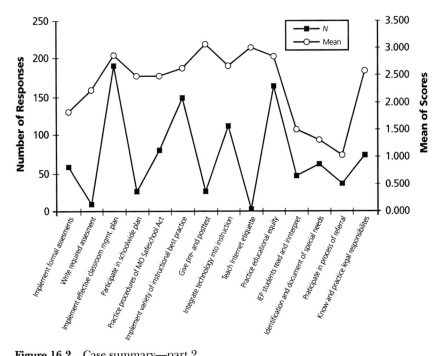

Figure 16.2 Case summary—part 2.

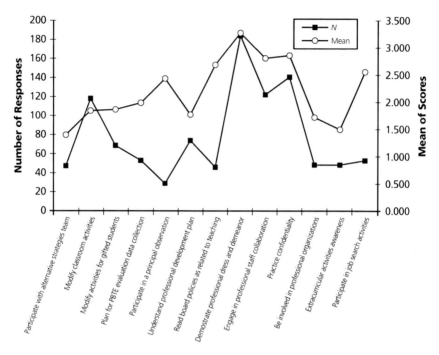

Figure 16.3 Case summary—part 3.

to try something out with guidance, the students could not be expected to perform these skills on their own during student teaching.

There were several individual items with means different from researcher expectations. One area of concern involved students with special needs. Out of a potential 192 Checklist completers, only 46 responded to item E1-IEP students ("read and interpret IEP"). The survey did not include a value of "0" (not discussed) since the expectation was that each item would be discussed; the issue was to what degree. The low number of students responding indicated that, perhaps, PDS interns did not significantly engage in dialogue concerning reading and interpreting IEPs. The mean for this item was 1.48, indicating that the 46 students who did respond reported teacher initiated discussion only.

Another item dealing with students with special needs was item E6 ("modify classroom activities"). One hundred eighteen students responded to this item with a mean value of 1.85 (indicating a closer to observing teacher modeling the skill, but without PDS student guided practice). Since PDS interns do have limited teaching responsibilities, the researchers expected most would indicate a value of at least "2" on this item. Item E2 ("identification and documentation of suspected special needs students"),

E3 ("participate in the process of referral"), E4 ("know and practice legal responsibilities"), E5 ("participate with alternative strategies team") had mean values as expected (see Case Summary 1, 2, 3).

Overall, PDS students were not engaged in guided practice of skills. However, there were three items that did achieve a mean value above "3". These were item A1 ("familiarity of facilities") with 192 respondents and a mean of 3.21, item F5 ("demonstrate professional dress and demeanor") with 185 respondents and a mean of 3.27, item D2 ("give pre-post tests for lessons") with 25 respondents and a mean of 3.08. The first two items received close attention by both university faculty and mentor teachers because the PDS experience was one of the first in a school setting. It was heartening to see that PDS interns recognized and practiced these professional skills. It should also be noted item D2 had a low response rate. It may be that while few of the PDS students had opportunity to even discuss pre-post tests, those who did were allowed to practice these companion skills.

One area of concern across teaching institutions and K–12 settings is in the area of classroom discipline and management. One item that addressed this topic was item C1 ("implement effective classroom management plan"). There were 191 responses with a mean of 2.85. It was interesting that, while this mean approached 3, a lower mean indicated that a large number of PDS interns did not engage in guided practice. Since classroom management is one area that requires extensive practice, student teaching will not provide adequate time to acquire optimal skill level in preparation for the first year of teaching. It would be more beneficial for PDS interns to practice classroom management skills.

DISCUSSION

As we move toward more innovative formats for student teaching, PDS, early field experiences (such as full year, flexible time coursework, and flexible student teaching), teacher dispositions and day-to-day performance expectations will become priority items. We will need an organized way to making sure that appropriate and thorough conversations are held between and among university faculty, university supervisors, mentor teachers, interns, and student teachers. The PDS experience seems the best venue for preparing our students in regard to expectations for highly qualified teachers. The collaboration demonstrated between university faculty and public school mentor teachers on the development and use of the Checklist is essential so that our future colleagues may demonstrate their readiness to be teachers.

The qualitative data supported the idea that the Checklist needed different items at each educational level. While many items could continue to be similar, some needed to be significantly modified. If the Checklist is to serve its purpose of preparing pre-service teachers, it must reflect the context of the educational level. It is noteworthy that teacher mentors at all educational levels felt the Checklist was an important conversation starter when educating pre-service teachers.

It is clear from the quantitative data that at least three immediate changes to the Checklist must occur. First, the Checklist should be amended to include the PDS intern's major. This will allow researchers to disaggregate data by major to note if kinds of experiences significantly differ across the various majors. Second, the Checklist must be revised to include a value to indicate "no discussion" on the topic. Some items received low respondent rates. It is possible that, since there was no way for the respondent to indicate no discussion had occurred, the PDS student chose to leave the item blank. Third, the Checklist should also be modified to include items to ascertain PDS student confidence in performing the various skills. Some skills required almost no practice while others require extensive practice. While the researchers realize that this item refers to PDS intern perception of ability only, confidence in abilities is associated with high teacher self-efficacy and, consequently, higher levels of success in teaching (Pajares, 1996).

Listening to many perspectives and collaborating with many stakeholders involved in the professional development school model improved communication and enriched the semester-long, pre-student teaching experience for interns, mentor teachers, and university faculty. We found that collaboration was a necessary element of PDS and the key to success (Cooper, 1998; Cowart & Rademacher, 1998). Consequently, through the development, use, and analysis of the Checklist, the authors believe we have fulfilled the cornerstone of the definition and concept of the professional development school, which is collaboration between school mentor teachers and university faculty to improve the education of P–12 students, pre-service teachers, and teacher education (CPDT, 1995; Holmes Group, 1990; Ishler, 1995). In addition, we believe this collaborative effort met the NCATE standard for collaboration (NCATE, 2001).

REFERENCES

Association of Teacher Educators. (1986). *Visions of reform: Implications for the education profession. The report of the ATE Blue Ribbon Task Force.* J. Sikula (Chair). Reston, VA: Author.

Carnegie Forum on Education and the Economy. (1986). *A nation prepared: Teachers for the 21st century.* New York: Author.

Center for Professional Development and Technology. (1995). *UNT CPDT: Program approval application.* Denton: University of North Texas.

Cobb, J. (2001). The impact of a professional development school on pre-service teacher preparation, inservice teachers' professionalism, and children's achievement: Perceptions of inservice teachers. *Journal of Teacher Education, 64–74.*

Cooper, M. G. (1998). Building a collaborative that will last. *Teaching and Change, 6*(1), 64–78.

Cowart, M., & Rademacher, J. A. (1998). In my opinion: What students say about professional development schools. *Teaching and Change, 6*(1), 119–131.

Darling-Hammond, L. (1998). Teachers for the 21st century. *Principal, 78*(1), 8.

Gall, M. D., Borg, W. R., & Gall, J. P. (1996). *Educational research: An introduction.* White Plains, NY: Longman Publishers USA.

Goodlad, J. I. (1993). *Teachers for our nation's schools.* San Francisco: Jossey-Bass.

Holmes Group. (1990). *Tomorrow's schools. Principles for the design of professional schools.* East Lansing, MI: Author.

Ishler, R. (1995). Tomorrow's teachers, schools, and schools of education. *National Forum, 75,* 4–5.

National Council for Accreditation of Teacher Education. (2001). *Standards of Professional Development Schools.*

Parjares, F. (1996). Self-efficacy beliefs in academic settings. *Review of Educational Research, 66*(4), 543–578.

APPENDIX

Pre-Service Teacher Observation Log Guide

Rationale: This guide is to be used to help the pre-service teacher grow professionally based upon constructive criticism and self-reflection. The intent is that the pre-service teacher will grow professionally based on modified behaviors.

Skill	Mentor teacher initiates discussion with pre-service teacher	Mentor teacher models the skills for pre-service teacher	Mentor teacher guides practice for pre-service teacher	Pre-service teacher independently demonstrates the skills
A. Routines				
1. Familiarity of facilities				
2. Maintain useful grade book and grading system				
3. Know how to take attendance and do daily record keeping				
4. Know how to start each day (bell work, opening activities, etc.)				
5. Dismissal procedures (planners, bus, notes home, etc.)				
6. Implement safety drill procedures				
7. Plan field trips				
8. Articulate expectations for individual students				
9. Implement non-teaching duties during the day				As applicable

10. Implement a variety of parent communications				
B. Curriculum				
1. Know how to access guides				
2. Use to build lessons plans				
3. Create assessments relevant for MAP experiences				
4. Revise lessons based on student assessment data				As applicable
5. Implement formal district assessments			As applicable	As applicable
6. Write required assessment reports	As applicable	As applicable	As applicable	As applicable
C. Discipline				
1. Implement effective classroom management plan	As applicable		As applicable	
2. Participate in school-wide plan		As applicable		As applicable
3. Practice the procedures of the Missouri Safe Schools Act plan				
D. Instruction				
1. Implement a variety of instructional best practices	As applicable	As applicable	As applicable	As applicable
2. Give pre-post tests for lessons				As applicable
3. Integrate technology into instruction across the curriculum				

Skill	Mentor teacher initiates discussion with pre-service teacher	Mentor teacher models the skills for pre-service teacher	Mentor teacher guides practice for pre-service teacher	Pre-service teacher independently demonstrates the skills
4. Teach internet etiquette	As applicable	As applicable	As applicable	As applicable
5. Practice educational equity (gender, ethnic, SES, etc.)				
E. Special needs and services				
1. IEP students—read and interpret IEP		As applicable	As applicable	As applicable
2. Identification and documentation of suspected special needs students		As applicable	As applicable	
3. Participate in process of referral		As applicable	As applicable	
4. Know and practice legal responsibilities			As applicable	
5. Participate with alternative strategies team		As applicable	As applicable	
6. Modify classroom activities		As applicable	As applicable	As applicable
7. Modify activities for gifted students		As applicable	As applicable	As applicable
F. Professional development				
1. Plan for PBTE evaluation data collection for professional portfolio/artifacts				

				As applicable
2. Participate in a principal observation				
3. Understand the professional development plan process				
4. Read board policies as related to teaching				
5. Demonstrate professional dress and demeanor				
6. Engage in professional staff collaboration				
7. Practice confidentiality				
8. Be involved in professional organizations (local, state, federal)				
G. Potential opportunities			As applicable	As applicable
1. Extra curricular activities awareness coaching, club sponsor				
2. Participate in job search activities (mock interviews, career services registration, MoREAP, references, etc.)				

Note. For PDS Interns: Ratings are scored by date for the first 2 levels and any other met level.
For Student Teachers only: For the last level, the student teacher will be rated on a Likert scale of 1–4 with 1 being poor and 4 being superior. An average level of 3 is the minimum expected of a satisfactory student teaching performance. Some skills are not expected to reach student teacher independence. These skills have been limited on the checklist.

CHAPTER 17

PORTRAITS OF AN INQUIRY STANCE TOWARD TEACHING

Exploring Explicit Relationships Between Inquiry and PDS

Jennifer L. Snow-Gerono

ABSTRACT

This chapter examines the stories of teachers for their understandings of the professional development school (PDS) model and how they cultivated their inquiry stance within a PDS site. A description of the PDS context is provided, as is its framework for "inquiry" and the research methodology. Three themes that emerged from the data are described and discussed; namely, collaborative relationships, mentoring interns and teacher education, and PDS partnership structure. Further discussions on teacher participation and agency are examined, followed by an analysis on the implications for PDS and the cultivation of an inquiry stance toward teaching.

University and School Connections, pages 295–317
Copyright © 2008 by Information Age Publishing

INTRODUCTION

Teacher inquiry, or teacher research, is an evolving movement in education that holds the potential for teachers to come to know and understand their individual "agency" as a means for educational change and their own professional development (Lieberman & Miller, 2001). Teachers who have agency recognize power within their own generation of knowledge and their contributions to classrooms and schools. Teacher researchers question the realities of their profession and their classrooms in order to make changes for the benefit of better teaching and learning environments. According to Little (2001), educational reform literature encourages the cultivation of a "culture of inquiry," and the literature on professional development underscores the importance of learning in and from practice (Lieberman & Miller, 2001).

The particular context for the study described in this chapter is an inquiry-oriented professional development school (PDS) (Darling-Hammond, 1994; Holmes Group, 1986, 1990; Teitel, 2003). Within this PDS partnership, prospective teachers and their mentors engage in teacher inquiry, either in accordance with a seminar and annual conference (where all participants present their inquiry projects) or as an integral aspect of their teaching persona (as identified by "living" an inquiry stance toward teaching).

When asked the question, "What is the relationship between inquiry and PDS?" the majority of the PDS teachers in this study made explicit connections between inquiry and this PDS model. Additionally, even in the case where one teacher denied the PDS's impact on her inquiry stance toward teaching, she identified situations specific to this PDS that subtly influenced her beliefs or experiences with teacher inquiry. The stories of these PDS teachers are portrayed in this chapter, including their understandings of this PDS model and how they cultivated their inquiry stance within a PDS site. The author describes the PDS context, its framework for "inquiry," and the research methodology. Then, three themes indicating the explicit connection between this PDS and inquiry are described: collaborative relationships, mentoring interns and teacher education, and PDS partnership structure. Two more discussions, (1) participation in PDSs and (2) raising teacher voices and taking up agency, are examined, followed by an analysis on the implications for PDSs and the cultivation of an inquiry stance toward teaching.

SITUATING THE CONTEXT: A FRAMEWORK FOR INQUIRY

Describing This PDS Model

The PDS collaborative in this study was the result of a Holmes Partnership commitment between a large university in the northeast and four elementary schools in a local school district. As the partnership evolved, the basis for teacher preparation remained the same (i.e., prospective teachers (interns) completed an undergraduate internship where learning to teach is accomplished through teaming with a mentor teacher for an entire school year [Silva & Dana, 2001]). Professional Development Associates (PDAs) served in a role that might be traditionally considered that of "university supervisor." Interns were required to complete teacher inquiry projects and present their findings at an annual PDS teacher inquiry conference. Mentor teachers participated in teacher inquiry in one of three ways: (1) by completing a teacher inquiry [individually or in collaboration with one or more colleagues], (2) by collaborating with an intern on teacher inquiry, and/or (3) by supporting his or her intern's teacher inquiry. PDS teachers in this partnership who were not mentor teachers were also encouraged to engage in teacher inquiry. An inquiry course was held each spring semester to support intern and mentor teachers' inquiry efforts. As the culture of inquiry within this PDS evolved (Dana, Silva, & Snow-Gerono, 2002) and several teachers began to cultivate an inquiry stance toward their teaching, some mentors or PDS teachers engaged in teacher inquiry without the support of the inquiry course. In fact, several PDS teachers (mentors and non-mentors) identified themselves as "living" an inquiry stance toward teaching and shared their perceptions of this experience in this study.

Defining Inquiry

As the movement of teacher inquiry has evolved, a variety of definitions have come into the foreground, thus giving rise to the danger of teacher inquiry becoming "anything and everything" (Cochran-Smith & Lytle, 1998). Therefore, for the purpose of this study, teacher inquiry is defined as the "systematic, intentional inquiry by teachers" (Cochran-Smith & Lytle, 1993) which becomes "a way of being" or professional positioning on the generation of knowledge and on one's own practice. An inquiry stance toward teaching is a continual state of problem-posing in order to effect change and reflection in education. It involves a disposition in which teachers search for and consider systematic evidence about the effectiveness of their practice. There is also a commitment to following that evidence and not dismissing it, even if it should bring discomfort. Finally, there is a desire to look beyond oneself for answers. When teachers cultivate an inquiry stance, they also hold promise for influencing cultures of inquiry within their professional contexts. Cochran-Smith (1991), drawing on earlier work (Lytle & Cochran-Smith, 1990, 1992), suggests that:

The way to link theory and practice is through a process of self-critical and systematic inquiry about teaching, learning, and schooling (Cochran-Smith & Lytle, 1990); this kind of inquiry is most effective within a larger occupational culture of collaboration wherein novices and experienced professionals alike work to learn from, interpret, and ultimately alter the day-to-day life of schools; power is shared among participants in the community, and knowledge about teaching is fluid and socially constructed; the wisdom, language, critique, and theoretical frameworks of school-based reforming teachers are as essential to a knowledge base for teaching as are those of university-based teacher educators and researchers (Lytle & Cochran-Smith, 1992); and, in the end, the power to liberalize and reinvent notions of teaching, learning, and schooling is located in neither the university nor the school but in the collaborative work of the two. (pp. 283–284)

Potential for collaborative resonance lies within partnerships designed around the conceptual framework for the PDS model; thus, they become a site for linking theory and practice in such a way that partners recognize and work within the tensions between theory, practice, and knowledge construction in educational research.

RESEARCH METHODOLOGY

The research described herein is a phenomenological case study (Merriam, 1998) that is aimed at determining what the experience of teacher inquiry means for PDS teachers. The research question that guided all of the data collection for this study was, "How do PDS teachers, who have an inquiry stance toward teaching and who teach in PDS sites intended as cultures of inquiry, understand and embody (or 'live') teacher inquiry?" Applying purposeful sampling, the author invited all PDS teachers involved in a local partnership to participate. Due to this study's purpose of describing the teachers' experiences and perceptions, the author did not wish to define inquiry and/or an inquiry stance for potential participants up front. Therefore, an invitation was issued "to talk with teachers who identify with the following characteristics:

- Teachers who are reflective; that is, teachers who question and deliberate about their decisions and actions and who recognize change and growth in themselves as a result of being reflective.
- Teachers who consider their questions and deliberations from various perspectives, including concrete evidence.
- Teachers who seek new ideas and understandings regularly and are willing to take risks in order to improve their classrooms and the teaching profession.

Teachers who responded agreed to engage in at least three long interviews (Merriam, 1998) in order to develop deep ethnographic understanding of their experiences. Data collection included field observations (Patton, 1990) in which the author entered the participants' classrooms or other professional environments where they indicated they lived out their inquiry stance toward teaching.

The primary data sources for this study were interview transcripts from three one-on-one, semi-structured interviews with each participant. Interviews were guided by a set of questions and issues to be explored (for example, "How do you define teacher inquiry?" and "How did you come to this understanding?") but controlled by the respondents and their understandings of teacher inquiry (Merriam, 1998). The interview protocols focused on issues connected to what an inquiry stance toward teaching "looks like"; how an inquiry stance toward teaching may be cultivated; and how an inquiry stance toward teaching impacts (or not) the teachers' classrooms, schools, and the PDS partnership. Field notes provided data for analysis and a means of triangulation when compared and contrasted with interview transcripts. Analysis of these data sources included reading and rereading interview transcripts and field notes while "memoing" the data with initial codes (Creswell, 1998). These initial codes generated themes and patterns within individual participant data, creating a "textual description" (Creswell, 1998) for each participant's understanding(s). The individual data analysis was shared with participants to conduct member checks and enhance "trustworthiness" (Lincoln & Guba, 1985).

Data sources for this study were used in attempting to create a "portrait of an inquiry stance toward teaching" for each of the participants. These portraits provided rich (Erikson, 1986), thick (Geertz, 1973) descriptions of the essence of inquiry for teachers who have cultivated a self-identified inquiry stance toward teaching. Likewise, in-depth descriptions of context and meaning lead to transparency and potential transferability, rather than generalizability (Breault & Adair Breault, 2007). After individual member checks, the portraits were used as data for cross-case analysis to generate a "composite description" of their experience of "living" an inquiry stance toward teaching.

The six PDS teachers who volunteered to participate in this study include Elyse, Heather, Lydia, Maggie, Penny, and Shelly. Their experience in this school district ranged from 6–18 years, and they had all worked in a PDS site since the partnership's inception. Five of the six teachers were active PDS participants, in the sense that they regularly worked as mentor teachers and participated in professional development teams and courses. However, one teacher, Lydia, had not participated as a mentor teacher, although she had conducted teacher inquiry as a means for alternative teacher evaluation.

Explicit Connection between Inquiry and PDS

Five of the six teachers in this study made an explicit connection between the PDS partnership and their cultivation of an inquiry stance toward teaching. Although Lydia was more reticent to credit this PDS partnership with her experiences with inquiry, she did include the PDS model and aspects of her school as a PDS site as largely influencing her introduction to teacher inquiry. Conversely, Shelly consistently credited this PDS partnership with influencing her understandings of inquiry and her professional development. She reported that the PDS inquiry course was her introduction to teacher inquiry as a formal process. She also mentioned she might not have taken this course had she not been working with an intern who was required to take the course and conduct an inquiry project. She claimed that this course "has given me a different perspective . . . on how I teach, and what I think about when I'm teaching" (Interview 2 transcript, p. 4). Shelly described her feelings about this PDS model and teacher inquiry as woven together. She explained,

> I think [PDS and inquiry] go together. I think they go together and comple-
> ment each other. The more you do in the PDS program, the more tools or
> experiences you have to help you with inquiry because they're so connected.
> (Interview 3 transcript, p. 2)

Shelly also saw her newfound passion for inquiry as keeping her involved in this PDS and its other activities. Shelly understood that their interconnectedness demonstrates that, for her, the PDS opened the door to inquiry—while at the same time, inquiry opened the door to the PDS.

Elyse also described this PDS's culture as integrating inquiry in an essential way for its teachers. Elyse claimed that inquiry was a vital component of this PDS program, and that emphasis made this program different from other PDS programs (in her estimation). Penny agreed with Elyse that this particular PDS partnership had intertwined inquiry in its definition of its PDS model in such a way that its participants benefited from a mutual understanding of inquiry as integral to the simultaneous renewal called for in PDS partnerships. Penny explained, "I think they go together. I think the way that this PDS is structured, I don't think they *necessarily* go together, but I think . . . that seems to be the thread that connects everything together for us" (Interview 3 transcript, p. 21).

The PDS teachers understood that there are several models of PDSs in practice across the United States, but they shared their personal understandings of this PDS model as a concept, as they told stories about their individual cultivation of an inquiry stance toward teaching. Three themes portray this explicit connection between inquiry and PDS: Collaborative

Relationships, Mentoring Interns and Teacher Education, and PDS Partnership Structure.

Collaborative Relationships

In general, these participants understood the PDS partnership to be an impetus for greater collaboration and collegiality with their colleagues, not only in their individual school sites but also across schools sites and the university. They recognized that this particular partnership provided opportunities for them to have access to a wide range of people and "experts" on various educational levels.

According to Penny, this PDS partnership was a model of "mutual respect and learning from each other" (Interview 3 transcript, p. 6). In this definition, she included PDS teachers and administrators, PDAs, interns, and elementary school children in the environment of respect and mutual learning. Maggie concurred with Penny's description of a PDS model. However, she also emphasized the power of relationships in reaching goals. She concluded, "It's the relationships that make us work. It's a relationship with [university faculty member] being in the building to make it work. . . . It is the relationship with your PDA" (Interview 3 transcript, p. 8). Maggie also recognized that the PDS partnership enhanced communication for teachers, principals, and university representatives. Again, she noted, "It's brought people out in the middle to talk about things" (Interview 3 transcript, p. 15). Maggie's metaphor of teachers coming out into the hall to "talk about things" implies the importance of dialogue in truly "living" an inquiry stance toward teaching. This dialogue creates the potential for raising teachers' voices and agency, as described in the opening paragraph, around issues they feel are important.

Heather appreciated this PDS partnership as a means for sharing ideas with new people and stimulating professionalism. She described this PDS as professional stimulation:

> It's kind of helped me intellectually survive sometimes. It's really fed me, and . . . I think it's more accessible . . . more of a presence of people who do understand teaching in a different way or look at it in a different way. I think . . . the PDA's, the instructors—they've done a lot to support us as professional, intellectual beings and treat us in a respectful way. (Interview 2 transcript, p. 8)

Heather considered this PDS a means for true collegiality. "To me it feels like more of a real collegiality in terms of what that can mean and what that can look like" (Interview 2 transcript, p. 13). She also connected PDSs to the "openness to learning," which she valued as an attitude that leads to inquiry and the scholarship necessary in the profession.

Maggie credited this PDS *partnership's emphasis on collaborative relationships with cultivating her inquiry stance* toward teaching. Although she grew professionally through her work with PDS interns, she understood the PDS model as a nurturing environment for practicing teachers. Maggie emphasized the importance of a professional learning community, or study group, that could support teachers in the inquiry process.

> There's got to be collaboration. And, there's got to be that nurturing environment that allows you to do that, and then an avenue to seek the answers . . . I really believe the avenue for me lately has been the professional development. . . . The collaboration helps because you have someone to say, "This didn't work, or I wonder about this, or where can I go?" And, somebody can give another professional information: "Well, try this or try this." What the PDS or a professional group can do is bring more professionals together to discuss things in a way that is nonthreatening. (Interview 2 transcript, p. 3)

Maggie voiced the theory that there was strength in numbers when collaborating, a notion furthered by Dana & Yendol-Silva (2003). Forming such professional groups may stimulate deeper conversations with more ideas about whatever questions the teachers were raising at meetings. Maggie recalled an experience she had with a study group lead by one of the PDS co-directors during her early years of PDS participation.

> I go back to that beginning group with Jack where we sat around and just talked. You know, "What's going on?" or "Have you worked on something?" And, it was very nonthreatening but so empowering to the young people that were in that group. They were professionals who questioned some of the things and then thought, "Oh, that's not bad, or maybe we could try that or we read some passages, quoted back." But, it was a way to have that guided . . . growth! (Interview 2 transcript, p. 13)

Maggie understood that this type of collaborative group nurtured an inquiry stance and the professional development of teachers.

When Elyse discussed the PDS community, she included her work of being a mentor teacher, her participation on the PDS mathematics team, attendance in the PDS inquiry course, and "being and working in contact with so many people who are in that inquiry state" (Interview 1 transcript, p. 4). Maggie appreciated the extension of her professional community that came with the PDS partnership. The new forms of participation that this PDS partnership offered teachers (collaborative planning of methods courses, for example) brought teachers together from across elementary schools and PDS sites. Maggie reported, "When you generate ideas in one building it's great, but pulling a couple from another building every once in awhile, it's like going to a conference, getting a little bit of new blood in there" (Interview 3 transcript, p. 15). She worried that the growth of the PDS has, ironically, sent people back to their own buildings.

> I think the PDS is growing a lot. So now each building . . . is trying to get together. Each building is trying to think, "Where are we going from here?" . . . but I really miss some of the colleagues we were thrown together with in pursuit of this excitement for generating ideas. (Interview 3 transcript, p. 15)

Maggie believed,

> The PDS should be inclusive, quality inclusive . . . to make the school grow, and people begin to take on some new roles, then how can we support each other with that? . . . I'd help out in some way, if I didn't work full time in the schools, I'd work to help out. But, I do believe that needs nurturing and support too, to get the quality we want. (Interview 2 transcript, p. 18)

This willingness to take on new roles demonstrated Maggie's openness to various forms of participation in her school and profession. She brought to light the idea that the safe, supportive environment necessary for change and risk-taking needed to be continually nurtured. Simply because a partnership or collaborative effort had grown should not mean that the initial nurturing of questions and relationships has been completed.

Mentoring Interns and Teacher Education

When Shelly first conversed about what the concept of a PDS meant to her, she immediately discussed the teacher preparation component of PDSs. She compared her experiences with traditional student teacher preparation with this internship program where interns learned to teach and inquire alongside their mentor teacher for the entire school year. Shelly was constantly working with other mentor teachers and PDAs on the teacher preparation component of this PDS partnership:

> We do the mentor teacher faculty planning together. . . . We offer those classes in the summer or take classes in the summer that are related to the PDS. And, then, we continue in the late summer planning for the fall. It's just a continuous circle relationship. As the year winds down, now, we are thinking of planning the next group. . . . So, it's kind of a wonderful, seamless thing. (Interview 3 transcript, p. 1)

The planning teams Shelly discussed are open to mentor teachers and others (even though Shelly saw them in connection with her role as a mentor). Shelly emphasized that being part of a PDS partnership opened opportunities for her to continually engage in professional development, while, at the same time, she was a teacher educator for her interns. Understanding this PDS model as about more than just initial teacher preparation leads this PDS to be seen as teacher education across the professional life span and opens the doors to a PDS being intimately connected to cultivating an inquiry stance toward teaching, whether it be through work with an intern's inquiry or not.

Maggie connected her beliefs about making changes and teacher agency to her work with PDS interns. She recognized the impact that the PDS context had on the interns who went through the program. She contrasted traditional teacher preparation programs with this internship.

> I truly believe it's the way the PDS is taught. It used to be, in order to be a teacher, you had to do A, B, C, and D . . . and, there was a right way to do it. Now, we want the novice teachers to certainly know how to write a plan, to know a lot of the basics . . . but this program allows a new teacher to fail, but more importantly to learn from their mistakes. If you learn, in a sense, you never fail. This program allows a student to say, "Well, that didn't work. What could I do?" And, it's not through a judgmental lens. If the judgments are left behind, I think that there's more than one way to do something. And, the students are able to see that too. (Interview 2 transcript, p. 10)

Consequently, work with interns influenced teacher education and professional development for educators at all levels.

Lydia, on the other hand, did not see herself as connected to this PDS because she had "not taken an intern." Although she recognized mentoring as an important PDS activity in which she did not currently participate, she did have understandings of this partnership not directly connected to work with interns, yet connected to teacher education in general. Lydia believed that this PDS was a place where teachers had more input into how their schools function as well as input into professional development opportunities. Lydia stated, "A PDS school has more teacher input . . . maybe room for more teacher growth" (Interview 3 transcript, p. 1). She described her vision of the ideal PDS: "To me, the ideal PDS school would be that the teachers are the ones [who] do a lot of the decision-making" (Interview 3 transcript, p. 2). However, she did not see that her school becoming a PDS had changed the faculty or the environment, other than the fact that there were more prospective teachers in the building. Similar to the manner in which Lydia saw inquiry as a label for something she already did, she viewed this PDS as a label for something her school already emulated.

I see that we've been the same school, we've just gotten a different label . . . it's just that, we've always been a school that's been labeled. [The PDS model] is just a philosophy that's been in the school forever . . . it's just another name. A big impact has been the amounts of student teachers or interns. (Interview 3 transcript, p. 1)

Lydia's dissonance in understanding inquiry as a part of her work in this PDS may stem from what Elyse termed the PDS mindset. When asked to describe a PDS culture, Elyse explained it as a mindset in which there is the outside influence of the program, but there is also a very important inside influence of an individual and her agency within that program. Elyse said, "that person involved in it also is a very integral part . . . they have to do it personally. They have to have ownership of it . . . PDS, I think, for me . . . it's just that idea of allowing that person to have a greater role" (Interview 3 transcript, p. 2). When considering Elyse's description of a mindset, Lydia seemed to have that mindset and the commitment to raising teachers' voices in her school and in education in general. However, she did not take "ownership" of this PDS model because she had experienced personal tensions in her participation with prospective teachers prior to the PDS "label."

Interestingly, Elyse described an almost inverse case of mentoring in her coming to understand teacher inquiry. She explained that it was working with an intern who was doing an inquiry project that really guided her understandings. She described her prior experience with interns:

It has really helped me to have an intern who's doing [an inquiry project]. And, it's not even that . . . because I haven't even been so involved in their writing it . . . it's me learning with them how to teach the subject matter. So they're learning, 'Well, this is what you could do in social studies, this is what you could do in science.' . . . yes, it directly correlates to having an intern in the room because I'm constantly forced to talk about myself and my teaching and think about my teaching and think about their teaching and . . . it has come from the culture, the PDS culture. (Interview 3 transcript, pp. 9–10)

Rather than interns leading her into inquiry as Elyse describes, Shelly talked about specifically modeling inquiry for her interns. She hoped that they would come to similar understandings of inquiry as an important process for change and growth in teaching. Therefore, lifelong learning and modeling inquiry were important characteristics of her inquiry stance toward teaching.

PDS Partnership Structure as Support for Inquiry

One of the most important influences on Elyse's understandings of teacher inquiry was her PDS teaching context. Elyse noted, "I definitely was influenced from the PDS community that has been established here. I think it was intrinsically in me to question, but . . . I wouldn't have come this far in it if I didn't have that structure there" (Interview 1 transcript, p. 4). Elyse viewed herself as a curious, inquiring teacher. She said, "I know that I had thoughts of inquiry." The PDS partnership provided structures for her work as a student in the inquiry course and as a mentor dedicated to supporting her intern's inquiry project in the classroom. These structures stimulated her awareness of inquiry and her conceptual understanding of the process.

> Until it bubbled to the surface and I really became aware of what it was, I was thinking about and really started analyzing it and [I] thought, 'I'm trying to do this,' and looking at myself, kind of a metacognition. But, I wouldn't have done that maybe as in depth and as soon as I have without the PDS. (Interview 3 transcript, p. 8)

Elyse described herself as "up on trying to make myself more inquiry-based." She continued to credit her association with this PDS community for creating the space for her to do that. She said, "How much better it was to have the PDS. . . . Of course, it [teacher inquiry and PDS] can be separate, but [the PDS] enhances it in such a better way that I believe it's better. [There are] people to talk to and people to help you" (Interview 3 transcript, p. 12).

Shelly connected her understandings of the cultivation of an inquiry stance with her work with PDS interns, but she more strongly credited the structure provided by the PDS inquiry course with her resulting inquiry stance.

> I don't think I would have had a chance to learn more about my teaching if I didn't have that course help me examine it. You don't always have time to examine it. You're so busy with your teaching, you're so busy with your life. You do the best you can, and you make it through the year . . . but, this course gave me opportunity to do more than wish I would have done better . . . this course gives you an opportunity to do something about it in a way that makes sense. (Interview 1 transcript, p. 12)

According to Shelly, not only would she not have engaged in teacher inquiry projects without this PDS but she understood her continued pull toward teacher inquiry as connected to the PDS partnership.

I think the inquiry has become, for me, more and more of the focus and more and more of an important part . . . I think it is a great way to reflect upon your teaching or reflect upon your teaching and what you do with your teaching. I think it gives you important tools to work on, areas you may feel that there's a need there. I think it also really provides a good opportunity for the intern to see that it's a lifelong journey. (Interview 3 transcript, pp. 1–2)

Inquiry's strong connection to this PDS for Shelly can be noted when she talks about the opportunities that it provided for her and the lifelong learning she sees necessary for teachers.

Maggie claimed that the opportunities of being part of a PDS partnership "really furthered [my inquiry stance]. It's just really, I think I questioned to begin with, and I questioned with a colleague . . . but PDS has supported it" (Interview 3 transcript, p. 13).

Heather also reflected on the relationship between her understandings of inquiry and PDS. She explained, "to get the most out of it, I would think [there is a necessary relationship]. Again, I think teachers . . . who see themselves as 'expert,' are going to be limited in what they get from the PDS" (Interview 2 transcript, pp. 24–25). In this comment, Heather recognized a tension in the PDS and inquiry; for example, how can you be an "expert" teacher and be open to questions and learning? Heather also cautioned about promoting the PDS model and inquiry with new teachers without first cultivating a safe, supportive environment (Snow-Gerono, 2005). Heather admitted that she was more comfortable or secure as a teacher than most new teachers. Therefore, she was more comfortable with opening her classroom to adults and publicly asking questions about her practice and teaching in general. She reflected, "You could feel less secure or you could get on the defensive and question yourself" (Interview 2 transcript, p. 33). According to Heather, this type of questioning could be damaging, as it is not done from a stance of inquiry but one of insecurity and doubt. Although uncertainty is important for an inquiry stance, a level of secure humility is also necessary. Heather found that this PDS helped to cultivate this atmosphere of safety in questioning, collaborating and talking. This caused Heather to feel that it is "better to see it as a district PDS" (Interview 2 transcript, p. 31) rather than simply four schools committed to a partnership with the local university. Thus, it was important to Heather that this PDS partnership was not viewed as site-specific but as a structure providing an extended community of learners.

Penny also understood this need for a safe, supportive environment as provided by a PDS partnership. In Penny's understanding, this PDS provided the environment that she and her colleagues needed to cultivate inquiry stances. "I would hope that most people who go into this field are people who want and think they need to grow as professionals. That you could cultivate it by providing an environment that supports it and encourages it and gives opportunities for it" (Interview 2 transcript, p. 6). Penny believed that this PDS collaborative provided these opportunities for her.

> I think teachers were committed to growth, but I think the PDS kind of en-
> hances that and gives more and better opportunities for the growth. But, I
> think you would still see people here trying to improve things, but this is sort
> of like the boost. The PDS makes it easier. It makes it easier, and it gives you
> better results! (Interview 1 transcript, p. 14)

Penny's impressions of the PDS's impact on her environment were connected to her views on the importance of a professional learning community for
teachers interested in inquiry and professional growth. Penny explained
that the PDS offered a "whole new support system." Penny described "a
network of people that you could go to. Like taking a course that sort of did
outline systematic steps" (Interview 3 transcript, p. 12).

Shelly provided an example of a specific PDS structure that helps to cultivate an inquiry stance toward teaching in these PDS teachers. At the annual PDS Teacher Inquiry conference, teacher inquirers shared their experiences and their knowledge generation in presentations focused on their
inquiry projects in this PDS partnership context, and Shelly celebrated her
inquiry stance in this public venue. She had presented at each PDS conference and found it a safe place for her to take risks and be uncertain
about her practice so that she could also demonstrate her questioning and
problem-posing as an impetus for change and her agency in education. Inquiry and this PDS conference were vehicles for Shelly (and other teacher
researchers) to share their beliefs on lifelong learning and growth.

"Representative" or "Participatory" Forms of Participation in this PDS

Connections between PDS and inquiry were also influenced by varying
degrees of participation in the PDS partnership. Problematizing participation is an important aspect of cultivating inquiry and PDS partnerships. Participation in democratic structures coincides with a "representative" versus
a "participatory" dialectic. PDS teachers may be *represented* by a core group
of teachers (or even only mentor teachers) in some people's eyes. However,
this understanding of participation limits the potential of a more *participatory* structure, where all PDS teachers' voices may be raised and heard.
Participation means engaging in PDS activity in some variation of its many
roles and responsibilities and choosing not to be represented by a larger
body of people. This participation may raise some opposition, at times, to
consensus in a PDS site, but the partnership should grow from engaging in
dialogue of multiple perspectives and participants.

An issue raised by the participants when discussing the PDS and teacher inquiry was on the varying degrees of participation in each experience at each of the PDS sites. Some PDS teachers were active in aspects of this PDS model (mentoring, collaborative methods course planning, PDS courses, and inquiry) while others, for whatever reason, selected not to participate as actively in the PDS experience. At the same time, some teachers were avid inquirers, although they may not have been involved in other experiences associated with PDS. Herein lies an inevitable tension in PDS work—is participation voluntary or is it an enforced, whole school commitment? Certainly, PDS participants were not forced to engage in any of the PDS activities. They were, therefore, voluntary. However, if an entire school faculty shares a PDS partnership commitment, how should participation be examined? These teachers appeared to be content to address PDS (and inquiry) participation as having varying degrees.

Penny saw both PDS and inquiry as opportunities in which some would relish and on which some would close the door. One aspect in which not all PDS teachers participated was working as a mentor teacher with an intern. However, Penny did not believe that this meant they may not participate in inquiry or in other PDS efforts.

> I think it takes more effort on your part because you don't have that young person in your room questioning you or coming up with ideas or saying, "This doesn't make sense. How can I teach this unit?" . . . But I think you could still [participate]. (Interview 3 transcript, p. 11)

This also demonstrates the idea of PDS participation beyond working with an intern and parallels the ideas of simultaneous renewal proposed by the Holmes Group (1990) and Darling-Hammond (1994).

Heather understood her PDS context as influenced by the individuality of the participants and their willingness or propensity to collaboration. Just like teacher inquiry was taken up in different ways so, too, was the PDS model in this partnership.

> It's that kind of openness or realization there are just all kinds of levels. You've got a lot of individuality there . . . I feel it's the place, time and space, and people that are interested. And, I feel like I'm not as isolated. I feel like I can kind of get people to get it. They're looking at it. It's that metacognition I guess. Looking at it from a different stance . . . (Interview 2 transcript, p. 25)

In the same vein, it could be better to view education, teaching, and learning as an appropriate place for inquiry and research into the profession, instead of simply a place where teachers have answers for eager students.

Elyse's description of this PDS model as a "mindset" intimated the individuality that influences PDS participation. She did not view this as a negative thing.

> It goes to say, even for some of the other mentors in the building, they don't have as much involvement in the PDS, but they are mentors. They might not serve on any other committee or anything else . . . so it's not necessarily if you're a mentor you're really involved, or if you're not a mentor, you're not as involved. (Interview 3 transcript, p. 5)

Elyse simply credited the PDS with her personal cultivation of an inquiry stance. Her participation in a PDS impacted her beliefs about teacher inquiry, but her school colleagues with similar PDS participation efforts may not have engaged as fully in the inquiry process or PDS mindset.

These PDS teachers had numerous ideas about ways in which teachers may participate in the "PDS mindset" for this partnership. They were also willing to suggest further connections between PDS participation and potential inquiry participation. For example, Shelly wondered if PDS teachers who were not mentor teachers (the ultimate PDS activity, according to Shelly) but who were engaging in teacher inquiry were next in line to work in the teacher preparation aspect of the PDS partnership.

> I think there's a real connection. I also kind of feel like teachers who are doing inquiry who don't have interns are doing a wonderful thing. And, I'm not sure if they really realize what an important component it is to the whole professional development school. I don't know, maybe it's preparing them for having an intern. (Interview 3 transcript, p. 3)

Shelly's wonderings here indicate her understanding that inquiry was the basis for this entire PDS partnership. Inquiry was encouraged as a means for continued professional growth for prospective teachers, practicing teachers, and teacher educators alike.

Certainly, Penny recognized how the PDS enhanced her professional growth, whether it was through conferences, courses, opportunities for talking with her colleagues, or her work as a mentor teacher. Taking advantage of these opportunities was evidence of an inquiry stance toward teaching for Penny. However, she also recognized that she and her colleagues were embracing these new opportunities with varying degrees of participation. It appeared acceptable to have a representative democracy or representative PDS participation for these PDS teachers. They stressed that the various forms of participation were open to everyone, but not everyone was taking advantage of a participatory PDS voice. This difference may merit further investigation, as PDS teachers question their curriculum, instruction, and professional environments, (for example, what is the reason some PDS teachers chose to engage in a representative rather than participatory structure?) Perhaps what Lydia called for in this PDS—teacher input—may be an answer to resolving this tension felt within PDS participation in this site. Lydia recognized mentoring as a PDS activity and understood that her role in this PDS site may not have been representative or participatory but may have been more of a teacher outside the PDS boundary.

Raising Teachers' Voices and Taking up Agency

Another important area of PDS participation returns to Lydia's perspective of what a PDS should be about—raising teachers' voices. Lydia claimed that the *teachers at her school had more input in what happened at their school.* And, unlike her experience with inquiry, she credited this new voice to the PDS partnership. Lydia stated, "Well, I think our faculty meetings came with PDS. Our faculty meetings are more geared toward professional development. . . . We've divided up into groups, and we're like study groups on something we want [to learn more about]" (Interview 3 transcript, p. 2). Lydia continued her idea of raising teachers' voices in schools by connecting PDS partnerships and inquiry with this transformative potential. She continued, "And, that's something I'd like to see come out of all this is . . . the teachers' voices" (Interview 3 transcript, p. 3). This setting for teacher dialogue and shared discussion mirrors Lydia's understandings of what was important in a context for inquiry. If these study groups became safe places for teachers to question their practice and their classroom contexts, teacher inquiry could become more embedded in the daily lives and stances of all PDS teachers. Likewise, this form of professional development could assist in the perception of the meaning of a PDS within this site as more than working with an intern.

When asked specifically if she thought inquiry could be a means for raising teachers' voices, Lydia said yes, explaining her view of inquiry and its potential for increasing teacher input into decisions in schools as follows:

Because I think that with teachers, with a school with a philosophy like the PDS, I think that to thrive, to make changes, to become a developed school, you need to have those things talked about. I think issues need to be spoken about. (Interview 3 transcript, p. 3)

Although Lydia's quote here is quite general and connected to inquiry, her advice (to have those things talked about) could spread to the issue of varying degrees of participation in her PDS site and why or how that might be changed, if, in fact, that is what the "teachers' voices" raise for discussion. In this sense, this PDS model and inquiry could provide environments where teachers come to understand their own individual agency in making changes in their schools and local communities. Perhaps inquiry is the tool teachers need to make a difference in or to discuss hegemonic educational structures with or to enter into the education policy arena with a stronger voice.

Penny provided a good example of a PDS teacher who enjoyed inquiry as a means for making changes. Her integrated perception of inquiry and PDSs was influenced by her personal convictions about inquiry, change, and growth as important for teaching and learning. In all of her conversations about inquiry, Penny, at some point, mentioned she does it "because it's fun!" She also appreciated that inquiry and the opportunities the PDS provided her helped her to "learn new things." Perhaps most prominent for Penny was that "in a small way [it] shows that you keep learning. You don't come to a point where you stop learning" (Interview 3 transcript, p. 17). Indeed, Penny and her openness for questions and change guided her into benefitting from PDS and inquiry in her profession. She summed it up best by saying,

> I took some things that I was doing, and it helped me to think about it in a systematic way and gave me some idea for how I could make changes. You know, it was more than just questioning and complaining—but giving me some ways to go about changing. (Interview 3 transcript, p. 12)

Penny epitomized the concept that PDS and teacher inquiry were both about change and growth in education. These ideas were also connected to a teacher with a strong voice in her classroom and on her faculty. When she had a question, she pursued it where the evidence took her. Penny understood that as an individual she may make changes, not only in her teaching but in education. This understanding demonstrated her belief in her personal agency. She believed she could and would make a difference in the lives of her students, interns, and colleagues, as well as the structures of education.

Maggie's analysis of the PDS program helped her to see the value of providing a safe environment for prospective teachers to make mistakes and learn from them. She also realized how she benefitted from working with interns and university representatives to cultivate a stance of questioning within educators in general. This questioning or inquiry stance set the stage for educators who question practice and educational systems in order to take up agency in a profession that has historically silenced teachers. Therefore, an inquiry stance toward teaching was imperative for these teachers. In Maggie's conversations, she, as an inquiring mentor teacher, provided space for the future generation of teachers to become "reformers" (Cochran-Smith, 1991). Maggie also claimed that she had "seen the program make change an integral yet fun thing to do" (Interview 3 transcript, p. 16). Maggie remembered that before this PDS partnership, most of her colleagues were working in their rooms and "there was sort of a way to do things." She also remembered a certain freedom in coming out in the middle to talk about things and collaborate together to make change. Penny and Maggie's perceptions of *inquiry and PDS as "fun" avenues for change* only make the case for a greater implication of PDS partnerships and teacher inquiry in the *honoring of teachers' voices and agency in education.*

Elyse discussed a cycle that included a tension between individual agency and the collective agenda. Understandably, this tension was also connected to her view of the PDS mindset.

Figure 17.1 indicates Elyse's idea of the dynamics in a PDS relationship. She said,

> I think it's kind of a back and a forth, and a circle, so it can't, it's not just that there's whoever is part of the PDS telling or working with these people who are involved in it. But, something that's constantly in a circular motion . . . and allowing them to make decisions in that realm in the PDS. So, giving [teachers] a voice, giving them a position is what made all the difference . . . it's not taken for granted that one person is making the decision. (Interview 3 transcript, pp. 2–3)

Elyse's understandings of the PDS community as dynamic with tensions among power and voice illustrated her understanding of the contradictions inherent in collaboration, where individual and collective agency need to be interrogated and balanced. Once again, Elyse went back to her description of the mindset of PDSs and that "no one is being forced to do these things." Her perception of this PDS and teacher inquiry coincided:

> Each person individually has some passion about something that they want to share, and they're willing to do it. And, it comes naturally because it is a passion. So I think that's the unique part. We're not always allowed or given the freedom to do what we want professionally . . . the PDS, this program anyway, has allowed people to do that. (Interview 3 transcript, p. 13)

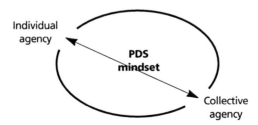

Figure 17.1 PDS mindset and agency.

In this discussion, Elyse was talking about the PDS program in which she was involved. However, her consideration for passion and natural inclination is also connected to scholarly literature on teacher inquiry (Hubbard & Power, 1993, 1999; Dana & Yendol-Silva, 2003). Her comments allude to the stifling of teacher inquiry in some education contexts. It is not always accepted to question or for teachers not to know the answer. Elyse believed this PDS allowed her and her colleagues to break out of stereotypical molds of the teacher as a technician and move toward the teacher as a creator of knowledge and a learner.

Heather described her experience as a mentor teacher and conversations she initiated in her learning community.

> I guess I do kind of struggle, I do think and I say these things, but oftentimes I wonder . . . I don't know that people get it . . . I really see the developmental levels for us as mentors. Does that mean I don't say it? No, because I'll always go along with, you know, I'll say things, but I will go along with what the group or the organization, what they decide. It doesn't take away from my individual thought. (Interview 3 transcript, p. 13)

Heather's voice here suggests the dialectic between individual agency and a collective agenda within collaborative partnerships. She believes that she must raise her voice and ideas even if they were not addressed by the group as a whole. This is similar to her belief that it was important to attempt to cultivate and nurture an inquiry stance with all teachers, even though individual personalities would effect what level it reaches. Heather clearly tried to inject her individual agency and raise her voice so that her colleagues could hear her. She understood that not everyone was ready for (or in line with) her type of thinking, and, because she was in a collaborative partnership structure, she would go along with consensus. However, she was willing to initiate "dissensus," a new critical form of consensus (Trimbur, 1992). "Dissensus" involves dialogue and democratic participation in educational issues, whether the partners agree or not. This type of dialogue would be indicative of a more participatory, public democracy where teacher voice and agency were integral components of educational change. Sehr (1997) writes about Dewey's thinking about public democracy:

> The process of people discussing their individual and group desires, needs and prospective actions, allows them to discover their shared interests in the consequences of their actions. This is what generates "social consciousness" or "social will" and creates the ability to act on collective goals. It is this process of communication and deliberation over collective goals that constitutes a democratic public. (p. 58)

Perhaps the same could be said about a democratic PDS partnership.

IMPLICATIONS

The variations in stories that came from these teachers when discussing the PDS model in connection with inquiry may stem from their personal definitions of PDS and how they believe they cultivated an inquiry stance toward teaching. Was inquiry always an innate part of their teaching persona, or did some event rupture experience so that they consciously developed this inquiry stance? The data demonstrates an explicit connection between the PDS and inquiry in this partnership. However, these PDS teachers also allow for varying degrees of connection and individuality in what "living" an inquiry stance toward teaching looks like. What would happen if there were more concrete expectations from and for PDSs and inquiry? To go even further, why might this be (or not be) a good thing to emphasize?

Although new roles and responsibilities came with the PDS, as well as the raising of teachers' voices within their school buildings, these new roles remain largely in the personal rather than the public domain. Valli, Cooper, and Frankes (1997) state:

> The majority of professional development initiatives within PDSs presently include new roles, new instructional methods, and increased decision-making opportunities for teachers that support their self-development, personal autonomy, and increased professional status; however, these reforms are most often linked to the narrow academic and personal consequences of teaching. Reflection, dialogue, and action pertaining to a broader set of social and political commitments are required of administrators, teacher educators, and teachers if the goal of educating everybody's children is to be achieved. (p. 275)

If a larger, collective social and political commitment is, in fact, necessary for a PDS model or for teacher inquiry, the PDS teachers in this study demonstrated that this commitment may not materialize immediately. Initially, these teachers needed to work through issues such as their understandings of PDSs, their participation in this PDS and inquiry, and, then, how they would take up their social and political commitments, both individually and as a collective. Knowing this up front, leaders within PDS partnerships may be able to structure more experiences to make explicit understandings of the PDS model and levels of participation so that all more quickly move to a united vision of social and political commitments to benefit all students.

Recognizing a strong tension between individual passions and collective goals or public and private purposes in these teachers' stories of a PDS and inquiry, suggests this is a place for further PDS research and development. Where are the social and political commitments? How might inquiry be connected to them? Certainly, it is important to contribute to the raising of teachers' voices and shared decision-making, but Cochran-Smith

(2002) identifies three aspects of inquiry: knowledge generation, professional development, and social activism. Cochran-Smith and Lytle's (2001) knowledge-*of*-practice is evident in teachers "living" an inquiry stance in this study. However, this knowledge is generated at an individual, or classroom, level. Teachers may share their experiences with each other, but not all of the teacher inquirers in this PDS partnership had yet realized their potential collective impact on education and society. How might "living" an inquiry stance toward teaching help educators at all levels navigate the pulls between the individual and the collective, and the personal and political purpose and action? Perhaps, more important, in the current political climate, how should PDS partnerships and teacher inquiry having an explicit connection be used to demonstrate collective purpose toward enhanced learning for K–12 students, prospective teachers, and their mentors? By using this connection, teacher educators at all levels should be able to encourage the individual and collective agency of teachers so that their voices are heard in policy and research contexts for education.

REFERENCES

Breault, R., & Adair Breault, D. (2007). *Warrantability and meaningfulness in PDS research: A content analysis.* Paper presented at the 2007 Annual American Education Research Association, Chicago, IL.

Cochran-Smith, M. (1991). Learning to teach against the grain. *Harvard Educational Review, 61*(3), 279–308.

Cochran-Smith, M. (2002). Inquiry and outcomes: Learning to teach in the age of accountability. *Teacher Education and Practice, 15*(4), 12–34.

Cochran-Smith, M., & Lytle, S. L. (1990). Research on teaching and teacher research: The issues that divide. *Educational Researcher, 19*(2), 2–11.

Cochran-Smith, M., & Lytle, S. L. (1993). *Inside/Outside: Teacher research and knowledge.* New York: Teachers College Press.

Cochran-Smith, M., & Lytle, S. (1998, April). *Knowledge for teaching: Where does it come from?* Paper presented at the Annual Meeting of the American Educational Research Association, San Diego, CA.

Cochran-Smith, M., & Lytle, S. L. (2001). Beyond certainty: Taking an inquiry stance on practice. In A. Lieberman & L. Miller (Eds.), *Teachers caught in the action: Professional development that matters* (pp. 45–58). New York: Teachers College Press.

Creswell, J. W. (1998). *Qualitative inquiry and research design: Choosing among five traditions.* Thousand Oaks, CA: Sage Publications.

Dana, N. F., & Yendol-Silva, D. (2003). *The reflective educator's guide to classroom research: Learning to teach and teaching to learn through practitioner inquiry.* Thousand Oaks, CA: Corwin Press.

Dana, N. F., Silva, D. Y., Snow-Gerono, J. L. (2002). Building a culture of inquiry in a professional development school. *Teacher Education & Practice, 15*(4) 71–89.

Darling-Hammond, L. (Ed.). (1994). *Professional development schools: Schools for developing a profession.* New York: Teachers College Press.

Erickson, R. (1986). Qualitative methods in research on teaching. In M. C. Wittrock (Ed.), *The handbook of research on teaching* (pp. 119–161). New York: Macmillan.

Geertz, C. (1973). *The interpretation of cultures.* New York: Basic Books.

Holmes Group. (1990). *Tomorrow's schools: Principles for the design of professional development schools.* East Lansing, MI: Holmes Group.

Holmes Group. (1986). *Tomorrow's teachers.* East Lansing, MI: The Holmes Group.

Hubbard, R. S., & Power, B. M. (1993). *The art of classroom inquiry: A handbook for teacher researchers.* Portsmouth, NH: Heinemann.

Hubbard, R. S., & Power, B. M. (1999). *Living the questions: A guide for teacher-researchers.* York, ME: Stenhouse Publishers.

Lieberman, A., & Miller, L. (Eds.). (2001). *Teachers caught in the action: Professional development that matters.* New York: Teachers College Press.

Lincoln, Y. S., & Guba, E. G. (1985). *Naturalistic inquiry.* Beverly Hills, CA: Sage.

Little, J. W. (2001). Professional development in pursuit of school reform. In A. Lieberman & L. Miller (Eds.), *Teachers caught in the action: Professional development that matters* (pp. 23–44). New York: Teachers College Press.

Lytle, S. L., & Cochran-Smith, M. (1990). Learning from teacher research: A working typology. *Teachers College Record, 92*(1), 83–103.

Lytle, S. L., & Cochran-Smith, M. (1992). Teacher research as a way of knowing. *Harvard Educational Review, 62*(4), 447–474.

Merriam, S. B. (1998). *Qualitative research and case study applications in education.* San Francisco: Jossey-Bass.

Patton, M. Q. (1990). *Qualitative evaluation and research methods.* Newbury Park, CA: Sage.

Sehr, D. (1997). *Education for a public democracy.* Albany: State University of New York Press.

Silva, D. Y., & Dana, N. F. (2001). Collaborative supervision in a professional development school. *Journal of Curriculum and Supervision 16*(4), 305–321.

Snow-Gerono, J. L. (2005). Professional development in a culture of inquiry: PDS teachers identify the benefits of professional learning communities. *Teaching and Teacher Education, 21*(3), 241–256.

Teitel, L. (2003). *Professional development schools handbook: Starting, sustaining, and assessing partnerships that improve student learning.* Thousand Oaks, CA: Corwin Press.

Trimbur, J. (1992). Consensus and difference in collaborative learning. In P. Shannon (Ed.), *Becoming political: Readings and writings in the politics of literacy education* (pp. 208–222). Portsmouth, NH: Heinemman.

Valli, L., Cooper, D., & Frankes, L. (1997). Professional development schools and equity: A critical analysis of rhetoric and research. In M. W. Apple (Ed.), *Review of research in education* (Vol. 22, pp. 251–304). Washington, DC: American Educational Research Association.

CHAPTER 18

A COMPARISON
OF EXPERIENCES OF YEAR-
LONG TEACHING INTERNS
AND TRADITIONAL
STUDENT TEACHERS
IN A PROFESSIONAL
DEVELOPMENT SCHOOL
SETTING

**Gary L. Willhite, D. John McIntyre,
and Kathy Thomas Willhite**

ABSTRACT

Research supports the notion that teacher candidates perceive their preparations programs' most powerful set of experiences as their field experience components. Our response to this research and to our own candidates' request for more time in the field was our development and implementation of an undergraduate teaching internship program in our professional development school

University and School Connections, pages 319–330
Copyright © 2008 by Information Age Publishing

(PDS) partnerships. Our research indicates that in the areas of planning, teaching and conferencing, Teaching Interns spent more time on each of these areas when compared to traditional student teachers in the same setting. Thus, more intense classroom interaction time was provided each Teaching Intern, resulting in a better-qualified candidate for the profession.

INTRODUCTION

Research supports the notion that teacher candidates perceive their preparation programs' most powerful set of experiences as their field experience components (Guyton & McIntyre, 1990; McIntyre, Byrd & Foxx, 1996). As a response to this research and to our candidates' request for additional time in P–12 classrooms, our teacher education program developed an undergraduate teaching internship program. This voluntary program, within a program, was developed through the professional development school (PDS) partnership forged with local public school districts. The Teaching Internship Program requires university students to double and sometimes triple the amount of time spent in their field placement the semester prior to student teaching and requires a mentor teacher to share their space, their time, and their students with a novice wanting to learn.

THE PROFESSIONAL DEVELOPMENT SCHOOL

Professional development schools (PDSs) are a product of educational reform trends and are viewed as a means to achieving some of the goals of educational reform. Known as professional development schools (Holmes Group, 1986), clinical schools (Carnegie Corporation, 1986), and professional practice schools (Levine, 1988), schools of this nature are exemplary school sites that have key components to improve student learning by improving teaching.

One of the major proponents of PDSs is the Holmes Partnership (2006), a consortium of universities, public school districts, and teachers associations, as well as national organizations. Since its inception, the Holmes Partnership has been dedicated to addressing issues associated with the low quality of teacher preparation in the United States. The organization defines itself as "a network of universities, schools, community agencies and national professional organizations working in partnership to create high quality professional development and significant school renewal to improve teaching and learning for all children" (online quote) and gives a list of six goals that are the foundation of the organization. These goals are Goal 1: High Quality Professional Preparation; Goal 2: Simultaneous Renewal; Goal 3: Equity, Diversity, Cultural Competence; Goal 4: Scholarly

Inquiry and Programs of Research; Goal 5: School and University-Based Faculty Development; and Goal 6: Policy Initiation.

The Holmes Partnership emphasizes the academic and field experience components of professional education, along with their close articulation and recommends the establishment of PDSs within public school districts in partnership with university teacher preparation programs. Lunenburg (1998) states, "The Professional Development Schools are unique in their ability to combine research, teacher training, and development of new models of teaching and learning simultaneously" (p. 401). In addition, the National Council for the Accreditation of Teacher Education (NCATE, 2006) states that PDSs are innovative institutions formed through partnerships between professional education programs and P–12 schools. PDS partnerships have a four-fold mission: (1) the preparation of new teachers; (2) faculty development; (3) inquiry directed at the improvement of practice; and (4) enhanced student achievement. PDSs improve both the quality of teaching and student learning. According to NCATE, there are five defining characteristics of PDSs. These are: Standard I: Learning Community; Standard II: Accountability and Quality Assurance; Standard III: Collaboration; Standard IV: Equity and Diversity; and Standard V: Structures, Resources and Roles (online quote).

Lunenburg (1998) reports that PDSs represent partnerships between schools and universities that come together for the following purposes: (1) to support the simultaneous renewal of schools and colleges of education; (2) to provide clinical education for new teachers in restructuring settings; (3) to support continuing professional development; and (4) to support inquiry directed at the improvement of practice. "And the following criteria have emerged already for identifying PDS sites: university and P–12 school faculty share a learner-centered approach to teaching and learning; there is parity between school and university within the collaboration, and issues of equity are addressed in the partnership" (p. 402).

Almost every commission and report on teacher education (Goodlad, 1990; Holmes, 1986, 1990; Levine, 1992) advocates the PDS as a strong vehicle for educational change. According to Linda Darling-Hammond (1994), professional development schools:

> aim to provide new models of teacher education and development by serving as exemplars of practice, builders of knowledge and vehicles for communicating professional understanding among teacher educators, enter professional practice by working with expert practitioners, enabling veteran teachers to renew their own professional development and assume new roles as mentors, university adjuncts, and teacher leaders. They allow school and university educators to engage jointly in research and rethinking of practice, thus creating an opportunity for the profession to expand its knowledge base by putting research into practice—and practice into research. (p. 1)

Darling-Hammond further describes PDSs as spaces where prospective and mentor teacher learning becomes (1) experimental, (2) grounded in teacher questions, (3) collaborative, (4) connected to and derived from teachers' work with their students, and (5) sustained, intensive, and connected to other aspects of school change. In 1996, Cassandra Book stated that PDSs "hold much promise as a means of reforming teaching and learning in schools, the preparation of novice educators, and the organization of schools" (p. 207). More than ten years later, the promise of the PDS movement—although not fully realized—is beginning to live up to its potential.

TEACHING INTERNSHIPS

The idea of teaching internships is not new. In 1990, Wise, Darling-Hammond and Gendler proposed that a paid internship be required for aspiring teachers. In place of the "sink or swim" approach to the teacher training of the past, the Rand Center for the Study of the Teaching Profession recommended a new, one-year formal training program similar to those for engineers, architects, and physicians. The new program was to provide hands-on training along with guidance, support, and, as the year progressed, increased responsibility. Under this plan, students would serve as teaching interns after they graduated from college but before receiving a teaching certificate. Primarily used as a weeding out mechanism, this type of plan has not proved popular. Although some teacher-training programs have adopted a fifth year, there are, however, few examples of a paid internship as suggested by these researchers.

The purpose of year-long teaching internships is to more significantly blend theory and practice during the candidates' preparation program. A significant portion of the instruction is "on the job." Wise, Darling-Hammond and Gendler (1990) believe that the major purposes of teaching internships are to select and prepare intern candidates and link education theory with classroom practice and to provide effective supervision, intensive support, and "artful blending" of the theoretical and practical aspects of good teaching. The concept of a network of support providers is important in internships. Nearly all intern programs are organized so that a group of interns enter and complete the program as a cohort. Previous studies of internship programs document the importance of the peer group in encouraging dialogue, lifting those who struggle, and developing reflective practitioners (McKibbin 1996, 1999; Wright, McKibbin, & Walton, 1987).

Research on Undergraduate Teaching Internships

Fischetti et al. (1999) describe a year-long student teaching internship at a high school PDS in Louisville, Kentucky. They report that the interns believed the program was successful because it allowed them to become comfortable with their classroom, knowledgeable about their teacher's planning, and helped them develop meaningful relationships with teachers and students. Interns also reported feeling less anxious about teaching.

Conaway and Mitchell (2004) reported on a year-long internship in a PDS at Baylor University and discovered that there were significant differences between the expectation of interns and traditional student teachers in the areas of instructional planning, classroom management, and social interaction between pupils and teachers. In short, interns were far more independent and assumed more responsibility than traditional student teachers.

Ridley, Hurwitz, Hackett, and Miller (2005) found that there were nonsignificant differences between traditional student teachers and year-long interns in teaching effectiveness. However, they did find significant differences during each group's first year of teaching. This was especially true for the instructional variables of managing student behavior, maintaining students' interest during instruction, and providing specific and immediate feedback.

Southern Illinois School University Partnership and Teaching Internship Program

The Southern Illinois School University Partnership was established in 1999. Since that time, the Partnership has established PDS sites in three local school districts and has implemented a number of collaborative initiatives. These PDSs were created to promote improved preparation of teacher candidates, improved professional development of practicing teachers, and improved learning opportunities for P–12 students.

One of the most recent initiatives has been the implementation of the Teaching Internship Program in elementary education in our PDS sites. The inertia for the Teaching Internship was from teachers and administrators at one of our PDSs who questioned why teacher candidates did not spend more time in the field. After many meetings and fruitful discussions within the partnership, the Teaching Internship Program was piloted in the fall of 2004 with one of the PDS sites and was then fully implemented in the fall of 2005 with an expansion to the other two PDS sites. The internship was designed for students to complete their Block 3 course work—the semester prior to student teaching—(Science, Math, and Social Studies methods and a Classroom Management course) and Block 4 student teaching in a PDS setting.

Once accepted into the Teacher Education Program, interested students must apply, meet the qualifications, and be matched with a mentor teacher for the Teaching Internship Program (their senior year or what is called Block 3 and Block 4). This year-long, inquiry-based internship is designed to immerse the prospective teacher into the school's culture, develop deeper understanding of student learning, and create a wider experience base from which the prospective teacher can draw when they enter the teaching profession as a first-year teacher.

The Teaching Internship Program differs from our traditional elementary teacher education program in a number of ways. First, Teaching Interns report to the school prior to the beginning of the school year in order to assist their Mentor Teachers in preparing their classroom. Second, Teaching Interns spend up to three full days in their public school classroom during the fall semester. This compares to one-half day for the traditional elementary education teacher candidates. In reality, interns accumulate 150–200 hours of field experience during Block 3 experience compared to 36–40 hours for the traditional elementary education teacher candidate. Third, Teaching Interns follow the school calendar. This means that the Teaching Interns complete their fall semester in the schools when the school district dismisses for Christmas rather than at the conclusion of university final exams. Likewise, the Teaching Interns begin their student teaching phase when the school district commences after Christmas Break and finish their student teaching on the school district's last day in May or June. This can result in as many as 7–8 extra weeks of full-time student teaching. Fourth, Teaching Interns complete an inquiry, action research project in the spring and present that project at a showcase presentation in late spring. Fifth, potential Teaching Interns must interview with teachers and administrators from the PDS schools in order to determine effective intern-mentor matches. Finally, all mentor teachers must have completed a workshop in teacher mentoring that is conducted through the PDSs.

The Teaching Internship Program, during the 2004–05 academic year, accepted nine students into the program, one of whom was a dual major in Special Education/Elementary Education. Seven of the nine successfully completed the program (one dropped due to illness and another dropped due to the distance in travel). This first-year pilot program placed all of the Teaching Interns in the same K–5 building.

During the second year (2005–06) of the Teaching Internship Program, 17 students were selected from 27 applicants. Applicants are forewarned that if a good match between the applicants and a mentor, grade level, or school cannot be made; they may not be selected for the program. Of the

17 who entered the program, two voluntarily stepped out of the program for personal reasons.

Mentor teachers had a five-hour beginning orientation, followed by monthly professional development seminars during the 2004–05 pilot year. The mentor teachers had a voice in setting the expectations and assessment procedures for the interns. The monthly mentoring workshops/seminars were designed as a place for the mentor teacher to express concerns, to determine solutions, and to have training in collaborative action research planning and implementation. In addition, the mentoring workshops served as a forum to design the assessment tools, learn how to work with adults (not just student teachers) in sharing ideas and in giving constructive feedback, and to brainstorm innovative ideas for the internship program. One idea was to have the Teaching Intern rotate through each of the mentor teacher's classrooms so that they were aware of the varied grade level expectations and became more familiar with the learning community in which they were involved. Interestingly, the mentor teachers asked to stop the rotation before it was completed for two reasons: (1) normal classroom disruptions for testing, substitutes and fall holiday activities, and (2) they had gotten used to the idea of having the intern as their co-teacher in their classroom and were unwilling to share them.

RESEARCH STUDY

The purpose of this study was to compare the experiences of Teaching Interns and traditional student teachers within a PDS site. More specifically, the study examined the potential differences between the Teaching Interns and traditional student teachers in the number of hours spent planning, the number of hours spent teaching, and the number of hours spent in conferencing with the mentor teacher/cooperating teacher. The traditional student teachers were also placed in schools within the PDS site.

Each week both interns and student teachers were asked to complete an instrument that asked them to estimate the amount of time they had spent during a given week in the areas of planning, teaching, and conferencing with their mentor or cooperating teacher during their student teaching semester. Data from the first two years of the program were used for the purpose of this study. Over the two-year period, 18 interns and 8 student teachers returned useable data.

In order to analyze the data, the 16-week semester was divided into 4-week quarters. The average or mean number of hours spent planning, teaching, and conferencing was determined for each student per 4-week period. Thus, it was possible to compare not only the differences between the interns and student teachers but also it was possible to analyze how the hours increased or decreased within these categories throughout the semester. Since the number of participants is small, no statistical analysis was conducted on the data. However, trends are evident that can inform the profession regarding potential benefits of a year-long teaching internship.

RESULTS

Table 18.1 indicates that Teaching Interns spent more time planning for their teaching activities than did their traditional student teaching peers placed in the same PDS site. These differences were 3.7 hours in the first quarter, 2.6 in the second quarter, 3.2 in the third quarter, and 4.8 in the final quarter. The reason for this difference in the amount of time spent planning is unclear. It could be that the interns had established a routine for planning during the fall semester since they would have spent substantially more time teaching in the semester prior to student teaching than their student teaching counterparts. This pattern may have simply continued during the student teaching semester. However, it may also be the result of spending more time teaching during student teaching than their traditional peers that would have necessitated the need for additional planning.

The same trends continue in the areas of teaching and conferencing. The data indicate that the Teaching Interns spent more time teaching than did their traditional student teaching counterparts. The differences seem to be more pronounced during the first half of the semester, are less noticeable during the third quarter, and then increase once again during the final four weeks of student teaching. One can only speculate as to why these

TABLE 18.1 The Average Number of Hours Teaching Interns and Student Teachers Spend Planning, Teaching and Conferencing During Student Teaching

	1st Qtr	2nd Qtr	3rd Qtr	4th Qtr
Planning				
Teaching Intern	10.5	10.5	10.7	11.5
Student teacher	6.8	7.9	7.5	6.7
Teaching				
Teaching Intern	20.9	23.1	20.6	19.6
Student teacher	11.3	14.7	17.7	12.2
Conferencing				
Teaching Intern	5.2	5.1	5.1	4.6
Student teacher	5.8	4.7	3.7	1.7

differences exist. However, it appears that the Teaching Interns were ready to accept teaching responsibilities during the student teaching semester sooner than their peers as a result of having spent a substantial amount of time teaching in their classrooms during the fall semester. Thus, there was no transition to or phasing in during the student teaching semester, as they appeared ready to assume teaching duties from the first day of the student teaching semester.

For all but the first quarter, Teaching Interns spent more time conferencing with their mentor teacher than did the student teachers. Student teachers spent slightly more time conferencing with their cooperating teachers during the first quarter. One item of note is the consistency of the time that Teaching Interns and mentor teachers spent conferencing throughout the semester. Perhaps this is the result of a pattern that had been established during the fall semester and then simply continued during student teaching, whereas, the student teachers had to establish a pattern or "rhythm" with their cooperating teachers since they most likely were not placed with that teacher for one of the early field experiences during the semester prior to student teaching.

ANECDOTAL DATA

In addition to the data collected from the teacher candidates, much was also learned from anecdotal data collected from mentor teachers. For example, mentor teachers related their beliefs that the Interns were much better prepared and ready for their student teaching experience than the traditional elementary education student teachers and that the Teaching Interns had become more fully integrated into the classroom and school environment than the traditional student teachers. In addition, mentor teachers mentioned that they often co-planned and co-taught with the Teaching Intern since they already had so much teaching experience entering the student teaching semester. Finally, many of the Teaching Interns shared that a major reason they were able to secure full-time teaching positions after graduation was the additional teaching experience they acquired during the internship.

DISCUSSION

The data collected on the Teaching Interns is fairly comparable to the aforementioned studies. The data indicate that Teaching Interns acquired more teaching experience during their student teaching semester than did traditional student teachers. Anecdotal evidence seems to reveal that this additional teaching experience has prepared the interns for the teaching profession. For example, one Teaching Intern said, "With the year-long internship, I have worked in the classroom all year long. I know how to start the school year and I know how to end the school year. I have had full control over the classroom for 3 plus months and know that I am more prepared than other student teachers." Another Teaching Intern stated, "The internship provided me with the extra time to know my students better which, in turn, allowed me to better instruct them. I had more quality time with my mentor teacher to discuss classroom management and techniques. I wouldn't have had time to do this otherwise. I had the opportunity to experiment and do inquiries that helped me to better understand unique scenarios."

The data also indicated that the Teaching Interns spent more time planning than the traditional student teachers placed in the same professional development school site. One possible reason for this difference in planning time is that since the Teaching Interns had been in the classroom from the beginning of the school year and had spent significantly more time in their classroom prior to student teaching, they were already involved in the classroom and school environment/programs and simply continued what they were doing as student teachers. For example, one Teaching Intern mentioned, "I chaperoned two field trips, I planned and delivered lessons and activities for family reading/family math and science nights. I actively participated in many child studies, IEP meetings, parent teacher conferences, and worked in cooperation with our "room grandma" to plan activities for the students."

Finally, the data reveal that the Teaching Interns spent more time conferencing with their mentor teachers than did the traditional student teachers. It is possible that the mentoring workshop required of all mentor teachers encourages additional conferencing, as suggested by Killian and McIntyre (1986). However, several of the cooperating teachers had also participated in workshops focusing on mentoring and/or supervisory skills. More likely, the relationship that developed between the mentor teacher and Teaching Intern during the fall semester simply continued to develop more fully throughout the student teaching experience. A Teaching Intern reinforces this notion by stating, "I was comfortable with my mentor teacher. By January, after working with her for almost 5 months, we had built a relationship that made me feel comfortable sharing new ideas for our classroom." Another said, "My mentor teacher has also been very helpful in preparing me for my student teaching experience. She has worked with me immensely the semester before student teaching. Therefore, we had a very well established relationship when I began student teaching. We both knew how each other worked."

CONCLUSION

In conclusion, it is our belief that an enhanced teaching profession can only occur with closer collaborative relationships between universities and public schools. Using vehicles such as professional development schools and programs such as year-long Teaching Internships can provide future, and current teachers with the tools to improve their practice and, as a result, improve the learning experiences and opportunities for their students. Year-long teaching internships provide future teachers with an immersion in the "real world" of classrooms that is not available through the traditional student teaching route. Benefits for the teacher candidate appear to be undergraduate co-teaching experience, in-depth field and reflective experience, professional development as a member of a learning community, and special recognition as a teaching intern. The emphasis on inquiry will, hopefully, provide both future and current teachers with the tools to cope with the ever rapidly changing world of knowledge and information. Clearly, the Teaching Interns, themselves, provide the best testimonials for this program. As one Teaching Intern stated, "All students should have to go through the internship at SIU to graduate. It was the most rewarding experience." A second suggested, ". . . make everyone do a year-long internship. I have gained so much real-life experience in the classroom from being in the same classroom for a whole year." As the profession continues to gather data on the success of year-long internships, it will behoove us to ask, "Why aren't all teacher education candidates involved in year-long experiences in the schools?"

REFERENCES

Book, C. (1996). Professional development schools. In. J. Sikula (Ed.), *Handbook of research on teacher education* (pp. 194–210). New York: Macmillan.

Carnegie Corporation of New York. (1986). *A nation prepared: Teachers for the 21st century.* New York: Carnegie Corporation of New York. ED 268 120.

Conaway, B. J., & Mitchell, M. W. (2004). A comparison of the experiences of year-long interns in a professional development school and one-semester student teachers in a non-PDS location. *Action in Teacher Education, 26*(3), 21–28.

Darling-Hammond, L. (Ed.), (1994). *Professional development schools: Schools for developing a profession.* New York: Teachers College Press.

Darling-Hammond, L., & McLauglin, M. (1995). Policies that support professional development in an era of reform. *Phi Delta Kappan, 76*(8), 597–604.

Fischetti, J., Garrett, L., Gilbert, J.I., Johnson, S., Johnston, P., Larson, A., Kenealy, A., Schneider, E., & Streible, J. (2000). This just makes sense: Yearlong experience in a high school professional development school. *Peabody Journal of Education, 73*(3/4), 310–318.

Goodlad, J. (1990). *Teachers for our nation's schools.* San Francisco: Jossey-Bass.

Guyton, E., & McIntyre, D. J. (1990). Student teaching and school experiences. In W.R. Houston (Ed.), *Handbook of research in teacher education* (pp. 514–534). New York: Macmillan.

Holmes Group. (1986). *Tomorrow's teachers.* East Lansing, MI: Author.

Holmes Group. (1990). Statement of principles. *Tomorrow's schools: Principles for the design of professional development schools.* East Lansing, MI: Author.

Holmes Group. (1995). *Tomorrow's schools of education.* East Lansing, MI: Author.

Holmes Partnership, (2006). *The Holmes Partnership: Working to improve teaching and learning.* Retrieved October 1, 2006, from: http://www.holmespartnership. org/

Killian, J. E., & McIntyre, D. J. (1986). Quality in the early field experiences: A product of grade level and cooperating teachers' training. *Teaching and Teacher Education, 2*(4), 367–376.

Levine, M., (1988). *Professional practice schools: Building a model.* Washington DC: Center for Restructuring, American Federation of Teachers. SP 031 702.

Levine, M. (Ed.). (1992). *Professional practice schools: Linking teacher education and school reform.* New York: Teachers College Press.

Levine, M. (Ed.). (1998). *Designing standards that work for professional development schools.* Washington, DC: National Council for the Accreditation of Teacher Education.

Lunenburg, F. C. (1998). Revolution in the teaching profession. *College Student Journal, 32*(3), 400–406.

McIntyre, D. J., Byrd, D. M., & Foxx, S. M. (1996). Field and laboratory experiences. In J. Sikula (Ed.), *Handbook of research on teacher education* (2nd ed., pp. 171–193). New York: Macmillan.

McKibbin, M. D. (1996). *The effectiveness of district intern programs of alternative certification in California: A longitudinal study.* Sacramento, CA: Commission on Teacher Credentialing.

McKibbin, M. D. (1999). Alternative Certification in Action: California's Teaching Internships. *Kappa Delta Pi Record, 36*(1), 8–11.

National Council for the Accreditation of Teacher Education (NCATE). (2006). Retrieved October 5, 2006, from: http://www.ncate.org/public/pdswhat

Ridley, D. S., Hurwitz, S., Hackett, M. R. D., & Miller, K. K. (2005). Comparing PDS and campus –based preservice teacher preparation. Is PDS-based preparation really better? *Journal of Teacher Education, 56*(1), 46–56.

Wise, A., Darling-Hammond, L., & Gendler, T. (1990). *The teaching internship: Practical preparation for a licensed profession.* Santa Monica, CA: Rand, Center for the Study of the Teaching Profession.

Wright, D., McKibbin, M. D., & Walton, P. (1987). *The effectiveness of the teacher trainee program: An alternative route into teaching in California.* Sacramento, CA: Commission on Teacher Credentialing.

PART IV

PROGRAM ASSESSMENT AND EVALUATION

CHAPTER 19

THE URBAN INITIATIVE PROFESSIONAL DEVELOPMENT SCHOOL'S INTERN ASSESSMENT SYSTEM

A Contextualized and Authentic Pre-Service Evaluation Method

Juliana M. Taymans, Kathleen P. Tindle, Maxine B. Freund, Lindsay A. Harris, and Deanna M. Ortiz

ABSTRACT

The Urban Initiative Professional Development School (UI-PDS) was a nine-year collaboration between The George Washington University's Graduate School of Education and Human Development and a high poverty District of Columbia public high school. The District of Columbia Public Schools (DCPS) provided the UI-PDS with Title II funding to formally study Interns and first-year graduates (Novices) during the final year of the collaboration.

University and School Connections, pages 333–358
Copyright © 2008 by Information Age Publishing

Findings from this study focused on identifying program features that lead to positive outcomes for Intern and Novice teachers. One of the conclusions of this study was that the UI-PDS Assessment System provided important information to guide the development of interns and the documentation of program outcomes. The purpose of this chapter is to describe the UI-PDS Assessment System and associated key outcomes.

INTRODUCTION

The poor social and academic outcomes of children in urban areas such as Washington, DC have long been a cause concern. A partnership between The George Washington University's (GWU) Graduate School of Education and Human Development and Cardozo Senior High School (Cardozo SHS), a District of Columbia Public School (DCPS), was developed to address the lack of well-qualified teachers prepared to serve the youth of Washington, DC. The partnership that emerged was called the Urban Initiative Professional Development School (UI-PDS). During the last year of the UI-PDS partnership, the DCPS provided Title II funding to support the UI-PDS Evaluation Study. This study investigated the effectiveness of the UI-PDS's teacher preparation program. Data collected for this study included results from the UI-PDS Assessment System as well as interviews, focus groups, and survey data from current UI-PDS interns (Interns), first-year graduates of the UI-PDS (Novices), and mentor teachers at Cardozo SHS (Mentors). One significant result of the UI-PDS Evaluation Study was evidence indicating the importance of the UI-PDS's Assessment System. This comprehensive, contextualized assessment system was designed to promote pre-service teachers' growth and development toward becoming successful educators of diverse students, professional collaborators, and student advocates willing to persist in challenging urban environments. The purpose of this chapter is to describe the UI-PDS Assessment System and discuss findings from the UI-PDS Evaluation Study that demonstrate the connection between the UI-PDS Assessment System and effective program outcomes.

This chapter provides information in five sections. The first section provides information on the history and attributes of the UI-PDS program. The second section presents the conceptual framework for the Intern Assessment System. The third section presents the components of the UI-PDS Assessment System, followed by a brief section describing the methodologies used in the UI-PDS Evaluation study. The final section of the chapter discusses key outcomes from the UI-PDS Evaluation Study linked to the UI-PDS Assessment System.

BACKGROUND

History of UI-PDS

GWU's Graduate School of Education and Human Development is committed to preparing professionals in education and human services who aspire to work in settings that broaden successful outcomes for children, youth, and families in the Washington, DC metropolitan area. As GWU's commitments to Washington, DC were long-standing, in 1994 several faculty and research staff decided to begin a professional development school (PDS) relationship with Cardozo SHS, a high school serving a high percentage of students living in poverty. The collaboration that emerged between GWU and Cardozo SHS's principal and staff was called the UI-PDS. In the fall of 1995, the UI-PDS began educating its first cohort of teachers, a partnership which continued for nine years. The UI-PDS graduated its final cohort in 2004 and was not continued due to lack of funding.

The main purpose of the UI-PDS was to prepare teachers to meet the demands of inner-city teaching, demonstrate effective practice, and remain in teaching, despite the usual 50 percent attrition rate within three years for new teachers in urban settings (Darling-Hammond & Snyder, 1999). In order to prepare for and remain in urban teaching, UI-PDS graduate students participated in a two-year master's degree program that included a year-long, full-time internship. This preparation cumulated in licensure in special education or dual licensure in special education and a content area (e.g., mathematics, science, English as a Second Language, etc.). The UI-PDS retention rate for graduates remaining in teaching since 1997 is 89 percent, with 68 percent of UI-PDS graduates continuing to teach in DCPSs since 2000. Of those UI-PDS graduates who have left DCPSs, 66 percent continue to teach in urban settings such as Los Angeles and Phoenix.

UI-PDS Key Attributes

To prepare graduates to work in urban schools, the UI-PDS incorporated five design features: graduate student choice, a focus on adolescent literacy, a social justice framework, consistent on-site support, and preparation for collaboration.

Graduate student choice. Unlike many PDSs, which at some universities are a standardized part of teacher preparation, the UI-PDS was one of many graduate teacher preparation options offered at GWU. This level of choice allowed prospective graduate students to apply to the UI-PDS based on their desire to work in urban secondary schools and to engage in a year-long, full-time internship.

Literacy focus.   Language and literacy development was a central theme across the two years of coursework required for UI-PDS Interns. As part of the PDS contribution to Cardozo SHS, the UI-PDS provided a literacy course for ninth- and tenth-grade students. The Literacy Curriculum for this course was designed to present students with a 'balanced literacy' program (Pressley, 2002) that included vocabulary development, word study, comprehension strategies, sustained silent reading, process writing, and multimedia presentations. Interns, working in pairs with guidance from a GWU literacy coordinator, co-planned and co-taught the literacy course one period a day from the first day of the school year. Interns were also required to infuse literacy instruction into their content area internship classes, which they co-taught with skilled Cardozo SHS teachers who served as Mentors.

To build students' thinking skills and address issues youth faced in their daily lives, the Literacy Curriculum focused on developing students' critical awareness of societal issues (Freire, 1993), called "critical literacy," which focused instruction on how texts reflect different social, cultural, and historical perspectives and biases (Taymans, Tindle, & Ortiz, 2005). Critical literacy asks teachers to pose challenging questions to students about societal inequities, to engage students in discussions, and to guide students to take subsequent action when possible (Provenzo, 2005). The critical portion of the Literacy Curriculum required Interns to tap into students' perspectives and background experiences that may not normally be included in academic instruction.

Social justice.   Social justice was embedded in the UI-PDS through a systematic approach to help address the adolescent literacy needs of an urban community as well as through Intern preparation in special education. While all UI-PDS Interns worked toward certification in special education, the majority also worked toward an additional certification in a content area. Working toward dual licensure and teaching the Literacy Curriculum promoted a student-centered view of instruction. In addition to working to provide appropriate instruction for all students, interns were often compelled to support and advocate for students with disabilities who were in need of more assistance in other classes.

Consistent on-site support.   Six professionals were responsible for guiding and sustaining the UI-PDS relationship. The two Cardozo SHS educators were the principal and an English teacher who also served as the ninth-grade team leader. The four GWU participating educators were the dean's liaison for partnerships, a special education faculty advisor, a project director, and a literacy coordinator.

The project director or literacy coordinator provided on-site daily support to Interns as they worked with students, taught lessons, and planned for instruction. Both the project director and the literacy coordinator conducted separate weekly seminars for Interns that addressed planning, instructional strategies, problem-solving related to student issues, collaboration, and preparation for non-instructional teacher responsibilities (such as conducting parent conferences, communicating with school staff, and building community relationships).

Collaboration and community. The UI-PDS was structured to build collaboration and community. The university-school collaboration was supported by the relationship between the UI-PDS project director and the ninth-grade team leader at Cardozo SHS. Collaboration and community were also enhanced physically through the Literacy Lab, a designated space for teaching the literacy course and a flexible work area utilized by Interns, UI-PDS staff, and Cardozo SHS teachers and students. The Literacy Lab provided a physical space that promoted collaboration and a sense of a learning community. Collaboration was further enhanced by the cadre of Mentor teachers which expanded over the years. Content internships with Mentor teachers were developed as co-teaching arrangements (Cook & Friend, 2005) to promote inclusive instructional practices. These individuals provided Interns with a semester-long structured and supported experience in content instruction.

Also, Interns were required to co-teach the literacy class on a daily basis. Grouped in teams of two or three, Interns were responsible for the 87-minute instructional block. Planning involved not only creating a good lesson or instructional unit but also collaborating with another Intern whose instructional style or philosophy of education may have differed greatly from their own. In addition to learning how to teach, co-teaching made their internship experiences significantly more complex by increasing the time and energy needed to negotiate ideas, build consensus, debrief lessons, and coordinate instructional responsibilities.

In summary, the UI-PDS's program "attributes and daily operations" firmly situated Intern preparation in a multifaceted and challenging urban school context in which Interns were able to experience a full range of urban experiences. The consistent daily support fostered Interns' development as teachers and collaborators skilled at meeting the diverse needs of urban students. Additionally, the UI-PDS provided the school and university partners with opportunities to learn from each other and work together toward improved educational experiences for all high school students attending Cardozo SHS.

THE CONCEPTUAL FRAMEWORK FOR THE UI-PDS ASSESSMENT SYSTEM

The UI-PDS Assessment System was developed to gauge Interns' development across the variety of demands faced by urban teachers. The conceptual framework for the UI-PDS Assessment System consisted of two interdependent concepts: authenticity and accountability (see Figure 19.1). The concept of authenticity defined the elements of the UI-PDS that represented the "real life" nature of teacher preparation work within an urban high school. The concept of accountability guided the array of assessments employed.

Authenticity

As displayed in Figure 19.1, the UI-PDS concept of authenticity was broadly based in research reflecting the reality of urban schools and the life of urban educators. Authenticity, as defined by the UI-PDS, also incorporated the tenets of Contextual Teaching and Learning (CT&L) (Sears & Hersh, 1998), a research and theory-based model of teacher preparation. Finally, the UI-PDS conception of authenticity was shaped by the UI-PDS Mission Statement that more specifically defined the aim of the program's work.

The reality of urban schools. Peterman (2005) has targeted some essential challenges of urban schools. These include organizational issues, funding,

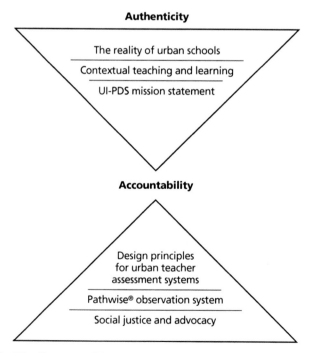

Figure 19.1 The Conceptual Framework of UI-PDS Assessment System grounded in authenticity and accountability.

diversity, and students' economic levels. Urban schools are bureaucratic and contradictory, which means that teachers experience multiple and changing directives. Some initiatives can appear to hold promise for improving students' school experiences and others do not. Such an environment demands that teachers have a strong inner compass to navigate their ways through shifting messages. These navigation skills require teachers not to necessarily give into ever-changing policy directives, to fight feeling victimized by chaotic school systems, and to teach in ways they know are effective. Urban schools are also often under-resourced at the school building level as evidenced by poor physical facilities and a lack of instructional materials. This necessitates that teachers become resourceful in finding ways to make instruction memorable and meaningful. Many urban schools are located in multilingual, multiracial, and multiethnic neighborhoods. This diversity has the potential for rich cross-cultural experiences when teachers know how to tap into students' cultures. This diversity often means that students possess varied levels of literacy and content knowledge, which requires teachers to find a way to build on students' prior knowledge and experiences when their backgrounds do not match the standard academic curriculum. Finally, many students who attend urban schools are living in high poverty communities. Teachers work with students who may be facing multiple out-of-school challenges due to their families' economic status and/or lack of neighborhood resources. Many urban educators believe that helping students to identify and address social justice issues is an important part of preparing them to be able to become productive and self-determined individuals. Thus, teacher preparation for urban schools must address these realities and provide experiences that allow pre-service teachers to learn how to effectively address these challenges and define the experiences they will find rewarding and self-sustaining.

Contextual teaching and learning. Contextual Teaching and Learning (CT&L) served as the UI-PDS's theoretical framework for teacher education (Sears & Hersh, 1998). CT&L incorporates multiple teaching and learning theories, including cognitive theories that stress the situated, social, and distributed nature of learning (Brown, Collins, & Duguid, 1989), constructivism (Simon, 1995), self-regulation (Bandura, 1986), problem solving (Albanese & Mitchell, 1993) and school-to-career theories (Hamilton, 1990). CT&L can be defined as teaching that uses a variety of in-school and out-of-school contexts to develop pre-service teachers' abilities to solve the real dilemmas they will face as teachers, while, at the same time, learning to work both alone and in various group structures. The real world nature of CT&L preparation is intended to promote pre-service teachers' abilities to self-regulate as they manage the many demands of a typical school day. One of the main tenets of the CT&L framework is the importance of employing authentic methods of assessment. This assessment practice is based on the recognition that teaching is a highly complex activity that is best developed when assessment is ongoing, multifaceted, and includes teacher reflection and action (as well as important evidence of student learning).

The UI mission statement. Based on urban PDS experience and the tenets of CT&L, the UI-PDS developed the following mission statement to guide the UI-PDS Assessment System:

> The Urban Initiative Professional Development School (UI-PDS) is a community of learners comprised of faculty, staff, graduate pre-service teachers, alumni, and school personnel working within urban schools. The UI-PDS community is committed to providing teacher preparation within the context of urban schools to develop competent, caring, collaborative, and reflective teachers who can effectively address the educational needs of adolescents with diverse backgrounds and learning profiles. The UI-PDS provides specific preparation to enable teachers to address the literacy needs of adolescent learners and to promote social justice through their teaching and advocacy for students' rights. (Tindle, Taymans, & Lander, 2004, p. 3)

Accountability

The UI-PDS held itself accountable, based on three main considerations. First, the Assessment System had to address the challenges of teaching in urban schools. Peterman's (2005) design principles for urban teacher assessment provided a clear description of the contextualized nature of the UI-PDS Assessment System. Although these principles were not available during the UI-PDS's assessment methods selection and design process, they serve as a clear description of the tenets that undergird the Assessment System. Second, the system needed to ascertain if Interns were able to demonstrate the basic competencies expected of any well-prepared pre-service teacher. Thus, the Educational Testing Service's (ETS) framework for pre-service teacher development as presented in Pathwise® (also known as Praxis III) (ETS, 2001) was selected because it is a concise, systematic, and research-based tool that describes the complex areas of development necessary for competent beginning teaching. The third consideration for the UI-PDS Assessment System was based on a growing recognition that Interns should be prepared to both cope and actively address systemic issues that they will face in urban schools, particularly in relation to special education.

Design principles for urban teacher assessment systems. Urban school systems are complex and demanding places often caught in competing political agendas, high staff turnover, and scathing critiques based on standardized test scores. These realities can easily discourage the most committed pre-service or in-service teacher. Based on these contextual variables, Peterman

(2005) has identified four principles for urban teacher assessment systems which are reflected in the UI-PDS Assessment System.

- The assessment system must be situated and responsive and take into account the urban school context and the conditions that pre-service teachers face once employed. A good assessment system is based on a solid conceptual framework which makes clear the mission and goals of the teacher education program.
- The assessment system should be longitudinal and reflective by capturing pre-service teachers' growth in negotiating the real-life, day-to-day challenges presented by urban schools. The assessment system should allow for ongoing feedback and reflection with input from individuals who are helping shape the pre-service teachers experience such as their peers, mentor teachers, and university faculty.
- The assessment system should be capacity building for all involved individuals. This means that the assessment system should be transparent to allow school and university-based partners to learn about the best ways to prepare and support new teachers for this challenging work.
- The conditions present in many urban schools are an outgrowth of social injustice experienced by families with low socioeconomic status. Preparing pre-service teachers to develop a critical mindset, as well as learning how to take action to address inequities, is important preparation for urban teaching. Thus, the assessment system must incorporate how well pre-service teachers develop connections to community and families and how they learn to address societal and institutional inequities.

The Pathwise® framework. The Pathwise® framework was developed by Educational Testing Services (ETS) based on extensive research on beginning teaching (Dwyer, 1994; Myford, 1993). It contains four assessment domains with specific criteria focused on planning, teaching, classroom management and teacher professionalism (see Table 19.1). The Pathwise® system provided a guiding framework for Interns, Mentor teachers, and UI-PDS staff to discuss and analyze Interns' daily work. The framework and accompanying assessment protocols allowed Interns to demonstrate their knowledge, skills, and abilities in pragmatic tasks within contextual assessments based on observations, interviews, presentation of artifacts, feedback, and teacher reflection (Goodman, 2002).

Social justice and advocacy. To compliment the four domains of Pathwise®, an additional fifth domain was created in order to evaluate the social justice and advocacy aspects of the UI-PDS Mission Statement. This additional domain examined Intern and Novice teachers' abilities to grapple

TABLE 19.1 Pathwise® Domains and Criteria

Pathwise® Domain	Domain Criteria
A: Organizing Content Knowledge for Student Learning	A1: Becoming familiar with students' background knowledge and experiences
	A2: Articulating clear learning goals for the lesson that are appropriate to the students
	A3: Demonstrating an understanding of the connections between the content that was learned previously, the current content, and the content that remains to be learned in the future
	A4: Creating or selecting methods, learning activities, and instructional materials or other resources that are appropriate to the students and that are aligned with the goals of the lesson
	A5: Creating or selecting evaluation strategies that are appropriate for the students and that are aligned with the goals of the lesson
B: Creating an Environment for Student Learning	B1: Creating a climate that promotes fairness
	B2: Establishing and maintaining rapport with students
	B3: Communicating challenging learning expectations to each student
	B4: Establishing and maintaining consistent standards of classroom behavior
	B5: Making the physical environment as safe and conducive to learning as possible
C: Teaching for Student Learning	C1: Making learning goals and instructional procedures clear to students
	C2: Making content comprehensible to students
	C3: Encouraging students to extend their thinking
	C4: Monitoring students' understanding of content through a variety of means, providing feedback to students to assist learning, and adjusting learning activities as the situation demands
	C5: Using instructional time effectively
D: Teacher Professionalism	D1: Reflecting on the extent to which the learning goals were met
	D2: Demonstrating a sense of efficacy
	D3: Building professional relationships with colleagues to share teaching insights and to coordinate learning activities for students
	D4: Communicating with parents or guardians about student learning

with systematic issues related to urban teaching and special education. The Pathwise® framework, combined with this additional UI-PDS domain, enlarged the context of the UI-PDS teacher preparation beyond Cardozo SHS and helped address larger systematic issues.

In summary, the UI-PDS Assessment System was grounded in contextual authenticity in order to capture the real-life experiences of the UI-PDS. Research-based standards and practices, which were enhanced and expanded with elements from the UI-PDS Mission Statement, provided the conceptual framework for the UI-PDS Assessment System. This system was operationalized in a way that held the program accountable for developing competent beginning teachers while it also addressed the challenging issues faced by urban teachers.

THE UI-PDS ASSESSMENT SYSTEM

The UI-PDS Assessment System was developed over time in order to assess the multifaceted skills needed by urban educators to be successful teachers, collaborators, and advocates who are resilient and committed to remaining in urban education despite its many challenges. The majority of the assessment processes in the UI-PDS Assessment System were designed to provide Interns with feedback and support for continued growth and development. The assessment process spanned the full-range of Intern experiences from the application process to coursework prior to their internships, internship work, and to post-graduation follow-up. Additionally, the UI-PDS Assessment System functioned as a way to provide ongoing evaluative feedback to the program in order to strengthen UI-PDS pre-service preparation practices.

Haberman Interview Protocol

Recruitment is a crucial activity for any teacher preparation program, but recruitment for pre-service teachers interested in working in urban schools is a specialized endeavor. The UI-PDS was committed to identifying candidates with dispositions supportive of working with students from complicated backgrounds who were attending school in a system needing reform. According to the literature on selecting candidates for urban education, mature individuals with diverse ethnic, cultural, and experiential profiles are the best candidates for working with urban students living in poverty (Haberman, 1995).

To identify such candidates, the UI-PDS used a multifaceted and holistic selection process. This process included an appropriate undergraduate grade point average, professional recommendations, and advocacy or social justice knowledge or experience. Additionally, the UI-PDS utilized the Haberman Teacher Selection Interview, an interview protocol designed to assess a candidate's capacity to teach urban students living in poverty (Haberman, 1995).

The Haberman Interview Protocol consists of a series of questions couched in behavioral terms with a corresponding scoring rubric. Applicants respond to questions by reporting actions they would take and reasoning they would use to address issues typical in urban schools. The protocol is supported by research that defines seven characteristics of effective teachers for students living in poverty: (1) persistence, (2) protecting learners and learning, (3) application of generalizations, (4) approach to at-risk students, (5) professional versus personal orientation to students, (6) fighting burnout, and (7) fallibility. The protocol was a measure beyond the typically-used selection methods such as standardized test score, previous grades, and letters of recommendation. Instead, it provided a standardized research-based measure of how applicants' previous experiences influenced their potential as urban teachers.

Coursework Prior to the Internship

Community Mapping—first experience. The UI-PDS integrated Community Mapping into graduate coursework as a way to assess future Interns before their internship year at Cardozo SHS. Interns were assessed on the insights they were able to articulate about the Cardozo SHS community and how they could use this knowledge in their teaching.

Community Mapping is a collaborative activity intended to broaden and deepen in-service and pre-service teachers' understanding and appreciation of their school community and to demonstrate that learning can be situated in the community (Tindle et al., 2005). The relationship between a community and a school should be a two-way street, since both have something to offer each other. However, making that a reality requires that teachers know both what is available in the community and how to make use of that knowledge. Community Mapping is a process of going out into the community to investigate, gather information, have experiences and conversations, and personally document the assets (as well as the issues) that are present in every community. In groups of three or four, participants walk through a predesignated area, equipped with writing materials, a digital camera, a bag to collect artifacts, and large pieces of paper with crayons for rubbings. Each group member has a designated role and objectives to accomplish, but every group member is responsible for observing, talking to people, asking questions, and deciding where to explore. Community Mapping becomes an assessment activity when teacher educators use the experience to determine the knowledge and insights gained as participants analyze the experience, present what they have learned, and connect it to future actions they will take.

Community Mapping was integrated into an instructional methods course that Interns attended prior to their internship year. This allowed Interns to develop baseline knowledge of the Cardozo SHS's community before they started their internship. It also provided them with the opportunity to begin to investigate how to connect their teaching with the greater community and learn about community assets that would be difficult to uncover through a more formal process.

Internship Work

The UI-PDS Assessment System focused on Interns' work during their year-long internship at the PDS site. Multiple means were used to provide feedback to Interns about their work with students and their ability to collaborate with others during their internship year.

Community Mapping—second and third experiences. The second use of Community Mapping required Interns to duplicate their initial mapping process with students. Interns planned a unit of study in the literacy course that connected with the community and culminated in taking students out in the community to explore, observe, interview residents, and document their experiences. Interns planned units that explored career opportunities, social service organizations, media images displayed in the community, gang violence, and neighborhood gentrification.

The second Community Mapping experience provided information on Interns' ability to plan a complex, community-based activity within a unit of study. It demanded that Interns plan student-mapping roles to accommodate individual student's learning strengths and needs. It also provided a means of assessing students' preparation to engage in a complex project that demanded higher-order thinking and presentation skills. Community Mapping consistently resulted in engaging students' interest and extending Interns' thinking about planning and executing multifaceted project-based learning.

The third use of Community Mapping targeted Interns' ability to connect with community agencies relevant to transition planning for special education students. In this instance, Community Mapping was used as an example of activism, an important skill for future special educators. Interns worked in collaborative groups to identify and contact organizations within Washington, DC that could support students and their families in preparing for life beyond high school. The Community Mapping steps were modified in this activity and, instead of physically walking the community, Interns explored resources through Internet research, phone calling, and face-to-face visits. Interns initiated relationships with agencies that could provide appropriate education and support services to students. Afterward, they analyzed the successes and challenges they faced in trying to develop working relationships with community organizations. Reaching beyond the school's current transition planning practices provided Interns with the experience of actively advocating for needed services and engaging in communication with agencies not usually accessed by school personnel.

UI-PDS staff also benefited from the Community Mapping experiences. Each Community Mapping experience deepened UI-PDS staff understanding of the Cardozo SHS community's demographics and cultures. UI-PDS staff members were also able to observe and support Interns as they engaged in the community in three different roles: learners, teachers, and advocates. This provided UI-PDS staff with an opportunity to observe Interns' growing confidence in connecting with the community and their increasing awareness and appreciation of its assets.

Work Sample Methodology

Western Oregon University's Work Sample Methodology (WSM) is a reflective instructional unit planning process that contextualizes instruction and relies on observable student outcomes (Western Oregon University College of Education, 2000). WSM requires pre-service teachers to: (1) consider the community and school context in which the unit will be taught; (2) conceptualize the unit's topic for appropriate goals and objectives; (3) provide a rationale for the unit's content; (4) pretest students to determine prior knowledge and cluster students based on pretest data in order to differentiate instruction; (5) design daily lessons, reflect on each lesson's outcomes, and alter planned lessons if needed; (6) posttest students and analyze and report results for clusters of students based on pretest data to determine student learning; and (7) reflect on the overall process of the teaching and learning cycle represented in the WSM. Initial research supports that teachers whose preparation emphasizes the connection between teaching and learning, such as the WSM requires, are more effective at impacting the learning of all students than teachers from programs that do not focus on the connection (Denner & Norman, 2006; Schalock & Schalock, 2006).

The UI-PDS required Interns to design a WSM unit in the fall and the spring. Interns taught their first WSM unit in the literacy course and their second in their content area classes. The WSM process focused Interns' unit planning on contextual variables, such as student learning profiles, community resources, and school policies. While teaching their unit, the WSM process incorporated daily reflections based on student performance. This required Interns to modify their plans to accommodate student needs. By the time their WSM unit was complete, Interns had developed detailed and sophisticated analyses of their unit's strengths and weaknesses related to the class as a whole, clusters of students, and individual students. This reflection activity, based on student data, allowed Interns to demonstrate sophisticated thinking about the complex variables that affect student performance.

Pathwise® Observation System

The Pathwise® observation and feedback system, which consists of four domains and related criteria (see Table 19.1), was used to guide the UI-PDS staff as they observed and gave feedback to Interns. This performance-based system evaluates a pre-service teacher's performance based on pre- and post-observation interviews, lesson observation, the pre-service teacher's detailed lesson plan, and a final reflection written by the pre-service teacher. This framework was incorporated into workshops for Mentor teachers, methods classes, and internship seminars to establish a common vernacular and a clear vision of competent, beginning teaching for all parties involved in the observation and feedback process. The Pathwise® system guided all UI-PDS formal and informal observations. It also provided a standardized evaluation tool to systematically determine Interns' areas of strengths and needs.

Ongoing informal observations. Ongoing observations happened on a daily basis in the UI-PDS. Instead of teaching behind closed doors, the Literacy Lab was a public place where observation, feedback, and problem-solving were daily processes supported by the project director and literacy coordinator. This made the act of teaching an open process. Interns collaborated together and with the literacy coordinator and project director to debrief after lessons and to develop weekly and daily plans. The consistency of the daily planning, along with the teaching and feedback cycle, provided a vehicle for benchmarking Interns' development in the four Pathwise® domains. This ongoing, daily work also provided a feedback vehicle for UI-PDS staff and school collaborators that promoted dialogue and inquiry to improve Intern development. Although informal observation and dialogue were not solidified into a formal process, they were important ongoing assessments that provided Interns frequent feedback on their planning, teaching, and collaboration.

Ongoing formal observations. Each Intern was assigned a UI-PDS staff member as a GWU university supervisor who conducted formal biweekly teaching observations throughout the year-long internship. When Interns were working in their content classes, their Mentor teacher was also included in the observation feedback process. The usual observation protocol involved Interns providing a lesson plan prior to the observation followed by a formal lesson observation and a post-observation conference, in which the GWU supervisor provided narrative feedback based on the four Pathwise® domains. The Intern would then write and submit a reflection within three days of the observation. These formal observations provided Interns, UI-PDS staff, and Mentors with a standardized feedback process for ongoing Intern support and development.

Pathwise® evaluations. Formal Pathwise® evaluations were conducted twice during the internship year, once in the fall and once in the spring. Observational systems such as Pathwise® that measure performance require observers to agree on collecting and scoring performance data in similar ways. Thus, GWU university supervisors received an initial training in the system for inter-rater reliability and then were paired with an experienced Pathwise® observer until both could score reliably. The Pathwise® system generates scores along a six-point scale for each of the criteria which can be aggregated to determine scores for each of the four domains. The first semester Pathwise® scores provided information to determine the strengths and needs of individual Interns and to investigate patterns of need across Interns so that these could be addressed in the subsequent semester. The scores were also used in conferences with each Intern to develop an Intern Development Plan used to build on areas of strength and address areas of need. The second semester Pathwise® scores documented Interns readiness for teaching both for their own knowledge of their current skill-set and as a program accountability measure. This formal observation process provided Interns and staff with detailed documentation of Intern progress and future goals.

Reflection

The UI-PDS utilized both critical and collaborative reflection as part of the UI-PDS Assessment System. Critical and collaborative reflection represents authentic contextualized assessment practices that ask developing teachers to assess their skills in the context in which they were used. By reflecting on contextualized experiences, Interns became aware of effective classroom teaching and their own roles in fostering student learning. Reflection also provided them with the opportunity to grapple with the impact of the larger school community on their students in order to address injustices. Reflection asks the developing teacher to examine not only the act of teaching but also the decision-making processes used in planning and implementing instruction, responding to student feedback, and assessment, and using that information to adjust practice. Secondly, reflection as an assessment tool allows pre-service teachers to examine their belief systems. By unpacking their current belief systems "pre-service teachers become better able to construct their own meaning of their situated practices and eventually understand what it means to be a teacher and how race, class, gender, sexual orientation, religion, ability, and so forth influence those belief systems" (Genor, 2005).

The act of reflection provided opportunities for Interns to consider issues related to classroom matters, collaboration with other professionals, and advocacy on the behalf of students. Engaging Interns in reflection was also a means to develop their teacher efficacy by encouraging them to consider their power and influence as teachers. Thus, the incorporation of a variety of reflective processes provided another type of assessment to indicate Interns' growth and development across the varied demands teachers face.

Ongoing individual reflection. Individual formative assessment involved: (1) reflections in the form of personal weekly e-mail journals to the project director, (2) daily reflective dialogue with UI-PDS staff about informally observed lessons, (3) written biweekly reflections on formally observed lessons, (4) written daily lesson reflections and overall final reflection during the WSM unit, and (5) a written lesson reflection as part of their Pathwise® evaluations.

This variety of reflection formats served to focus Interns' attention on the various components of teaching. Interns often discussed school context issues and student advocacy in e-mail journal entries. They used this format to express their joy and frustration as they negotiated relationships with Cardozo SHS teachers and administrators and discussed how the school context was impacting their thinking about what it means to be a teacher. Student advocacy was also explored as Interns reflected on student reactions to lessons taught. The WSM units and the Pathwise® reflection revealed Interns' connections with curriculum knowledge, showed their development leading to culturally relevant lesson planning, and provided evidence of how they were coming to understand the how teachers blend theory and practice. Through the various individual reflective assessments, Interns' thinking and belief systems could be brought to the surface for self-examination and feedback. Ultimately, this would lead to growth and development toward professional practice.

Formal individual self-assessment. Interns participated in a formal reflective self-assessment at the end of their first semester internship. The self-assessment required Interns to reflect on their development in the Pathwise® domains. They developed an action plan with benchmarks for each area of improvement and shared this plan with their GWU university supervisors. This shared plan provided supervisors with information to focus their attention and feedback for future observations. Prioritizing and focusing on specific skills allowed the Interns to guide their development process with a clear conception of their strengths and areas of need. At the midpoint of the second semester, Interns revisited the plan and assessed their progress. They reviewed the observational feedback and refined either the action plan to better improve the skills initially identified, or they documented success and targeted new skills for improvement. By initiating their own development plan (targeting skills and dispositions they wanted to improve), Interns were developing reflection skills that could carry over to their initial years of teaching when observation and feedback is less available. This individual reflection also helped to build a strong sense of teacher efficacy and involved an opportunity for Interns to advocate for support in areas they had identified as needing improvement.

Collaborative reflection. Collaborative reflection for Interns included participation in two problem-solving forums: a standardized protocol for group discussion called Critical Friends (2005) and an electronic blog designed to allow Interns to express issues of concern and brainstorm possible solutions. Critical Friends and blogging centered on feedback to and from peers, resulting in an effective vehicle for Interns to articulate their concerns, consider their peers' multiple perspectives, and engage in either oral or written dialogue.

In sum, the formal, informal, and collaborative reflection strategies used in the UI-PDS were time consuming for both UI-PDS staff and Interns. The personal attention to each Intern's development provided ongoing individualized assessment related to how Interns constructed meaning based on their dispositions, prior experiences, theory from their graduate classes, and the realities of school. Embedded contextualized reflections were used to demonstrate to Interns a variety of means for reflection that could be carried into their lives as teachers. Additionally, reflective processes were used to foster a sense of collaboration through community thinking and problem-solving.

Graduate Follow-Up

The intense nature of the year-long internship facilitated a strong collaborative community. Each year the UI-PDS community experienced the joys, challenges, frustrations, and tragedies inherent in working in a high poverty urban school. Through trial and error, laughter and tears, and mentoring and learning, a bond formed between committed professionals who worked to untangle the complex learning and literacy needs of adolescents and collaborate on strategies to meet these needs. To sustain this community, the UI-PDS staff developed ways to support graduates as new teachers so that they could continue to strengthen their knowledge and experience gained as Interns. This graduate follow-up was mostly comprising of ongoing, informal communication.

UI-PDS staff invited graduates for informal support sessions held after school, either at Cardozo SHS or a restaurant in the community. These sessions allowed the Novice teachers to discuss the successes and challenges they faced as new educators. At times, participants chose to use the Critical Friends protocol to engage in collaborative problem-solving. Discussion topics included the impact of the school's climate and political context, social justice issues related to special education service delivery, and the differences in motivating middle school males versus females. Given that these issues were beyond basic survival concerns typical of many first-year teachers, these sessions provided positive feedback about the appropriateness of the UI-PDS preparation.

In addition, graduates were invited to lead classes, serve as guest speakers, or participate on panels in seminars or GWU university-based classes for current Interns. More formal relationships were sustained with teachers who were employed at Cardozo SHS, with many serving as Mentor teachers once they passed the novice teacher phase. This more formally supported relationship also extended to graduates who entered advanced graduate programs at GWU with the aim of providing leadership in urban education.

THE UI-PDS EVALUATION STUDY

The UI-PDS Evaluation Study was conducted during the 2003–2004 school year in order to explore the relationship between factors in the UI-PDS experience and the perceptions and performances of Intern and novice teachers prepared by the UI-PDS.

This study collected data in response to the National Council for the Accreditation of Teacher Education's (2001) PDS standards which addressed the particular nature of the PDS as a format for preparing teachers. Project staff and researchers external to the UI-PDS collected evaluation data.

Project staff collected data using the UI-PDS Assessment System. For example, a formal Pathwise® evaluation was conducted twice on each Intern and once on each novice in order to quantitatively measure instructional and collaborative effectiveness. Project staff also assessed Interns' Work Sample Methodology instructional units (Western Oregon University College of Education, 2000) during fall and spring semesters in order to measure Interns' impact on student learning. Three individuals external to the UI-PDS collected quantitative and qualitative data from individual interviews, focus groups, and surveys conducted with Interns, Novices, and Mentors. These data provided information on the utility of the UI-PDS Assessment System (Taymans et al., 2006a).

Quantitative data were analyzed using descriptive statistics and qualitative data were analyzed through three stages of coding including: (1) the creation of conceptual categories (Merriam, 1998) based on Pathwise® domains, CT&L attributes, and UI-PDS program components; (2) compilation of descriptive matrixes (Miles & Huberman, 1994) to generate explanations and interpretations found in the data; and (3) using axial coding (Strauss & Corbin, 1998) to reassemble data and describe emerging phenomena. For the purposes of this chapter, only findings related to the utility of the UI-PDS Assessment System are discussed.

KEY OUTCOMES FROM THE UI-PDS EVALUATION STUDY

Three main factors, clearly linked to the UI-PDS Assessment System, were identified as contributing to the effectiveness of UI-PDS teacher preparation program. These factors were: (1) Intern dispositions and background experiences, (2) support and feedback for daily lesson planning, and (3) reflection tied to addressing issues faced by urban teachers.

Intern Dispositions & Background Experiences

The UI-PDS Assessment System provided the means to analyze the dispositions and background experiences of the individuals applying to GWU's UI-PDS teacher preparation program. The pre-selection process was one factor identified in data analysis that supported the UI-PDS's effectiveness. Guided by Haberman's research (1993, 1995), the UI-PDS application and acceptance process allowed for the selection of Interns who evidenced dispositions supportive of successful urban teachers. UI-PDS Interns were selected on the basis of their background experiences and demographic characteristics associated with successful teachers for students in poverty. For example, Interns in the final two UI-PDS cohorts came from culturally-diverse backgrounds (20 percent Asian and 30 percent African American), and most had previous experience with advocacy work which included Peace Corps service, volunteer work with children, and employment with educational and community advocacy organizations. Exhibiting characteristics of successful urban educators before entering the UI-PDS preparation program, Interns and novice teachers were able to build connections between their prior experiences and beliefs about teaching to the actions they took while teaching. The appropriateness of the selection process was evident in the completion rates of UI-PDS Interns. Throughout the nine years, only two of 72 Interns did not complete the program. Program evaluation data from the UI-PDS Evaluation Study indicated that both Interns and staff identified the experiences and dispositions that Interns brought to the UI-PDS program as significant factors in understanding and connecting to students (Taymans et al., 2006a).

Daily Lesson Planning & Teaching

Data analysis from the UI-PDS Evaluation Study revealed that the daily expectation and experience of lesson planning, teaching, and receiving feedback were a major factor that contributed to the success of UI-PDS teacher preparation. Through the UI-PDS Assessment System, Interns were supported and held accountable for producing daily and weekly plans for the literacy course and for planning with their cooperating teachers in content classes. Interns' responsibility for teaching the literacy course from the first to the last day of school was a major factor in their pre-service teacher development. The project director or literacy coordinator assisted Interns in this process by providing daily planning, observation, and feedback support. Daily supported planning allowed Interns time to work through their initial confusion and misconceptions about teaching and to progress toward putting into practice the knowledge and skills presented in their graduate classes. The combination of teaching responsibility with feedback provided Interns with an extended and intensive experience that is not commonly reported in the research literature.

The consistent on-site support, organized by the UI-PDS Assessment System, helped move Interns through important developmental processes. For example, during the fall semester, interns reported great frustration with the continual process of developing and revising plans, given the rigors of the daily responsibility of teaching the literacy course. In the moment, Interns did not always perceive their accountability for daily lesson planning to be a supportive process (with one Intern describing it as 'abusive'). However, by the end of the internship year, Intern interview data and formal Pathwise® observations indicated that Interns were competent and efficient in lesson planning. One Intern noted:

> It was hard, at the beginning, to turn in a set of objectives and then get rejected, and turn another set in, and get rejected again. The process for one hour of instruction, it could take three days to plan. But now, I'm very competent in my ability to do that [plan], and I know that next year, it's not going to be a difficulty. . . . I think that is a very valuable skill that I have developed over the course of the year. (Taymans et al., 2006b, pp. 20–21)

Interns' work in literacy was also a powerful social justice experience. On a daily basis, Interns grappled with figuring out how to engage their students in literacy development that both honored the experience and the intelligence that students brought to school while, at the same time, taking on the challenge of developing adolescents' reading and writing skills that were well below grade level. Community Mapping, Work Sample Methodology unit planning, consistent use of the Pathwise® framework, and reflective practice helped Interns learn about, accept, and engage in problem solving to reach their students. The result was Interns' acceptance of students' diverse literacy levels. Rather than blaming students for the literacy challenges they presented, Interns learned that varied literacy levels were to be expected in urban schools, and they consistently demonstrated a problem solving approach to literacy instruction (Taymans et al., 2006b).

Formal Pathwise® evaluations also provided important information for UI-PDS partners on Interns' common strengths and areas of need related to planning and teaching. An analysis of the second semester Pathwise® scores indicated that, as a group, Interns tended to exit the UI-PDS program with the greatest strength in Pathwise® Domain B: Creating an Environment for Student Learning. This domain can often be a challenge for new teachers in chaotic, bureaucratic, under-resourced, and culturally and linguistically diverse urban schools serving impoverished communities (Peterman, 2005). Interns' positive Domain B Pathwise® scores were supported by data from the UI-PDS Evaluation Study, which identified Intern and Novice teachers' commitment to developing relationships with their students as the most consistent theme across all data sources (interviews, focus groups, and surveys). Each Intern and Novice teacher clearly wanted to know students for two purposes: to be instructionally effective and to be a supportive and positive adult in students' lives. Their commitment to these goals was evident in the lack of negative descriptions of students with many examples of actions each Intern and Novice had taken to get to know students (Taymans et al., 2006a).

Analysis of Pathwise® scores also indicated that Interns were still developing skills related to planning and teaching. Data revealed that they could benefit from additional experience in designing and analyzing evaluation methods to determine student progress, which was a highly complex process given the diversity of student strengths and needs. Another area of need identified by the Pathwise® scores addressed one of the foci of the UI-PDS teacher preparation program. Even though the UI-PDS focused on adolescent literacy development, this was an area that Interns, Novices, and Mentors all identified as an ongoing challenge they faced in their current roles (Taymans et al., 2006a).

Reflection Related to Collaboration and Special Education

Intern reflection on issues related to collaboration and social justice were significant factors present in UI-PDS Assessment System that contributed to the success of the UI-PDS teacher preparation program. Collaboration and social justice were stressed throughout the UI-PDS experience and incorporated into the UI-PDS Assessment System. The UI-PDS Evaluation Study provided a means to investigate novice teachers' reflections on their experiences related to preparation for collaboration during their internship year. Some enjoyed collaboration even though they acknowledged that it was hard work; others struggled greatly with it. One Novice who did not find collaboration a natural way of working during the internship reported:

> I'm inclined to go with myself and handle things on my own. That was one of my biggest problems last year, [to learn] that you just can't do that in this setting, you really need to reach out for help. Otherwise, you will lose your mind. And at the time, it seemed like a ridiculous, busy kind of activity when [the project director] or someone would send us out to talk to someone else. . . . Anyway, we learned that it was really important to get out there and get input from somebody else. (Taymans et al., 2006b, p. 28)

Findings from the UI-PDS Evaluation Study revealed that all of the Novice teachers were involved in formal and/or informal collaborative activities during their first year teaching. For example, one Novice was on a literacy task force and taught reading strategies to colleagues. Another reported developing informal communication networks with general educators teaching unsupported special education students. However, in general, collaboration related to special education seemed to be challenging for Novices. All expressed disappointment in the lack of systems or procedures for collaboration between special and general educators at their schools and reported taking action to promote this important type of collaboration. Novices were also disappointed that the school district did not follow its policy to provide new teachers with school-based mentors, which resulted in a missed opportunity for collaboration and support. This lack of systemic support accentuated the need for new teachers to enter their first year of teaching with the knowledge and skills to seek out and build collaborative relationships with talented and committed educators in their schools.

Embedded year-long reflective practice in the UI-PDS Assessment System provided Interns with opportunities to formally and informally grapple with complex social justice issues that urban teachers face. Data from the UI-PDS Evaluation Study revealed that the Interns' reflective practices prepared them to exit the program with a clear sense of urban school issues and how they, as first-year teachers, were prepared to address the myriad issues they would face. As one Novice teacher explained:

> I think that it [social justice] is very important. . . . I think because they had such a focus on that throughout the [UI-PDS] program, I think it helps me understand where the kids are coming from, and that the world of the students is very different from the world of my experience, and the experience of many of the other teachers in the school, and knowing that and using those principles to help, I can understand that, while a teacher may see it one way,

a lot of times, the student is totally seeing it a different way, simply based on the cultural experiences that they've had . . . it has impacted my relationships with the students, and it helps me to understand the relationships between students, and between students and teachers, and my understanding of social justice issues definitely helps me strengthen those relationships that I have with the students. (Taymans et al., 2006a, p. 20)

Data from the UI-PDS Evaluation Study indicated that novices and Interns reported feeling "very prepared" to work in the often-chaotic environments of urban schools after their year-long internship at Cardozo SHS. One Novice explained, "Yeah, most definitely, it [the internship] acquainted me with the realities of DCPS." This same idea was shared by another Intern who described a personal mantra for working in DCPS as, "Assume nothing; expect the unexpected" (Taymans et al., 2006b, p. 32).

In conclusion, the power, utility, or effectiveness of the UI-PDS Assessment System was in its firm situation in the contextualized reality of an urban school. The System facilitated multiple means of communication between Interns and those who were focused on their development. Because assessment and feedback were embedded in the daily life of Interns and their students, the assessments and feedback were authentic and useful tools for both the Interns and the professionals dedicated to helping develop those skills to become competent urban teachers. The UI-PDS Assessment System provided GWU personnel, Cardozo SHS partners, Interns, and Novices with opportunities to build communities of learners with no one person or group having all the answers. Instead, all parties became more aware of the essential functions of urban teaching and the varied ways professionals can work to better serve students in under-resourced and challenged schools.

REFERENCES

Albanese, M. A., & Mitchell, S. (1993). Problem-based learning: A review of literature on its outcomes and implementation issues. *Academic Medicine, 68*, 52–81.

Bandura, A. (1986). *Social foundations of thought and action. A social cognitive theory.* Englewood Cliffs, NJ: Prentice-Hall.

Brown, J. S., Collins, A., & Duguid, P. (1989). Situated cognition and the culture of learning. *Educational Researcher, 18*, 32–42.

Cook, L., & Friend, M. (2005). Co-teaching: Guidelines for creating effective practices. *Focus on Exceptional Children, 28*(3), 1–16.

Darling-Hammond, L., & Snyder, J. (1999). Authentic assessment of teaching in context. In W. M. Sherman (Ed.), *Contextual teaching and learning: Preparing teachers to enhance student success in and beyond schools* (pp. 253–294). Columbus, OH: Eric Clearinghouse on Adult, Career, and Vocational Education and Eric

Clearinghouse on Teaching and Teacher Education. (ERIC Document Reproduction Service No. ED427263)

Denner, P., & Norman, A. (2006). *Credibility evidence for teacher work sample assessments from the renaissance partnership.* Paper presented at the 2006 Teacher Work Sample Conference, Portland, Oregon.

Dwyer, C. (1994). Criteria for performance-based teacher assessments: Validity, standards, and issues. *Journal of Personnel Evaluation in Education, 8,* 135–150.

Freire, P. (1993). *Pedagogy of the oppressed.* New York: Continuum Books.

Educational Testing Service. (2001). *Pathwise®: Classroom observation system.* Princeton, NJ: Educational Testing Service.

Genor, M. (2005). The assessment of urban teaching in a not-so-urban setting. In F. P. Peterman (Ed.), *Designing performance assessment systems for urban teacher preparation* (pp. 97–126). Mahwah, NJ: Lawrence Erlbaum Associates Inc.

Goodman, G. (2002). Implementing and researching teacher education programs in PDSs. In I. M. Guadarrama, J. Ramsey, & J. L. Nath (Eds.), *Forging alliances in community and thought: Research in professional development schools* (pp. 31–64). Greenwich, CT: Information Age Publishing Inc.

Haberman, M. (1993). Predicting the success of urban teachers (The Milwaukee Trials). *Action in Teacher Education, 15*(3), 1–5.

Haberman, M. (1995). *Star teachers of children in poverty.* Bloomington, IN: Kappa Delta Pi.

Hamilton, S. F. (1990). *Apprenticeship for adulthood: Preparing youth for the future.* New York: Free Press.

Miles, M. B., & Huberman, A. M. (1994). *Qualitative data analysis.* Thousand Oaks, CA: Sage.

Merriam, S. B. (1998). *Qualitative research and case study applications in education.* San Francisco: Jossey-Bass.

Myford, C. (1993). *Formative studies of Praxis III: Classroom performance assessments—An overview. The Praxis Series: Professional assessments for beginning teachers.* (Report No. ETS-RR-94-20). Princeton, NJ: Educational Testing Service. (ERIC Document Reproduction Service No. ED 395977)

National Council for Accreditation of Teacher Education. (2001). *Standards for Professional Development Schools,* NCATE: Washington, DC.

Peterman, F. P. (2005). Design principles for urban teacher assessment systems. In F. P. Peterman (Ed.), *Designing performance assessment systems for urban teacher preparation* (pp. 49–63). Mahwah, NJ: Lawrence Erlbaum Associates Inc.

Pressley, M. (2002). *Reading instruction that works: The case for balanced teaching.* New York: Guilford Press.

Provenzo, E. (2005). *Critical literacy: What every American ought to know.* Boulder: Paradigm.

Sears, S., & Hersh, S. (1998). Contextual teaching and learning: An overview of the project. In W. M. Sherman (Ed.), *Contextual teaching and learning: Preparing teachers to enhance student success in and beyond schools* (pp. 1–18). Columbus, OH: Eric Clearinghouse on Adult, Career, and Vocational Education and Eric Clearinghouse on Teaching and Teacher Education. (ERIC Document Reproduction Service No. ED427263)

Schalock, D., & Schalock, M. (2006). Tracing connections among teaching, teacher preparation, and K–12 learning: Four decades of development and research at Western Oregon University. Paper presented at the 2006 Teacher Work Sample Conference, Portland, OR.

Simon, M. A. (1995). Reconstructing mathematics pedagogy from a constructivist perspective. *Journal of Research in Mathematics Education, 26,* 114–145.

Strauss, A., & Corbin, J. (1998). *Basics of qualitative research: Techniques and procedures for developing grounded theory.* Thousand Oaks, CA: Sage.

Taymans, J. M., Tindle, K. P., Freund, M. B., Harris, L. A., & Ortiz, D. M. (2006a). *Opening the black box: Influential elements of an effective urban professional development school.* Manuscript submitted for publication.

Taymans, J. M., Tindle, K. P., Freund, M. B., Ortiz, D. M., & Harris, L. A. (2006b). *Evaluation research to sustain and expand an established PDS.* Paper presented at the 2006 the American Educational Research Association (AERA) Conference in San Francisco, CA.

Taymans, J. M., Tindle, K. P., Ortiz, D. M. (2005). *Urban initiative: Sustaining and expanding a PDS.* Unpublished manuscript, The George Washington University.

Tindle, K. P., Leconte, P., Buchanan, L., & Taymans, J. M. (2005). Transition planning: Community mapping as a tool for teachers and students. *Improving Secondary Education and Transition Services through Research: Research to Practice Brief, 4*(1), 1–6. Retrieved August 8, 2004 from http://www.ncset.org/publications/viewdesc.asp?id=2128

Tindle, K. P., Taymans, J. M., Lander, R. (2004). *Urban initiative handbook.* Unpublished manuscript. George Washington University.

Western Oregon University College of Education. (2000). *Teacher work sample methodology.* Retrieved September 15, 2006 from http://www.wou.edu/education/worksample/twsm/index.htm

CHAPTER 20

USING NCATE PDS STANDARDS TO CONDUCT PROGRAM EVALUATION AND CHANGE PARTNERSHIP CULTURE

Jonatha W. Vare, Crystal L. Small, and Wendi S. Dunlap

ABSTRACT

Winthrop University's Professional Development School (PDS) partnership implemented a program evaluation system based on the *NCATE PDS Standards* at six professional development schools (PDSs) from 2000–2005. During 2000–2002, the partnership used Phase I data to establish a baseline and set future goals. From 2002–2005, Phase II activities were designed to promote growth in elements of the standards related to accountability and to establish local benchmarks for future PDS performance. Phase II data from three years across six PDSs were aggregated in a meta-matrix to facilitate cross-site analysis. The results provide a basis for determining the best ways to use benchmarks to guide local PDS performance, direct partnership efforts to collect evidence of accountability, and set future goals. Sample benchmarks and critical factors for success are provided.

University and School Connections, pages 359–375

359

INTRODUCTION

Professional development schools (PDSs) evolved during the 1990s to provide innovative sites where school–university partnership faculty could collaborate in the simultaneous renewal of teacher preparation and P–12 schooling (Clark, 1999; Goodlad, 1990; Holmes Group, 1995). For PDS partnership sites affiliated with the National Network for Educational Renewal (NNER), professional development schools establish goals that reflect the NNER's mission for education in a democracy (Fenstermacher, 1999). These are: (1) a commitment to parity between school and university partners; (2) a focus on equity for diverse learners; (3) the embodiment of democratic principles in curricula, structures, roles, and organizational processes; (4) and, ultimately, the promotion of public education for the good of the commonwealth. The NNER's goals extend the focus of PDSs in some areas not well represented in the NCATE PDS Standards, such as outcomes related to participation in a democracy (Vare, 2004). The NNER also encourages its school/university partnership sites to collect evidence of their impact on teacher preparation, professional development, and P–12 students' achievement.

While PDSs continue to evolve as structures of educational renewal, evaluating their effectiveness in meeting their goals persists as a crucial challenge (Teitel, 2001a,b; 2003, 2004). During the past few years, researchers have lamented the dearth of evidence supporting the effectiveness of PDSs and have called for a focus on accountability (e.g., Abdal-Haqq, 1998; Teitel, 2000, 2004). In 2001, the National Council for Accreditation of Teacher Education (NCATE) published standards to frame assessment, evaluation, and research pertaining to PDSs (NCATE, 2001). Before development of the *NCATE PDS Standards*, most school–university partnerships focused on the preparation of new teachers and neglected the inquiry portion of their mission (Levine & Trachtman, 2005).

The *NCATE PDS Standards* (2001) provide a useful tool for all PDS partnerships to use in structuring longitudinal program evaluation of simultaneous efforts to renew teacher preparation and impact student achievement. In conjunction with the increased calls for evidence, these PDS standards provide guidance for partnership faculty in setting rigorous goals and evaluating the results of their work. The *NCATE PDS Standards* hold the development of accountability, assessment, and analysis of data as elemental. The standards incorporate Accountability and Quality Assurance as the second of five standards and reference accountability, evaluation, or assessment in at least four of the 21 elements. Self-assessment, using the *NCATE PDS Standards,* enables participants to collect authentic data for comparison of their partnership's work to rigorous standards of quality (Vare, 2004). Collaborative assessment methods, such as empowerment evaluation (Fetterman, 2001), promote ownership of goals and procedures that provide evidence of accountability for a school/university partnership. Thus, a partnership's use of the *NCATE PDS Standards* to conduct collaborative program evaluation can hold great potential for collectively creating a culture of accountability.

PROGRAM EVALUATION IN THE WINTROP UNIVERSITY PDS PARTNERSHIP

The present research reports an analysis of the Winthrop University partnership's program evaluation activities at six PDSs from 2000–2005. The analysis also provides a means of deriving implications for partnership success from the evaluation process. Since 1992, Winthrop University has been a member of the South Carolina Network for Educational Renewal (SC-NER), a collaborative that is a charter member of the National Network for Educational Renewal (NNER). Winthrop University's school–university partnership defines a PDS as a site where partners engage in the simultaneous renewal of teacher preparation and public schooling (Goodlad, 1994). Four purposes guide each PDS, according to the mission of the NNER (Clark, 1999; Fenstermacher, 1999): (1) the collaborative preparation of teachers; (2) professional development for all partnership faculty; (3) school renewal that promotes equity for diverse learners; and (4) collaborative, improvement-oriented inquiry. Using Teitel's (2001a,b) assessment framework as a guide, the Winthrop University PDS partnership implemented a program evaluation plan based on the NCATE PDS Standards in two phases during 2000–2005.

PROGRAM EVALUATION

Phase I

During Phase I (20000–2002) of the program evaluation cycle, the PDS partnership's evaluation activities were collaboratively designed using democratic principles of empowerment evaluation (Fetterman, 2001). Collaborative design emphasized parity between partners and promoted ownership of the evaluation process. In addition, the partnership employed methods of authentic assessment (such as portfolios and site-based artifact selection) to add validity to data collection procedures as recommended in the measurement literature (Darling-Hammond & Synder, 2000; Moss, 1992). Phase I data were collected each year during 2000–2002. Table 20.1 contains a complete description of the 2000–2005 program evaluation cycles.

TABLE 20.1 2000–2005 Program Evaluation Cycle

Phase I		Phase II		
2000–2001	2001–2002	2002–2003	2003–2004	2004–2005
Collaborative design				
Baseline data collection		Analysis of baseline data		
Distribution of sample benchmark indicators	Distribution of form for aggregation of data		Construction of local benchmarks	Revision of local benchmarks
Authentic assessment (portfolios, artifacts)	Authentic assessment (portfolios, artifacts)	Authentic assessment (portfolios, artifacts)	Authentic assessment (portfolios, artifacts)	Authentic assessment (portfolios, artifacts)
Use of NCATE PDS Standards as scoring rubrics	Use of NCATE PDS Standards as scoring rubrics	Use of NCATE PDS Standards as scoring rubrics	Use of NCATE PDS Standards as scoring rubrics	
Post-then-pre self-assessment	Post-then-pre self-assessment	Post-then-pre self-assessment	Post-then-pre self-assessment	
	Principals' end-of-year interviews	Principals' end-of-year interviews	Principals' end-of-year interviews	Principals' end-of-year interviews
		Title II mini-grants	Title II mini-grants	
			PDS Committee accountability presentations	
				Cross-site analysis using meta-matrix of data

The evaluation design for baseline data collection in Phase I followed benchmarking procedures similar to those described by Denner, Salzman, and Bangert (2001). Six PDSs, ranging from three to seven years in existence, participated in the study. Such a range provided examples of performance along all stages of the NCATE PDS developmental continuum of "Beginning," "Developing," "At Standard," and "Leading." Each school year, the PDSs assembled portfolios of evidence to document attainment of

Recommendations from Paratore, 1995	Winthrop Partnership's PDS Portfolios
1. Benchmarks (goals)	1. *NCATE PDS Standards* (21 elements)
2. Benchmark indicators (observable behaviors)	2. List of sample artifacts to use as evidence
3. Aggregation form for review of artifacts	3. Sample matrix to use for organization of data
4. Rubrics used to rate performance	4. Post-then-pre assessment with *NCATE PDS Standards*

Figure 20.1   Process for standardization of evidence in PDS portfolios.

outcomes for the 21 elements of the five NCATE PDS standards. Standardization of portfolio evidence was achieved by adapting recommendations of Paratore (1995): (1) using core elements as benchmarks, (2) defining benchmark indicators, (3) constructing a form for aggregation of data, and (4) providing scoring rubrics. See Figure 20.1 for a comparison of Paratore's (1995) benchmarking recommendations to the Winthrop partnership's process. The 21 elements of the NCATE PDS standards served as initial benchmarks. In the fall of each year, the PDSs received a document containing examples of evidence to provide as benchmark indicators and a sample matrix to use for organizing data.

In addition, the NCATE descriptions of developmental levels of PDSs served as self-scoring rubrics for each PDS. Each May, teams of school–university partners used the post-then-pre method to self-rate their PDS's developmental status on the 21 elements of the NCATE standards. Studies have shown that retrospective pre-assessment is often more accurate because participants rate both post and pre-items from the same frame of reference, an advantage that offsets potential threats to internal validity such as response-shift bias (Howard & Dailey, 1979; Howard et al., 1979).

Results from the Phase I analysis of data established a baseline of PDS performance (Vare, 2004), a recommendation of Teitel (2000; 2001a,b). Significantly, results also revealed that all six PDSs, and thus the whole partnership, showed a weakness in NCATE PDS Standard II.D., "Develop Assessments, Collect Information, and Use Results" (NCATE, 2001). In this instance, "weakness" was defined as a lack of growth on an element of the PDS Standards within the partnership as a whole. Growth was indicated by a movement of at least one developmental level on an element of the NCATE PDS Standards. Table 20.2 depicts a summary of Phase I strengths and weaknesses across the partnership.

TABLE 20.2   2001–2002 Program Evaluation Baseline Data

Assessment Rubric: Developmental Levels of *NCATE PDS Standards*

Weakness = Lack of movement across levels
- I.D. Learning Community: Serve as Instrument of Change
- II.D. Accountability and Quality Assurance: Develop Assessments, Collect Information, and Use Results

Strength = Growth of at least one level
- II.C. Accountability and Quality Assurance: Set PDS Participation Criteria

Phase II

Phase II (2002–2005) of the program evaluation process involved use of the NCATE standards to establish benchmarks for PDS performance and implement activities that would promote growth in Standard II.D, a partnership weakness identified in baseline data from Phase I. Astin's (2001) theoretical framework for institutional transformation was adapted to create a model for systemic change in the partnership's culture and structures. Figure 20.2 provides a description of the model for changing partnership culture. Phase I results of the program evaluation indicated a need for change in the collective partnership culture to valuing the use of assessments in collecting evidence of impact on professional development and P–12 student achievement. Therefore, program evaluation facilitators focused on the exterior factors of personal actions and partnership structures to create change within the collective culture during Phase II.

Using the *NCATE PDS Standards* as a guide, school–university partnership faculty continued to gather assessment data (i.e., annual portfolios and post-then-pre assessments based on NCATE standards) to establish benchmarks of acceptable performance along the PDS developmental continuum. Following exterior components of the model adapted from Astin (2001), evaluation facilitators used the main partnership structure of the PDS Committee to feature personal actions of faculty teams who were committed to collecting accountability data. Several partnership teams were asked to present information about procedures for collecting evidence of accountability at three meetings of the partnership's PDS Committee during 2003–2004. Presentations included the following: a quantitative study of means of increasing science interest among third graders at a "Leading" PDS; a quantitative study in progress of writing instruction at one "At Standard" PDS; and a qualitative evaluation of professional development seminars for interns at another "At Standard" PDS. During the meetings, partnership faculty shared instruments for data collection and aspects of their various research designs. At the end of Phase II, researchers aggregated data from the six sites in a meta-matrix and conducted a cross-site

	Interior	**Exterior**
Individual	*Personal consciousness* (Values, beliefs, expectations)	*Personal actions* (Teaching, inquiry, service, planning, etc.)
Collective	*Partnership culture* (Shared values, assumptions, beliefs, etc.)	*Partnership structures* (Committees, centers, special groups, policies, etc.)

Figure 20.2   A Model for Creating Systemic Change in the Partnership's Culture and Structures [Adapted from: Astin, A.W. (2001). *Toward a theory of institutional transformation in higher education.* Paper presented at the Institute on Campus Leadership for Sustainable Innovation, Leesburg, VA.]

analysis (Miles & Huberman, 1984, 1994). The results provide a basis for determining the best ways to use benchmarks to guide PDS performance, direct partnership efforts to provide evidence of accountability, and set future goals.

Phase II Data Analysis

Sources of evidence for the initial analysis in Phase II included three sets of portfolios (2002–2005) and two sets of self-ratings (2002–2004) provided by each PDS. Tabulations of portfolio artifacts and self-ratings were included in a within-site analysis for each PDS. To provide data triangulation, researchers collected additional documents that could test and confirm analytic findings (Miles & Huberman, 1984, 1994). Documents included: (1) transcripts of hour-long, semi-structured interviews with each PDS principal from 2002–2005; (2) PDS Title II mini-grant applications, guidelines, and evaluation reports for 2002–2004; (3) copies of published articles and selected presentations generated by partnership faculty during school years 2002–2005; and (4) copies of the partnership's PDS Handbook for school years 2003–2005.

All data were combined by school for within-site analysis and aggregated in a site-ordered, descriptive meta-matrix for cross-site comparisons following procedures recommended by Miles and Huberman (1984, 1994). An analytical conceptual framework was developed from iterative coding of patterns in the data (Glaser & Strauss, 1967; Miles & Huberman, 1984, 1994). Five research questions provided a boundary for the analysis: (1) To what extent did each PDS report evidence of accountability? (2) What was the nature of the data reported? (3) What is the relationship between the extent and type of data reported and the developmental level of the PDS?

(4) What recommendations can guide future implementation of evaluation components of the *NCATE PDS Standards*? (5) Did the partnership culture change and, if so, how?

Results of Phase II Data Analysis

Aggregated results of the portfolio artifacts, self-assessment ratings, principals' interviews, and other documents enabled a comprehensive view of growth across the partnership. Three aspects of the results will be discussed here: (1) the construction and revision of benchmarks; (2) the extent of growth in the provision of accountability data and change of partnership culture; and (3) areas for future growth of the partnership.

CONSTRUCTION AND REVISION OF BENCHMARKS

Triangulated evaluation data from self-ratings with NCATE rubrics, portfolios, and principals' interviews were used to construct local benchmarks that may guide future partnership growth. Whereas the NCATE PDS Standards are professional criteria that define developmental progression toward excellence as a PDS, locally-constructed benchmarks are annual goals differentiated according to years of experience as a PDS. Thus, benchmarks provide goals derived from contextualized data and represent reasonable expectations for the partnership.

To construct benchmarks for the partnership, data were displayed in a site-ordered, meta-matrix, showing each PDS's developmental status and types of evidence provided for the 21 elements of the NCATE standards. These data were reported by number of years as a PDS and converted to narrative profiles that serve as local benchmarks. (For illustration, see the chart of revised benchmarks in the Appendix.) A draft of data-based benchmarks was constructed after the first year of Phase II data collection. The initial draft included a table of activities common to PDSs divided by year to show expected commonality among those schools who had been PDSs for the same length of time. Researchers used summative results from the three years of Phase II data collection and analysis to modify both the benchmarks and the timeframes. For example, the developmental levels were overlaid to reflect differential rates of progression within annual timeframes. Also, year one was divided into two semesters to enable a focus on activity that will construct a baseline of data for assessment of progress, a school improvement plan based on disaggregated data, and an action plan with a specified timeline and identification of funding sources.

Significantly, researchers noted that another PDS cycle of activity is necessary to complete the benchmark chart. Although summative Phase II data provided a basis for modifying the initial draft of benchmarks, specification of benchmarks for all developmental levels was limited by the extent of PDS growth (i.e., there was only one "Leading" PDS available for analysis). Therefore, sample benchmarks are not provided for three elements in year three or for 13 elements in year four. Consequently, additional partnership growth data are necessary, and the revised draft will be modified further as future partnership assessments become available.

ACCOUNTABILITY DATA AND PARTNERSHIP CULTURE

Aggregated data provided some evidence that the partnership culture changed to value collection of accountability data. During 2003–2005, the Winthrop University PDS partnership achieved limited growth in addressing PDS Standard II.D., "Develop Assessments, Collect Information, and Use Results" (NCATE, 2001). Analysis of portfolio artifacts and principals' interviews revealed that schools frequently focused on reporting activities rather than analyzing assessment data as evidence of progress. Schools' portfolios typically contained copies of the State Report Cards that use standardized tests as an indication of performance. However, three of the six schools did link improvements in test scores to specific activities implemented as PDS initiatives (i.e., links were provided by the "Leading" PDS and two of the four "At Standard" PDSs). For example, one "At Standard" PDS reported a significant narrowing of the racial achievement gap in mathematics on state tests and a slight narrowing of the gap in English/language arts. Another "At Standard PDS" reported a narrowing of the racial achievement gap in English/language arts and attributed the results to a specific PDS initiative.

Notably, the most rigorous evaluative data were contained in articles co-authored by university PDS liaisons and included as portfolio artifacts. Six articles and presentations examined student achievement relative to PDS activity. Three studies at the "Leading" PDS tracked the impact of specific professional development on teaching practices in reading, writing, and science. One study at an "At Standard" school explored issues of validity in assessing PDS impacts, and a study at the same PDS documented the impact of training on improvements in students' writing skills. One small case study at another "At Standard" school explored the value of interning in a PDS. Therefore, researchers concluded that the programs on accountability presented to the PDS Committee appeared to impact the partnership's progress in NCATE PDS Standard II.D. PDS principals networked with one another to exchange ideas, and university liaisons connected with colleagues to share ideas related to their PDS research projects.

Change in the collective partnership culture was indicated through patterns of networking among PDSs regarding accountability data. Growth patterns indicate that the "Leading" PDS, a school which had been a PDS for seven years, generated ideas that spread to less-developed PDSs. Principals' interview data showed that the "Leading" PDS was the first to analyze state test score data and link results to PDS initiatives as evidence of impact on student achievement. Also, two "At Standard" PDSs replicated an initiative designed to impact growth in teacher candidates' professional development. In this instance, the "Leading" PDS initiated seminars for interns, an idea that spread to two other schools. In addition, two university liaisons began to collaborate on a project designed to improve students' writing. After one PDS liaison experienced success initiating the writing project at an "At Standard" PDS, another liaison replicated the project at a less-developed PDS in an adjacent county.

Directions for Partnership Growth

Results of final self-ratings with NCATE PDS rubrics provided clear directions for future partnership activities. Each PDS examined its portfolio of evidence and self-rated growth along the developmental continuum for each of 21 elements of the *NCATE PDS Standards.* As indicated in Figure 20.3, data were aggregated from all six PDSs to provide an indication of growth for the partnership. Areas in which PDSs perceived greatest growth were in Standards I.A., I.B., I.E., II.C., II.D., and III.C. Significantly, PDS partners perceived growth in an earlier area of weakness identified in Phase I, (i.e., II.D. "Accountability & Quality Assurance: Develop Assessments, Collect Information, and Use Results").

The aggregated data from Phase II also provided a summative assessment of the partnership's relative weaknesses. The lowest areas of combined self-ratings on the 21 elements of the *NCATE PDS Standards* point clearly to priorities for partnership growth. As shown in Table 20.3, areas of priority for future partnership activities include Standards I.C., III.B., V.A., V.C., and V.D. When partners set goals and plan subsequent activities, they should target areas such as the following for refinement and further development: (1) develop a common shared vision, (2) design collaborative roles and structures, (3) establish governance and support structures, (4) create specific PDS roles, and (5) identify resources to support the partnership.

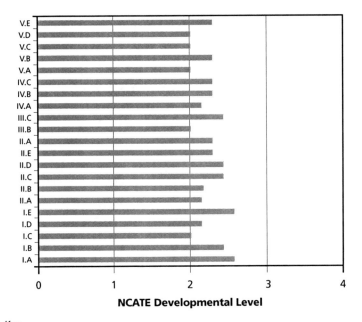

Key

NCATE PDS Standards	NCATE Developmental Level
I. Learning Community	1. Beginning
II. Accountability and Quality Assurance	2. Developing
III. Collaboration	3. At Standard
IV. Diversity & Equity	4. Leading
V. Structures, Resources, & Roles	

Figure 20.3   Final Combined PDSs' Self-Ratings on 21 Elements of the NCATE PDS Standards (N = 6).

Critical Factors for Future Success

The importance of Winthrop University's program evaluation derives from lessons learned as a result of analysis of comprehensive data collected during Phase II of the partnership's evaluation cycle. The partnership's key lessons center on the importance of factors crucial to the successful provision of accountability data. The following factors are discussed in further detail: (1) consistency of university liaisons, (2) differences in the accountability focus of principal partners, (3) the usefulness of like-kind networks among principal partners, (4) the need for peer models in other partnerships, and (5) the need for goal-based planning and assessment.

TABLE 20.3 Areas of Priority for the Partnership Based on 2002–2005 Phase II Data

Assessment Rubric: Developmental Levels of *NCATE PDS Standards*

Strength = Highest areas of combined self-ratings on 21 elements of the *NCATE PDS Standards*

- I.A. Learning Community: Support Multiple Learners
- I.B. Learning Community: Work and Practice are Inquiry-Based and Focused on Learning
- I.E. Learning Community: Extended Learning Community
- II.C. Accountability & Quality Assurance: Set PDS Participation Criteria
- II.D. Accountability & Quality Assurance: Develop Assessments, Collect Information, and Use Results
- III.C. Collaboration: Systematically Recognize and Celebrate Joint Work

Weakness = Lowest areas of combined self-ratings on 21 elements of the *NCATE PDS Standards*

- I.C. Learning Community: Develop Common Shared Professional Vision
- III: B. Collaboration: Design Roles and Structures to Enhance Collaboration and Develop Parity
- V: A Structures, Resources, and Roles: Establish Governance and Support Structures
- V.C. Structures, Resources, and Roles: Create PDS Roles
- V.D. Structures, Resources, and Roles: Resources

Consistency of University Liaisons

Consistency within the assignment of university liaisons selected to work with PDSs appears to be a crucial factor for success. However, it is a necessary but not a sufficient condition for the provision of adequate accountability data. The partnership appeared to flounder at one individual school site when no consistent relationship was maintained across the four years of PDS activity from 2001–2005. Of the three PDSs that provided specific accountability data, each school had the same university liaison for all four years of partnership activity. In contrast, of the three PDSs that failed to provide sufficient accountability data, only one had the same university liaison across the four years of partnership activity. Of the two remaining schools, each lacked the assignment of a university liaison during the first year of the PDS partnership, and each experienced the lack of a consistent working relationship with the same university liaison across the remaining three years. The five years of Winthrop University partnership data underscore the importance of one factor noted by Levine and Trachtman (2005), that of an initial period in which partners establish relationships and build a foundation of trust. PDS partnerships find it difficult to recover from initial lags in time or from starts and restarts in the development of relationships among representatives.

Differences in Accountability Focus of Principal Partners

In all PDSs, school partners and university liaisons focused on different types of accountability data. Whereas school partners used disaggregated No Child Left Behind data mandated for use in State Report Cards and indicators of Adequate Yearly Progress, university liaisons focused on more specific data linked to individual project outcomes. All three PDSs that provided accountability data in their portfolios and end-of-year interviews did so by referencing improvements in scores of state-mandated tests. Perhaps state test scores provide ease of use, which may be an important consideration for school personnel whose workplace culture proceeds at a different tempo (Brookhart & Loadman, 1990, 1992). Even so, the accessibility of standardized achievement test scores has also been noticed by university partners. For example, Cooper's (2005) description of systematic evaluation in one partnership's PDS-centered teacher preparation program references State Report Card data as evidence of P–12 student performance. In contrast to the PDS provision of State Report Card data, however, Winthrop University liaisons provided evidence of impact keyed to specific projects. For example, measures of P–12 student improvement included science interest inventories and assessments of word fluency, reading comprehension, and writing skills. Nonetheless, both standardized test scores and project-specific assessments are useful indicators of progress. When used in tandem, standardized and criterion-referenced measures provide a more complete picture of partnership accountability.

Like-Kind Networks among Partners

Professional development school leadership appears to emanate from a strong team of school principal, university liaison, and teacher leaders who network with other like-kind PDS leaders. These constituents are what Levine and Trachtman (2005) refer to as the "principal partners" or the key faculty and administrators who actually perform the daily work of the PDS. Accountability projects were strongest in the "Leading" PDS with a stable, four-year team of principal partners. Ideas about projects coupled with provision of accountability data tended to spread through principal-to-principal, liaison-to-liaison, and teacher-to-teacher networking. For example, the use of intern seminars spread from initiation at the "Leading" PDS to implementation at two other PDSs after principals shared information at networking sessions. Also, information about a specific project to improve students' writing skills spread from initiation at one PDS to replication at another when university liaisons began to collaborate after a PDS committee accountability presentation. Partnerships should consider arranging frequent formal and informal opportunities for networking among principal partners in like-kind groups.

Peer Models in Other Partnerships

Program evaluation data indicate that "Leading," "At Standard," "Developing," and "Beginning" PDSs could be limited in the accuracy of their self-assessments from lack of peer comparisons. Self-assessments using the *NCATE PDS Standards* were helpful to the PDSs within the partnership in locating strengths, identifying areas for improvement, and deepening understanding of the standards. Earlier reports about the partnership's PDS evaluation noted the limitations inherent in self-assessments (such as the potential for bias in self-reporting growth) and recommended supplementing the information with more objective views from an external evaluator (Vare, 2004). However, the data in this study indicate that it may be more helpful for the partnership's PDSs to examine activities of developmental peers in other partnerships. The lack of comparative perspectives could explain, for example, why the "Leading" PDS self-assessed at that level, yet there were no local partnership data to provide examples of 13 of 21 elements for a fourth-year PDS in the benchmark chart. Perhaps representatives of the partnership's PDSs could visit other sites and interact with school–university faculty about PDS activities. Such visits could provide a basis for comparison and enhance the accuracy of future self-assessments.

Goal-Based Planning and Assessment

In order to provide sufficient evidence of impact on the learning of P–12 students, partnerships must implement goal-based planning and assessment to provide consistency in evaluation across individual PDSs. Results of the partnership's Phase II evaluation show that evaluating PDS activities with rigorous assessments and providing evidence of accountability is conceptually challenging for schools. According to the study, most school personnel adhere to a paradigm of assessment using standardized achievement test data provided by State Report Cards. In the present study, the partnership gathered additional accountability data in studies lead by university liaisons to assess the impact of activities on P–12 students' learning and interns' development as teachers. Nonetheless, only three of six schools provided sufficient accountability data. Thus it appears likely that future PDS benchmarks should include a template for accountability data collection to which all PDSs must adhere, a recommendation of Teitel (2003). This recommendation contrasts with a lesson learned in earlier partnership work (i.e., the need to live with goal-free planning, action, and evaluation which promotes parity in collaboration among partners [Patterson, Michelli, & Pacheco, 1999]). Whereas goal-free planning, action, and evaluation may allow spontaneous initiation of collaborative projects, goal-based planning and assessment across the partnership promotes the collection of accountability data in each PDS.

SUMMARY AND CONCLUSION

A major goal of the program evaluation system was to establish local benchmarks for Winthrop University's PDS performance along stages of a developmental continuum. Results of a cross-site analysis were used to set authentic benchmarks that can anchor future expectations for PDS performance. The benchmarks are based on local partnership data, describe reasonable goals within a realistic timeline, and provide essential guidance for new and existing PDSs as partnership faculty set and evaluate their goals.

A second goal during Phase II of the program evaluation was to change the Winthrop University PDS partnership's culture so that partners increased their use of data to provide evidence of accountability. Summative results indicate that school–university partners can collaborate to provide evidence of accountability in their quest to accomplish simultaneous renewal of schooling and teacher preparation. Fenstermacher (1999) notes that the NNER carefully chose the term "renewal" rather than "repair" or "reform" because it embodies the idea of building on the strength of each partner to create systemic change. Although school principals emphasized standardized test scores and university liaisons focused on criterion-referenced measures, the two perspectives complemented one another to provide more complete evidence of impact. In the instance of this partnership, the tension between national standards and the voices of empowered participants seemed to dissolve in the daily collaborative activities of effective partnerships. It seems feasible that both site-specific projects and goal-based assessment across the partnership can coexist to provide evidence of accountability and quality assurance.

A third goal of the program evaluation was to use summative data to set future goals for the PDS partnership. Compilations of six PDSs' self-ratings on 21 elements of the *NCATE PDS Standards* reveal areas of relative strength and weakness and provide clear direction for partnership activities. Areas of priority for refinement include developing common goals for future growth and designing structures, resources, and roles to achieve the shared vision of Winthrop University's Professional Development School partnership.

In conclusion, the partnership must reassess how it implements empowerment evaluation. As a method, empowerment evaluation purports to develop ownership of the collaborative process because it privileges all participants' voices in the selection of goals and strategies for the assessment of accountability (Fetterman, 2001). One researcher speculated in an earlier paper that an external check of PDSs' self-evaluation responses would counteract the potential for bias (Vare, 2004). However, given the nature of the data reported in schools' portfolios, it seems more critical to include the voices of individual PDSs in the development of consistent data requirements. A natural tension exists for empowered partners between authentic, site-based data collection and the national press for accountability. Individual PDSs can retain some unique projects and assessments, but to achieve comprehensive assurance of accountability, the partnership must implement common assessment procedures. Such a challenge is an important priority for partners to embrace as they plan activities to achieve future goals.

REFERENCES

Abdal-Haqq, I. (1998). *Professional development schools: Weighing the evidence.* Thousand Oaks, CA: Corwin Press, Inc.

Astin, A. W. (2001). *Toward a theory of institutional transformation in higher education.* Paper presented at the Institute on Campus Leadership for Sustainable Innovation, Leesburg, VA.

Brookhart, S. M., & Loadman, W. E. (1990). School–university collaboration: Different workplace cultures. *Contemporary Education, 61,* 125–128.

Brookhart, S. M., & Loadman, W. E. (1992). School–university collaboration: Across cultures. *Teaching Education, 4*(2), 53–68.

Clark, R. (1999). *Effective professional development schools.* San Francisco: Jossey-Bass.

Cooper, M. G. (2005). Systematic evaluation in PDS-centered educator preparation: Turning state and national accreditation standards to program advantage. In J.E. Neapolitan and T.R. Berkeley (Eds.), *Staying the course with professional development schools* (pp. 127–142). New York: Peter Lang.

Darling-Hammond, L., & Synder, J. (2000). Authentic assessment of teaching in context. *Teaching and Teacher Education, 16*(5–6), 523–545.

Denner, P. R., Salzman, S. A., & Bangert, A. W. (2001). Linking teacher assessment to student performance: A benchmarking, generalizability, and validity study of the use of teacher work samples. *Journal of Personnel Evaluation in Education, 15*(4), 287–307.

Fenstermacher, G. (1999). Agenda for education in a democracy. In W. Smith and G. Fenstermacher (Eds.), *Leadership for educational renewal* (pp. 3–27). San Francisco: Jossey-Bass Publishers.

Fetterman, D. M. (2001). *Foundations of empowerment evaluation.* Thousand Oaks, CA: Sage Publications, Inc.

Glaser, B. G., & Strauss, A. L. (1967). *Discovery of grounded theory: Strategies for qualitative analysis.* New York: Aldine de Gruyter.

Goodlad, J. (1990). *Teachers for our nation's schools.* San Francisco: Jossey-Bass Publishers.

Goodlad, J. (1994). *Educational renewal: Better teachers, better schools.* San Francisco: Jossey-Bass.

Holmes Group. (1995). *Tomorrow's schools of education.* East Lansing, MI: Author.

Howard, G.S., & Dailey, P.R. (1979). Response-shift bias: A source of contamination of self-report measures. *Journal of Applied Psychology, 64*(2), 144–150.

Howard, G. S., Ralph, K. M., Gulanick, N. A., Maxwell, S. E., Nance, D. W., & Gerber. S. K. (1979). Internal validity in pretest-posttest self-report evaluations and a re-evaluation of retrospective pretests. *Applied Psychological Measurement, 3*(1), 1–23.

Levine, M., & Trachtman, R. (2005). Co-constructing an accountability system for professional development schools. In J.E. Neapolitan and T.R. Berkeley (Eds.), *Staying the course with professional development schools* (pp. 97–126). New York: Peter Lang.

Miles, M. B., & Huberman, A. M. (1984). *Qualitative data analysis: A sourcebook of new methods.* Newbury Park, CA: Sage Publications.

Miles, M. B., & Huberman, A. M. (1994). *Qualitative data analysis: An expanded sourcebook.* Thousand Oaks, CA: Sage Publications.

Moss, P. A. (1992). Shifting conceptions of validity in educational measurement: Implications for performance assessment. *Review of Educational Research, 62*(3), 229–258.

National Council for Accreditation of Teacher Education. (2001). *Standards for professional development schools.* Washington, DC: Author.

Paratore, J. R. (1995). Assessing literacy: Establishing common standards in portfolio assessment. *Topics in Language Disorders, 16*(1), 67–82.

Patterson, R. S., Michelli, N. M., & Pacheco, A. (1999). *Centers of pedagogy: New structures for educational renewal.* San Francisco: Jossey-Bass.

Teitel, L. (2000). *Assessing the impacts of professional development schools.* Washington, DC: American Association of Colleges for Teacher Education.

Teitel, L. (2001a). An assessment framework for professional development schools: Going beyond the leap of faith. *Journal of Teacher Education, 52*(1), 57–69.

Teitel, L. (2001b). *How professional development schools make a difference: A review of research.* Washington, DC: National Council for Accreditation of Teacher Education.

Teitel, L. (2003). *The professional development schools handbook: Starting, assessing, and sustaining partnerships that improve student learning.* Thousand Oaks, CA: Corwin Press, Inc.

Teitel, L. (2004). *How professional development schools make a difference: A review of research* (2nd ed., revised). Washington, DC: National Council for Accreditation of Teacher Education.

Vare, J. (2004). Empowerment, vision, and voice: Building an assessment system for professional development schools. *The Teacher Educator, 40*(2), 133–148.

CHAPTER 21

USING NATIONAL STANDARDS TO EXAMINE PROFESSIONAL DEVELOPMENT SCHOOL PARTICIPANTS' BELIEFS AND VALUES REGARDING THEIR PDS PARTNERSHIPS

Diane M. Truscott, Lydia Criss Mays, and Brandi Wells

ABSTRACT

This study centered on the voices of urban school partners examining their perceptions, values, and beliefs regarding professional development school (PDS) work. Participants from seven schools and a local teacher education department responded to a survey and interview aligned with the PDS level criterion used by National Council for Accreditation of Teacher Education (NCATE). Descriptive statistics were employed using survey data for each item by developmental level and across NCATE standards. Interviews were coded for the value and understanding of the PDS partnership and activities. Reported PDS activities centered on classroom teaching and learning, and

University and School Connections, pages 377–390
Copyright © 2008 by Information Age Publishing

the partnership was viewed as a way to enhance school climate and culture. No differences were found between university and school personnel in what was reported as valuable. Preparing quality future teachers was observed as a shared goal. The PDS model was viewed as a value-added partnership centered on student learning.

INTRODUCTION

Adapted from an apprenticeship model in the medical field, professional development school (PDS) partners are committed to teaching and learning within situated practice and collaboration with school educators, university stakeholders, and other community members. Operationally defined, the PDS model is a mutual partnership between an institution of higher education and birth–12 schools (Holmes Group, 1990; Teitel, 2001). Because the development of pre-service and in-service teachers is key to quality teaching and learning for all children, PDSs have gained interest and momentum in the higher education community. Increased attention in PDS partnerships grounded in research and guided by a shared vision of educational excellence defines new ways of university and school personnel working together (Levine, 2002).

After its inception in 1990 by the Holmes Group (now called the Holmes Partnership) the PDS movement has been lauded by various organizations such as the National Education Association (NEA) and the National Council for Accreditation of Teacher Education (NCATE). The purpose of PDS partnerships is to build and sustain a community of educators dedicated to helping children succeed and is typically guided by four areas of collaboration: (1) exemplary school-based experiences for teachers in training; (2) applied inquiry designed to improve practice; (3) new teacher mentoring; and (4) quality professional development. Extending beyond traditional relationships with schools, PDS partnerships ". . . encourage the school to undergo a structural reform that allows for collaboration between school and university faculty and supports changes in teaching and learning" (Book, 1996, p. 195). Indeed, PDS models that commit to school improvement are more than just a "collaborative affiliation driven by mutual concerns in teacher preparation, innovation of practices, and professional development" (Murrell, 1998, p. 28). Instead, PDS programs extend beyond traditional partnerships and work toward creating quality schools and enhancing learning opportunities in the contextual needs of the communities where our children live.

Although partnership work commonly defines itself in terms of collaboration between various stakeholders, those key components or features that characterize partnership activities often vary significantly (Book, 1996; Kochan, 1999; Leonard et al., 2004). For example, Book noted a range of networks, including the Ford Foundation, the Rand Corporation, and the American Federation of Teachers Task Force on Professional Practice Schools, that defined and described PDS partnerships differently. Even though NCATE (2001) developed guidelines for PDSs, partnerships continue to struggle with self-identities. Some of the PDS partners in our study wondered whether they were a professional development school in light of specific criterion and, instead, described the state of ebb and flow that typifies working together.

There has been a surge of research available on the PDS partnership over the last decade (Book, 1996; Kochan, 1999; Pritchard & Ancess, 1999; Teitel, 1998), particularly on its role in improving teacher education (Gimbert, 2002; Levine & Rock, 2003; Taylor & Sobel, 2003). These studies have closely examined the collaboration between university-school partnerships and their commitment to preparing and supporting pre-service teachers. Recent work by Castle, Fox, and O'Hanlan Souder (2006) reveals positive impacts for pre-service teachers who are prepared in PDS settings versus non-PDS settings. While no differences were found among teacher candidates (PDS or non-PDS) in their abilities to plan for instruction, PDS teacher candidates were evaluated significantly higher on their depth of understanding and level of sophistication in integrating teaching standards in their practice. Equally important is that research in teacher education has long recognized the connection between the quality of teacher preparedness and learning outcomes for children. New research connecting PDS activities with academic increases in student learning is being conducted, suggesting that students show higher gain scores when compared to students in non-PDSs (Basile, 2005). True to the intent of the PDS model, research asserts that quality teaching and learning through the creation of democratic learning communities where all children participate is possible (Holmes Group, 1990).

Georgia State University's teacher education program, like many other higher education institutions, is vested in collaborating with school partners to provide site-based learning for pre-service teachers. These local university-school partnerships are reflective of committed PDS stakeholders who share a common goal of quality teaching and learning. This study examines the perceptions, understandings, and values of educators associated with PDS work. Our study is guided by an interest in what matters most to school partners as they consider and commit to collaborative PDS relationships. We explore how school partners view themselves in response to defining external PDS criteria and what this may mean in terms of our mutual vision, goals, and work together. The research takes into account that the lack of success in some PDSs is the "... different perceptions individual staff members hold with regard to the goals of PDSs and their individual roles" (Leonard et al., 2004, p. 577). In the spirit of the original intent of a democratic learning community, the study centers on the voices of the partnership participants as they explain what matters most.

THE STUDY

During the time of the study, the Department of Early Childhood Education partnered with seven elementary schools from four districts in the metro-Atlanta area. Each university faculty liaison collaborated with a PDS school on various projects, programs, and professional development opportunities, including site-based courses, undergraduate fieldwork, teacher action research, participation in large grant-funded research, and collaborative inquiry projects.

One school administrator, one teacher, and one university faculty liaison (N = 21) from each of the seven PDS sites were selected based on their participation in the school partnership during the 2004–2005 school year. Recommendations from the university liaisons, in consultation with the school principal, resulted in the purposeful sample selection of teachers from each PDS site. We hoped that those teachers who were active participants in the partnership activities would be the most knowledgeable about the work and have opinions about its value. All schools are considered urban and high-need based on their poverty levels and high concentrations of diverse learners. Across schools, the average percentage of children eligible for free and reduced lunch was 77 percent (range 59–92 percent) with 89 percent of the student population identified as minority (range 79–99 percent). This study reports on the perceived values and beliefs of 27 PDS participants; all participants were female except one.

Survey Instrument & Interview

The National Council for Accreditation of Teacher Education (NCATE) developed and published standards to guide school and university PDS partners in 2001. The NCATE standards are designed to highlight core components of a PDS partnership that can improve student learning. Table 21.1 delineates each NCATE standard, defined by elements that represent beliefs, practices, and policies. Four developmental levels that can be used to describe a PDS demarcate each element: beginning, developing, at-standard, or leading.

A 30-item survey was designed using the NCATE (2001) Standards for Professional Development Schools, to explore perceptions, values, and beliefs found in urban schools relating to their PDS partnerships. In developing the survey, researchers analyzed and independently coded each

TABLE 21.1   NCATE Standards and Elements for Professional Development Schools

Standard I: Learning Community

Elements:

1. Support multiple learners
2. Inquiry-based work
3. Common shared vision
4. Serve as instrument of change
5. Extended learning community

The learning community includes the university, school district, and the teacher union or professional education association. It supports the integrated learning and development of P-12 students, teacher candidates, and PDS partners through inquiry-based practice grounded in research and practitioner knowledge.

Standard II: Accountability & Quality Assurance

Elements:

1. Professional Accountability
2. Public Accountability
3. PDS Participation Criteria
4. Formative Assessments
5. Engage with PDS Context

PDS partners are accountable for upholding professional standards for teaching and learning. They collaboratively develop assessments, collect information, and use results to systemically examine their practices and establish outcomes goals.

Standard III: Collaboration

Elements:

1. Engage in joint work
2. Roles & structures
3. Celebrate joint work

PDS partners commit to joint work implementing the PDS mission. They collaboratively design roles and structures and systemically recognize and celebrate collaborations and partner contributions.

Standard IV: Diversity & Equity

Elements:

1. Equitable learning opportunities
2. Policies and practices
3. Recruit & support diverse participants

PDS partners develop and demonstrate knowledge, skills, and dispositions resulting in learning. They ensure that policies and practices result in equitable learning outcomes. PDS partners include diverse participants and diverse learning communities for PDS work.

Standard V: Structures, Resources and Roles

Elements:

1. Governance & support structures
2. Ensure goal progress
3. Create PDS roles
4. Resources
5. Effective Communication

PDS partnership uses its authority and resources to articulate its mission and establish governing structures and partner institutions ensure that structures, programs, and resources decisions support the partnership's mission. They create new roles and modify existing ones. Lastly, the partnership effectively uses communication for coordination and linkage.

NCATE standard and corresponding elements for each developmental level (beginning, developing, at-standard, leading) for key terms by two of the researchers. Key terms resulted in a survey item pool. Survey questions resulted in items, which represented each standard and corresponding elements within each developmental level. For example, the survey had seven items devoted to NCATE Standard II (Accountability and Quality Assurance). Of these, two items corresponded to Element 1 (collecting data) at the at-standard and developing levels; another two items for Element 2 (parent involvement) for beginning levels. One item focused on Element 3 (participating in professional development) for the category at-standard. Another item focused on Element 4 (data collection and reflection) at the developing level, and a final item for Element 5 (engaging with PDS partners to share work) at the leading level. This resulted in all elements covered within a standard and items targeting each of the four developmental levels: 8 beginning, 6 developing, 10 at-standard, 6 leading. Survey items were randomly ordered and masked so no standard, element, or developmental level was detectable.

Survey items responses were twofold: (1) how much that particular goal/activity mattered to the school (4-point scale); (2) where the respondent currently saw the school in response to the goal/activity (3-point scale). Each respondent rated each survey item correspondingly. Figure 21.1 illustrates a sample of a survey item and Likert scale for both categories.

Survey reliability and validity was determined by field-testing the original survey with a group of teachers from local urban schools and doctoral students in educational-related fields in order to determine items of ambiguity. Only two content changes were made as a result of this field test: (1) one item was determined "wordy" and was reworded, and (2) the addition of the word "research" with items asking about "inquiry." The addition of the question "Did you have any difficulty answering any of these items?" concludes the survey and serves for reliability purposes.

Each PDS participant met individually with one of the researchers at the school or university at a prearranged time convenient to the subject to conduct the interviews. Surveys were provided to participants prior to the interview and collected after the interview. Each subject was asked four interview questions (two forced-choice response questions and 2 open-ended questions) regarding his/her understanding of PDS, where he or she saw the school in terms of NCATE levels, and additional probing on what mattered most in the PDS work. On average, each survey and interview session lasted 30 minutes. Immediately after the interview, each researcher

What PDS goals and/or activities matter most to you?	The following matters...				Our school is...		
	Least	A little	A lot	Most	Envisioning	Gearing up	In progress
5. Planning supportive environment for students, teacher candidates, faculty and other professionals	☐	☐	☐	☐	☐	☐	☐

Figure 21.1 Sample of a survey item and Likert scale.

transcribed the interview notes. Each subject was given a subject code to maintain confidentiality, and each interviewer was trained in conducting the interview prior to the study using a university faculty liaison from a PDS school not active at the time of the study.

Analysis of Data

Descriptive statistics were performed on the initial 4-point scale for items' value related to the school. The second 3-point scale (see Figure 21.1), indicating where the respondent saw the school at that point in time in response to the goal or activity, are being used in a secondary study. Frequency responses, means, and percentages for each item by developmental level (beginning, developing, at standard, and leading) and across the five standards were calculated. Glaser and Strauss' (1999) constant comparative method was employed to analyze semi-structured interview data. All interviews were read independently by two of the three researchers and coded explicitly for three *a priori* themes: (1) value of the PDS, (2) understanding of the PDS, and (3) PDS activity. After independent coding, the researchers had 61 percent consensus. Operational definitions of "value of the PDS" and "understanding of the PDS" were determined ambiguous, requiring redefining the terms "value" and "understanding." Items were then recoded with new operational definitions and 100 percent consensus was reached on 186 meaning units. Meaning units were defined as individual words (e.g., "understanding") or short phrases (e.g., "extra hands") which related to the categories. This coding technique helped to capture all relevant discussion during participant interviews. One *a priori* category was modified after initial coding. "Understanding of PDS" was changed to "Understanding/Misunderstanding of PDS" due to interview statements exemplifying confusion surrounding the purpose of the PDS partnership. All meaning units were then collectively compared by all three researchers across and between these categories and analyzed for themes. Emerging themes were compared to the frequency percentages for what was rated as most and least valuable on the survey.

FINDINGS

Prior to completing the survey, each participant was asked to rank four PDS components (teacher candidate preparation, faculty development, student learning, and inquiry/research) in order of importance to their partnership. The majority of respondents (81 percent) ranked student learning as the most important priority in the PDS partnership. No differences were found between rankings of university versus school personnel. Contributing to the development of new teachers was ranked second by 71 percent of the respondents. Interview data supported these rankings evidenced by various descriptions of PDS activities centered on classroom teaching and learning. Many participants reported that they saw the partnership as a way to enhance school climate and build relationships. One classical example provided by participants was the additional support of "extra hands" in the classrooms from student teachers and interns. Likewise, the focus on producing quality new teachers was within the context of student learning. Educators stressed the need for good teachers who can support children in challenging educational settings. Moreover, interviews revealed that the partnership works diligently to align school practices and theoretical beliefs and that the partnership does not end with solely supporting pre-service teachers. There was an overarching theme of preparing quality future teachers, as reflected in one of the PDS participant's comment, ". . . we recruit and hire many pre-service teachers who are now in-service teachers within our school community." Focus on research or inquiry as a PDS element ranked last by 76 percent. Consistent with the surveys, discussion regarding research or inquiry were notably absent throughout the interviews.

Little variation for separate ratings of "most" and "a lot" among the five standard areas as referenced in Table 22.2 was noted. However, when combined, what appeared to matter to PDS participants was a commitment to equity and diversity (85 percent), accountability (79 percent), and building a learning community (79 percent). Participants described powerful relationships between the school and university, with both stakeholders illustrating a strong commitment to the principles of a learning community. Though equity and diversity ranked among the highest standard of what mattered the most, none of the participants spoke to the importance of equity and diversity or discussed activities currently implemented which relate to issues of equity and/or diversity. Interestingly, most questions addressing equity and diversity on the survey focused largely on student learning. For

TABLE 21.2   Frequency Percentages of Participant Responses to Standards That Matters Most

Standard	Most f%	A lot f%	Both f%
I. Learning Community (8 items)	39	40	79
II. Accountability and Quality Assurance (7 items)	30	49	79
III. Collaboration (4 items)	28	38	66
IV. Equity and Diversity (3 items)	43	42	85
V. Structures, Resources & Roles (7 items)	22	55	77

example, "Assessing PDS partnerships' influence on student learning" was a question addressing Standard IV: Student Equity and Diversity.

Accountability was rated high as an element of the PDS work that mattered; however, explanations of why this was important or how this facilitates the PDS work were absent from the interview data. "Involving parents, policymakers, and business community in sharing responsibility for student learning," is an example of one of the survey items in this category.

Table 21.3 shows that frequency percentages for participant responses to what mattered least ranged from 9 percent to 22 percent. Combining ratings of "least" and "a little" resulted in collaboration as the standard area that was reported as having little value. This finding may be more reflective of PDS school participants desiring to engage more in the collaborative decision-making process with university faculty. In addition, the definition of "collaboration" was dictated, in part, by the survey items that focused on producing joint work for teacher candidates and children, allocating additional resources for PDS partners and receiving recognition and rewards for joint PDS work. However, inconsistent with the survey findings, interview data suggested that the school-university partnership is, in fact, highly regarded for its value in improving the school culture by providing collegial and school-based support and by implementing quality professional development that is tailored to the specific school-related needs.

Interview analyses resulted in five emergent themes which reflected PDS participants' attitudes toward the partnership: (1) a valuable relationship; (2) a resource providing tangible and personal support; (3) a shared, strong commitment to preparing quality future teachers; (4) a feeling of separatism between the school and university, and (5) PDS identity within NCATE standards. Overall, the PDS was viewed as a value-added partnership, that centered primarily on student learning and a dedication to pre-service and in-service teachers. Ultimately, these added-values, or gains, were viewed through their ability to support and guide teaching and learning efforts and provide the tangible resources needed to participate in unique experiences. For example, one of the participants noted the additional benefits

TABLE 21.3 Frequency Percentages of Participant Responses to Standards That Matters Least

Standard	Least	A little	Both
I. Learning Community (8 items)	16	5	21
II. Accountability and Quality Assurance (7 items)	16	5	21
III. Collaboration (4 items)	22	9	31
IV. Equity and Diversity (3 items)	0	15	15
V. Structures, Resources, & Roles (7 items)	19	3	22

of a university liaison on their school campus, reporting, "We have huge benefits from having a faculty liaison who can offer guidance to benefit students and their families."

Moreover, within the same context, PDS participants viewed these added values as enhancing the school climate as well as building relationships. In other words, tangible support was valued because of financial contributions, additional support from the student teachers and interns, and implementation of professional development activities. Personal support reflected the interpersonal relationships of PDS participants. For example, the university liaisons noted they were able to "build deeper relationships with teachers and it established a sense of family between the schools and faculty liaison." In addition, most schools reported the PDS relationship assisted with the facilitation of school goals and plans. The interns were also seen as a part of the school community. Lastly, PDS participants reported positive feelings toward the PDS partnership reflecting wholesome attributes such as support, commitment, and nonthreatening experiences. Participants were excited about their work and relationships, comfortable in their school communities, and proud to be a part of the school community.

A strong commitment to preparing future teachers emerged as a theme throughout both interview and survey data. In-service teachers discussed being able to connect their "old ways" to new practices introduced to them by their interns. Faculty liaisons reported a stronger relationship with their PDS partner because of the intern placements in the school. One faculty liaison said, "We want the interns to have a valuable experience and get them ready for teaching in the future." The same sentiment was shared by administrators in the PDSs. Many administrators expressed using the field-based placement as a resource for hiring new teachers.

One area of concern found was the theme of separatism, which emerged from the data. School partners discussed a sense of disconnect from the university in various ways. Finding common ground, including schools in university decision-making regarding the PDS and aligning school goals with PDS goals are just a few statements eliciting the theme of separatism. A quote from a teacher expressing this frustration exemplifies the struggle, "Teachers want the school/university partnership to feel more like a relationship because they feel the school is doing a lot and the university is getting the benefits."

Lastly, school identity emerged as a critical theme. PDS partners found it difficult, or "problematic," to identify their position within one of the NCATE development levels (at beginning, developing, at-standard or leadership). "It's hard to pinpoint a specific level between the four . . . cannot place our school in one stage or the other . . . some things are in place, while others are developing." Often times, as exemplified in the previous quote, participants believed they were participating in two or more developmental levels simultaneously as described by the NCATE standards.

DISCUSSION

As illustrated by survey and interview data, findings suggest, that pre-service teacher training and student learning are the most important components of the PDS partnership. Most PDS partnerships are initiated by institutions of higher education that typically take the lead in building the structures, roles, and design (Boudah & Knight, 1999). Teacher development research informs us that PDS programs positively affect the performance of pre-service teachers, particularly by the extended practicum experiences students are afforded (Darling-Hammond, 1996). Pre-service teachers may experience unique teaching and learning opportunities (such as co-instruction by classroom teachers and a university professor, demonstration lessons, field-study groups, teacher action research, and/or induction activities). Such site-based PDS experiences allow interns to readily apply theory to practice with more meaning (Castle et al., 2006). Likewise, schools place an importance on student learning especially in the advent of high stakes testing and standardized accountability measures. Interview respondents continually referenced the importance of student achievement related to state mandated tests and other student performance measures. Thus, any partnership activities must mutually address the preparation of, and continued professional development of, quality educators who can provide learning opportunities for all children. The shared vision of the Holmes Group (1990) proposition was to provide opportunities for teachers and administrators to dialogue on problems with student learning and produce possible solutions while engaging in collaborative research on the problems of educational practice. This vision is in direct support of linking teacher preparation with student learning.

There are several possible reasons that inquiry and research were rarely described in PDS activities and ranked among the lowest in the four components. The first explanation could be a matter of having sufficient time; work in PDS schools is time-consuming for most participants. University faculty members view school research essential to their roles in academe. Teachers, while valuing action research and the continual process of reflection and refinement, may find prioritizing research difficult to do. Leonard et al. (2004) found that PDS schools practiced and valued the overarching concepts of improving the quality of instruction and collaboration but were resistant to investing the time and energy associated with collaborative inquiry-based research (Leonard et al., 2004). A second explanation is associated with the maturity of the PDS relationship (as measured by NCATE, a level 4 versus a level 1) and hence the opportunities afforded. PDS participants reported that they were at different stages within the PDS partnership. Some saw themselves as a well-established PDS and could talk about the interplay between field placements, induction, research, and professional development. Some PDS personnel did not think of themselves as a PDS, even though they had partnered with the university for many years and had in place all the elements described. As PDS partners struggle to place themselves within the NCATE developmental levels, interview data support the emerging theme that identifying one "level" of partnership (beginning, developing, at-standard, leading) may not be the most appropriate criterion in self-identification or actualization. Indeed, Daniel, Brindley, and Rosselli (2000) found that the PDS standards should "extend their scope" and evolve to be more reflective of the complexities of working in schools.

Contrary to the low ratings from our survey data, the theme of collaboration permeated throughout all participant interviews as paramount to the success of PDS partnerships. These findings are supported and well documented in the PDS literature (Boudah & Knight, 1999). Collaboration was described in tangible ways through the resources that were provided via the personal relationships, connections to outside sources of information and support, and the ways partners work together. The low survey ratings may be attributed to specific definitions by NCATE in characterizing collaboration. For example, one survey item generated from Standard III asked respondents to rate the importance of "receiving recognition and awards for joint work at district and state levels." Given the day-to-day challenges and concerns that face urban educators, this aspect of collaboration did not take precedence. Instead, our findings suggest that PDS partners acknowledge collaboration as an important component within learning communities.

Finally, this study represents the first part of an exploratory study with PDS partners in seven schools. Findings are limited, based on two converging data sets from self-reporting instruments. Our next steps include examining what respondents indicate as valued compared to the activities they participate in or were afforded (Scale B on survey). We also plan to validate the survey instrument nationally which has now been used in the earlier preliminary study (Truscott, Wells, & Mays, 2006) and the one reported here. A research void remains between specific PDS components and learning outcomes. Specifically, we wish to investigate what elements of the partnership (climate, relationships, resources) are associated with positive impacts for teachers, students and children.

Our findings suggest that although determining an NCATE developmental level of partnership appears to be difficult for PDS participants, there are incontrovertible similarities when it comes to "what matters most" to PDS partnership (Truscott et al., 2006). Student learning emerged as the foundation upon which building a learning community that supports the development of teacher candidates, their educators, and community constituencies is driven. *Tomorrow's Schools* of the Holmes Group (1990) are the reality of today's public schools. In light of NCLB and continuing pressure for education reform, partnerships are needed now more than ever. A PDS can be one whole-school reform model attempting to enrich the school culture during a time when educators are currently required to do more with less. While PDS partnerships will naturally vary, they all aim for the same goal: increased student achievement. While the long history of America's attempt to reform public schools perpetuates itself, the PDS model of the Holmes Group fails to waiver in its commitment to join forces with universities, schools of education, and public schools to build communities of practice and inquiry that will endure over time.

REFERENCES

Basile, C. G. (2005). *Building intellectual capital in professional development schools: A comparative study of teacher quality in PDS and non-PDS.* Paper presented at the meeting of the American Educational Research Association, Montreal, Canada.

Book, C. L. (1996). Professional development schools. In J. Sikula (Ed.), *Handbook of research on teacher education* (2nd ed., pp. 194–210). New York: Association of Teacher Educators.

Boudah, D. J., & Knight, S. L. (1999). Creating learning communities of research and practice: Participatory research and development. In D. M. Byrd & D. J. McIntyre (Eds.), *Research on professional development schools, teacher education yearbook VII* (pp. 97–114). Thousand Oaks, CA: Corwin.

Castle, S., Fox, R. K., & O'Hanlan Souder, K. (2006). Do professional development schools (PDSs) make a difference? A comparative study of PDS and Non-PDS Teacher Candidates. *Journal of Teacher Education, 57*(1), 65–80.

Daniel, P. L., Brindley, R. N., & Rosselli, H. C. (2000). The goodness of fit between the voices in the field and the NCATE PDS draft standards. *Teaching and Change, 7*(4), 372–391.

Darling-Hammond, L. (Ed.). (1996). *Professional development schools: Schools for developing a profession.* New York: Teachers College Press.

Glaser, B. G., & Strauss, A. L. (1999). *The discovery of grounded theory: Strategies for qualitative research.* New York: Gruyer.

Gimbert, B. G. (2002). *Mastery of teaching in a school-university partnership: A model of context-appropriation theory.* Philadelphia, Pennsylvania: Teaching and Teacher Education. (ERIC Document Reproduction Service No. ED471194).

Holmes Group. (1990). *Tomorrow's schools: Principles for the design of professional development schools.* East Lansing, MI: Holmes Group.

Kochan, F. (1999). Professional development schools: A comprehensive view. In D. M. Byrd & D. J. McIntyre (Eds.), *Research on professional development schools, teacher education yearbook VII* (pp. 173–190). Thousand Oaks, CA: Corwin.

Leonard, J., Lovelace-Taylor, K., Sanford-DeShields, J., & Spearman, P. (2004). Professional development schools revisited. Reform, authentic partnerships, and new visions. *Urban Education, 39*(5), 561–583.

Levine, M. (2002). Why invest in professional development schools? *Educational Leadership, 59*(6), 65–69.

Levine, B. B., & Rock, T. C. (2003). The effects of collaborative action research on preservice and experienced teacher partners in professional development schools. *Journal of Teacher Education, 54*(2), 135–149.

Murrell, P. C. Jr. (1998). *Like stone soup: The problem of the professional development school in the renewal of urban schools.* Washington, DC: AACTE.

National Council for Accreditation of Teacher Education. (2001). *Standards for professional development schools.* Washington, DC: National Council for Accreditation of Teacher Education.

Pritchard, F., & Ancess, J. (1999). *The effects of professional development schools: A literature review.* New York: National Partnership for Excellence and Accountability in Teaching. (ERIC Document Reproduction Service No. ED448155).

Taylor, S. V., & Sobel, D. M. (2003). Rich contexts to emphasize social justice in teacher education: Curriculum and pedagogy in professional development schools. *Equity & Excellence in Education, 36*(3), 249–258.

Teitel, L. (2001). *Handbook for the assessment of professional development schools.* Washington, DC: National Council for Accreditation of Teacher Education. (ERIC Document Reproduction Service No. ED470235).

Teitel, L. (1998). Professional development schools: A literature review. In M. Levine (Ed.), *Designing standards that work for professional development schools* (pp. 33–80). Washington, DC: National Council for Accreditation of Teacher Education. (ERIC Document Reproduction Service No. ED426052).

Truscott, D., Wells, B., & Mays, L. (2006). Exploring what matters to professional Development school partners. *Journal of the Georgia Association of Teacher Education, 17*(1), 32–42.

PART V

PAST AND FUTURE CONSIDERATIONS

CHAPTER 22

ELEVEN YEARS AND COUNTING

The Lasting Impact of PDS Experience on Teaching Careers

Roger Brindley, Patricia L. Daniel, Hilda Rosselli, Cindy Campbell, and Dorian Vizcain

ABSTRACT

The authors surveyed 348 graduates of the College of Education within the last ten years who had an early field experiences and/or a final internship in a PDS. The final response rate of 86 (24 percent) revealed that the PDS graduates who responded to the survey are retained in the profession at much higher numbers than the national average. The authors concluded that PDS internship placements can positively affect the continuing professional development of pre-service teachers after they graduate and enter into teaching themselves.

University and School Connections, pages 393–409
Copyright © 2008 by Information Age Publishing
All rights of reproduction in any form reserved.

INTRODUCTION

For the past eleven years a large metropolitan university in the southeast United States has partnered with four professional development schools (PDSs) over a two-county area. Over the history of these PDS partnerships the relationship has ebbed and flowed, but all four schools have achieved the threshold conditions of the NCATE standards for PDS work, and throughout their history, the sites have offered exemplary internship experiences to pre-service educators enrolled at the university.

Two of the four PDSs, one a middle school with 850 children and one a Title One elementary school, are located in an adjacent rural county and have been in a PDS partnership for eleven years and nine years respectively. The other two schools, both Title One elementary schools, are located in the same urban county as the university. Both these schools serve high transient communities with significant limited English proficient populations.

All four of the schools have moved beyond the pre-threshold stage as defined by the National Council for the Accreditation of Teacher Education (NCATE, 2001) standards, and this would not be possible without a strong support system that includes school faculty and administration, district-wide resources, and both departmental and college assistance. However, each school has its own distinct PDS history, and each has been effective in its work to varying degrees. The research study reported herein started out documenting whether the pre-service teachers who graduated from our teacher preparation programs having had a PDS internship experience found success and satisfaction in their teaching careers, and, if so, to what extent they have continued their professional development and become leaders in their schooling communities.

THE VULNERABILITY OF THE PDS LITERATURE

The body of literature is replete with detailed and well-explained descriptions of the work of individual PDS initiatives. Many of these pieces of research articulate school cultures, administrative structures, and collaborative systems that are distinctive or even unique to a particular context (Breault, 2006; Byrd & McIntyre, 1999). The PDS literature frequently portrays a successful partnership, usually in the early stages of development. Some of this context-specific work has been questioned as it lacks quantifiable data sources (Tietel, 2000; Zeichner, 2004) and has even been portrayed as simplistic and lacking true community focus (Boyle-Baise & Mcintyre, 2006). Teitel (2001) asserts that, without some standardized assessment framework, entering into PDS work is akin to taking a leap of faith. In response to these concerns, recent large scale data studies across

PDS partnerships are purposefully beginning to address this gap in the literature (Root et al., 2004; Siers et al., 2006; Watson et al., 2006), and this study also seeks to respond to the need for larger data sets.

There are some profound reasons why the impact of PDS work remains unclear. As with any initiative where substantial resources are allocated, accountability and a review of PDS outcomes have followed (Teitel, 2000). However, given that PDSs are still developing institutions that are open-ended, they can be expected to produce *unexpected* results, and this raises dilemmas with regards to the accountability processes and the sustainability of PDSs (Daniel, Rosselli, & Brindley, 2001; Neapolitan & Berkeley, 2006). For example, teachers at a PDS may engage in more reflection on their own professionalism as they articulate their craft knowledge to pre-service teachers, while PDS stakeholders may participate in more collaborative discussions, professional development experiences, and action research activities (Byrd & McIntyre, 1999). Unfortunately, these types of outcomes may not produce measurable impacts of significance.

The evasive nature of PDS outcomes leads us to ask if, for instance, it is reasonable to expect student test scores to increase significantly as a result of the establishment of a PDS and, if so, the extent to which the PDS initiative is responsible? Furthermore, the traditional style of scholarship that characterizes educational research at the university may not be achievable within the PDS environment. The relative value assigned to the nature of inquiry often differs when comparing the views of school-based personnel with university-based personnel. With the distinctive individuality of much of the PDS work, school-university partnerships are often difficult to present through meta-analysis consistent with the United States Department of Education call for "scientific research."

At our university, the authors recognized the concerns of Ismat-Haqq (Teitel, 2000) who believed that, "If professional development schools are to prosper, or even survive, the call for credible evidence of accomplishment cannot be dismissed" (p. v). Keen to influence the debate in our own college on the ways in which school-university partnerships should be emphasized in strategic planning, the authors designed a study intent on identifying if and how a PDS internship placement affects the continuing professional development of pre-service teachers after they graduate and enter into teaching. In short, we wanted to know to what extent graduates with a PDS experience have been retained in the profession and whether the reflective and continuous learning emphasized in our PDS sites translated to these graduates seeking additional professional development and leadership roles. In our own college planning, we recognized that this "credible" data would be helpful in identifying the role that the PDS initiative is to play in future school partnership efforts and in the task of considering how mature PDS relationships should continue to evolve over time.

METHODOLOGY

Graduates of the College of Education over a ten-year period who had an early field experience and/or a final internship in a PDS were identified through alumni data. These 348 graduates were sent a 47-item survey that they were asked to complete and return (see Appendix A for the full survey). The final response rate of 86 (24.7 percent), demonstrated how easily schools of education can lose touch with their graduates after a decade! We had more than 50 surveys "returned to sender" indicating the addressee had left that address at least eighteen months earlier, and we were sad to be informed that three of the graduates were deceased.

Thirty-one of the survey items use a Lichert Scale five-point design, and the consequent quantitative data were compiled as simple descriptive statistics into frequency tables. Sixteen of these 31 questions also sought a narrative explanation. In order to demonstrate the longitudinal effects of PDS pre-service teacher preparation, the analysis focused specifically upon the narrative of 36 graduates from the two longest serving PDS sites (eleven and nine years respectively). The qualitative content analysis of the open-ended narrative responses used Hycner's (1985) protocol for identifying units of meaning and emergent themes. These were categorized and are shared within the category labels.

RESULTS

In order to report on the research data, Likert scale responses and narrative explanations are separated in this section of text.

Likert Scale Responses

The following summarizes the quantitative data received from the PDS graduates. The data shared here are based upon the key emergent themes of career retention and attrition, job satisfaction, retrospectives of the PDS experience, continuing education, and self-evaluation of practice.

Retention in the teaching profession. Of the 86 survey respondents 74 percent are presently classroom teachers, and 6 percent are working in some other instructional or administrative capacity in education. Only 20 percent of the respondents stated they had left the profession over the previous decade. Furthermore, of the 69 active educators among the 86 respondents, 73 percent ($n = 50$) believe they will remain educators in the long term with 28 percent anticipating career moves within education. Only 4 percent

($n = 3$) of these 69 educators stating they planned to leave the profession in the future.

Preparation and job satisfaction.   Results indicate a positive sense of how well prepared our PDS graduates felt. Just one of the 86 respondents felt "inadequately prepared." Furthermore, 70 percent (n = 60) considered their job satisfaction to be "above average" or "excellent." Only two respondents considered their job satisfaction as "poor," while one rated his/her job satisfaction "below average."

Retrospectives of the PDS experience.   Asked to reflect back on their PDS experience, 76 percent reported they "would definitely" recommend the university with an additional 19 percent stating they "probably would" for a 95 percent positive response. Further, there was a 90 percent positive response when asked if they would recommend a PDS internship specifically, with 56 percent asserting they "definitely would" and 34 percent responding that they "probably would."

Educational Status.   Asked about their educational status, working as they do in a state that does *not* require graduate-level professional development, 46 percent were pursuing and 17 percent had completed graduate work (6 percent at the doctoral level). When combined with the 10 percent who had added a second certification endorsement, 74 percent of all our PDS graduates had extended their education beyond the baccalaureate level.

Self-evaluation of practice.   Respondents were also asked to self-evaluate their collaboration with other teachers, collaboration with their students' families, their involvement in school improvement, their experience with mentoring, their ability to provide leadership, their practice with action research, and their role as a student advocate. The results are presented in Table 22.1.

The PDS graduates in general consider themselves to be effective teachers. They take their roles as collaborators very seriously and are universally

TABLE 22.1 Self-Evaluation of Practice

	Excellent	Above Average	Average	Below Average	Poor
Teacher Collaboration	55	26	5	—	—
Family Collaboration	46	26	14	—	—
School Improvement	26	35	25	—	—
Mentoring	13	34	35	3	1
Leadership	25	14	34	9	4
Action Research	9	15	40	14	6
Student Advocate (3 responses blank)	30	28	21	3	1

involved in school improvement. Mentoring, leadership, advocacy, and research are usually associated with veteran teachers, and most of our PDS graduates report some experience in these three areas, although some report that the behaviors associated with leadership and action research are in need of further development.

The authors' recognize the dangers in analyzing self-report data, but we can deduce that these teachers, many of whom are now in their mid-careers, retain a predominantly positive 'image of self as teacher' (Fuller & Bown, 1975).

Items 32 through 46 of the survey requested narrative responses. Again, the authors focused on the narrative responses from graduates of the two longest serving PDS sites in order to provide the perspectives of mid-career teachers now firmly established in their careers. There were 36 graduates from these two sites, and eight (22 percent) had been nominated for the "Teacher of the Year" at their schools; six of the eight received the award. In addition, other graduates had received the Council for Exceptional Children *Mainstream Teacher of the Year Award*, the state of Florida *Technology Education Teacher of the Year*, and the school district *Technology Teacher of the Year* awards. Finally, two teachers had received their school's *Rookie Teacher of the Year Award*, one of whom went on to receive the accolade as the State of Florida *Rookie Teacher of the Year*. All told, 11 of the 36 teachers (30 percent) had received significant accolades.

Narrative Responses

The narrative focused upon three general categories: the benefits of PDS work, the disadvantages of PDS work, and the PDS culture.

The benefits of PDS work. Three themes emerged within this category. "The professionalism of the school faculty" was a prominent theme, as documented in the following selection of comments:

> The teachers at the school were willing to help and let the interns try new things in their classrooms.

> Being surrounded by passionate teachers and other interns who cared so much about children, and the innovative techniques learned . . . were among the benefits of being at a PDS.

> Teachers were more motivated and cared more about their teaching than normal schools.

> There was specialist direct one-on-one attention. I felt the administration was very supportive and involved, and that the other teachers genuinely wanted interns there and were willing to help us.

An environment where *all* teachers are working with the interns—encouraging interdependence.

Another theme in the category of benefits of PDS work was "the school/ university collaboration." The following observations by PDS graduates are a representative sample:

The [university] professors and school staff were very supportive.

I felt like the school and [the university] worked closely to provide for all of the needs of the interns. I also felt like the relationship . . . allowed for better communication between the school faculty and [the university].

The interns received more and better feedback. The teachers could also communicate more effectively with supervisors and interns.

The collaborative environment was wonderful.

The third theme identified within this category of benefits was the "access to university faculty." Examples of illustrative comments include:

Having the university liaison on the campus of the school. Mentors were always at hand.

Seeing the liaison on a regular basis.

Easy access to university faculty.

I saw the conferencing sessions with our supervising instructor as the most beneficial part of the learning because of the reflection.

It was very beneficial to have the [university] professors at the school. They were available to discuss the experience and provided me with much needed support.

Disadvantages of the experience.   Two themes emerged, although we will later discuss how the second theme should be viewed as complimentary. The first theme involves "geographical inconvenience" and speaks to the fact that pre-service teachers placed at a PDS site often had to travel farther from the university campus. Sample responses include:

Distance to travel [to the PDS site].

Having to travel so far, driving between school and [the university] for other classes.

I was *so* far [50 miles] from my home.

The second theme relates to "the quality of the PDS experience compared to subsequent teaching placements." Graduates felt they had been spoiled at the PDS site. Sample reflections include:

> Not every school is as good—you get spoiled.

> I was used to the aid of other teachers.

> Not like the real world of teaching!

> Not all schools are run so smoothly and have available all that was at our fingertips.

> Other schools poorly compared to the PDS (i.e., technology, teachers, administration support, attitude of students).

> It created high expectations of what a school environment should be like when the reality is very different. Resources such as materials, additional help when trying new lessons, etc., are limited elsewhere—too protected [at the PDS].

> I perceived that mentors were *always* at hand—realistically, this is not true. In the real world it is hard to find someone for advice, or to talk out a situation.

> My expectations were set too high (not really a *bad* thing), and I have found myself displeased with the administrators that I have worked with (at other schools).

The distinctiveness of the PDS Culture. We also asked PDS graduates to share in what ways the PDS culture had influenced their professional development. *Every* response was positive; if there were negative perceptions among the 36 mid-career teachers from our two longest serving PDS sites, *none* of the graduates chose to express them. Many responses reiterated the notions of the positive nature of the experience and the professionalism of the faculty and staff, and the sensitivity to student diversity at the PDS sites:

> I think being at a school with so many interns in such close contact with [the university] gave the teachers at the school a more mentoring feeling. Everyone was very helpful when it came to brainstorming solutions to any classroom problems. They were also very open to being observed.

> The PDS culture helped my development because I had such a POSITIVE experience with all of the staff, administrators, and even the district. The PDS really cares about turning out *good* teachers.

> The support and experience of the other teachers. It was like a hotbed of progressive teaching ideas and experiences constantly being exchanged.

> The climate was designed to make intern teachers feel welcome and supported. In many respects, the PDS helped me become a better teacher than I could otherwise have become. All the teachers at my PDS were great role models!

The culture fueled my passion toward teaching. The positive atmosphere made children eager to learn and teachers eager to teach.

Wow! What a culture shock. The childrens' backgrounds were so different from mine. Children working in the field before school, a child whose arm was torn off, the language difference.

The culture of the student body was highly Hispanic LEP [limited English proficiency] children. This helped me learn LEP strategies that I use at my school with LEP kids.

Finally, we asked the PDS graduates what leadership roles had they assumed in the profession. The responses indicated that of the 36 PDS graduates from these two PDS sites, 17 (47 percent) had become department heads or team leaders in their schools, while other leadership roles included being district teacher trainers, school committee members and chairs, PTA Presidents, union representatives, district text book adoption committee members, and officers in state teaching organizations.

DISCUSSION

With a response rate of 24.7 percent (86 out of 348) we cannot claim that these graduates represent all our PDS graduates over an eleven-year period. However, we do believe that these 86 responses from PDS graduates give substantial insight into the work of PDS partnership, given that large sample data is rare in the body of PDS literature. The data is consistently positive, and frequently reflects the successful adoption of professional values articulated in the PDS mission.

As a fundamental indicator of the effectiveness of pre-service preparation, our retention data, indicating that 80 percent of the PDS graduate respondents are still working in K–12 education, is outstanding, given that 40 percent of all new teachers will leave in the first four years in the profession, with up to 66 percent of teachers seeking certification through alternative pathways leaving in the first three years (Berry, 2003; Graziano, 2005). Within the local context, the surrounding school district reports that the loss of teachers in the *first* year ranges from 10 to 21 percent (Ave, 2002). Given this background and the fact that almost three-quarters of our respondents foresee remaining educators well into the future, the authors assert PDS preparation was a significant influence on their professional induction.

We suggest that part of the reason they have remained as educators speaks to the quality of their preparation. The exceptional retention numbers are echoed by the 98 percent of respondents who felt well prepared. Not surprisingly, the majority of PDS graduates consider their job satisfaction to be "above average" or "excellent" while three quarters have committed to extend their education beyond the baccalaureate level. While we fully accept that multiple variables influence a teaching career, their PDS preparation is a constant across this population. This assertion is borne out by the 90 percent of respondents who would in retrospect recommend a PDS internship to pre-service teachers today.

Among the 36 graduates from our two longest serving PDSs, eleven (30 percent) received professional recognition and awards. We are pleased that so many PDS graduates perceive themselves as taking leadership roles in their schools and that 95 percent of the respondents (all of whom had PDS experience with at-risk populations) considered their child advocacy skills as "average" or higher. Indeed, 70 percent reported "above average" or "excellent" child advocacy behavior. Again, while the authors treated this data cautiously, we contend that, given a pre-service experience at PDS sites that reflect a great range of ethnic, socioeconomic, and linguistic cultures, our graduates hold a professional sensitivity for the needs of children.

The authors are also wary of the "victory dance" trap, but the 86 respondents uniformly value the PDS preparation they received. Now experienced teachers in their own right, they looked back and identified numerous benefits of the PDS internship and how that experience shaped their professionalism today. In contrast, when asked to consider the disadvantages of PDS work they focused on the inconvenience of travel, and, tellingly, they also declared a sense of being spoiled in their PDS placement. It seems they remember PDSs where teachers support each other, resources are organized, administration runs smoothly, and mentors were available. Unfortunately for some graduates, upon entering the profession these experiences were not mirrored in their school setting. The experience of our graduates seems to suggest the PDSs demonstrate what can be, not necessarily what is. If the reader accepts the positive survey data from these 86 PDS graduates, then simultaneously the data raises general questions about the culture of professionalism in the K–12 schools, the quality of teacher preparation in the university, and supports the notion of school-university partnerships as central to teacher education as the rule—rather than as the exception.

SUMMARY

We have concluded through this study of 86 PDS graduates that PDS internship placements can positively affect the continuing professional development of pre-service teachers after they graduate and enter into teaching themselves. Our results confirm that PDS graduates who responded to the survey are retained in the profession at much higher numbers than the national average. The narrative responses, together with the quantitative data, illustrate that among these 86 respondents the reflective and continuous learning emphasized in our PDS sites translated into our graduates seeking additional professional development and leadership roles.

Further research is needed to compare this data set to norms among our "traditional" graduates to see if the PDS data are representative of the larger student body or are distinctive. As future partnership decisions are made, it remains to be seen how the PDS model and wider school-university partnerships in general will evolve, but we can assert that, within the context of teacher preparation at this large university, the PDS model is a viable partnership model and that this data should be helpful in strategic planning for the continuing development of school-university partnerships.

REFERENCES

Ave, M. (2002, July 28). County prepares to debut 9 new schools. *St. Petersburg Times*, p. B1.

Berry, B. (2003). *The need for large scale data research*. Paper presented at the annual conference of the Holmes Partnership, Washington DC.

Boyle-Baise, L., & McIntyre, J. (2006, April). *What kind of experience? Preparing teachers in a PDS or community settings*. Paper presented at the annual meeting of the American Educational Research Association, San Francisco.

Breault, J. (2006). *Power and position: Discourse and rhetoric in PDS literature*. Paper presented at the annual meeting of the American educational Research Association, San Francisco.

Byrd, D., & McIntyre, D. (1999). *Research on professional development schools: Association of Teacher Educators Yearbook VII* (Eds.). Thousand Oaks, CA: Corwin.

Daniel, P., Rosselli, H., & Brindley, R. (2001, February). *Issues of sustainability in professional development schools: Examining transitions in leadership*. Paper presented at the annual meeting of the American Association of Colleges for Teacher Education, Dallas.

Daniel, P., Brindley, R., & Rosselli, H. (2000). The goodness of fit between voices in the field and the NCATE PDS draft standards. *Teaching & Change, 7*(4), 372–391.

Fuller, F., & Bown, O. (1975). Becoming a teacher. In K. Ryan (Ed.), *Teacher education: 74th yearbook of the National Society for the Study of Education, part II* (pp. 25–52). Chicago: University of Chicago Press.

Graziano, C. (2005). Schools out. *Edutopia, 1*(3), 38–44.

Hycner, R. (1985). Some guidelines for the phenomenological analysis of interview data. *Human Studies, 8*, 279–303.

National Council for the Accreditation of Teacher Education. (2001). *Standards for Professional Development Schools*. Washington, DC: Author.

Neapolitan, J., & Berkeley, T. (2006). *Where do we go from here? Issues in the sustainability of professional development school partnerships*. New York: Peter Lang.

Root, E., Grasmick, N., Smeallie, J., Pilato, V., & Ehrlich, R. (2004). *Professional development schools in Maryland*. Baltimore: Maryland State Department of Education.

Siers, S., Madden, M., Wittman, C., Dunkle, M., & Hopkins, L. (March, 2006). *Can seagulls soar with swallows? A model for a multiple-partner regional professional devel-*

opment school council. Paper presented at the annual meeting of the National
Association for Professional Development Schools, Orlando.

Teitel, L. (2000). *Assessment: Assessing the impacts of professional development schools.*
Washington, DC: American Association of Colleges for Teacher Education.

Teitel, L. (2001). An assessment framework for professional development schools:
Going beyond the leap of faith. *Journal of Teacher Education, 52*(1), 57–69.

Watson. S., Miller, T., Johnston, L., & Rutledge, V. (2006). Professional development
school graduate performance: Perceptions of school principals. *The Teacher
Educator, 42*(2), 77–86.

Zeichner, K. (2004, March). *Professional development schools in a culture of change.* Key-
note address at the annual meeting of the National Association for Professional Development Schools, Orlando.

APPENDIX

Survey of Alumni Who Completed Field Experience(s) at a Professional Development School (PDS)

Directions: Please indicate your answers by filling in the corresponding
bubbles.

Demographics:

Graduation year		Degree program associated with internship	Ethnicity (optional)
1 1990	7 1996	1 Bachelor's	1 Caucasian
2 1991	8 1997	2 Master's	2 African-American
3 1992	9 1998		3 Hispanic
4 1993	10 1999		4 Asian
5 1994	11 2000		5 Native American
6 1995			6 Other

Current educational status	Sex
1 Bachelor's Degree	1 Female
2 Bachelor's plus 15	2 Male
3 Pursuing Master's Degree	
4 Master's Degree Completed—Program Area: _____	
5 Beyond Master's Degree—Program Area: _____	
6 Second Certification/Endorsement—Subject Area: _____	

PDS Placement History:
Early Field Experience(s):

PDS site	**Grade Level(s) Taught**	
1 ***** Elementary	1 Pre-K	6 Grade 4
2 ***** Elementary	2 Kindergarten	7 Grade 5
3 ***** Elementary	3 Grade 1	8 Grade 6
4 ***** Middle	4 Grade 2	9 Grade 7
5 A Non-PDS School	5 Grade 3	10 Grade 8

Number of semesters at a PDS during early field experience(s)	**Time Spent Per Week * Check all that apply**
1 Not at a PDS	1 Not at a PDS
2 1 semester	2 Less than 1 day per week
3 2 semesters	3 1 day per week
4 3 semesters	4 2 days per week
	5 More than 2 days per week

Final Field Experience/Internship:

PDS site	**Grade Level(s) Taught**	
1 Centennial Elementary	1 Pre-K	6 Grade 4
2 Cypress Creek Elementary	2 Kindergarten	7 Grade 5
3 Pizzo Elementary	3 Grade 1	8 Grade 6
4 Weightman Middle	4 Grade 2	9 Grade 7
5 A Non-PDS School	5 Grade 3	10 Grade 8

Specialization(s) During Field Experiences(s):
* Check all that apply

1 Early Childhood	8 Instructional Technology	14 Behavior Disorders
2 Elementary	9 Math	15 Gifted Education
3 Art	10 Music	16 Mental Retardation
4 Business	11 Physical Education	17 SLD
5 English	12 Science	18 Varying Exceptionalities
6 Foreign Language	13 Social Studies	19 Counselor Education
7 Industrial Arts		20 School Psychology

Recommending [this university]:

*Would you recommend ***** to others considering teaching?*

1 definitely no   3 probably yes
2 probably no   4 definitely yes

Would you recommend internship placement at a PDS to future interns?

1 definitely no   3 probably yes
2 probably no   4 definitely yes

Current Career Status:

1 Classroom Teacher
2 School Administrator
3 Support Services
4 Other field in education
5 Career outside education*

* If after graduation you did not pursue a teaching career, please go to question #26.

Current Educators:

Directions: Using the following 5-point scale, rate your current teaching performance in each area listed below. Bubble the response that best describes your evaluation.

1 = Poor (P); 2 = Below Average (BA); 3 = Average (A);
4 = Above Average (AA); 5 = Excellent (E)

	P	BA	A	AA	E
1. Adaptation of instructional strategies to meet individual students' learning styles and abilities, including those with special needs.	1	2	3	4	5
2. Ability to work effectively with other teachers and staff in the school.	1	2	3	4	5
3. Ability to work collaboratively with parents and families to meet student needs.	1	2	3	4	5
4. Engagement in self-improvement and professional development activities.	1	2	3	4	5
5. Participation in school improvement initiatives/activities.	1	2	3	4	5
6. Mentorship of other teachers.	1	2	3	4	5
7. Providing leadership in my school/district.	1	2	3	4	5

	P	BA	A	AA	E
8. Engagement in inquiry or action research.	1	2	3	4	5
9. Collaboration with a local college of education.	1	2	3	4	5
10. Advocating for students rights and needs.	1	2	3	4	5

To what extent did you see your PDS:

	P	BA	A	AA	E
11. Improving teacher preparation?	1	2	3	4	5
12. Supporting teachers' professional development needs?	1	2	3	4	5
13. Helping improve education?	1	2	3	4	5
14. Supporting research that helps schools become even better?	1	2	3	4	5
15. My present job satisfaction is:	1	2	3	4	5

Directions: Please choose the response that best describes your opinions.

16. Compared to other teachers in your current school, how well prepared do you think you are?

      1 inadequately prepared   3 generally well prepared
      2 minimally prepared   4 very well prepared

17. What are your long-range career plans?
    1 continue teaching
    2 move into another career within education
    3 leave education temporarily with the intent to return later
    4 move to a career outside of education
    5 not sure yet

Directions: Please provide responses to the following questions. If you are unable to respond, please mark N/A.

18. Please describe your transition from student teacher to teacher. To what extent was your PDS field experience(s) helpful to that transition?

19. Are there any skills or strategies in your teaching repertoire that you credit to your experience at a PDS?

20. Have you completed Clinical Education Training qualifying you to supervise interns? If not, do you intend to?

21. Have you supervised an intern? If so, how many? In what ways did your own experiences at a PDS influence your supervision of interns?

22. Please list and describe any awards or special recognition you've received as an educator.

23. Please list any presentations you have done or publications you have authored or co-authored.

24. Please list and describe any grants or grant writing in which you have been involved.

25. Have you applied for National Board Certification? If not, do you intend to?

All Survey Participants:

Directions: Please provide responses to the following questions.

26. Please describe your current career status, whether in education or another field?

27. Where do you see yourself in 5 years?

28. What do you perceive were the *benefits* of being at a Professional Development School?

29. What do you perceive were the *disadvantages* of being at a Professional Development School?

30. In what ways did the PDS *culture* help or hinder your professional development?

31. What leadership roles have you assumed in your career? To what extent did your experience(s) at a PDS help you develop your leadership skills?

32. At any point in your career have you worked at a PDS? If not, would you choose to work at a PDS if you could? Why or why not?

33. Other comments:

Thank you for completing this survey. *If you would like to be considered for participation in an interview or round-table discussion pertaining to this research,* please provide your name, telephone number, and email address below.

CHAPTER 23

EXAMINING THE QUALITY OF INQUIRY IN THE RESEARCH ON PROFESSIONAL DEVELOPMENT SCHOOLS

Editors' Analysis

Irma N. Guadarrama, John M. Ramsey, and Janice L. Nath

ABSTRACT

This chapter examines the research studies on PDSs by both practitioners and researchers and specifically analyzes the quality of inquiry and its potential impact on teacher education. The selected research studies were published in two previous volumes of PDS research in 2000 and 2005 (Guadarrama, Ramsey, & Nath, 2000, 2005). The authors, also the editors of the current volume, conclude that the results of their investigation affirm the vision of Goodlad and others that universities and schools working together to educate teachers and improve school performance are poised to impact educational reform in profoundly positive ways.

University and School Connections, pages 411–424
Copyright © 2008 by Information Age Publishing

INTRODUCTION

The call for systemic reform in our nation's schools has also embraced the need for change in teacher education. The persistent demands for a new paradigm took on a distinctive perspective two decades ago with John Goodlad's influential work on university and school partnerships (1984, 1988, 1990, 1996) along with the Holmes Group (1986) declarations that, in hindsight, recognized and sought after professional development schools (PDSs) as a cornerstone in the educational change landscape. While it may be premature to make a complete analysis on the historical significance of PDSs and deliberate on the full extent to which PDSs have impacted teacher education and school reform, it is quite appropriate to illuminate and examine the advances made by practitioners and researchers on their successes with PDSs. The substantial amount of studies on PDSs that have yielded data that inform practitioners and researchers can be analyzed to determine the quality of the inquiry and its potential for substantive change in teacher education and beyond. This chapter offers readers an analysis of the quality of inquiry in the research and its potential impact on teacher education based on selected articles published in two volumes of PDS research in 2000 and 2005 (Guadarrama, Ramsey, & Nath, 2000, 2005). The results of our investigation affirm the vision of Goodlad and others that universities and schools working together to educate teachers and improve school performance (simultaneous renewal) are poised to impact educational reform in profoundly positive ways.

THE COLLECTION OF PAPERS: OUR PERSONAL JOURNEY

The two volumes of research papers on professional development schools were published in 2000 and 2005. As members of the editorial team, we each had accrued substantial experience with professional development schools as faculty members and/or administrators. Additionally, our involvement in the PDSs Special Interest Group of the American Education Research Association provided us with the opportunity to engage in a book series project that resulted in the publication of the two volumes with a total of 36 articles and a third volume in progress. Through the process of working with the collection of papers on a myriad of related topics on PDSs, we developed a framework that served to organize and synthesize the information and, thus, acquire a perspective from which to re-analyze the data.

COMPONENTS OF THE ANALYSIS PROCESS

Each of the 12 papers selected for this analysis was organized into five components: (1) defining statements of PDS and the main sources cited; (2) research methodology, including a description of their subjects; (3) the purpose of their research in the form of research questions; (4) data collected; and (5) findings. In this chapter we discuss statements 1, 3, and 5, although we include all of the data in table form. The following sections discuss the components in the following order: (1) how the researchers define or describe their PDSs, (2) the research questions and the findings of each study, and (3) the results of our analysis.

Evolving Constructs that Define PDSs

During the first readings of the collection of research papers, we were struck by the diverse contexts depicted in the PDSs studies. Our initial preoccupation with an operational definition of PDSs was not an important issue with the researchers, as we had anticipated. Basically, the research projects focused on the quality of the working relationship between the school and the university and the research gains from inquiry established within the project. Thus, it became immediately apparent to us that the PDSs tended to have strong contextual ties to the specific goals and activities of the school and/or university. Indeed, the uniqueness of each PDS setting relied on the way the program parameters were tied together to accomplish their specific goals and objectives.

Another important observation made during our initial analysis was the extent to which the PDSs were described in terms of their vital roles in their efforts to conduct systemic reform in teacher education. Whether this was part of the PDSs' initial agenda or whether it was a result of their research or inquiry was not immediately evident, unless it was clearly stated by the researchers (which was rarely the case). Regardless of the researchers' intentions, the majority of the PDS researchers made references to effective practices in teacher education and, in many cases, couched their findings within the context of school and teacher education reform.

Even though the findings were specific to each PDS case, there are several common themes related to the goals and mission of PDSs that resonate throughout the studies.

In the following tables, the first column contains the titles of the articles in Volume 1 (Table 23.1) and Volume 2 (Table 23.2); the second column contains one or two statements: (1) statement #1, or no number, contains direct

TABLE 23.1 Descriptions of PDSs from Volume 1

Study—Volume 1	PDS Description—Excerpts
A. *Village of Learners: Collaborative Research at a Professional Development School*—D.V. Craig (pp. 67–86)	1. The concept of the PDS is intended to *connect theory and practice* in education so that they reciprocally inform each other. Working collaboratively with an educational community, the PDS operates as a school that values and seeks to use the full range of knowledge and skills of classroom teachers, school administrators, future teachers, and professors to determine the goals and pathways of success for the school, the teacher preparation curricula, and the teaching and learning process. 2. One of the most intriguing and revealing means of gleaning information that assists in informing practice in the educational community is through *reflective dialogue.*
B. *Building an Inquiry Oriented PDS: The Journey Toward Making Inquiry a Central Part of Mentor Teachers' Work*—N. F. Dana, & D. Y. Silva (pp. 87–104)	1. *Research or inquiry* should be an essential and ongoing force within the PDS, as university faculty and school practitioners work together to examine shared concerns. 2. Inquiry might focus on issues of teacher education, professional growth, curriculum, and the improvement of pedagogy. . . . Hence, *teacher inquiry* becomes a crucial component of life in a professional development school that is largely missing from the PDS literature.
C. *Paradigm Pioneers: A Professional Development School Collaborative for Special Education Teacher Education Candidates*—B.C. Glaeser, B.D. Karge, J.Smith, & C. Weatherill (pp. 125–152)	1. The goal of the PDS is to draw *closer connections* between school and teacher training institutions so that responsibility for teacher candidate education is *shared.* In this way, teacher education candidates participate in direct, organized experiences with children rather than non-interactive observations. 2. Teacher education candidates bring recent *research-based* ideas and practices from their university courses to the PDS. Veteran teachers at the school sites provide the opportunities for the candidates to *apply* these practices and learn the profession through *first hand experience.*
D. *How an Integrated Unit Increased Student Achievement in a High School PDS*—John Fischetti & Ann Larson (pp. 227–258)	1. Goals of the PDS: improving the lives, learning, and opportunities of all students; enhancing the curriculum structures, school culture and community ties for the high school and the University of Louisville staff and faculty; preparing new educators in a *professional, collegial environments* within the context of experiences that they will likely face in their early years; 2. . . . *researching, assessing, reflecting upon and/or disseminating* the results of our work.
E. *Principals as a Learning Community*—W. Malloy (pp. 259–284)	University–school partnerships should be viewed as *evolving social experiments* where the participants, with their own philosophy and practices, struggle to develop alternative ideas, organizational arrangements, and collaborative activities.

Study—Volume 1	PDS Description—Excerpts
F. *Collaborating for Urban School and Teacher Education Renewal: Perspectives on the Development of a School-University Partnership*— Zhixin Su (pp. 331–376)	. . . the biggest change is that the school teachers and administrators are now, through inquiry, social justice meetings, and community involvement, consciously and deliberately questioning and challenging their existing practices and exploring changes to create a more *socially just education for all children.* As a result, they have become more reflective of their own practices, more aware of diversity issues, and more analytical of schooling and the larger context for education.
G. *The Facilitators of and Barriers to the Collaboration Process in Professional Development Schools: Results of a Meta-ethnography*— E. K. Hess & H. Afman (pp. 377–406)	1. The *collaboration process* [between schools and universities] is one of the most important elements in the formation and maintenance of a PDS. It is the cornerstone of the development of the spirit of PDS work and often emerges as a key theme and challenge that must be addressed. 2. PDSs are fast becoming a significant trend in teacher *education reform.*
H. *The Status of Early Theories of Professional Development School Potential*— C. Mantle-Bromley (pp. 3–30)	1. The greatest potential of the Professional Development School appears to lie in the willingness of its experienced participants, both school and university-based, to use their different perspectives and skills to improve their *collective work.* 2. While teachers and teacher educators enthusiastically help novice teachers improve their teaching and expand how they view their work, they are decidedly uncomfortable doing the same *for each other.*

excerpts that allude to the researchers' concepts or visions of the PDSs' functions, forms, dynamics, praxis, etc.; (2) statement #2 contains information on the researchers' perception(s) of effective practices or strategies in relation to teacher education reform. The highlighted words in bold are deliberately emphasized for their meaning or for clarification purposes.

The data in these tables illustrate the consistency to which the researchers are in concordance with one another. Indeed, they have similar understandings of the value of: (1) genuine, deeply integrated collaboration; (2) the challenge of raising the bar by creating professional, collegial environments whereby the players fully exercise their expertise; and (3) through inquiry-oriented structures, have the opportunity to learn from their experiences and from each other. The lens by which they examine their PDSs are contextually unique; however, their individual voices reiterate similar views on how cutting edge is the PDS design, and, while the challenge can be overwhelming, the view from every angle points to the feasibility of institutionalizing PDSs. With the concerted efforts of the key players, PDSs are poised to create

TABLE 23.2 Descriptions of PDSs from Volume 2

Study—Volume 2	PDS Descriptions—Excerpts
I. *Examining How School-Based Partners Bring PDS to Life: NCATE Standards in Their Own Words*—H. Thornton (pp. 3–28)	1. Mutual agreement among school, school district, union/professional association, and university of the basic mission of a PDS: "the preparation of new teachers, support of children's learning, continuing professional development, and *practice-based inquiry* within a school setting." 2. Moving from a traditional, cooperative, relationship between universities and school partners to one that is more truly *collaborative, jointly owned, and institutionalized* is a *challenge.*
J. *Conditions of Inquiry Within PDS Relationships*—D.A. Breault	1. The study seeks to address ways in which universities can establish effective PDS relationships that are dynamic, productive, sustainable, and *inquiry or reflective thinking* is the driving force of their relationships. 2. *Inquiry* is the defining element within successful PDSs.
K. *Are New Teachers Prepared in a PDS-Based Certification Program Really Better?*—D. S. Ridley, M.R. Hackett, K. Landeira, & P. Tate (pp. 47–63)	Ultimately, the key outcome goals for the *full-service PDS* (increased student achievement through teaching that is exemplary and data-driven and the preparation of effective new teachers) are *interdependent.*
L. *Creating a Quantitative Snapshot of a Learning Community Using Dynamics*—C. Balach & G. J. Szymanski (pp. 65–83)	Since PDSs represent systemic reform, the idea of a *learning community* in PDSs is fundamental to reform.

a viable means by which to vastly improve education for K–12 schools as well as for teacher education programs in four-year colleges or universities.

In the following section, we analyze another aspect of the research studies by posing questions on the quality of the research inquiry and the preponderance of evidence. Then, we develop indicators that we use to examine the extent to which PDSs actually impacted change in the K–12 schools and teacher education programs or, at least, had these goals as intended outcomes. We also use these indicators to describe how they achieved their goals and/or objectives.

THE RESEARCH QUESTIONS AND FINDINGS

We isolated each study's research questions and the findings in Table 23.3 (Volume 1) and Table 23.4 (Volume 2) for the purpose of analyzing each,

TABLE 23.3 Research Questions and Findings—Volume 1

Title of Study (w/author)	Research Questions	Findings
A. *Village of Learners: Collaborative Research at a Professional Development School*—D.V. Craig	What can teachers and pre-service students learn via *personal interactions with high school students?* Can reflective dialog between pre-service and HS students aid in teacher development? Can HS student involvement aid in their empowerment as learners within a community?	As a result of the study, positive changes were made in the following areas; *staff development*—Socratic Seminars added; *Instruction*—collected suggestions for improvement; *alternative assessment* forms were added; uses of *technology* expanded; field placements improved.
B. *Building an Inquiry Oriented PDS: The Journey Toward Making Inquiry a Central Part of Mentor Teachers' Work*—N.F. Dana, & D.Y. Silva	How do *teachers* develop as *inquirers?* What do teachers inquire about? How do teachers feel about inquiry? In what ways can professional development schools facilitate the development of an *inquiry-oriented culture?*	Fourteen inquiry projects completed, at first through the inquiry-support mode. The summaries of inquiries indicate that as a result of the commitment to inquiry, *new pedagogies* were tried and examined and existing pedagogies were refined, improved, and enhanced. Needs identified to *further improve and support inquiry* process.
C. *Paradigm Pioneers: A Professional Development School Collaborative for Special Education Teacher Education Candidates*—B.C. Glaeser, B.D. Karge, J.Smith, & C. Weatherill	How can PDS address the needs as created by the Individuals with Disabilities Education Act of 1997: to *set goals and meet standards* for children with disabilities; to *collaborate* with all players to ensure disabled children have equitable and equal access to the curriculum; to *provide professional development* for teachers & administrators about special needs of children.	Collaboration between university and schools provided a "*heightened sense of community development* among administrators, college faculty, teacher education candidates, teachers, and staff. The greatest challenge…is to *show over time* that these relationships have led to what Fullan refers to as 'second-order changes' in which the *schools are altered in fundamental ways* rather than merely temporary innovations…."
D. *How an Integrated Unit Increased Student Achievement in a High School PDS*—John Fischetti & Ann Larson	What is the impact of *integrated curriculum and teaming* on teacher growth? How do teachers and students perceive their work? How do teachers best serve *students* in achieving at *high levels*—performance tasks?	In spite of external demands on every aspect of the curriculum, the "PDS [university and school] relationship has been able to create *unique opportunities to support teaming and teacher invention.*"

(continued)

TABLE 23.3 Research Questions and Findings—Volume 1 (continued)

Title of Study (w/author)	Research Questions	Findings
E. *Principals as a Learning Community*—W. Malloy	To what extent is the *learning organization* or the community concept useful to an entire group of principals in a rural school district undergoing system wide reform?	"If there is to be real systemic change, principals must be given opportunities to *learn and grow together* while addressing these changes. . . . principals can no longer be seen as visionaries but must develop the capacity to *facilitate sharing of ideas* on which to negotiate the reality of *shaping and reshaping the purpose of the organization.* . . . The partnership provided university participants ample opportunities *to enrich graduate student pre-internship experiences* and expand the knowledge base and *research agenda of the professor* involved."
F. *Collaborating for Urban School and Teacher Education Renewal: Perspectives on the Development of a School-University Partnership*—Zhixin Su	What are the *perspectives* of participants in the collaboration-in-progress between a university and school district? What *conclusions* can be drawn from the data on the *re-structuring of the pre-service and beginning teacher education* program at the university?	"Both the school and the university people *want the partnership* to move *beyond its present structural* relationship into the more substantive reform issues on curriculum, on the culture of the school and the university, and on creating a 'third space' whereby the school and university people can work together in a *true and equal partnership.* A center of pedagogy very much like the one proposed by Goodlad (1994) *has been envisioned* out of which *schools will become exemplary sites* for school reform and teacher education. . . ."
G. *The Facilitators of and Barriers to the Collaboration Process in Professional Development Schools: Results of a Meta-ethnography*—E. K. Hess & H. Afman	What are the *facilitators and barriers* to the collaboration process in PDSs?	*Facilitators are identified* as obtaining external resources, administrative support, establishing a vision about the goals of the PDS, and connecting PDSs with increased professional development. *Barriers are* time, lack of rewards, the change process, district mandates, and space issues. *Few recommendations* were advanced for both *beginning* and *sustaining* a PDS.
H. *The Status of Early Theories of Professional Development School Potential*—C. Mantle-Bromley (pp. 3–30)	What are the early program [PDS] theories advocating PDS implementation? To what degree are the early theories of *PDS potential being realized?* What are the *conditions* that led to or inhibited such realization?	Theory 1 of 4 was supported (i.e., *improvement of teacher preparation*). Theory 2—*professionalization of teaching*—no major changes observed; theory 3 and 4—clearly lack of progress observed; however, when the *hypothesized conditions are in place,* could lead to *renewal of schooling and of teacher education.*

TABLE 23.4 Research Questions and Findings—Volume 2

Title of Study (w/author)	Research Questions	Findings
I. *Examining How School-Based Partners Bring PDS to Life: NCATE Standards in Their Own Words*—H. Thornton	How was each of the PDS *functions* evidenced in each PDS site?	Teacher preparation questions generated primarily two themes: *redefined and newly emergent roles* within the PDS structure and differences from traditional structures; and *decision-making* grounded in *ownership and power*. Another emerging theme was the importance of *dialogue and communication*. Inquiry was defined by *relationships* that were *fundamental to developing trust and commitment*. "Creating genuine partnerships requires *reconsideration of roles* that individuals play and their *functions*." (p. 8)
J. *Conditions of Inquiry Within PDS Relationships*—D.A. Breault	To what extent does *inquiry* play a role in the *operational quality* of the PDSs examined?	Two of the three PDSs revealed STRONG evidence of inquiry; the third revealed a WEAK evidence. Thus, two of three PDSs met all 5 *conditions of inquiry*; the third faltered in #2—in that the pre-service teachers' experiences were one-dimensional, more limited and standardized, thus, non-transformative; in #1—it lacked evidence of transformative communication due to over reliance on standards, policies, and procedures; and #5—no efforts were evident to suggest that the partnership extended beyond its operational goals.
K. *Are New Teachers Prepared in a PDS-Based Certification Program Really Better?*—D. S. Ridley, M.R. Hackett, K. Landeira, & P. Tate	What are the differences between teachers prepared in three programs—traditional, PDS, and Teach For America in regards to *teacher effectiveness* and *student outcomes* as measured by Stanford-9 reading and math scores?	Study 1—First-year, *PDS trained teachers did better than traditional program trained teachers in performance-based measures; among second-year teachers from both programs there was no significant difference*. Study 2—Students taught by first-year *PDS graduates scored higher in reading than their peers taught by TFA teachers; students taught by second year PDS trained teachers* scored *lower in math* compared to their peers taught by second year TFA teachers. Findings suggest that PDS and TFA teachers have different entry level strengths and pose another question: When pitting pedagogy with content area knowledge—"what would happen if PDS graduates had **both strong content knowledge and pedagogical skills?**" (p. 61)
L. *Creating a Quantitative Snapshot of a Learning Community Using Dynamics*—C. Balach & G. J. Szymanski	What are the **dynamics** of a *learning community* that address systemic change in PDSs? How do these PDSs' dynamics impact *student achievement*? (Note: student achievement was not treated in this first part of the study.)	Data from PDS site A reveal that it is the *closest* to an "*ideal*" learning community; Site C is the *most distant*; site B is in *between*. No analysis was provided and since student achievement data was not used in the study, the authors were not able to compare the learning community scales with student achievement.

TABLE 23.5   Research Models or Types of PDSs

Focus of Research	Description or Indicators
Type I Function/partnership/ structure	The study type examines certain areas selected from the *effective practice* categories that are perceived to be vital to the development/sustainability of a university–school partnership. One of the major or overreaching goals is to improve teacher education and K–12 schools.
Type II Partnership/function/ structure	The main focus of this study type is to bring university and school together; the quality of collaboration is vital to what they want to accomplish (e.g., improve the education of children with special needs or disabilities). The study is framed within an explicit understanding that the efforts will lead to substantial structural changes like those in school reform.
Type III Partnership/structure/ function	This study type relies on the improvement of the school/university collaborations so that school reform can take place. By targeting the efforts in both partnership and structural improvements, K–12 school and university staff will be able to successfully accomplish their goals and objectives.
Type IV Function/structure/ partnership	In this study type, the efforts are squarely placed on the accomplishment of an activity (e.g., getting principals to "learn and grow together") with the ultimate outcome of improving or affecting systemic change. Collaboration between school and university is a secondary objective and has no bearing on whether the goal of the study is successfully accomplished or not.

and then drawing comparisons between the research questions, findings, and the descriptions from the previous tables. We also drew comparisons across the 12 studies so that we could develop snapshot descriptions that could serve as referents. This resulted in the development of four research models, described in Table 23.5. Thus, the research models served as indicators that allowed us to frame the research studies as well as to organize, describe, and analyze them.

RESULTS

The descriptions of the studies in relation to the research models that we have identified (Table 23.5) are not significantly tied to an assessment scale that determines the rigor or accuracy of the investigation. Rather, our approach to examining the studies is one that recognizes the value of each according to its specific outcome and offers a paradigm perspective by which to analyze the collective contributions of the research.

The research models described in the following Table 23.5, represent the perspectives of the studies in question and serve to profile the kinds of research conducted by the researchers. Then, in the subsequent tables (23.6, 23.7, 23.8, and 23.9), the studies are organized according to their research model type described accordingly.

The research model type is based on the primary focus or key issues of the researchers. Type I researchers initiated their investigation by focusing on the effectiveness of a particular strategy or sets of strategies or practices (Table 23.6). Their primary inquiry dealt with a particular function

---

TABLE 23.6   Type I Research Models: Function, Partnership, Structure

Study	Description
B	*Function:* The study focused on how teachers can develop inquiry skills. *Partnership:* The inquiries indicated that new pedagogies were developed and existing ones were re-visited. *Structure:* The question of how PDSs can facilitate the development of an inquiry-oriented culture?
D	*Function:* The focus is on examining the impact of integrated curriculum and teaming on teachers and students. *Partnership:* As a result of the collaboration, unique opportunities to support teaming emerged. *Structure:* Implicit.
G	*Function:* The study examined the facilitators and the barriers of starting up and sustaining a PDS. *Partnership:* As a result of the collaboration, recommendations were developed to assist in the development and sustainability of PDSs. *Structure:* Implicit.
H	*Function:* The focus of this study was on the assessment of PDSs based on the initial theories on PDSs. *Partnership:* Four theories centered on collaboration, the improvement of teacher education and student performance formed the framework for determining the implementation success of the PDSs in question. *Structure:* The study assessed the extent to which the PDSs generated outcomes of the kinds in systemic change.
I	*Function:* The study assessed the quality of a PDS in relation to its functional roles. *Partnership:* As a result of the partnership the researcher identified areas of importance such as the need to redefine the roles of players, to re-consider decision-making process, and new or different ways to communicate and dialogue. *Structure:* The study assessed the various needs in the change process in establishing a sustainable goal in the school and university relationship.
J	*Function:* The study assessed how three PDSs implemented inquiry as a sustainable process. *Partnership:* The quality of the partnership was assessed on the same level as were the players in the pre-service teacher education program. *Structure:* Implicit.
K	*Function:* The study compared the training and performance of teachers who were trained in a PDS and those trained in Teach for American Program. *Partnership:* The collaboration was assessed along the same lines as were the teachers' performances. *Structure:* Implicit.

within the context of the university and school collaboration or PDS. If the researchers extended their goals or vision as part of a school reform effort, the description is noted. However, if it is implicitly instead of explicitly stated, the description is noted as such.

Type II researchers began their investigations by focusing on the collaboration component between the university and school (Table 23.7). Their inquiry relied on the outcome of the quality of collaboration to yield the desirable effects. Particular strategies, practices, or change are realized as a result of the collaboration process. As in the previous Type I, the goals of the research study may extend beyond a localized agenda to include long-term systemic reform that produce structural changes in the curriculum of both the K–12 setting and the university teacher education program.

Only one example in our collection of articles fell into the third category of research models. The Type III model researchers started with an inquiry into the collaboration process as in the previous Type II model, however, the research study was focused on the extent to which the collaboration would affect systemic change in their curriculum structure (Table 23.8). As a result of the investigation, the researcher identified certain practices or strategies that were directly connected with a specific model that represented systemic reform.

Finally, Type IV research models focused on a specific function that was identified as part of a systemic change agenda (Table 23.9). The research studies were similar to Type I models, except that Type IV studies were linked directly to the desired structural changes whereas Type I studies were linked with the goals and objectives in the university and school collaboration process. Whether the Type IV studies included implicit or explicit goals for improving their relationships between the university and school was noted accordingly in the "Structure" comment.

TABLE 23.7   Type II Research Models: Partnership/Function/Structure

Study   Description

A	*Partnership:* The pre-service students collaborated with the high school students and their teachers that resulted in improvements. *Function:* As a result of the collaboration improvements were made in staff development, instruction, assessment, and use of technology. *Structure:* Implicit
C	*Partnership:* Collaboration between school and university was the main focus. *Function:* As a result of bringing key players together from both sites, objectives to meet the needs of disabled children were met. *Structure:* An important goal is to sustain collaborative relationships and bring them to a higher level.

TABLE 23.8   Type III Research Models: Partnership/Structure/Function

Study	Description
F	*Partnership:* The collaboration between school and university was examined to determine the extent to which such a union affects the systemic change. *Structure:* The study determined that the key players accepted the need for change at the structural level. *Function:* As a result of the partnership and the examination, the study concluded with a list of goals and objectives that would operationalize their vision.

TABLE 23.9   Type IV Research Models: Function/Structure/Partnership

Study	Description
E	*Function:* The study examined learning organization as a concept to facilitate principals as change agents. *Structure:* The study was primarily based on how a learning community can lead to structural changes in the system. *Partnership:* The results of collaboration between university and school were perceived as a positive but secondary outcome.
L	*Function:* This study focuses on the dynamics of a learning community. *Structure:* The analysis was centered on certain characteristics of what the researchers deemed as comprising an ideal community and how these approximated systemic change. *Partnership:* Implicit.

CONCLUSION

Our work as editors of a book series on professional development schools research has rendered us an opportunity to address the contributions of researchers, specifically their efforts in advancing our understanding of the role of PDSs in educational reform. In examining the quality of inquiry in the research articles we selected for this purpose, we deliberately chose to avoid analyzing the studies from the perspective of an external evaluator. Rather, we determined that our best efforts should be concentrated on understanding the research from the researchers' points of view. After all, making a judgment about which research designs are superior and inferior is not in our best interest when the primacy in the agenda is to encourage research that informs and improves our efforts in PDSs. Indeed, the research models we developed from our analysis are insightful because each gives us a sense of what's going on in the field. But the information also serves to help nascent developers in their efforts to implement the best designs for their specific situation. However, we realize that the analytical approach we ascertained as informative and full of possibilities also represents an initial effort, the first steps in a long process of examining PDSs. It is our hope that the contributions toward the development and improvement of PDSs herein will add to the growing momentum in actualizing the vision of professional development schools.

REFERENCES

Goodlad, J. I. (1984). *A place called school.* New York: McGraw-Hill.

Goodlad, J. I. (1988). School-university partnerships for educational renewal: Rationale and concepts. In K. A. Sirotnik, & J. I. Goodlad (Eds.), *School-university partnerships in action: Concepts, cases, and concerns* (pp. 3–31). New York: Teachers College Press.

Goodlad, J. I. (1990). *Teachers for our nation's schools.* San Francisco: Jossey-Bass.

Goodlad, J. I. (1996, November). Sustaining and extending educational renewal. *Phi Delta Kappan* pp. 228–233.

Guadarrama, I. N., Ramsey, J. M., & Nath, J. L. (Eds.). (2000). *Forging alliances in community and thought: Research in professional development schools.* Greenwich, CT: Information Age Publishing.

Guadarrama, I. N., Ramsey, J. M., & Nath, J. L. (Eds.). (2005). *Professional development schools: Advances in community thought and research.* Greenwich, CT: Information Age Publishing.

Holmes Group. (1986). *Tomorrow's teachers: A report of the Holmes Group.* East Lansing, MI: Author.

CONTRIBUTING AUTHORS

Jerry Akins is a retired Superintendent of Schools for the Crest Ridge R-VII School District, Centerview, Missouri. Dr. Akins led the educational community and the elected officials in supporting an on-site Professional Development School program located in the Crest Ridge R-VII School District.

Jennifer E. Aldrich, Ed.D., Associate Professor of Early Childhood Education and Associate Chair of the Department of Curriculum and Instruction, University of Central Missouri, began the first early childhood PDS and continues as university faculty at the site. Her research interests include professional development schools, teacher education, and early childhood.

David Allsopp is Associate Professor of Special Education in the College of Education at the University of South Florida. His research and writing interests include effective practices for struggling learners in the areas of mathematics, social-emotional/behavioral development, strategy instruction for adolescents and adults, and the integration of technology in teacher preparation/professional development.

Sima Behshid is a teacher at University Preparation School at CSU-Channel Islands. She assists with research and the facilitation of professional development for teachers at UPS.

Robert E. Bleicher is an Associate Professor of Science Education at CSU-Channel Islands. Professor Bleicher specializes in classroom communication, science education, and professional development school research.

Anita Perna Bohn is an associate professor of social studies education and coordinator of the elementary education program in the Department of

University and School Connections, pages 425–433
Copyright © 2008 by Information Age Publishing
All rights of reproduction in any form reserved.

Curriculum and Instruction at Illinois State University. She has been extensively involved in teaching, leadership, and research in ISU's PDS partnerships for the past eight years.

Roger Brindley is Associate Professor in Childhood Education and Interim Department Chair at the University of South Florida. The Professional Development Schools movement represents a major focus of his work, and he is currently the Senior Editor for the NAPDS journal, *School–University Partnerships*.

Merilyn Buchanan is an Assistant Professor of Education at CSU Channel Islands. She has served as the University Liaison to UPS for five years. Professor Buchanan specializes in mathematics education and professional development school research.

Cindy Campbell, recently graduated from the University of South Florida, the Department of Secondary Education. She co-authored the PDS chapter in this volume with Brindley, Daniel, Rosselli, and Vizcain.

Sherri Carter is a 16-year veteran classroom teacher who has mentored over 100 pre-service teachers. She taught third grade and she served as PDS site coordinator. She currently teaches at Warrensburg Middle School in Warrensburg, Missouri. Sherri has a BS and MS in education from Missouri State University.

Karen Colucci, Ph.D., is an instructor with the Department of Special Education at the University of South Florida. She co-authored the PDS chapter in this volume with McHatton, Allsopp, Doone, DeMarie, and Cranstron-Gingras.

Ann Cranstron-Gingras, Ph.D. is Professor of Special Education and Director of the Center for Migrant Education. She directs federal and privately funded projects serving students from migrant farmworker families and conducts research and publishes in the areas of special education and migrant education. She teaches classes in special education and supervises doctoral student research.

Thomas P. Crumpler is an Associate Professor of Reading and Literacy at Illinois State University where he teaches graduate courses in education. His research has investigated how multiple literacies inform the education of teachers. Currently, he is examining how innovative pedagogies might enrich teachers' literacy instruction with young children.

Fern Dallas is an Assistant Professor of Education at Lenoir-Rhyne College. She is the coordinator of the Middle Grades and K–12 Literacy programs with research interests in staff development in elementary and middle school faculties and PDS partnerships.

Nancy Fichtman Dana is Professor of Education and Director of the Center for School Improvement at the University of Florida. She has authored three books with Diane Yendol-Hoppey, including *The Reflective Educator's Guide to Mentoring* as well as articles on teacher inquiry, teacher leadership, school–university collaborations, and professional development schools.

Patricia L. Daniel is Associate Professor in Secondary Education at the University of South Florida. She serves as the Director of the Tampa Bay Area Writing Project, teaches English education courses, and invests considerable time at schools mentoring teachers and students.

Darlene DeMarie teaches educational psychology/child development courses to early childhood/elementary/special education majors at the University of South Florida. She earned a Ph.D. in Developmental Psychology from the University of Florida in 1988 and researches childrens' study strategies. Her current research utilizes childrens' photography as a way to see schools through childrens' eyes. Currently, she is a Fulbright Scholar at the University of Limpopo in South Africa.

Marie Donnantuono is a National Board Certified Teacher with 20 years experience as an elementary school teacher. Teaching the course *Literacy and Learning* onsite enables Marie to observe readers and writers in their learning environment, promote best practices in language arts literacy instruction, and model effective teaching strategies.

Elizabeth Doone, Ph.D., is an instructor with the Department of Special Education at the University of South Florida. She co-authored the PDS chapter in this volume with McHatton, Allsopp, Colucci, DeMarie, and Cranstron-Gingras.

Wendi S. Dunlap, a teacher at South Middle School in Lancaster County Schools, South Carolina, holds a Master of Arts in Teaching Secondary Social Studies from Winthrop University. She has assisted with data analysis and benchmark construction in the evaluation of Winthrop's Professional Development Schools.

Charmon Evans is a teacher and the Special Projects Coordinator at University Preparation School at CSU-Channel Islands. She acts as a liaison between the school and the University and assists with research and the facilitation of professional development for teachers at UPS.

Dorothy Feola, Ph.D., is Professor and Associate Dean in the College of Education at William Paterson University of New Jersey. Research interests include literacy and teacher preparation with a particular focus on preparing teachers within professional development school settings.

JoAnne Ferrara is the chair of Curriculum and Instruction at Manhattanville College. She is a former elementary teacher and school administrator. Her research interests include professional development schools, pre-service teacher education, and new teacher induction.

Christina Flynn graduated from William Paterson University in 2003. She is currently a second grade teacher in Passaic, NJ. Christina also serves as a mentor for practicum and student teachers and co-teaches the course *Literacy and Learning* which has allowed her to work with candidates in the teacher education program at William Paterson University.

Martha M. Foote is Associate Professor and Head of the Curriculum and Instruction Department at Texas A&M University–Commerce where she has been a teacher educator for 11 years. Her areas of research include Reggio Emilia inspired approaches to education, student-centered approaches to teacher education, and family involvement and literacy.

Maxine B. Freund is a Professor of Special Education, Director of Special Projects and Associate Director of the Institute for Education Studies at the Graduate School of Education and Human Development at The George Washington University.

Marion Godine spent a number of years as a public school teacher before coming into higher education at the University of Houston–Downtown as a mathematics education specialist. She has recently returned to public education as an assistant principal in Detroit.

Fran Greb is an associate professor at Montclair State University's Department of Early Childhood Elementary Education and Literacy. Dr. Greb is a liaison to two MSU partner schools.

Carl Grigsby is Associate Professor of Secondary and Middle Level Education in the Department of Curriculum and Instruction at the University of Central Missouri. He currently is responsible for one of the Middle School Professional Develop School Programs at the University of Central Missouri.

Irma N. Guadarrama is Associate Professor in the Department of Curriculum and Instruction at the University of Houston. She is co-editor with Ramsey and Nath of the Professional Development Schools Research Book

Series. Besides PDS research, she also conducts research in pre-service bilingual education and service learning.

Lindsay A. Harris was a former research assistant with the Urban Initiative Professional Development School. Currently she works at PHILLIPS Program for Children and Families overseeing staff development and community outreach. Her research interests include pre-service and inservice teacher education, educational services for youth with emotional or behavioral disabilities, self-determination, and transition.

Tina L. Heafner, Ph.D., is an assistant professor at the University of North Carolina at Charlotte. She is the social studies methods instructor for undergraduate and graduate programs in the Department of Middle, Secondary, and K–12 Education and serves as a PDS liaison. Dr. Heafner's research focus is social studies education.

Alisa Hindin is Assistant Professor at Seton Hall University in South Orange, New Jersey. She co-authored the PDS chapter in this volume with Lourdes Z. Mitchel.

Suzanne Horn is Assistant Professor of Education with a dual focus of Secondary Education and Reading Education. She is the Director of Secondary Education at Spring Hill College and focuses her research efforts in schools of poverty.

Robert Kladifko, an assistant professor in the Department of Educational Leadership and Policy Studies at California State University, Northridge, has an extensive background in P–12 leadership at both school and district office levels. His research, teaching, and publishing interests focus on the principalship, school safety, and successful school site leadership.

Sharon L. Lamson, Ph.D. and Chair of the Department of Curriculum and Instruction, University of Central Missouri, has been involved in the university school partnerships since PDSs began at UCM. She served as the university faculty member at two PDS sites. She is now on the advisory board for the PDS collaboration.

Mary L. Lebron is an elementary school teacher with 14 years experience. She graduated from Fairleigh Dickinson University in 1984 with a BA in Psychology. She furthered her education at The University of Puerto Rico where she was certified as an English teacher and worked for seven years. She is currently an elementary school teacher in Passaic, NJ.

Lydia C. Mays is a doctoral fellow in the Department of Early Childhood Education at Georgia State University and a member of the Urban Graduate Research Collaborative.

Patricia Alvarez McHatton is Assistant Professor at the University of South Florida, teaching at both the undergraduate and graduate level. Much of her work is grounded in school university community partnerships and focuses on teacher preparation, cultural competency, school experiences of Hispanic families and learners, and service learning.

John D. McIntyre is a professor in the Department of Curriculum and Instruction at Southern Illinois University–Carbondale. He specializes in the area of teacher leadership and has published widely in the areas of teacher education, field and clinical experiences, and school university partnerships.

Lourdes Zaragoza Mitchel is a professor at Seton Hall University in South Orange, New Jersey. She co-authored the PDS chapter in this volume with Alisa Hindin.

Gilbert Naizer is Associate Professor in the Department of Curriculum and Instruction at Texas A&M University–Commerce. He teaches field-based courses and graduate courses in science education for elementary and middle level teachers. Areas of interest include integration of mathematics and science.

Janice Nath, Associate Professor in the Department of Urban Education and Associate Dean at the University of Houston–Downtown, has co-edited a number of books and articles on PDSs, including *Forging Alliances in Community and Thought: Research in Professional Development Schools* and *Professional Development Schools: Advances in Community Thought and Research.*

Linda Ngarupe is the Superintendent/Principal of University Charter Middle School at CSU-Channel Islands and the University Preparation School at CSU-Channel Islands. She has extensive experience in implementing a collaborative model of teachers' professional development.

Deanna M. Ortiz is a doctoral candidate in Special Education and graduate research assistant at The George Washington University. She is a graduate of GWU's Urban Initiative Professional Development School. Her research interests include urban education, systems change, and socio-cultural issues in the lives of people with disabilities.

John M. Ramsey is Associate Professor in the Department of Curriculum and Instruction at the University of Houston. He specializes in Science Education and is co-editor with Guadarrama and Nath of the Professional Development Schools book series.

Julie L. Rosenthal, Ph.D., is Assistant Professor in the College of Education at William Paterson University of New Jersey. She teaches and coordinates the College's initial certification elementary reading course, that is taught on-site in the partner schools. Her research focuses on best practices for preparing teachers to teach reading.

Hilda Rosselli serves as Dean of the College of Education at Western Oregon University, and her career has spanned early childhood, special education, middle school teaching, university teaching, administration, and professional development school partnerships. She earned her degrees at Florida Southern College and the University of South Florida.

Eileen Santiago is currently the principal of Thomas A. Edison Elementary School. Her professional expertise includes building community in schools and designing comprehensive and integrated programs that draw upon the resources of the community. She has been instrumental in transforming Edison into a national demonstration site for full-service schooling.

Christina Siry is an instructor at Manhattanville College and a doctoral student at the City University of New York Graduate Center. She has experience as an elementary school teacher as well as an informal educator. Her research interests include pre-service elementary teacher education for science and urban ecology education.

Crystal L. Small, a teacher at Jefferson Elementary School in York District 1, South Carolina, holds a Master of Education in Reading from Winthrop University. She has assisted with data analysis and benchmark construction in the evaluation of Winthrop's Professional Development Schools.

Belinda Smith, Ph.D., is a clinical faculty member at the University of Missouri and art education faculty member of Columbia College, in Columbia, Missouri, where she teaches and supervises pre-service elementary, early childhood, and art education students and interns in teacher training courses and programs. Her research has focused on pre-service students' use of sketchbooks in a campus Child Development Lab and work in the MU Professional Educational Renewal Programs.

Marie Smith, a veteran teacher for over thirty years, is a cooperating teacher and District Coordinator for the Montclair State University/ Knollwood partnership as well as the as the school-district's coordinator of placement of MSU practicum students.

Tara Snellings, a fifth-year elementary education teacher at Knollwood School, completed her undergraduate and graduate degrees at Montclair

State University. She is the site-based coordinator for the Montclair State University/Knollwood partnership and adjunct MSU professor.

Jennifer L. Snow-Gerono is Assistant Professor in Curriculum and Instruction at Boise State University. Her research focuses on school university partnerships and teacher inquiry. She teaches graduate courses in curriculum theory and teacher education and undergraduate courses in an elementary education program while working with interns and teachers in a new PDS partnership.

Melba Spooner is Associate Professor and Coordinator of Professional Development Schools at the University of North Carolina at Charlotte. She is also currently serving as Interim Chair of the Department of Middle, Secondary, and K–12 Education. Dr. Spooner's research interests spans the continuum of teachers' professional development and university school partnerships.

Juliana M. Taymans, Ph.D., is Professor in Special Education in the Department of Teacher Preparation and Special Education at the George Washington University in Washington, DC. She specializes in cognitive behavioral interventions and teacher development for work with at-risk students. Dr. Taymans currently directs three funded projects in special education teacher preparation.

Matt Thomas is Associate Professor of Reading in the Department of Curriculum and Instruction at the University of Central Missouri. He teaches courses on content area literacy using online delivery, hybrid formats, and traditional classroom modes. His research focuses on content area literacy, reading maturity, and technology integration.

Kate Tindle has been in education for 25 years. Fifteen years of teaching students in middle schools fostered her research interests in supporting students' literacy needs to access curriculum, preparing teachers to meet the needs of students from high-poverty backgrounds, and creating learning environments that value social justice.

Diane M. Truscott is Associate Professor in the Department of Early Childhood Education at Georgia State University.

Kathy Unrath is Assistant Professor of Art Education at the University of Missouri–Columbia. Her qualitative research interests center on reflective practice, National Board Certification, and pre-service art teacher training and induction. She is a fibers artist whose work is exhibited widely.

Jonatha W. Vare is Professor at Winthrop University and Director of the Center for Pedagogy in the Richard W. Riley College of Education. She holds a Ph. D. in Educational Psychology from the University of North Carolina at Chapel Hill and has researched aspects of school/university collaboration since 1990.

Dorian Vizcain received a Master's Degree in Education and a Ph.D. in Curriculum and Instruction with a Specialization in Educational Research and Evaluation from the University of South Florida. Dr. Vizcain's research interests concentrate on gender, ethnicity, equality, efficacy, and achievement as related to education nationally and internationally.

Carole Walker, an associate professor of Curriculum and Instruction at Texas A&M University–Commerce, coordinates the Greenville Center of the NET CPDT. Previously she had extensive school and district level experience with the Duval County (Florida) public schools. Her research focuses on the impact of mentoring on professional growth.

Beverly Wallace, Ph.D., is Associate Professor of English at Shippensburg University. She was the university faculty member who worked with secondary educators during her time at University of Central Missouri.

Brandi J. Wells is a doctoral fellow in the Department of Counseling and Psychological Services at Georgia State University and a member of the Urban Graduate Research Collaborative.

Nina Wasserman is an elementary school teacher in Passaic, NJ. She graduated in 1990 from Barnard College and received her teaching certification in 2003 from WIlliam Paterson University. She also has an ESL certification from New Jersey City University.

Gary Willhite is a professor in the Department of Curriculum and Instruction in Southern Illinois University in Carbondale.

Kathy Thomas Willhite is a professor with the College of Education Student Services in Southern Illinois University in Carbondale.

Diane Yendol-Hoppey is Associate Professor of Education in the School of Teaching and Learning at the University of Florida. She has written extensively on professional development schools, teacher leadership, and mentoring, and is recent recipient of the American Educational Research Association/Kappa Delta Pi, Division K, Early Career Research Award.

Catherine K. Zeek is associate professor and chair of the Education Department at Lasell College in Newton, MA. Her research interests include the role of narrative in encouraging teacher candidates' reflection and strategies that support connections between college and public school partners.

Printed in the United States
117270LV00002B/43/P